CW01637171

The Invention of Northern Aesthetics in 18th-Century English Literature

The Invention of Northern Aesthetics in 18th-Century English Literature

By

Yvonne Bezrucka

Cambridge
Scholars
Publishing

The Invention of Northern Aesthetics in 18th-Century English Literature

By Yvonne Bezrucka

This book first published 2017

Cambridge Scholars Publishing

Lady Stephenson Library, Newcastle upon Tyne, NE6 2PA, UK

British Library Cataloguing in Publication Data
A catalogue record for this book is available from the British Library

Copyright © 2017 by Yvonne Bezrucka

All rights for this book reserved. No part of this book may be reproduced, stored in a retrieval system, or transmitted, in any form or by any means, electronic, mechanical, photocopying, recording or otherwise, without the prior permission of the copyright owner.

ISBN (10): 1-5275-0302-X
ISBN (13): 978-1-5275-0302-1

This book is dedicated to my beloved husband Sergio
and our daughter Theodora Giovanazzi

CONTENTS

PREFACE

The Invention of Northern Aesthetics in 18th-Century English Literature examines the complex and intertwined semiotic, ideological, visual and cultural operations that took place during the 18th century and that were to be conducive to and culminate in the creation, or 'invention', of an aesthetics that would be promoted as if it were genuinely English, in a limited sense, and Northern in an extensive one.[1]

Essentialism,[2] the move towards a reactionary and populistic invention of characteristics believed to be inherent in a geographical region, is the vehicle through which the English culture of the 18th century marked the necessity to be free, original and independent from an outside influence that the English people did not perceive to be adherent to the aesthetic necessities of 'their' nation.[3] British intellectuals, amongst others Thomas Warton, felt the need to free themselves from the yoke of the 'Latin' (Greek and Roman) solar aesthetics that imposed on them the rules and forms they used, and were expected to continue to use, respect and imitate but which they felt to be foreign and not adequate to their unique geographical region and culture. In rejecting this system, they did not fully realise that what they were doing was just substituting the former cultural, regional and geographical Southern focus with a Northern one. By choosing to favour the contemplation of the Northern elements of their region, i.e. rejecting the also present Southern ones, they were applying an essentialist perspectival choice, equivalent to the one they were trying to dismantle.

To make their claims stronger, English intellectuals recovered what they believed to be their autochthonous literary origins and traditions. This origin they set in a mythical past, prior to the effect of the melting pot of cultures and literature and the engrafting of peoples on peoples – Celts, Britons, Iberians, Belgae, Romans, Anglo-Saxons, Danes, Norwegians, Scandinavians, French, etc. – of which the English people are the result. This origin they chose to set in their 'mythical' and real Celtic past.

Why they decided, of the various peoples they are made up of, to focus on this specific identity core, positing the Celtic literary ancestry line at their origin, this book will try to explain in the terms of their search for an alternative to the classic Southern mythology and aesthetics. This they did to highlight their different political and religious points of view. English intellectuals decided thus to focus on their autochthonous common Celtic identity core, which provided them with the opportunity to highlight their different aesthetic, political and religious stance, i.e. different from the values provided in the previously adopted classic Southern mythology and aesthetics.

To set themselves free from an aesthetics they felt discriminative and negative, they pinpointed all their distinct natural landscape characteristics, *de facto* 'creating' a Northern aesthetics. Thomas Warton's *History of English Poetry* (1774-1781), in positing the autochthonous canon of English Literature in Chaucer (partly), Spenser, Milton and Shakespeare, provides an answer to Oliver Goldsmith's request, expressed in his *An Enquiry into the Present State of Learning* (1759),[4] that "English taste, as English Criticism, should be restrained by laws of its own promoting" (OGE: 90), and, accordingly, that criticism should consider "the nature of the climate and the country before it gives rules to direct taste. In other words, every country should have a national system of rules" (OGE: 95), giving him the opportunity to conclude thus:

> it may be objected, that *this is setting up a particular standard of taste in every country*; this is *removing that universal one*, which has hitherto united the armies and enforced the commands of criticism; by this reasoning the critics of one country, will not be proper guides to the writers of another; Grecian or Roman rules will not be generally binding in France or England; but the laws designed to improve our taste, by this reasoning, must be adapted to the genius of every people, as much as those enacted to promote morality. WHAT I propose as objections, are really the sentiments I mean to prove, not to obviate. I must own it as my opinion, that if criticism be at all requisite to promote the interests of learning, its rules should be taken from among the inhabitants, and adapted to the genius and temper of the country it attempts to refine. (OGE: 88-90, my emphasis)

Furthermore, Goldsmith raises Milton above both Homer and Virgil, which had represented the elite of the Neoclassicists. Interestingly he also looks North, praising Sweden and Denmark for their sense of freedom: "They have, I am told (...) a jealous sense of liberty, and that strength of thinking, peculiar to northern climates, without its attendant ferocity" (OGE: 66-67).

Goldsmith, that is, anticipates strongly the request for 'aesthetic regionalism' promoted later in the century, in 1788, and this time only in aesthetic terms, by Francis Grose – an intellectual whose importance is unrecognised.[5] Grose strongly avoids all claims of any, falsely, universal aesthetics – rejecting thus aesthetic absolutism, and the Southern one with it, in order to avoid hierarchic peaks of 'civilization' (for example, that of the Greek aesthetics) in opposition to the idea of 'cultures' (pertaining to all different cultures of the world). The theory had enormous consequences, anticipating postmodern aesthetic regionalisms in the wake of which we still live today.

Thomas Warton, on the other hand, in indicating Spenser as one of the founding fathers of the English tradition, would initiate one of the most interesting discussions of 18th-century literature regarding the issue whether *The Faerie Queene* belonged to the elite works of English literature, being anti-classical in its design. The invective was to involve many critics and ultimately lead to the promotion of the Saxon-Gothic style as 'the' characteristic English style, and as the *par excellence* anti-classical 'Northern' one. Accordingly, *The Faerie Queene* was read as a Gothic Northern poem.

These elements are at the core of the choice made by the English intelligentsia to define their autochthonous aesthetic perspective. Fabricated to permit them to set themselves aside from the continental influence, they invented their own roots, which they chose to set in a distant, faraway past. This was done on purpose, to increase the difficulty of finding evidence, to permit them to engraft onto their Celtic past a mythological, invented, political superstructure in which King Arthur and his Round Table of the Knights figure prominently. The chivalric ethos then was to be visibly symbolised and reified in the Round Table of the knights, which would become the image for the democratic union of paratactic equals and no presiding authority: not even King Arthur. All 18th-century constitutionalists (Hughes, Hurd, Percy, Warton) would adopt and insist on this image to contrast the still-unresolved Glorious Revolution and the Jacobean Catholic crises and their related political problems, which were linked to the authoritarian claims of the Catholic kings, the Stuarts.

One of my contentions is that the Gothic novel and the a-religious Graveyard Poetry provide an indirect critique, from an enlightened English standpoint, and scorn those places of Europe (epitomised by Italy and France) where people could still believe in spirits and acquiesce to the fears of damnation. This permitted this religion and the Catholic kings, who considered themselves to be anointed by God, to dominate and manipulate people for their own interests. *The Castle of Otranto,* and the Gothic novel in general, is here, therefore, interpreted as a mock-heroic work – which is also why the first edition is unsigned – set against all demonologists, one of the works through which the Enlightenment declared war on *all religions* that proclaim obedience or acquiescence to a higher authority beyond the private and personal one.

In this way, the dichotomy North *vs.* South became, besides an aesthetic and literary contention, the site of a religious, political and philosophical debate, polarised as a fight between Catholic and Protestant countries, with Italy, Austria and France, the lands of authority, against the Northern countries, where the Reformation reigned: England, Germany and, partly, Holland, which set empiricism and the imagination against belief.

The 18th century was therefore to represent the rational critique of the religiously authoritarian South (implicitly and at a safe distance, providing an exposition of their own religions as well) through the mock-heroic and the rational Gothic, genres able to contrast the obscurantism of the still-in-the-dark lands. These forms of writing also attracted attention to the real, anti-universal and anti-exemplary humankind: eventually portrayed in the "comic-epic poem in prose"– the novel – as real 'characters' and not belittled as *caricaturas,* an enterprise on which Hogarth and Fielding jointly decide to embark. Sylphs, gnomes, and nymphs were, therefore, assigned zero power in Pope's *Rape of the Lock* (1712, 1714), where they appear but, significantly, do not give advice and do not have norms of behaviour to impose, limiting themselves to warning and helping people indirectly, without any possibility of direct intervention.

Celtic mythology came to represent the counter-tradition to that of the saints, successful in providing the people of the 18th century a recognisable system of chthonic elements made up of spirits and deities of extremely limited powers, completely different from the vindictive classic Greek and Roman gods, and different also from the authoritative God of the monotheistic religions and their hierocracy to which the English had been converted, up to the Reformation, and were not still entirely free from. Celtic spirits, having no religion to proselytise people into and pretending no conformity acts, represented liberty. They embodied the Protestant response to the abuse of power of Catholicism. An issue resumed, in paradigmatic terms, also in the Gothic novel, references to Italy being a shorthand for Catholicism or the South in general and its derivative from religion, authoritative political models.

Sylphs, the *sylvestri nymphae*, gnomes, descendants of the mythic Norwegian and Scandinavian trolls that reside in rocks and caves, and the fairies of the underworld of Elfame alongside the witches in Welsh, Irish and Scottish folklore constituted the core of this endeavoured cohesion literature and the complex literary historiography of the myth connected with it.

Chthonic and airy minor deities, derived from the primeval and the nature-bound elemental understanding of the world, based on air, fire, earth and water, also guaranteed the just and fair protection of the specificities of this northern land on which these creatures presided and protected from evil human intrusions. These intermediary beings, independent from the mythology, lived in English nature and were the strongest tie literature could possibly envisage to connect people to their home*land*, providing a strong identity trope. In the 18th century, the Celtic mythology was revived and recovered to create pride in an autochthonous literary tradition, stating implicitly and explicitly that there was no need to adopt a model that was external or inconsistent with local necessities.

As we shall see, the Celtic world provided a chivalric political model clearly connected to a non-authoritarian political rhetoric that strongly resembled the constitutional monarchy, thus creating strong links with the tradition of the ancient German law and the tradition of equity. This is also the core referred to in Matthew Arnold's defence, in the 19th century, of what he defined as "Englishism pure" qualifying it as "faith (…) in its [UK's] untransformed self".[6] Arnold, in contesting the Welsh decision to maintain their language, tries to defend his personal nationalistic and anti-regionalist aim to prevent the splitting of the nation, recovering the purpose of the 18th-century's scholars. This ideological background collides, nevertheless, with today's agenda when the same linguistic issues are insisted upon but must be framed within a closed or strong regionalism rather than a critical and open one.[7] A secessionist framework that does not correspond to the 18th-century national agenda and tried to evade internal regionalisms, the Celt origin provided a good, shared bait. Indeed, this mythology cast a spell that is seemingly active even in our own contemporary world, as the recent Brexit from the European Union due to law divergences has demonstrated, and is confirmed by the successful revival of recent fiction and TV series on the early Saxon period promoting strong muscular leaders and chivalric values, but also violence.[8] It is also for this reason that this book will look at the past to try to find an origin for the present, beside the more pointed legal origin, the populistic resurgence of insularity-bound values that were at work then, different from today for cohesive reasons and that, most likely, constitute the core premises for the understanding of the complex issue of Britishness and the Brexit from Europe.

In the 18th century, Thomas Warton thought that a shared foundation and the provision of Celtic roots and myths would be able to unite an internally split nation, this, notwithstanding the recent union with Scotland (1707) and the partly autonomous Irish Island that would find a formal union with the UK only in 1800. Warton's essentialism was guided by a centripetal issue, fostering an isolationist insular move to unite the nation against outward continental homogenising cultural influences. It is an isolationist matrix that has recently repeated itself, but is today complicated by strong internal regionalisms that assume a contrary centrifugal turn, aimed at acquiring political independence, dividing from within, likely because the national homogenising stance is perceived as a menace or cancellation of some groups' relative diversity. The cohesive, rather than the secessionist, aim was also the core of Matthew Arnold's reading of Alfred Lord Tennyson's recovery of the Arthurian legend in *The Idylls of the King,* that he – in thoroughly anti-Southern terms – defines as an "*unHomeric*" poem, recovering the older autochthonous tradition and repeating the issues pursued in the 18th century,[9] without mentioning it but along the lines of Northern aesthetics.

The popular mythological perspective runs parallel to the history of British empiricism and its defence of rationality. The founding fathers of British empiricism, Bacon, Locke and Hume, to whom I propose adding Addison and de Mandeville, represent the attack of culture against superstitions and religious belief. In their focus on the senses and the external world, and on how the senses apperceive external reality, they fostered a sense-related, nearly scientific and epistemological understanding of the world rather than a merely emotional one.

The man who did more than any other to popularise Locke's system and his idea that the mind is a *tabula rasa* is, paradoxically, Joseph Addison. With his series of essays on *The Pleasures of the Imagination* (1712), he attached an unprecedented importance to personal reception and its analysis so he could be termed the spiritual father of English Romanticism. Indeed, if Romanticism existed, it existed because there was an Addison who, with William Duff, democratised the idea of ingeniousness (from Lat. *ingenium* or inborn talent), seeing it not as a gift of the gods but counterpoising the idea of the imagination as one of the faculties present in humans, a faculty that could be improved through training: an esemplastic faculty, as Coleridge, who derives his theory from Addison, defined it, a creative faculty capable of changing the world.

Addison, thus, as we shall see, taught artists to look with their own eyes and change what they did not like. Through the imagination, as Addison says, "[the artist] has the modelling of Nature in his own hands".[10] Romanticism takes over this responsibility: in England, this is to collect the most varied stances and viewpoints – avoiding continental coteries of shared beliefs and shared philosophical stances – aiming at being a transversal declaration of independence of both the imagination and the artists. In stating the liberty and possibility for everyone to become the sole stakeholder, artist, moulder and creator of one's own life, it took free will back from religion. Accordingly, as a new English Renaissance, it celebrates a new humanity that uses free will, freedom and the imagination to envisage the new utopian worlds of the future, like Blake's *New Jerusalem* (1820-1827).

As can be seen, Romanticism is not an unexpected result but has been prepared by the 18th-century new literary and philosophical values that upset the Renaissance-oriented Neoclassicism, and this from Addison's essay of 1712 onwards, giving rise to what I prefer to call 'The Long Enlightened Romanticism'[11] rather than 'The Long Eighteenth Century'.

The issues that culminate in Blake are the result of the revolt of the empiricists against the rationalists, an attack they set on various fronts (religion, free will, empiricism, the imagination) to affirm an English Northern chthonic democratic past against the hypotactic, hierarchical and authoritarian mythology, founded in religion, politics and ethics, and ingrained and hidden in the Greek and Roman tradition, a tradition safely exported abroad via the Southern aesthetics.

If this hypothesis of a conscious focus on a Northern tradition during the 18th century has been examined at all, it has most certainly not been given its proper importance and place in the history of literature.[12]

This book aims to provide this new hypothetical perspective in the hope that it will result in a fresh outlook on the history of literature, identifying unheeded or misinterpreted popular trends recognisable in the timespan ranging from the 18th century to the present day, where such themes are widespread in contemporary literature.

The Northern elements connected to the elemental creatures, the recovery of the Saxon-Gothic laws and its political system, the picturesque, the sublime, the new line of beauty of Hogarth's aesthetics of the shell, the Domestic Anti-Grand-Tour, Gainsborough's and Constable's studies of clouds (nephology) and the emphasis on the dark night elements rather than the, apparently, clear and solar ones, once identified, become so evident throughout the literature of the century, and even after, to justify the feasibility of the Northern hypothesis as the master cyphered symbolism and identity politics of the 18th century.

All the above-mentioned aesthetic Northern elements draw constant attention to the different English nature that, as these theorists think, requires and deserves an aesthetics of its own. A good material proof is Wordsworth's *Prelude* (1798-1799), significantly subtitled the "Growth of a Poet's Mind", which depicts the evolution of nature as a spiritual entity come to envisage the biological *natura naturans* of physics.

The fairy way of writing, which Addison promoted, once re-established was never to be abandoned again, reappearing in the 19th, the 20th and 21st centuries. Recent works, like J.R.R. Tolkien's *The Lord of the Rings* and more contemporary ones like J.K. Rowling's *Harry Potter* and G.R.R. Martin's *A Song of Ice and Fire,* belong to the tradition established in the 18th century, grounded in the Middle Ages and in the Renaissance, through Thomas Warton's appositely created canon and his emphasis on the qualities of Chaucer, Spenser, Milton and Shakespeare. When, between 1774 and 1781, Thomas Warton published his *History of English Poetry*, these writers had lost their appeal with the public and were recovered by the Moderns, against the Southern tradition of the Ancients. Warton, being an academic, became instrumental in the creation of the new insular canon, an aim he pursued with the publication of the first *History of English Poetry*.

To sum up: although Addison was instrumental in the recovery of the Northern elemental magic spirituality, through his promotion of the fairy way of writing, and even if the myth of King Arthur represented a modern emblem of equity without a religion as a reference, without the *History of English Poetry* (1774-1781), the Northern tradition might not have made its way into this book. Thomas Percy's work (1765), Thomas Warton's Arthurian poetry (1777)[13] and Macpherson's appropriation of the Irish Celtic elements in his 'invented' *Ossian Poems* (1739)[14] gained entry in literature through Warton's *History of Poetry*. The democratic spirit of the Arthurian political model (read the English constitutional monarchy), on the contrary, that appears in emblematic and symbolic terms – as do other cyphered emblematic readings, the Rosicrucian and Freemason traditions being two of them – was offered as material evidence, seen in the blueprint and design of the English Garden (Addison, Pope, William Temple, Kent, Bridgman, Knight, Price, Repton), in Gothic architecture (the Saxon-Gothic) and in its first application as a design-oriented, structural and formal reading of literature in Spenser's *Faerie Queene* (Hughes, T. Warton, R. Hurd).

The development of this tradition can also be examined in the 19th century through Tennyson, the Pre-Raphaelites, in Charles Kingsley; and in the 20th century through J. Barrie, W.B. Yeats and the previously highlighted tradition of the fairy novel, which testifies its relevance in English literature.

The analysis will follow this outline:

• Chapter One examines the premises of the empiricist tradition (Locke and Hume and de Mandeville) that undermined the belief in inborn knowledge. Innatism represented the indirect short-cut to the creationist hypothesis and its related hierarchical and authoritarian reading of society. This outlook interpreted ingeniousness as the result of God's gift to his chosen emissaries, poets, writers and prophets. The premise of this fixed system (the *Scala Natura*) was based on the idea that knowledge was inborn and it could only be recovered by *anamnesis* (Plato). The genius theory reflected, thus, directly a principle of authority which was already inflected in religion (God) and in the body politics of the age (the king seen as God's representative on earth), i.e. the alliance of church and state, best expressed in the *Basilikon Doron* by James I.[15] The English responded to innate knowledge with the counter-claim of originality and inventiveness, grounded in the empiricist senses-revolt against the primacy of ratio and deduction considered to produce fallacies if they were not endorsed by inductive proofs.

• Chapter Two revises the history of literature, attributing to Joseph Addison's work the appropriate centrality and importance that has so far been neglected. It examines the focus on the senses and their bodily *ratio* as applied in the ground-breaking *ante litteram* Romantic aesthetics in his *The Pleasures of the Imagination* (1712). Addison popularises Locke's principle that there is no innate knowledge and that the mind is a *tabula rasa* on which the senses inscribe impressions that are then reworked into ideas. Ingeniousness is not seen as a gift of God but is reworked into the imagination-faculty, interpreted as being present in all human beings, and seen as a pliable organ that has the potential to be exercised and perfected by everyone.

Without this undermining of the theory of *ingegnum*, Romanticism would not have existed as it represents the most direct consequence of its dismissal, replacing God with the human artist as the creative entity of the world and thus returning accountability for the universe to humankind and to their abilities. Furthermore, in contrast to the Southern tradition of the Greek and Roman classics, Addison provided a different, autochthonous tradition, which was that of the fairy way of writing, linked to the use of "Fairies, Magicians, Demons, and departed Spirits" (JA: 419, 84), in which Milton and Spenser show "an admirable Talent in Representations of this kind" (JA: 419, 87) but where Shakespeare "has incomparably excelled all others" (JA: 419, 86). Thus, Shakespeare's and Spenser's use of the Celtic tradition is examined, keeping the pairing of the Celtic tradition with Englishness in mind, in the belief that, as Addison says: "the Genius of our Country is fitter for this sort of Poetry. For the English are naturally Fanciful, and very often disposed by that Gloominess and wild Melancholy of Temper, which is so frequent in our Nation, to many wild Notions and Visions, to which others are not so liable" (JA: 419, 86) "wild Notions" at which the Gothic novel was to poke fun, and to which, in a different way, also the invented fake-works by James Macpherson, in his *Poems* by Ossian, testify.

• Chapter Three examines the invention of the North as the product of an imaginary geography that leads to a wealth of consequences[16] from aesthetic, climatic and cultural perspectives. This chapter examines the way the invention translated itself into the fully rational literature of the Graveyard Poets and into Horace Walpole's mock-heroic Gothic novel, *The Castle of Otranto*, the Italian environment where superstitions take the place of rationality – i.e. into the "pleasing kind of Horrour"[17] that the English fear no more.

• Chapter Four turns to the way the Northern perspective discourse was first translated into aesthetic categories that were then applied to works of art. The chapter examines the centrality of Reverend Gilpin's 'picturesque', a focus that gave rise to the Domestic Anti-Grand-Tour travel tradition and which also informed the political reading of the English garden. This hinges on William Hogarth's double vision and his revolutionary conceptualisation of Variety through his line of beauty: issues that Burke translated into his study of the Sublime that dismantles, once and for all, the idea of perfection in art, which had guided the aesthetics of the beautiful since the Greeks. Furthermore, the chapter establishes the aesthetic relevance of Francis Grose, who breaks down all claims of aesthetic absolutism, unequivocally establishing the revolutionary claims for aesthetic regionalism.[18]

• Chapter Five considers Thomas Warton's role in backing up the Northern aesthetics in three important moves.

Firstly, he revises the *stemma codicum* of the Arthurian Romance and sets the English Anglo-Saxon romance tradition as the distinguished core of English literature and its democracy by linking it to the shared power model of King Arthur's version of the chivalric values based on the tradition of Equity Law. Secondly, in writing the first history of the literature of England, he establishes the first English canon, institutionalising the founding poets of the Northern tradition – Chaucer, Spenser, Milton and Shakespeare (the rise of the novel is contemporary to this work). Thirdly, he sets the Saxon-Gothic as the 'English' autochthonous and muscular 'architectural' style. This will encourage the readings of the *Faerie Queene* as a 'Gothic' poem (Hughes, Warton, Hurd, Walpole), and promote the 'Gothic' as a stark literary style that dismisses religion and superstitions, producing the a-religious Graveyard Poets and Horace Walpole's mock-heroic "pleasing kind of Horrour" tradition (JA: 419, 85) of the anti-Catholic Gothic fiction that the English fear no more. The creation of the English canon provides us also with the opportunity to examine and focus our attention on the differences between types of essentialisms, ranging from the invention of tradition (Ossian's poems) to the favouring of cultural standpoints and differences between a strong and a critical regionalism.

The book closes with Emily Brontë's *Wuthering Heights* (1847). Even though this novel was produced in the mid-19th century, it has been chosen because the book uses the Northern aesthetics to present the perils of an upgrade of a North/South essentialist logic. Brontë's early awareness, that these dichotomies produce non-collateral damage if they undergo an essentialist escalation in the ethnic direction, is strong. And this, more often than not, fatally happens, imaginary geographies being all too easily transformed by means of ethnic and nationalistic filters, as history has taught us,[19] into ethnic typologisations always lurking on the doorstep, even though they may on the surface appear to be merely matters of aesthetics and geography. Emily Brontë's *Wuthering Heights* provides the results, in fact, of the ethnic escalation of these filters.

Notes

[1] The proxemic term 'Northern' can mean anything if it is not qualified through a centre of reference; every place is north of somewhere else. The centre of reference in this book is Europe, and to be absolutely clear from the beginning, I am fully aware that the 'North' on a map is always the South of something more North than the place in question.

[2] Gayatri Chakravorty Spivak uses the term "strategic essentialism" to describe a negative, but sometimes necessary, sort of mystic union brought about by a focus on some shared 'essential' cultural properties that provisionally erode the differences between the people within a group, in this case Subaltern groups, or even of a nation, to contrast with an outside enemy, so to gain, as a minority, more dialogic force within the majority. See Sara Danius, Stefan Jonsson (1993) 'An Interview with Gayatri Chakravorty Spivak', *Boundary 2*, 20 (2): 24-50, and G.C. Spivak (1988) 'Can the Subaltern Speak?'. In (eds) (1988) L. Grossberg, C. Nelson *Marxism and the Interpretation of Culture* (Basingstoke: Macmillan), pp. 271-313.

[3] In this sense, the philosopher to be quoted here is Johann Gottfried Herder, who in his work (1784-1791) *Ideen zur Philosophie der Geschichte der Menschheit* became the first theorist of the idea of a 'characteristic' beauty different for each culture and related to its peculiar tradition, history and education; thus not something inherently there, but a product of experience. On the subject of *Cultur* [the old word Herder uses for Kultur], he says: "Nothing is more indeterminate than this word, and nothing more deceptive than its application to all nations and periods"; see Raymond Williams' (1983, 1976) *Keywords: A Vocabulary of Culture and Society* (Oxford: Oxford University Press, p. 89), in which Herder is quoted to dismantle an overarching idea of Europe if its meaning is to cancel the difference within the cultures composing it: "Men of all the quarters of the globe, who have perished over the ages, you have not lived solely to manure the earth

with your ashes, so that at the end of time your posterity should be made happy by European culture. The very thought of a superior European culture is a blatant insult to the majesty of Nature."

[4] Goldsmith, O. (1759) *An Enquiry into the State of Polite Learning in Europe* (London: Dodsley), hereafter referred to in the text as OGE: and p. no.

[5] I have pointed to the importance of Francis Grose's aesthetics in Y. Bezrucka (2002) *Genio ed immaginazione nel Settecento inglese*, Università di Verona (Verona: Valdonega), pp. 116-123. See also Stephen Bending (2003) 'Every Man is Naturally an Antiquarian: Francis Grose and Polite Antiquities'. In (eds) Dana Arnold and Stephen Bending (2003) *Tracing Architecture* (Oxford: Blackwell), pp. 100-110.

[6] M. Arnold (1891) *Celtic Literature* (London: Smith, Elder, & Co) Kindle version, p. 139.

[7] I have examined the issue of 'critical' and 'strong regionalism' in Bezrucka, Y. (2008a) '"The Well-Beloved": Thomas Hardy's Manifesto of "Regional Aesthetics"', *Victorian Literature and Culture*, 36.1, 227-45; Y. Bezrucka (ed.) (1999a) *Regionalismo e antiregionalismo* (Trento: Luoghi/Edizioni); Y. Bezrucka (ed.) (1999/2) *Forme e caratteri del regionalismo. Mitteleuropa ed oltre* (Trento: Luoghi/Edizioni); Y. Bezrucka (ed.) (1997) *Le identità regionali e l'Europa* (Trento: Luoghi/Edizioni); Y. Bezrucka (1995) *Tra passato e futuro. Assaggi di teoria dell'architettura*, (Trento: Autem).

[8] See the transposition of Martin, George R.R. (1996) *A Song of Ice and Fire*, a number-one *New York Times* bestseller in 2011, transcoded into the successful TV-series (2011) *Game of Thrones* by David Benioff.

[9] See M. Arnold (1862) *On Translating Homer: Last Words* (London: Longman, Green, Roberts), pp. 54-57, here 55. Indeed, Arnold admired the Arthurian revival works by Tennyson, *Idylls of the King*, the set of 12 poems on the Arthurian cycle published between 1856-1885.

[10] See Joseph Addison (1907 [1711-1714]) *The Pleasures of the Imagination*, *The Spectator,* 4 vols., (ed.) G. Gregory Smith (London: Dent) vol. 3, no. 418, p. 83, hereafter referred to in the text with JA: essay no. and page no.

[11] A new name for what Northrop Frye has called the "Age of Sensibility" (1959) 'Towards Defining an Age of Sensibility'. In (ed.) James L. Clifford (1955) *Eighteenth-Century English Literature. Modern Essays in Criticism* (Oxford: Oxford University Press) pp. 311-18. See also Tuveson, E. (1960) *The Imagination as a Means of Grace: Locke and the Aesthetics of Romanticism* (Berkeley: University of California Press).

[12] The only book that I have been able to trace is Fjagesund, Peter (2014) *The Dream of the North: A Cultural History to 1920* (Amsterdam: Rodopi), which presents a historical study of the Scandinavian region. The other work that elaborates on this perspective and should be read as an important adjunct to my perspective is the work by (ed.) Berger, M. (1964) *Madame de Staël. On Politics Literature and National Character* (New York: Doubleday), which focuses on the same North/South issues from the point of view of philosophy and religion, that I comment upon in ch. 3.2. Scattered Northern references appear in Howard D.

Weinbrot, (1993) *Britannia's Issue. The Rise of British Literature from Dryden to Ossian* (Cambridge: Cambridge University Press) but are not completely developed.

[13] Thomas Warton, 'Ode X: The Grave of King Arthur', in (1777) *Poems: A New Edition, with Additions* (London: T. Becket) pp. 62-71: the poem relates King Arthur's death as told to Henry II in Wales by Welsh Bards. One minstrel sets the tomb of King Arthur before the high altar at Glastonbury Abbey, where it is said his body was later found. In the same edition, on p. 82, his other important Arthurian poem, 'On King Arthur's Round Table at Winchester', also appears. This last poem is at the same time a eulogy of Spenser and a tribute to King Arthur and his "capacious" Round Table of equals, the knights, with whom he democratically shares power. If the table – the Druid frame – will corrupt under blind Time, in "Spenser's page, that chants in verse sublime// Those Chiefs, shall live, unconscious of decay."

[14] Macpherson, James (1762 [1761]) *Fingal, An Ancient Epic Poem, in Six Books: Together with Several Other Poems, Composed by Ossian, the Son of Fingal*, tr. from the Galic Language by J. Macpherson (London: T. Becket and P. A. De Hondt). See also his other works: Macpherson, J. (1760) *Fragments of Ancient Poetry Collected in the Highlands of Scotland, and Translated from the Galic or Erse Language* (Edinburgh: Hamilton Balfour); see also Macpherson, J. (1818 [1763]) *Temora: An Epic Poem by Ossian* (Perth: Morison).

[15] "The State of Monarchie is the supremest thing upon earth. For Kings are not only God's Lieutenants upon earth, and sit upon Gods throne, but even by God himselfe they are called Gods. There bee three principall similitudes that illustrate the state of Monarchie. One taken out of the word of GOD; and the two other out of the grounds of Policie and Philosophie. In the Scriptures Kings are called Gods, and so their power after a certaine relation compared to the Divine power. Kings are also compared to Fathers of families: for a King is truely Parens patriae, the politique father of his people. And lastly Kings are compared to the head of this Microcosme of the body of man." James I (1599) *Basilikon Doron. Or his Majesty Instructions to his dearest Sonne Henry the Prince* (Edinburgh) reprinted from the edition of 1616 in (1887) (ed.) Charles Howard McIlwain, *The Political Works of James I* (Cambridge MA: Harvard University Press), p. 307.

[16] Cf. Edward W. Said, (1995 [1978]) *Orientalism. Western Conception of the Orient* (London: Penguin).

[17] See Joseph Addison (1907 [1711-1714]) *The Pleasures of the Imagination*, *The Spectator,* 4 vols. (ed.) G. Gregory Smith (London: Dent), no. 419, p. 85, hereafter referred to in the text with JA: essay no. and page of this edition. Noteworthily, vol. V, of the internal subdivision of volumes of *The Spectator*, in vol. 3, is dedicated to Thomas Warton, cf. pp. 1-2.

[18] Cf. Y. Bezrucka (2002) *Genio ed immaginazione nel Settecento inglese*, Università di Verona (Verona: Valdonega), pp. 116-23.

[19] Cf. Said, E.W. (1995 [1978]) *Orientalism. Western Conception of the Orient* (London: Penguin).

CHAPTER ONE

INNATISM *VS.* EMPIRICISM

Knowledge is not from maxims.
—John Locke

1.1 Innatism vs. Empiricism

The intellectual battle fought in the 18th century was based on a contention between an epistemology that envisaged an ordered, holistic universe – a world that could be brought back to a single explanation (e.g. the creationist hypothesis) – and the opposing one that envisaged a varied universe that needed space-time-specific (scientific) explanations relative to issues: in short, a battle between past and present. Innatism became the main point of contention discussed by the new philosophers. In claiming that people were born with universal innate ideas on which they could faithfully rely, innatism postulated and presupposed that the ideas that the mind innately possessed had been provided before birth. Plato, Plotinus and, in more recent times, Descartes and Leibniz, in fact, posited that these derived from God himself.

This idea was defended by the rationalists, who believed in the capacity of reaching conclusions about reality via the process of mere syllogistic reasoning, without the necessity of scientific proof to back up one's argument. The choice of the inductive perspective, in contrast to the deductive one, runs parallel to and has its basis in the history of British empiricism.

Bacon, Locke and Hume, to whom I propose to add de Mandeville, are, of course, the founding fathers of empiricism: the founding of the Royal Society dating back to 1660. Empiricism, as I want to demonstrate, is one of the core elements of Britishness. The innovative choice, which was ahead of its time, that the English made to trust in science and not in religion, notwithstanding the deists, was a stance that differentiated them from the people on the continent who hindered this kind of progress. As a result of the new orientation, English intellectuals and scientists perceived themselves as pertaining to the most advanced society of their time. This is a core conviction behind the intelligentsia's choice to distance themselves from the continent that was influenced also, later, by Addison and the invention of 'their' own literary roots, choices that need to be taken into careful consideration. These roots, Addison and others, as we shall see, set in a distant and faraway past, using literature as a powerful persuasive medium to spread their point. The founding of the moment in the past and the connected scarcity of evidence allowed them, building on their real Celtic past, to create the superstructure of a foundational mythological moment set in a democratic, invented political past. Writers, antiquarians and historians, following the lead of Addison's choice of setting the fairy way of writing as the English way of writing, connected it thus to the mythological King Arthur and his Round Table of Knights. The self-evident proxemics of the Round Table bears witness to the absence of an imposed hierarchical leader and is presented as the icon of a democratic union of paratactic equals, a cogent amalgam of ethos and medievalism, whose message is that the knights are not inferior to the king. This emblem became the symbol of British democracy, embodying the communal and democratic equity law system, the negotiable and pliable jurisprudence based on precedents. This is a system pliable to change if change is needed. The choice of adopting the Common Law, where it is the judge who modifies the law according to a changed reality, despised the continental 'once and for all' letter of the law.

The acquisition of national pride, which paved the way for this mythological foundation and is involved in the stance the British intelligentsia adopted in the 18th century, is therefore likely to be linked to core philosophical issues that have been debated from the 17th century, starting with Francis Bacon's discussion of the inductive method. The method was later developed in the ground core of Locke's attack on innatism, based on his requirement for the evidence of the senses and material proofs for hypotheses made about reality– and not only about *reflection*, as the rationalists claimed.

In John Locke's *An Essay Concerning Human Understanding* (1690),[1] senses were given a primary role in the development of understanding and knowledge: "it is *not possible*, for anyone *to imagine* any other *qualities* in bodies, howsoever constituted, whereby they can be taken notice of, besides sounds, tastes, smells, visible and tangible qualities." (JL: 122, Bk. 2, ch. 2, § 3). Senses were for Locke the filters for the apprehension of reality in our species. Aware of the critique that would be levelled against his theory of the mind as a *tabula rasa*, a blank slate, rather than a repository of innate ideas, he set his system in direct contrast to the creationist hypothesis, "spirits", of which God is one, being strongly present in his work.

Locke, therefore, firmly grounds his epistemic theory of understanding on "sensation and reflection," which are the basis for simple ideas (JL: 284, Bk. 2, ch. 23, § 32). The two are nevertheless markedly different. Sensations are self-evident and come first, and they direct reflections such as creating the complex idea of God, which is itself only the result of simple ideas:

> For whensoever we would proceed beyond these simple ideas, we have from sensation and reflection, and dive further into the nature of things, we fall presently into darkness and obscurity, perplexedness and difficulties; and can discover nothing further, but our own blindness and ignorance. But whichever of these complex ideas be clearest, that of body, or immaterial spirit, this is evident, that the simple ideas that make them up, are no other than what we have received from sensation or reflection; and so it is of all our other ideas of substances, even of God himself. (JL: 284, Bk. 2, ch. 23, § 32) (...) For though in his own essence, (which certainly we do not know, not knowing the real essence of a pebble, or a fly, or of our own selves) God be simple and uncompounded; yet, I think, I may say we have no other idea of him, but a complex one of existence, knowledge, power, happiness, etc. infinite and eternal: which are all distinct ideas (…) all which being, as has been shown, originally got from *sensation* and *reflection*, go to make up the idea or notion we have of God. (JL: 285, Bk. 2, ch. 23, § 35)

The idea of God is, therefore, the result of the sensations our species have and of the reflection springing from the observation of the variety and excellence of "this fabric", the universe (JL: 122, Bk. 2, ch. 2, §3). "[T]he Supreme Being" is thus the product of the enlargement of simple ideas "with *our* ideas of infinity" (JL: 284, Bk. 2, ch. 23, § 284, my emphasis); which, together, make up our complex idea of God. Locke, however, clearly sees it as the product of *reflection* only: "all our ideas of the several sorts of substances, are nothing but collections of simple ideas, with *a supposition* of something, to which they belong, and in which they subsist; though of this supposed something, we have no clear distinct idea at all" (JL: 285, Bk. 2, ch. 23, § 37, my emphasis).

Reflection, as we have seen, is thus linked solely to hypothetical thinking, Locke reminding us that we need to have evidence from our sensations to back up our reflections when we speak of spirits, "even of God himself." (JL: 284, Bk. 2, ch. 23, § 32). He then closes the argument of how simple ideas can be 'enlarged' by reflection via a metaphor:

> most of the simple ideas, that make up our complex ideas of substances, when truly considered, are only powers, however we are apt to take them

> for positive qualities; *v.g.* the greatest part of the ideas, that make our complex idea of gold, are yellowness, great weight, ductility, flexibility, and solubility in *aqua regia, etc.* all united together in an unknown *substratum* all of which ideas are nothing else but so many relations to other substances, and are not really in the gold, considered barely in itself." (JL: 286, Bk. 2, ch. 23, § 37)

Thus, he marks the difference between the spontaneous, unwilled acquisition of the senses – for example, seeing *vs.* watching – i.e. of sensations, and the way reflection reworks them into more complex ideas that do not belong to the object of thought itself, as the complex ideas of gold demonstrate.

Locke is thus demystifying all ideas of spirits rather than directly that of God, notwithstanding God being one.[2] Considering these entities as the result of only (unproven) reflections, he seems to be keeping the idea of God as a principle of general goodness, as a sort of positive regulatory system that facilitates the peaceful cohabitation of people. As for proof of the existence of God, he clearly says we can rely only on "revelation", that is, by "assent on the credit of the proposer" even though these "cannot introduce any (…) formerly unknown simple ideas" (JL: 608, Bk. 4, ch. 18, § 2, 3), relying thus, again, only on, untrustworthy, reflection, and not on:

> simple ideas (…) which are the foundation, and sole matter of all our notions, and knowledge, we must depend wholly on our reason, I mean, our natural faculties [the senses] and we can by no means receive them, or any of them, from *traditional revelation*, I say, *traditional revelation*, in distinction to *original revelation*. By the one, I mean, that first impression, which is made immediately by God, on the mind of any man, to which we cannot set any bounds; and by the other, those impressions delivered over to others in words (…) yet nothing, I think can, under that title, shake or overrule plain knowledge (...) in a direct contradiction to the clear evidence of his own understanding (JL: 609-10, Bk. 4, ch. 18, § 3),

pertinently adding: "In Propositions (…) whose certainty is built upon clear perception (…) we need not the assistance of *revelation*" (JL: 609-610, Bk. 4, ch. 18, § 5).

To this conclusion, to rely on knowledge merely based on "clear perception", we should compare what he says in chapter 10, where Locke discusses the unreliability of "intuitive knowledge" (JL: 547, Bk. 4, ch. 10, § 1) of our idea of "*a most perfect being*" (JL: 549, Bk. 4, ch. 10, § 7) that appears to us as "certain" but that he clearly sees as the product of reflection: "a knowledge (...) a man may frame in his mind" (JL: 549, Bk.

4, ch. 10, § 6-7). The interesting choice of the verb he uses here, "framing", is to me evidence that those who proceed merely by reflection, proceed by choosing a perspective through which they would then construct their argument, their framed perspective, excluding other possible points of view and, therefore, already implying the conclusion they aim to reach.

Of the effort to establish whether there is enough evidence of God's existence, his stance relies on the fact that "God has given us no innate ideas of himself (...) wherein we may read his being", so we can only rely on "our intuitive knowledge" (JL: 547, Bk. 4, ch. 10, § 1). All his further argument is then constructed upon hypothetical clauses – if, whether, let us suppose, perhaps it will be said – and adversative ones – but, notwithstanding, others would have, etc. – aimed at dismantling the tenets of the innatists; but, and this needs to be strongly underlined, inspired by his awareness of the consequences of any position, knowing that innatism, which he dismantles, is the core tenet of ethics: "this being so fundamental a truth, and of that consequence, that all religion and genuine morality depend thereon" (JL: Bk. 4, ch. 10, § 7).

In his "Epistle to the Reader", he focused on innatism, pointing out how dangerous the issue was and the censure it could cause: "I have been told, that a short epitome of this treatise, which was printed in 1688, was by some condemned without reading, because innate ideas were denied in it (...) concluding that if innate ideas were not supposed, there would be little left, either of the notion or proof of spirits" (JL: 11), of which God is one.

Whenever the creationist hypothesis is called in, it is always to foster ethics and justify a principle of order based on goodness among humankind.[3] When, for example, Locke speaks about the divine law, he explains it thus: "*divine* law (…) [is] promulgated (...) by the light of nature [the *Codex Dei*, a "framing" also merely based on an 'intuitive' knowledge he distrusts], or by the voice of revelation [thus unreliable, and that he, again, as seen, distrusts]"; God can exercise his law because "we are his creatures" [a hypothesis which has no proof for those who do not believe], enforcing it via: "rewards and punishments, of infinite weight and duration, in another life" (JL: 317, Bk. 2, ch. 28) but whose compliance produces the victory of virtue over vice.

Basil Willey, rightly, in his study of the 17th century, points out that the system of positive spirits was upheld also by the contrary spirits, the demonic ones, and thus used by religions to foster belief. A system of good and evil that:

> was tapping a reservoir of traditional supernatural belief which lay deeper in the national consciousness than Christianity itself, and deeper, certainly, than the new ice-crust of rationalism which now covered it. Christianity, as is well known, had not abolished the older divinities, it had merely deposed and demonised them; and Protestantism, aiming at the purification of Christianity from the 'pagan' accretions of the middle ages, had produced at first not a diminished but a greatly heightened Satan-consciousness, so that the later sixteenth and earlier seventeenth centuries, when witch-burnings reached their maximum, were Satan's palmiest time in England. By the time of More, it is true, this Puritan horror which had persecuted without pity much that had been tolerated in the less self-conscious pre-Reformation days, had greatly weakened, under 'philosophic' influences. But primitive picture-thinking is not destroyed at a blow, and the persistent if furtive acknowledgement of things undreamed of in the 'new philosophy' was now unexpectedly available as a reinforcement to *the philosophic defence of the faith*. It may be, one may now conjecture, that in making the most of this crude material the defenders of religion were guided by a sound instinct. They may have obscurely felt, though they could not have realised or admitted it, that the ancient springs of popular demonology were also those of religion itself, and that in the emotion of the supernatural, however evoked, they had a surer foundation for faith than all the 'proofs' of philosophic theism. (Willey: 1968 p. 167, my emphasis).

Most certainly, one of the "*the philosophic defence[s] of the faith*" was the tenet of innatism.

Locke sustains his theory of the enormous difference between sensation and reflection, basing his conclusion on the capacity the mind has for enlarging what it acquires through the senses by focusing on its ability to create unembodied forms, the products of 'reflection' and its specific capacity for enlargement, or what we would call imagination. I base my contention that Addison will become the populariser of Locke on the fact that Addison will precisely underline the 'creative' ability of the imagination on two grounds: first, that the imagination is powerful and able to envisage non-existent reality, and second that this non-existent reality should be used positively to foster pleasures, and not to transport the mind thus losing the "sight of Nature" as happens with "superstitious" people, who "fall in with our natural prejudices" and who, "very well versed in legends and fables, antiquated romances", make "fairies, witches, magicians, demons, and departed spirits (...) talk like people of his own species, and not like other sets of beings", this being a world created by the artist "out of his own Invention" (JA: 419, 84-85).

Nevertheless, Locke's stance on everything concerned with the colliding principle of nativism is restricted to the sensations that children might retain from the life in their mothers' womb: sensations of hunger or warmth but "*not* the least appearance of any settled ideas at all in them; especially of *ideas, answering the terms which make up those universal propositions*, that are esteemed innate principles" (JL: 91, Bk. 1, ch. 4), ideas he rejects. Indeed, in ch. 11, Locke makes the point that innatists have been led to their conclusions for want of any knowledge of why certain propositions are universally accepted; these ideas should rather be referred to our capacity for discerning and not seen as the result of inborn ideas set in our mind by a Designer or Maker:

> On this faculty of distinguishing one thing from another depends the evidence and certainty of several, even very general propositions, which have passed for innate truths; because men, overlooking the true cause why those propositions find universal assent, impute it wholly to native uniform impressions; whereas it in truth depends upon this clear discerning faculty of the mind, whereby it perceives two ideas to be the same, or different. (JL: 152-53, Bk. 1, ch. 11)

And this conclusion can also be applied to Locke's dismantling chapter on the existence of God, which is a perfect example of a rhetorical, eristically set, philosophical thesis where all conclusions are admitted (existence and non-existence) but one of them is refuted by the master syllogistic premise that, talking about spirits (of which God is one), no facts can be asserted so there can be no proof about their existence.

I disagree with those who conclude that Locke belonged to "the contemporary reconcilers of science and religion" (Willey 1967, 279), deists like Boyle and Joseph Glanvill; nor is he searching for a 'Mechanic' like the one Newton proposes. Seen from the point of view of innatism, a standpoint not examined by Basil Willey, there is no doubt about Locke's conclusion.

Innatism, as we have seen, is a highly controversial notion, which primarily means claiming proof of God's existence and for the creationist hypothesis. Nevertheless, the truth claims of the various religions cannot dependably be ascertained. Locke proposes the standpoint of tolerance in his work: *Letters Concerning Toleration* (1689–1692). In the essay, he says: "If any idea can be imagined *innate*, the idea of God may of all others, for many reasons, be thought so; since it is hard to conceive, how there should be innate moral principles, without an innate idea of a Deity: without a notion of a law-maker, it is impossible to have a notion of law, and an obligation to serve it." (JL: 93, Bk. 1, § 8). The last remark on the obligation is extremely significant in that it expresses clearly that moral restrictions must be imposed by an authority. The passage continues with a list of peoples of the world where the concept of a God does not exist, the humankind of *nulla idola*, concluding with the remark that in "civilized" countries, if people did not fear "the magistrates' sword, or their neighbour's censure, (...) apprehensions of punishment [they] would as openly proclaim their atheism, as their lives do." (JL: 94, Bk. 1, § 8). This notation was probably the origin of Swift's pointed remark that people of the Church were apprehensive about the fact that: "People are likely to improve their understanding much with Locke; it is not his 'Human Understanding', but other works that people dislike, although in that there are some dangerous tenets, as that of [no] innate ideas."[4] Sir Thomas Browne, in *Religio Medici* (Bk. 1, 30), wrote: "For my part I have ever believed, and do now know, that there are Witches: they that doubt of these, do not only deny them, but Spirits; and are obliquely and upon consequence a sort not of Infidels, but Atheists."

The connection between innatism and theology was presented in its clearest way in Gottfried Leibniz's *Theodicy*, where the presence of evil in the world is justified by the unknown-to-man teleological and theological finality of God, which is always oriented to the best possible outcome. Therefore, humankind must, in this way, submissively accept (partial) evil, always the minimum possible one, because God, who can holistically encompass infinite time, is always oriented to a future good and what is best for us. Alexander Pope, who accepts and embodies Leibniz's Design Theory in his *Essay on Man*, concludes Epistle 1, devoted to the nature of the universe, with the self-evident words: "Whatever is, is Right." These words constitute the most laconic expression of the acquiescence theory implied in the old, hierarchical and fixed, *Scala Natura*,[5] based on a fixed and unchangeable order-and-degree world model. The other convinced proponent of this internal, innate, gnoseological system of the mind was Descartes, who believed that the mind had inborn, intuitive clear ideas that could, and should, be recovered.

If innatism was an unavoidable notion for dismantling deduction and instituting induction, it was also strongly linked with the Genius theory. It is thus crucially important for literature, where it has been used to maintain that artists differ from common humankind. Indeed, ingeniousness was interpreted as if it were a gift of God to his chosen emissaries, artists, saints and prophets and, circularly, the theory of inborn genius was then taken as proof of God's existence. A counter confirmation of this is the Greek myth of Prometheus, who is forever punished by the Gods, for having autonomously chosen to help humankind with the gift of fire, which produces light – metaphorical rationality – without being authorised by them.

Plato, in his dialogues *Ion* and *Phaedrus*, sees the human body of the artist or genius as the intermediary for God, who speaks through it, a notion that was later developed into the theory of the *furor poeticus* of the Latins. According to Plato, people, having previously lived in a world of forms, bring with them knowledge that only needs to be recovered. Innatism can be seen to be at work in Plato's "Myth of the Cave" (*Republic* VII, 514b-520a), and in his theory of the immutable and eternal forms expressing transcendental truth (*Sophist* and *Parmenides*). Forms can be recovered through an *elenchus*, or maieutic process, related to obstetrics – Socrates' mother's profession – a process followed to help people give new birth to those truths already present in them. Innatism of abilities is also present in people's *physis*, and mostly in people endowed with superior inherent capacities, the *megalophues* or the greatsouled: "for centuries thereafter nurture and nature (*ars* and *ingenium*) were most often seen as complementary, and the same is true of the belief in natural endowment and the theory of the poetic inspiration."[6] Aristotle rejected innatism and favoured the experience provided by reality itself over this deductive or rational – if not metaphysical – a priori system of knowledge.

Another group of innatists, against whom Locke, de Mandeville and Hume react, is, the Cambridge Platonists,[7] who had posited the innatism of the idea of God in human beings deriving from it the innate concept of morality. This group was led by Herbert of Cherbury, the advocate of the innate quality of 'common notions', universally admitted to be true.[8] Other members of the group were Henry More, who saw nature as a *Codex Dei* and wrote a *Manual of Ethics* (1666) and a *Manual of Metaphysics* (1671), and Ralph Cudworth, author of *The True Intellectual System of the Universe* (1678), who saw nature as the 'plastic' archetype of God[9]; they had recovered Plato's innatism[10] through Marsilio Ficino and Origen.[11] These concepts are also present in Lord Shaftesbury, who maintains a balanced position,[12] and in Francis Hutcheson.[13] Both analyse 'common sense'[14] and the notions of 'sympathy' and 'benevolence'.[15] Sympathy and benevolence left their mark on literature via Henry Mackenzie's *The Man of Feeling* (1771).

Hutcheson postulates an inborn moral sense, which makes one approve of benevolence and hate its contrary. This is due to love, or benevolence, on which this moral sense is founded. He claims the same to be true for beauty, the moral sense being beauty in action or applied affection, thus confirming the Platonic triad. The universe is therefore ordered and harmonious, God having set virtue as our guiding principle. The fact that Hutcheson criticises de Mandeville's *Fable* in the title of his work testifies to the Neoplatonists' attack on the materialistic scepticism de Mandeville maintains in matters of morality and towards the priesthood in general.[16]

Innatists found the grounds for their belief in God via what they thought were the self-evident universals with which God had endowed humankind, and that they saw confirmed in their belief that everybody had a distinct, intuitive, knowledge of beauty, God and morality. De Mandeville's "The Fourth Dialogue Between Horatio and Cleomenes"[17] contests these tenets. In this dialogue, Horatio affirms: "there are no innate Ideas, and Men come into the World Without any Knowledge at all"; Cleo confirms it, saying that it is only a matter of Education into which "we are so industriously and so assiduously instructed" (BM2: 149). Horatio would rather see pride as an inborn passion and a capacity for good government as an acquired talent (BM2: 205). The two friends also discuss the role of religion, and to the question of how it came into the world, Cleo responds: "From God, by Miracle." To which Horatio answers: "*Obscurum per obscurius*. [An unclearness explained through an even obscurer one, my tr.] I don't understand Miracles" (BM2: 205).

After the empiricists' attack on inborn knowledge and their championing of the senses as the unique means for the acquisition and reflective elaboration of primary ideas, the innatists attempted to defend the creationist hypothesis by means of the stronghold of the Scottish branch of Neoplatonism, which asserted that humankind possessed an inborn sense of morality.[18] Without considering the 'cultural' background of myths, traditions, communities, nations and education, on which de Mandeville strongly insists,[19] they claimed that everybody was born with an innate moral faculty that permitted them to judge whether an action, a deed or an idea was morally good or bad. This was reinforced by the other stronghold they championed and maintained: their belief in the universality of "common sense". Lord Shaftesbury wrote:

> Do you maintain then, said I, that these mental children, the notions and principles, of fair, just, and honest, with the rest of these ideas, are innate? (…) this I am certain of, that life and the sensations which accompany life, come when they will, are from mere nature, and nothing else. Therefore, if you dislike the word Innate, let us change it, if you will, for Instinct; and call Instinct, that which Nature teaches, exclusive of Art, Culture, or Discipline." "Content," said I.[20]

Bernard de Mandeville, in *The Fable of the Bees,*[21] confutes and invalidates this citadel of the innatists' tenets and their 'common sense' hard core. He clearly states that morality and ethics are not universal but only space-time-specific in that peoples' principles are the result of their cultural environments, an affirmation further validated by the differences in the evaluations of deeds in the various, and sometimes violent, religions.

Being the philosopher who dismanted this holistic universe, Bernard de Mandeville demonstrated how religious and secular powers go hand in hand in the promotion of their joint project of keeping people deferential, acquiescent and submissive. He showed that this system was upheld through instilled fears of retaliation and revenge: either in hell or prison or through death and damnation. Indeed, the implied issue, in all inborn arguments, is the defence of authority. The old medieval *Scala Natura* was based on the non-disputability of God's authority and that of his anointed representative on earth, the king. This model was further sustained by the Bible, used as the word of God, and by nature, seen as an open visual book, there to be read to ascertain the hidden structure of God's design, which Newton seemed to confirm with his findings. The creationist hypothesis was further backed by the guidelines set by Charles Batteux, who instructed artists to choose of all manifestations only the ones pertaining to *la belle nature* that confirmed the intrinsic beauty of God's universe, leaving aside other manifestations like earthquakes, floods or avalanches.

De Mandeville contested the ideological use of nature to claim law's 'naturalness'. The assumptions of the existence of a natural or innate law in the universe had been proposed by de Mandeville's countryman, Hugo Grotius, and by the Scottish Neoplatonist School, which claimed the existence of a 'natural' right, present both in nature and in the mind. As we have seen, Neoplatonists based the premises of the supposed innatism of morality on the assumption that all people instinctively knew whether an action was right or wrong. De Mandeville, on the other hand, demolished abstract universal morality by insisting on space-and-time-specific principles, that is, on cultural values that pertain to specific cultures and their different systems of education.[22] Dismantling the implicit holistic principles on which authority was set – the hierarchy of order and degree (i.e. rank) of the *Scala Natura* and the specular secular one on earth – de Mandeville revises holism[23] into utter particularism. He pared society down to the mere sum of egoistic individuals but, in contrast to Hobbes's materialistic, repressive and deterministic view, he ingeniously sees 'egoism' as a passion that needs to be positively directed and exploited for the profit and the good of a community, not by a king but by the people's representatives devoted to the common good and to the *res publica*. De Mandeville, indeed, questions the intrinsic justification for the necessity of an abidance by the laws set by an undebatable, imposed authority from which 'forced' laws derive. In contrast to this, he asks for a negotiation of the law, directed by all stakeholders and actors: the people and the sovereign, like in the constitutional monarchy, where the queen sitting in the hive is just one of the sharers and not on top of them.

In this sense, it is not by chance that de Mandeville's emphasis on people's inclination towards self-interest, on which the wellbeing of his hive rests would, soon after, be translated into the collective *laissez-faire* principle of economic liberalism by Adam Smith.

De Mandeville is thus the follower of Bacon and Locke, who had jointly deconstructed innatism from within, dismantling deduction and preconceived ideas, what Bacon called the *idola* of the mind.[24] In this way, de Mandeville anticipates Hume, who, in his *Treatise of Human Nature* (1739), further deconstructs metaphysics gradually from within.

De Mandeville, therefore, proves to be one of the detractors of natural jurisprudence, which was based on the idea of the existence of a 'natural' law, or *ius naturale*.[25] In "Remark C" of *The Fable of the Bees*, he strongly relies on the cultural power of the environment and its educational values (that of a specific space-time environment), which he sees as the real vehicle of ethics, values and behaviours, dismantling the belief in the innate sense of morality that deists and Neoplatonists in this version only called 'law':[26]

> The Multitude will hardly believe the excessive Force of Education, and in the difference of Modesty between Men and Women ascribe that to Nature, which is altogether owing to early Instruction: Miss is scarce Three years old, but she is spoken to every Day to hide her Leg, and rebuk'd in good Earnest if she shews it; while Little Master at the same Age is bid to take up his Coats, and piss like a Man. (FB1: 72)

De Mandeville confutes the champions of common sense[27]: believing, like Hobbes, that humanity is driven by egoism and passions, he sees morality as an artificial construct, the result of a process of acculturation that can also fail, as the past demonstrates. Said in his own words, it is the outcome of the "bewitching Engine" of "Flattery" (FB1: 43, FB1: 42) used by "Lawgivers and other wise men" (FB1: 42),[28] probably those of the Church, just the effect of a cultural rhetorical discourse – certainly not the outcome of an inborn moral sense (exactly as Darwin would later claim) but rather the mere result of one's environment, i.e. one's cultural context, the beliefs acquired and absorbed in one's family, such as its religion, set out at school and presumed and defended as if they were the Truth by a specific community, region, society or nation. De Mandeville says:

> I differ from my Lord Shaftesbury entirely, as to the Certainty of *Pulchrum & Honestum*, abstract from Mode and Custom: I do the same about the Origin of Society, and in many other Things, especially why a man is a Sociable Creature, beyond other Animals.[29]

Indeed, this might be read as a response to what Shaftesbury wrote in *Characteristicks*, where he claimed that "any fashion, law, custom or religion which may be ill and vicious itself (…) can never alter the eternal measures and immutable independent nature of worth and virtue."[30] Two other ideas are innate for Shaftesbury: *divinity* and *beauty*, both confirming the Platonic triumvirate.[31]

The false justifying authority of a supposed universal 'natural' ethics is thus freed from the aura of metaphysics it had always had. In "An Enquiry into the Origin of Moral Virtue", Shaftesbury dismantles why this has happened:

> The first Rudiments of Morality, broach'd by skilful Politicians, to render Men useful to each other as well as tractable, were chiefly contrived that the Ambitious might reap the more Benefit from, and govern vast Numbers of them with the greater Ease and Security. (FB1: 47)

David Hume, coming after de Mandeville, in his *Treatise on Human Nature* (1739), confirms Locke's focusing on how the mind reworks perceptions to create knowledge. Memory and the imagination are shown to be faculties present, in quality but not in quantity, in all human beings. Downplaying ingeniousness, now seen as the result of chance and experience in contrast to the idea of it being a gift from God or the gods, the new trust in creativity of the imagination will make every human being a possible artist, a possible utopian re-writer of the universe and its laws; a revolution that was, soon after, called 'Romanticism'. Hume also repeats Locke's nominalist conception of language, seeing universals only as hypothetical constructions of the mind and thus as mere names for 'ideal' things. Nevertheless, these do not exist and cannot be rationally proven to exist, and their material existence, independent of thought, is linked to their single, distinct, unique and not typological forms. Hume, therefore, inaugurates sceptical empiricism and directs it against 'universal' notions in general and metaphysics specifically.

But who then has the right to analyse the passions and the egoistic drives of people? According to de Mandeville, only the community of the state has this right through its social, laic ethics, predicated by its negotiated laws. The state guarantees that egoism is kept within safe limits and wealth is also distributed to those in need. Indeed, if benefactors act, they usually act only to bolster their own self-esteem or to be recognised by their peers as generous, with the aim of augmenting their public virtue, the private one remaining private and thus unascertainable. As a result, their acts are far from guaranteed. If public virtue is not the outcome of private virtue, what needs to be worked on is the ostensible contradiction in de Mandeville's *Fable*'s subtitle: "Private Vices, Public Benefits". Indeed, if "Private Vice by the dextrous Management of a skilful Politician may be turned into Public Benefits" (FB1: 369) and "these Qualifications [private vices], which we all pretend to be asham'd of, are the great support of a flourishing Society",[32] the paradox to be reached is exactly the transformation of vices into virtues, i.e., into social virtues.

Who can direct this inclination of egoistic private interest into a social benefit? For de Mandeville, it is not the king but the state and, during his times, parliament. This is clearly not the state indicated in *Leviathan*, where the king passes laws for his own and his retinue's prosperity, as exemplified in Abraham Bosse's famous etching (1651),[33] a state that maintained the order-and-degree hierarchy of the *Scala Natura*, guaranteeing the top power and an inequality system. According to de Mandeville, the means to paradoxically turn private interests into social pluses will be, and is, a different state, which would probably comprise what we today call the Welfare State.

This new anti-Leviathan state already existed in England – the constitutional monarchy, set up in 1689, foresaw the king – or queen, as in the case of the hive – sitting on top of the arena but not hierarchically imposing their will top-down. Instead, they were within the hive, like everybody else, as it is the hive itself that, bottom-up, puts them in this position: a most remarkable difference even though not fully exercised at that time.[34]

Against the devaluation of the material world, de Mandeville proposes a new understanding of ethics based on reason rather than religion, or mysticisms of sorts, defending its rational necessity and importance against the recourse to the external grace or wrath of God, as stated in Bosse's emblem. The queen partakes of the destiny of the state. The state, comprising all its representatives, will, therefore, become the supreme good, with politics seen cynically as a necessary evil: a matter related to the calculus people use to judge laws with and made in terms of a *do ut des* logic. State welfare will be regulated through the taxation system, by means of which the common good is redistributed to those that are in need, a first request for what would later be called the Welfare State:

> It may be said, that Virtue is made Friends with Vice, when industrious good People, who maintain their Families and bring up their Children handsomely, pay Taxes, and are several ways useful Members of the Society, get a Livelihood by something that chiefly depends on, or is very much influenc'd by the Vices of others, without being themselves guilty of, or accessory to them, any otherwise than by way of Trade, as a Druggist maybe to Poisoning, or a Sword-Cutler to Blood-shed. (FB1: 85)

Furthermore, in 1714, when de Mandeville's book was published and the Hanoverian dynasty was called to reign over Great Britain – as is made clear in a later Victorian emblematic visual example[35] – the Queen of Bees was now a constitutional queen: she does not preside over the hive from the outside. She has no privileged status but sits with her bees inside the hive and, moreover, the bees can get rid of her if she puts the interest of the hive-society in peril.

The only peril of politics is eristics, the rhetorical use or misuse politicians make of persuasiveness for ideological reasons or manipulation. Only Private Vices can create Public Virtues for de Mandeville, as Adam Smith was quick to understand and translate into its furthest possible development, the free-trade *laissez-faire* policy, liberalism, supported by the certainty that the market self-regulates. On the other hand, Jeremy Bentham, conscious of the risk implicit in this type of geometrical excess, mitigated it, translating it into the hazy ethical formula that favours, as a standard of wellbeing, the uncountable qualitative principle of happiness rather than other countable and quantitative elements of economics. This was synthesised in: "The greatest happiness for the greatest numbers ... is the measure for right and wrong"; the hedonic formula that became the basis for the economic utilitarianism of John Stuart Mill, who tries to generalise by glossing the principle that morality of personal pleasure should entail pursuit of the greatest amount of happiness altogether. At any rate, he continued to strongly assert the liberty of the people, who need to be protected in their freedom provided they do not harm others.[36]

To sum up: the argument of the Scottish Neoplatonists, like Shaftesbury and Hutcheson, was that every man possessed a self-evident and innate standard of behaviour, a natural ethics, the basis also of the natural law idea: 'natural' meaning an instinctive, innate or inborn sense of morality. Indeed, exerting a sort of social innatism, this school of thought claimed that, in case of doubt, one could safely rely on common sense.[37]

Enticing as this might seem, indeed it is not in that common sense, in hypostatising nature, does not consider nurture. Common-sense champions, unaware of regionalism, erected their regional, limited space-time-specifics – those of the *status quo* or of the *doxa* of their culture – mistaking their beliefs for universal values. Cultures, on the contrary, produce all sorts of beliefs, each culture producing its own. Common sense is thus no guarantee of ethical behaviour; rather, it betrays its cultural bias. Furthermore, common sense, being different for each culture and not being common at all, implicitly denies a natural or innate sense of ethics. Indeed, in his *Essay*, Locke defined 'custom' as "a greater power than nature" (JL: 89, Bk. 1, ch. 3, § 25). Since then, innatism as a notion had a hard time; Bacon, Locke, de Mandeville and Hume, the pragmatists, having won the intellectual battle against it. Another of its tenets was dismantled by philosopher William Duff, as we shall see in our next chapter.

1.2 The Dismantling of the Genius Theory

Addison devotes a great deal of attention to the imagination, considering it a faculty present in all human beings, able to create new original, unprecedented ideas. He distinguished between the primary pleasure, derived from the imagination as the result of something which, once seen, pleases us, shrewdly recovering Augustine's dictum on beauty, *id quod visum placet*,[38] and the secondary imagination, which is produced by associations of what we already know and evocation through descriptions, using evocative words (see JA: 416, 74-75), proposing both the ancient and the modern view as viable models.

When we turn to Homer, Pindar and Shakespeare, Addison considers them to be "Prodigies of Mankind" that are "wild and extravagant" and can, therefore, be considered "natural Genius's" who cannot be compared with the artificial "Polishing" of the French "*Bel Esprit*" (JA: 160, 283). According to Addison, Shakespeare belonged to the class of natural geniuses, who did not conform to "Rules" (JA: 160, 285), unlike Milton and Bacon, artists who "submitted the Greatness of their natural Talents to the Corrections and Restraints of Art" (JA: 160, 285). For Addison, both types achieve success, the quantity of their genius being the same, but Milton and Bacon "cramp their own Abilities too much by Imitation" so their results will be different.

> In the first, it is like a rich Soil in a happy Climate, that produces a whole Wilderness of noble Plants rising in a thousand beautiful Landskips, without any certain Order or Regularity. In the other, it is the same rich Soil under the same happy Climate, that has been laid out in Walks and Parterres, and cut into Shape and Beauty by the Skill of the Gardener. (JA: 160, 285)

Artists who follow rules neglect "the full Play to their own natural Parts", not permitting themselves to be "Original", ending up as "great Genius's (...) thrown away upon Trifles" (JA: 160, 286); still geniuses but based on "wonderful Perseverance and Application" (JA: 160, 286).

Addison's theory is also used in an important work on the topic of genius written by William Duff.[39] In his examination, Duff distinguished between the imagination as a creative power capable of conception, and fancy as a capacity exerting only an "extensive combination of ideas", thus combining the ideas of Addison and Hartley.[40] Addison, democratically, like the later William Duff,[41] sees the imagination as a communal faculty, present in each human being to be used as a treasure and activated to render it productive in its creative and esemplastic function – as Coleridge, who only comments without quoting Addison's theory, would say – so as to proactively create and envisage new images, forms, ideas and utopian solutions to change an unsatisfactory reality. In Essay No. 417 of *The Pleasures of the Imagination*, Addison states: "A poet should take as much Pains in forming his imagination as a Philosopher in cultivating his Understanding" (JA: 417, 78). If, as Paul Hunter[42] says, the Counter-Reformation created the reader by giving over to the people the tasks of interpreting the book of God themselves and following their own understanding, Addison, we could say, created the artist, the critic, the dissenter and the utopian revolutionary, an individuality perfectly embodied by Blake, the imaginative creator of his own grand cosmogony. Famous are his words in his utopian work *Jerusalem. The Emanation of the Giant Albion* (1804-1820): "I must create a system, or be enslaved by another man's. I will not reason and compare: my business is to create".[43]

The core motif that started the polemic around the conception of the genius involved philosophers, literary critics, poets and writers, who confronted each other from two opposing factions and two opposite camps, fighting for completely different visions of the world: those siding with change and originality, opting for acquired and nurtured ingeniousness, and those siding with stasis and the imitation of the Ancients, supporting its innatism. On the one hand, we find William Duff, with his book *Essay on Original Genius* (1767), and Alexander Gerard, who voices his theory of originality in his *Essay on Genius* (1774); Helvétius's *De l'esprit*: *or, Essays on the Mind and its Several Faculties* (1758),[44] with his merely environmental theory, represents the cultural argument, while on the other extreme we find the Neoplatonists. William Sharpe, an Anglican clergyman, in his work *A Dissertation upon Genius: or, an Attempt to shew that the Several Instances of Distinction, and Degrees of Superiority in the Human Genius are not, fundamentally, the result of Nature, but the Effect of Acquisition* (1755),[45] which, despite its promising title, uses the vocabulary of the empiricists, twisting it against them by reversing their argument and proposing working on one's innate ingeniousness so as to reach the best results by absorbing the extraordinary abilities *engrafted* in "abstract nature"[46] (p. 5, my emphasis) and to implement one's nature with the "necessity of instruction and information" (p. 6) so as to reach increasingly better results.[47] Kant, the authority on philosophy at the end of the 18th century, in his *Critique of Judgement*[48] says:

> *Genius* is the talent (natural endowment) which gives the rule to art. Since talent, as an innate productive faculty of the artist, belongs itself to nature, we may put it this way: Genius is the innate mental aptitude (*ingenium*) through which nature gives the rule to art. (I, § 46, 168)

Notes

---

[1] John Locke (1997 [1690]) *An Essay Concerning Human Understanding* (London: Penguin), cf. Bk. 2, ch. 1, § 2, where imagination is said to derive from experience, and in book 2, ch. 2, § 3, where a possible sixth sense is posited. In book 2, ch. 11, § 2, he distinguishes between imagination and reason, positing imagination as a faculty that, in exercising wit, unites and composes similar ideas, thus having a synthetic power, whereas judgement is a faculty that divides and separates ideas that might even be similar.

[2] John W. Yolton (2004) *The Two Intellectual Worlds of John Locke: Man, Person, and Spirits in the Essay* (Cornell: Cornell University Press).

[3] See John Locke, (1999) *The Reasonableness of Christianity and Paraphrases of St. Paul's Epistles* (ed.) John Higgins-Biggle (Oxford: Clarendon). Yolton, commenting on a passage of this work, says: "In a well-known passage, Locke remarks on the difficulty of 'unassisted Reason, to establish Morality' (p. 148). It is, he says, "at least a surer and shorter way, to the Apprehensions of the vulgar, and mass of Mankind, that one manifestly sent from God, and coming with visible Authority from him, should as a King and Law-maker tell them their Duties (...) The 'train of reasoning' probably reflects his suggestion in the *Essay* that a demonstrative morality could be constructed, deriving moral rules by reason. His early *Essays on the Law of Nature*, claimed that reason together with sense-perceptions could discover the law of Nature." (p. 145).

[4] Jonathan Swift (1898) *The Prose Works of Jonathan Swift* (ed.) Temple Scott (London: Bell and Sons), 2 vols., originally vol. 3: 'Swift's Writings on Religion and the Church', in vol. 1, p. 224.

[5] Cf. Tillyard, E.M.W. (1981 [1943] *The Elizabethan World Picture* (Harmondsworth: Penguin).

[6] Darrin McMahon (2013) *Divine Fury: A History of Genius* (Philadelphia: Basic Books), p. 17.

[7] See C.A. Patrides (ed.) (1980) *The Cambridge Platonists* (Cambridge: Cambridge University Press).

[8] Basil Willey (1967), in his *Seventeenth Century Background; Studies in the Thought of the Age in Relation to Poetry and Religion* (New York: Columbia University Press), writes: "Herbert discovers the principle of certainty in the 'natural instinct', the 'common notions' of mankind. Whatsoever (…) is received

by universal consent, that, and that only, is Truth." Willey then quotes Herbert himself: "universal consent will be the sovereign test of truth (...) and there is nothing of so great importance as to seek out these common notions, and to put each in their place as indubitable truths." (p. 123). His doctrine of innate notions was influential on Leibniz.

[9] Cf. Alain Petit, 'Ralph Cudworth, un Platonisme Paradoxal: La Nature dans la 'Digression Concerning the Plastick Life of Nature'. In G.A.J. Rogers, J.M. Vienne, J.C. Zarka (eds) *The Cambridge Platonists in Philosophical Context. Politics, Metaphysics and Religion*, Dordrecht: Kluwer, 1997, pp. 101-10. See also G.A.J. Rogers (1979) 'Locke, Newton, and the Cambridge Platonists on Innate Ideas' *Journal of the History of Ideas*, 40, pp. 191-215.

[10] The Cambridge Platonists considered reason to be the authority on all issues in that it was "a Seed of Deiform Nature" and thus "a natural revelation" that Revelation proper (Nature) had only to confirm. See Willey, Basil (1967) op. cit., p. 72, and his (1980 [1940]) *The Eighteenth-Century Background: Studies on the Idea of Nature in the Thought of the Period* (London: Chatto & Windus). See also: Ernst Cassirer (1953) *The Platonic Renaissance in England* (Austin: University of Texas Press); John W. Yolton (1956) *John Locke and the Way of Ideas* (Oxford: Oxford University Press), see ch. II, and for a nearly religious view about Locke's *Essay*, see his other book (2004) *The Two Intellectual Worlds of John Locke: Man, Person, and Spirits in the* 'Essay' (Ithaca, London: Cornell University Press); D.P. Walker (1972) *The Ancient Theology* (London: Duckworth); John Tulloch (1872) *Rational Theology and Christian Philosophy in the Seventeenth Century* (Edinburgh and London: W. Blackwood), 2 vols. See also Jonathan E. Lowe (1995) *Locke* (London: Routledge). Important for a reasoned study of Locke is Roland Hall & Roger Woolhouse (1983) *Eighty Years of Locke Scholarship: A Bibliographical Guide* (Edinburgh: Edinburgh University Press), and Kenneth MacLean (1962) *English Literature of the Eighteenth Century* (New York: Russell & Russell).

[11] See C.A. Patrides (1980) *The Cambridge Platonists* (Cambridge: Cambridge University Press).

[12] Cf. Anthony Ashley Cooper, Earl of Shaftesbury (1709) *Sensus Communis. An Essay on the Freedom of Wit and Humour* (London: Sanger) to be found also in his major work *Characteristicks of Men, Manners, Opinions and Times* (ed.) Douglas Den Uyl (Indianapolis: Liberty Fund, 2001), 3 vols., vol. 1, pp. 32-49, references to page no. appear in brackets. Here it says: "The Lovers of Mankind respect and honour Conventions and Societies of Men" (32). Speaking of the subjects of Morality and Religion, one of the speakers affirms that many people take the liberty to appeal to 'common sense': "If by the word Sense we were to understand Opinion and Judgment, and by the word common the Generality or any considerable part of Mankind; 'twou'd be hard (…) to discover where the Subject of common Sense cou'd lie. For that which was according to the sense of one part of Mankind, would be against the Sense of another (…) for some Virtue and Vice

being a mere matter or Fashion and Vogue" (40). The establishment of common principles for religion, policy and morals is therefore impossible, there being no agreement on a common system (40). Shaftesbury's character therefore relies on "endless Scepticism" (41). In Part II, section I, the same speaker comments on ethnic differences and on systems created by "Conjurers" that try, in principle, only to appear as fair as possible so "to better conceal their Practice", claiming thus "excellent moral Rules (…) greatest Purity of Religion (…) greatest Integrity of Life and Manners" (42) knitted together with "By-Laws and Political institutions" (43) in substance a "Cheat" (43) productive of "Fierce Prosecutors of Superstitions" (43). These facts, he continues, induce modern reformers to tell us that there is no "natural Faith or Justice (…) that there was no such thing in reality as Virtue; no Principle of Order in things above, or below; no secret Charm or Force of Nature, by which every-one was made to operate willingly or unwillingly towards publick Good" but rather only "Force and Power which constituted Right" (44). The addressee, at this point, responds, ironically, that it is better to keep the cheat that there is a "natural Affection (...) an *Art* by which we are happily tam'd, and render'd thus mild and *sheepish*", an attitude that in section II is comprised within "common Honesty" (44) a principle that works towards the publick Good and which is in contrast to a belief that "*by Nature* we are all *Wolves*" (44) which would, as a consequence, produce the giving over of Power "into one hand" (45) rather than having "a right Division and Balance" that would prevent mankind from "Subjection". In section III, Shaftesbury opposes Truth to Authority, and speaking of Virtue, often made into a mercenary thing, sees it as "estimable in it-self" and as a "*right* Inclination", "Love of Doing Good" should not, therefore, be connected to a Reward (46). He then speaks of the Jewish religion where Virtue is a free choice (47). In Part III, sect.1, he unites Virtue to "Publick Good" and praises the Britons, who possess a Sense in Morals that translates itself into a "Common sense in Politicks" (49) which respects a "Society being founded on a Compact; the Surrender made of every Man's private unlimited Right, into the hands of the Majority, or such as the Majority shou'd appoint", which is the result both of free Choice and of a Promise. (49) my emphases.

[13] In 1724, Frances Hutcheson (1694-1746), a pupil of Shaftesbury, wrote *An Inquiry into the Originals of our Ideas of Beauty and Virtue; in Two Treatises. In which the Principles of the late Earl of Shaftesbury are Explain'd and Defended, against the Author of the 'Fable of the Bees': and the Ideas of Moral Good and Evil are establish'd, according to the Sentiments of the Ancient Moralists. With an Attempt to introduce a Mathematical Calculation in Subjects of Morality* (Zürich: Georg Olms 1990).

[14] On common-sense notions, Locke comments: "It is not easy for the mind to put off those confused notions and prejudices it has imbibed from custom, inadvertency, and common conversation." (JL: 174, Bk. 2, ch. XIII, § 27). See M. Ben-Chaim (2000) 'Locke's Ideology of "Common Sense"', *Studies in History and Philosophy of Science*, Part A, 31, 3, 473-501.

[15] Thomas Reid (1764) *Inquiry into the Human Mind, on the Principles of Common Sense* (London: A. Millas).
[16] To confirm this, there is the subtitle of Hutcheson's major work: 'An Inquiry into the Original of Our Ideas of Beauty and Virtue' in his *Two Treatises, in which the Principles of (…) Shaftesbury are (…) defended against (…) 'The Fable of the Bees'* 1725 (cf. Bezrucka: 2016).
[17] In F.B. Kaye (1924) *The Fable of the Bees by Bernard de Mandeville*, II vol., 'The Fourth Dialogue', pp. 148-93 and 'The Fifth Dialogue', pp. 194-265, embodied hereafter in the text as BM: and p. no.
[18] For a comprehensive overview on de Mandeville, cf.: Irvin Primer (ed.) (1975) *Mandeville Studies: New Explorations in the Art and Thought of Dr. Bernard de Mandeville* (The Hague: Martinus Nijhoff). On the innate sense of morality, see William Law (1732) *Origin of Honour*, commented by F.B. Kaye (1924), in de Mandeville's *Fable of the Bees*, Book II (Oxford: Oxford University Press) on p. 185, n. 1, where he says: "[W. Law] asserted the divine origin of morality and society against Mandeville's argument that morality and society are the results of human endeavour (...) for human convenience". On page 92, de Mandeville explicitly speaks of Honour as an "acquir'd" standard. On the contrary, it is stated ironically in his work that only the seeds of Passions are inborn: in 'An Essay on Charity, and Charity-schools' he says: "But the Seeds of every Passion are innate to us and no body comes into the World without them" (*Fable of the Bees* Book 1, Part I, 253-322, p. 281).
[19] Locke, for his part, specifies that words "charm (...) men into notions" and that one has to be very careful particularly of how the people we are meant to trust use them: "father or schoolmaster, the parson of the parish, or such a reverend doctor" (JL: 444, Bk.III, ch. 10, § 16).
[20] Cooper, A.A, Lord Shaftesbury (1976) 'The Moralist, a Recital of Certain Conversations on Natural and Moral Subjects', Part 3, Sect II. In Albert Hofstadter, Richard Kuhns (eds) *Philosophies of Art and Beauty: Selected Readings in Aesthetics from Plato to Heidegger* (Chicago: Chicago University Press), p. 253.
[21] Bernard de Mandeville (1924 [1732]) *The Fable of the Bees, or Private Virtues, Publick Benefits* (ed.) F.B. Kaye (Oxford: Clarendon Press) 2 vols. [which uses the 1732 edition, the last authorised one during de Mandeville's life]. References, hereafter, to this edition will be given directly inserted in the text as FB1 or FB2: and page number. *The Fable* is preceded by *An Inquiry into the Origin of Moral Virtue, and Remarks*, present in FB1.
[22] Robertson, John M. (1900 [1711]) in his 'Introduction' to Shaftesbury's *Characteristics of Men, Manners, Opinions and Times* (London: Grant Richards) 2 vols., vol. I, xxxviii, comments that it is due to de Mandeville if we think that: "all our relish for beauty (…) is either from advantage, custom or education; and the argument of morals was on all fours."
[23] I have examined the dismantling of holism in the first half of the 18th century

extensively in Y. Bezrucka (2002) *Genio and immaginazione nel Settecento inglese*, op. cit., pp. 17-77.

[24] Francis Bacon's *Novum Organum*, presents a series of *idola*, idols of the mind, that he contests as being the result of old ways of thinking that he wants to dismantle: the rational and inferential way of reasoning that, according to him, is based on unproven and taken-for-granted ideas: indeed, *idola* of the mind. *Idola* or "illusions", as he calls them, can be either artificial or innate: "inherent in the nature of the intellect itself, which is found to be much more prone to error than the senses"; see F. Bacon (2000) *The New Organon* (eds) L. Jardine, M. Silverthorne (Cambridge: Cambridge University Press), p. 40 and 19. Bacon attacks Aristotle's syllogistic method and proposes to substitute this inferential or *idola* way of reasoning with the inductive scientific method, corroborated by the evidence of material proofs and experiments. *Idola* are wrongly venerated gods, forms of reasoning that need to be iconoclastically dismantled. These were for him congenital reasoning cages, present "in the poor structure of the mind" (p. 19), which resulted in ingrained and taken-for-granted truths, like the common-sense notions that Neoplatonists insisted one should rely upon in case of doubts. They needed to be refuted because people accept them as *idola*, truisms that needed, on the contrary, to be questioned. Bacon identifies the *idola* of the Cave, Tribe, Marketplace and Theatre and dismantles them by showing that they have no claim to truth. The idola of the Cave are subjective acquired notions that reflect time-space idiosyncrasies that people tend to apply to reality as a whole. The *idola* of the Tribe are notions that man infers from reason and sense but that are "relative" to the mind, that is – rewriting Plato's Myth of the Cave – "an uneven mirror receiving rays from things and merging its own nature with the nature of things, which thus distorts and corrupts it" (41). The *idola* of the cave can be personal or educational notions that one pretends to be universally valid without recognising their time-place specificity. The *idola* of the Marketplace are the cultural community-notions produced by "agreement and from men's association with each other" that produce a sort of semantics (a dictionary) that Bacon says can produce "violence to the understanding" (42). Bacon is probably referring to the eristic, rhetorical, persuasive and manipulative use of words merely to convince one's addressee without considering the truth value of the predicate. The *idola* of the Theatre are the philosophical constructions that have become *dogmas*, a synonym for *idola*. Metaphysically accepted as such, they are "axioms (…) which have grown strong from tradition, belief and inertia" (42); notions that do not even need anymore to claim truth-value deductively, being already so much ingrained as to be taken for granted. These last are the most dangerous for rationality and science.

[25] David Hume, in his work (1779) *Concerning Natural Religion*, defined "natural religion" as "so delicate a subject", cf. his letter 'Pamphilus to Hermippus', Gutenberg text, June 20, 2009 [EBook #4583]. In this work, he dedicates twelve discussions among friends who hold different opinions to ascertain whether a deistic position is tenable. Even though he did not come to a certain inductive

conclusion about the issue, he dismantles its 'naturality', which seemed, even up to then, still obvious.

[26] B. de Mandeville, 'The Introduction' to *An Enquiry into the Origin of Moral Virtue*, 1723, II ed. of *The Fable*, in FB1, 39-40.

[27] Common sense was invoked whenever a difficult answer was failing; see A.A. Shaftesbury, *Sensus Communis. An Essay on the Freedom of Wit and Humour*, Sanger, London 1709; to be found also in *Characteristics*, op. cit.

[28] In this sense, deists relied heavily on John Toland's (1696) *Christianity not Mysterious* (London: Buckley), which tried to eliminate every mystery from Christianity.

[29] B. de Mandeville (1732) *Letter to Dion,* p. 47, quoted in the 'Introduction to Mandeville's Thought' in FB1:§3, p. lxxv, note 1.

[30] Anthony Ashley Cooper, Earl of Shaftesbury (2001) *Characteristicks of Men, Manners, Opinions and Time* (ed.) Douglas Den Uyl (Indianapolis: Liberty Fund), 3 vols., vol. 2, sect. 3, p. 17.

[31] *ibid.* vol. 3, p. 18. In another note, on p. 171, Shaftesbury qualifies innate ideas further: "If we should speak accurately, there may be no conceptions imprinted on our minds by nature, nevertheless no one would deny that the faculties of our minds have been *shaped by nature* so that as soon as we start to use reason we begin to distinguish in some fashion truth from falsity, evil from good"; on p. 75, he affirms: "In nature, nevertheless, there are natural Standards (...) according to which we perpetually approve or disapprove and to whom in all natural appearances, all moral actions (whatever we contemplate, whatever we have in debate) we inevitably appeal, and pay our constant Homage."

[32] B. de Mandeville, 'Introduction' to *An Enquiry into the Origin of Moral Virtue*, 1723, II ed. of the *Fable*, in FB1:39-40.

[33] Cf. Bezrucka Y. (2016) 'Beehive-Images and Politics in Bernard de Mandeville's 'The Fable of the Bees': Empiricism *vs* Innatism', Cardozo Research Paper Series, *Cardozo Electronic Law Bulletin*, 1-26, see image on p. 6.

[34] Members of Parliament were elected by constituencies around the country, which clearly reflected the distribution of power: "After the Act of Union with Scotland in 1707 (…) there were 558 MPs elected by 314 constituencies, 245 of which were in England (…) with 45 in Scotland and 24 in Wales." Cf. James Vernon (2017) *Modern Britain: 1750 to the Present* (Cambridge: Cambridge University Press), p. 16.

[35] Cf. the image by Gabriel Shire Tregear (29.8.1837) *The Queen Bee in her Hive*, in Bezrucka Y. (2016) 'Beehive-Images', op. cit., p. 19.

[36] J. Bentham, in (1789[1780]) *An Introduction to the Principles of Morals and Legislation* (Oxford: Clarendon Press), worked on this topic along the lines of previous thinkers, amongst whom were Francis Hutcheson, William Paley and John Gay, but he was the first to propose a formula that envisaged personal pleasure and pain. This he connected to his famous *felicific calculus*: "the greatest happiness of the greatest number (…) is the measure of right and wrong" that, as

seen, had been anticipated by Hutcheson's similar attempt at a calculation of the results of moral principles. The interesting point is that this introduces an ethical qualitative corrective in a quantitative market economy – the hedonistic or *felicific calculus* – i.e. a thoroughly personal and individualistic concept since happiness is connoted differently for each of us.

[37] A.A. Shaftesbury (1709) *Sensus Communis. An Essay on the Freedom of Wit and Humour* (London: Sanger), re-edited in Shaftesbury (1981) *Sämtliche Werke* (eds) G. Hemmerich, W. Benda (Stuttgart: Frommann-Holzboog), I, 3, pp. 14-129, present also in *Characteristics of Men, Manners, Opinions and Times*, J.M. Robertson, op. cit.

[38] "What, once seen, pleases", my tr.

[39] Cf. Duff, William (1994 [1767]) *Essay on Original Genius* (London: Routledge/Thoemmes). On the importance of the depreciation of the previous theory of the genius through the theory of the imagination, see Bezrucka: 2002.

[40] Cf. William Duff, *Essay on Original Genius*, op. cit., p. 59.

[41] William Duff, in his *Essay on Original Genius*, op. cit., turns the concept of ingeniousness into that of invention, giving prominence to the imagination in its, common to all, ability to create and invent new original forms (Bezrucka: 2002, pp. 25-54).

[42] Hunter, J. Paul (1990) *Before Novels. The Cultural Contexts of the Eighteenth-Century English Fiction*, (London: Norton).

[43] W. Blake (1998 [1804]) in Paley, Morton D. (ed.) *Jerusalem. The Emanation of the Giant Albion, the Illuminated Books*, vol. 1, The William Blake Trust (Princeton: Princeton University Press). In 'To the Christians', p. 258, Blake makes his *peana* for the imagination that he sees as the fount of liberty for mankind: "I know of no other Christianity and of no other Gospel than the liberty both of body & mind to exercise the Divine Arts of Imagination / Imagination the real & eternal World of which this Vegetable Universe is but a faint shadow & in which we shall live in our Eternal or Imaginative Bodies, when these Vegetable Mortal Bodies are no more. The Apostles knew of no other Gospel. (...) What is the Divine Spirit? Is the Holy Ghost any other than an Intellectual Fountain?"; the task being indeed that of personal evolution: "Answer this to yourselves, & expel from among you those who pretend to despise the labours of Art & Science, which alone are the labours of the Gospel: Is not this plain & manifest to the thought? Can you think at all, & not pronounce heartily! That to Labour in Knowledge is to Build up Jerusalem: and to Despise Knowledge, is to Despise Jerusalem & her Builders. And remember: He who despises & mocks a Mental Gift in another; calling it pride & selfishness & sin; mocks Jesus the giver of every Mental Gift, which always appears to the ignorance-loving Hypocrite, as Sins, but that which is a Sin in the sight of cruel Man is not so in the sight of our kind God."

[44] In Essay III of his work, Helvetius combines a natural gift with the effects of education, and identifies the natural "gifts" of the mind with the "delicacy of the senses, extent of memory, and capacity of attention", which are unequally

distributed. In ch. XXX of the same Essays, he clearly states: "All men well-organised, have the natural power of acquiring the most exalted ideas, and the difference of genius observable in them, depends on the various circumstances in which they are placed and on the different education they receive. This conclusion discovers the full importance of education." This also gives him the opportunity to say that "it is not then from the different temperature of climates, but from moral causes that we ought to search for the reason of the inequality of genius." C.A. Helvétius (1810 [1758]) *De L'esprit: or, Essays on the Mind, and Its Several Faculties* (London: Albion Press), p. xxxv.

[45] William Sharpe (1755) *A Dissertation upon Genius: or, an Attempt to shew that several Instances of Distinction, and Degrees of Superiority in the human Genius are, not fundamentally, the Result of Nature, but the Effect of Acquisition* (London: C. Bathurst).

[46] *ibid.* p. 5.

[47] *ibid.* p. 6.

[48] Immanuel Kant (1911 [1790]) *Kant's Critique of Aesthetic Judgement* (ed.) Henry Frowde (*Kritik der Urteilskraft*), tr. J.C. Meredith (Oxford: Clarendon Press).

CHAPTER TWO

EMPIRICISM APPLIED

There is more Beauty in the Works of a true Genius who is ignorant of all the Rules of Art,
than in the works of a little Genius, who not only knows, but scrupulously observes them.
(JA: 92, 128)

2.1 Addison and *The Pleasures of the Imagination*

The first critical attack on Southern European Aesthetics was launched by Joseph Addison. When he published in his journal *The Spectator* a series of papers with the title "The Pleasures of the Imagination", Nos. 411-421 (21st June - 3rd July 1712),[1] he was likely unaware of the long-standing revolution in aesthetics that he was ushering into English literature.[2]

The title is, significantly, self-explicit. Focusing on the word "pleasures", Addison eludes the morally edifying *niveau* of ethics – that art had, up to then, protected – to move towards the examination of subjective feelings and the direct, i.e. emotional, reactions art might produce, such as pleasure, disgust or even pain, *de facto* anticipating Burke by nearly half a century (1757). Authorising pleasures as such, Addison[3] was the first scholar to open the precincts of art and aesthetics to – up to then – hidden subjects and topics. In this way, and this is the foremost advance of Addison's aesthetics, he legitimises all kinds of idiosyncratic pleasurable responses in aesthetic matters, anticipating a 20th-century reader-response criticism or reception theory.[4]

This move from ethics to aesthetics is the result of the application of the empiricist method, strictly based on the senses, to the domain of art and literature. The new aesthetics, focusing on emotions rather than rationality, favours the specific feelings of "embodied" people, and not of spiritual entities. The new sensory focus produced two results: besides inaugurating, little by little, the deconstruction of the so-called universal typologisations of people – abstract and unembodied, so as to hide their differences – that had been set as the model addressees of the philosophical and literary works of the past, the new orientation enabled a progressive move towards the artistic representation of these particular, and even unedifying, characters that were, idiosyncratically, who they were: unique individuals leading unique lives. This is a shift we can follow and measure clearly in the new 18th-century novel, and it has been the focus of Ian Watt's canonical work on the representational realism of the novel (1957) and of McKeon's[5] amplification of the panorama, seeing realism as one amidst the other coexisting plural forms of the 18th century: idealism, empiricism and scepticism (McKeon: 1987, 1-3). These are trends that climaxed in the individual poetry of the totally different poets and writers of the canonical, end-of-century, Romantic Age: Blake represents the symbol and synthesis of all McKeon's novelistic tendencies, even though transposed and applied to poetry, and becomes, in my opinion, the matrix of what was to follow, the *par excellence* proto-romantic. These are artists that ideally complete and are comprised within Addison's perspectival focus on the world, that is, subjectively seen through "the Eye of the Beholder" (JA: 412, 61).

The distance that was growing between innatism and empiricism, universality and subjectivity, can also be clearly marked on the *niveau* of ethics. If we compare the subjective particularism of Addison's *Pleasures* (1712) to Francis Hutcheson's recovery of Shaftesbury's innate morality (*Characteristicks,* 1711), rewritten into a geometrical *super-partes* morality (*Attempt to introduce a Mathematical Calculation in Subjects of Morality*, 1724),[6] we have the two extremes of the spectrum. Nevertheless, it is the focus on mere self-interest and the economic liberalism of the free-trade axiom of Hutcheson's pupil Adam Smith (*Theory of Moral Sentiment*, 1759) that fostered a mitigation of personal pleasures or drives, marked in exact terms by Jeremy Bentham's *felicific calculus* and Greatest Happiness Principle (*An Introduction to the Principles of Morals and Legislation,* 1780), glossed by J.S. Mill (*Utilitarianism*, 1863) into the non-personal greatest happiness altogether. J.E. Crimmins writes:

> In IPML [*An Introduction to the Principles of Morals and Legislation*], Bentham directed this analysis against a host of ethical propositions he sought to eliminate as competing alternatives to the utility principle, such as "moral sense", "common sense", "law of reason", "natural justice", and "natural equity". All are dismissed on the grounds that they are merely empty phrases that express nothing beyond the sentiment of the person who advocates them. Not representing verifiable reality, such phrases could not be considered useful. Indeed, they were surely pernicious, serving as a "pretense, and aliment, to despotism; if not (…) in practice, a despotism however in disposition" (1970, 28n). By comparison, "utility" was a principle rooted in the empirical and verifiable facts of the felt

experience of pains and pleasures.[7]

If we examine Jeremy Bentham's reversal of issues with his utilitarian but thoroughly idiosyncratic attempt to establish a calculation on the most personal concept possible – that of happiness, the keyword of his *felicific calculus* – we exactly measure the distance between Shaftesbury's and Hutcheson's impersonal rationality and Addison's and J.S. Mill's focus on sentiments. This underlines the fact that rationality could not fully describe the complexity of real people, being concerned only with universal typologies and perfect inexistent types. Subjective and utterly personal feelings – e.g. *happiness* – needed to be considered murky but all-important elements for the justification of an ethical – i.e. fair – dimension of economics – again, as has already been said, nuances of the gamut between innatism vs. empiricism.

Pleasures, as such, were notoriously feared in that, philosophically, they were always linked to egotistic, privately driven feelings and desires or passions that society needed and attempted to curb to maintain control. Hobbes, for example, in *The Leviathan*, characterises all passions and idiosyncratic inclinations as sinful desires.[8] The personal and subversive individual dimension, whereby pleasures abide, was also the negative crux for those who defended the authority of the Ancients against the Moderns, praising their sifted and tested models of artistic beauty. They were *literati* that wanted these overly personal feelings to be prevented by favouring pure beauty and what they considered to be ideal, trustworthy and neutral characters and characteristics. In England, this was marked by the absorption of the continental *Querelle des Anciens et des Modernes,*[9] with intellectuals siding for either stance. To defend novelty and the Moderns, Addison ingeniously devised a new understanding of aesthetics, based on the application of Locke's senses-apparatus, to authorise a personal and therefore bodily understanding of the meaning of beauty. He thus holds, like Locke and later Hume, that perception precedes reflection: "It is but opening the eye and the scene enters" (JA: 11, 57); senses being the filter through which human beings apprehend the world and the means for the inscription in the *tabula rasa* of the mind, as Hume would later rename what Locke had defined "the white paper" or the blank slate of the unprejudiced mind of children that "receives any character" (JL: 88, Bk. 1, ch. 3., §22).[10]

The senses were the bricks of knowledge also for Francis Bacon, who stated that only observation and experiment can be considered guarantees of truth. The consequence of this was his notorious and influential move of setting the scientific value of induction (proofs) over deduction (reasoning). Only facts, not rational thoughts or reasoning, and their gathering so as to predict hypotheses, to be confirmed by experiment, guaranteed scientific truth, as he says in *The New Organon* (1620), the extant part of his, uncompleted, *Instauratio Magna* (1620).[11] All empiricist philosophers focus their attention on the ideas that result from perception – the filter through which we apprehend reality – activated by looking, tasting, hearing, touching and smelling rather than focusing on the final principle that would have activated or created the senses in the first place.

To summarise: why is it, then, that all these people deem it important to debunk innatism? Because they see innatism as the hardest stronghold and core of the Design theory and the old idea of the *Natura Naturata*, or created nature, that had been used, via the formula *Natura Codex Dei,* to justify creationism, but it was also – and, unfortunately, still is – the premise for the various declinations into a variety of religious beliefs that all claim their unique divine rightfulness. Innatism is also mirrored in the theory of the natural genius that reads ingeniousness as an inborn gift of God, or in alternative declinations as directly inspired by him or his intermediary, the Holy Spirit, or, in secular versions, the divine Muses.[12] As a result of Addison's theory, imagination was finally totally linked to the body, and while it was only one of the faculties of the mind, it was the one that provided the greatest possibilities for change and understanding, humankind being made accountable for their actions, and for the world itself. The imagination was no longer the innate gift of a superior Being. Indeed, nature itself had been one of the cyphered signs that imposed a filter to interpretation through the master premise of a creator, a superimposition on the objectivity of facts. As a result, nature, circularly, was interpreted as upholding creationism. In the words of Abrams:

> Some Neoclassic critics were also certain that the rules of art, though empirically derived, were ultimately validated by conforming to that objective structure of norms whose existence guaranteed the rational order and harmony of the universe. In a strict sense, as John Dennis made explicit what was often implied, Nature 'is nothing but that Rule and Order, and Harmony, which we find in the visible Creation'; so 'Poetry, which is an imitation of Nature', must demonstrate the same properties.[13]

This is a circularity that is further sustained by an unprecedented synergic confluence of the sister arts, pictorial art and writing, as J.H. Hagstrum underlines: "Lord Chesterfield urged his son to read Ariosto because 'his painting is excellent.' Of Shakespeare, Gray says, 'Every word in him is a picture.' Uvedale Price found *Gulliver's Travels* to be a picture. Boswell called his 'Life of Johnson' a 'Flemish picture' of his revered friend."[14]

Such transcoded artistic works, using *la belle nature* (only), tended to reinforce the message of this being God's open book.

Addison, therefore, sees God as "the great sovereign of Nature" (JA: 531, 211), implying a deistic stance that nevertheless is not always convincing. In *The Spectator,* he summarises Locke almost *verbatim* and quotes him specifically on the idea of God as being: "made up of the simple *Ideas* we receive from *Reflection*; *v.g.* (...) from what we experiment in our selves (...) we enlarge every one of these with our *Idea* of Infinity; and so, putting them together, make our complex *Idea of God*" (JA: 531, 211). This explanation, he says, is confined to "the Light of Reason and Philosophy. If we would see him in all the Wonders of his Mercy, we must have Recourse to Revelation (...) But, as this is a Theory which falls under every one's consideration (...) I shall here only take notice of that habitual Worship and Veneration which we ought to pay to this Almighty Being" (JA: 531, 212-13). Quoting from a funeral sermon, Addison's argument should be interpreted as an eristic discourse whose real meaning is the critique enclosed in its antiphrastic structure, i.e. only its antiphrastic structure shows Addison's real stance:

> We should often refresh our minds with the Thought of him, and *annihilate* our selves before him, in the Contemplation of our own *Worthlessness* (...) This would imprint in our Minds such a constant and uninterrupted *Awe and Veneration*, as that which I am recommending, and which is in reality a kind of *incessant Prayer*, and reasonable *Humiliation of the Soul* before him who made it. This would *effectually kill in us all the little Seeds of Pride, Vanity and Self-conceit*, which are apt to shoot up in the Minds of such whose Thoughts turn more on those comparative Advantages which they enjoy over some of their Fellow-Creatures, than on the infinite Distance which is placed between them and the Supreme Model of all Perfection. It would likewise *quicken our Desires* and Endeavours of uniting our selves to him by all the Acts of Religion and of Virtue. (JA: 531, 213, my emphasis)

Devotion and religious worship, he said, "must be the effect of a Tradition from some first Founder of Mankind, or that it is conformable to the Natural Light of Reason or that it proceeds from an Instinct implanted in the Soul it self" (JA: 201, 123), proposing thus all possible explanations for the creationist hypotheses: the religious, the rational and the innatist.[15]

In conclusion, concerning Addison's attitude towards religion, one must consider one of his final essays on it. In No. 574, he says: "there was never any System besides that of Christianity, which could effectually produce in the Mind of Man (...) Virtue. (...) Religion bears a more tender Regard to humane Nature (...) It prescribes to every miserable Man the

Means of bettering his Condition; nay, it shews him, that the bearing of his Affliction as he ought to do will naturally end in the Removal of them: It makes him easie here, because it can make him happy hereafter: Upon the whole, a contented Mind is the greatest Blessing a Man can enjoy in this world." (JA: 574, 69)

Previously, he had undermined, without directly mentioning it, Leibniz's *Theodicy*, another system providing a theological and teleological answer about life telling us that: "whatever Evil befalls us is derived to us by a fatal Necessity, to which the Gods themselves are subject; (...) others very gravely tell the Man who is miserable, that it is necessary he should be so as to keep up the Harmony of the Universe, and the *Scheme* of Providence would be troubled and perverted were he otherwise. These, and the like Consideration, rather silence than satisfie a Man. They may show him that his Discontent is unreasonable, but are by no means sufficient to relieve it. They rather give Despair than Consolation" (JA: 574, 69).

Speaking about the origin of the Discontent in Men in the same essay, he said: "Men of Sense have at all times beheld with a great deal of Mirth this silly Game that is playing over their Heads, and by contracting their Desires, enjoy all the secret Satisfaction which others are always in quest of. The Truth is this ridiculous Chace [chase] after *imaginary Pleasures* cannot be sufficiently exposed, as it is the Source of those Evils which generally undo a Nation" (JA: 574, 67, my emphasis), where the inversion of the previous 'bodily' Pleasures of the Imagination should be noted.

To summarise: in Essay No. 590, he says that God:

> is indeed a Thought too big for the Mind of Man, and rather to be entertained in the Secrecy of Devotion, and in the Silence of the Soul, than to be expressed by Words. The Supreme Being has not given us Powers or Faculties sufficient to extol and magnifie such unutterable Goodness. It is however some Comfort to us, that we shall be always doing what we shall never be able to do, and that a Work which cannot be finished, will however be the Work of an Eternity. (JA: 590, 123)

Let us come then to *The Pleasures of the Imagination,* which are a counterpart to the just-seen "Imaginary Pleasures" but that might be related, as Addison hints, to the faculty that promotes all kinds of inexistent powers that, in this instance and in contrast to the previous ones, produce immediate and not future pleasures.

Imagination, or fancy, as Addison uses the terms "promiscuously" (JA: 411, 56), will hereafter no longer be the same. Indeed, future conceptions of the idealistic romantic subject are comprised within his conception of the imagination, a faculty democratically present in everyone, i.e. providing everyone a right to use it. This belief debunks thus the last tenets of innatism, implicitly and inherently present in the old theory of the genius. Addison, following John Locke strictly and championing his idea of the mind as a *tabula rasa* as developed in his *An Essay Concerning Human Understanding* (1690),[16] nearly quotes him *verbatim* when he states: "we cannot indeed have a single Image in the Fancy that did not make its first Entrance through the Sight" (A:537), nobody having set anything in the mind beforehand.

This perspective supports the thoroughly original understanding of the century's *Weltanschauung*, focusing on the epistemic process that passes from innatism to empiricism and, with it, from the ancient imitative Neoclassical theory of art to the creative Romantic one. Most certainly, the new orientation did not directly cancel out previous conceptions but they had to vie with this challenging new epistemology. The importance of the shift from innatism to empiricism is an unseen connection even in the ground-breaking studies of the Romantic theory, for example, in M.H. Abrams' studies (1953, 1973) who speaks of "the secularization of inherited theological ideas", considering it simply as an "assimilation and reinterpretation (...) from a supernatural to a natural frame of reference" (1953: 12).

Addison focuses on natural geniuses as those "who by mere strength of natural parts, and without any assistance of art or learning have produced works that were the delight of their own times, and the wonder of posterity" that he sees as "nobly wild and extravagant (...) infinitely more beautiful than all the turn and polishing of (...) a Bel Esprit (...) a Genius refined by Conversation. The Greatest Genius which runs through the Arts and Sciences, takes a kind of Tincture from them, and falls unavoidable into Imitation", whereas the natural geniuses "were never disciplined and broken by rules of Art" (JA: 160, vol. 1, 283).

John Locke and Addison, with their emphasis on the creative capacity of the imagination to envisage inexistent systems, fostered people to take direct action in order to change reality. This new focus could authorise us to rename and revise the periodisation of Romanticism. By starting it in 1712, concomitantly with the publication of Addison's *Pleasures*, we could call it "The Age of the Imagination", and thus rename the whole period "The Long Enlightened Romanticism", definitions which comprise apart from the initial ten years, almost the entire 18th century.

This periodisation and these definitions correspond more adherently to a still-lingering Neoclassicism but the emphasis is focused on the successive blooming of the imagination. We are aware that there is always a coexistence of issues present in each period under examination but we also think that, seen with the advantage of hindsight, a major general development can always be traced and this general trend should be determined.

In England, the emphasis on the senses that empiricism set in motion and the attention paid to the possibilities provided by the imagination fostered, little by little, the creation and definition of a Northern aesthetics and tradition. This was the result of the effort of seeing whether a shared feeling of unity and identity existed in England, besides the external one provided by the Southern aesthetics.

Through the invention of common roots, based on the adoption of a merely Northern perspective on the country, Northern aesthetics was *de facto* created – for example, by pointing out the cold atmosphere of English nature (*Wuthering Heights*), or its clouds (present both in Gainsborough's and Constable's studies),[17] the night rather than day, the moon rather than the sun (elements that Gothic Graveyard Poetry and the Gothic novel exploited). This favouring of Northern geographical and climatic elements, rather than the also present Southern solar ones, was reinforced by Addison's emphasis on the particularities of English nature and Gilpin's picturesque. These represented the groundwork of the Manichean aesthetics of Burke's sublime deployed against the classical idea of a pacifying beauty, and with it came all the related corollaries of artistic consequences: the invention of the Domestic Tour in contrast to the Grand Tour, the exploitation of fear, the favouring of intricacy above symmetry, the aesthetics of the English garden, Hogarth's new line of beauty, the triumph of variety.

These are all perspectival choices based on the emphasis placed on unique individuals, on their differences, on their unique peculiarities. This would bloom into Romanticism but would be applied in overarching terms to define people and nations, focusing on their differences rather than on the shared humanitarian conceptions that, for example, appeared in the cosmopolitism of this age and its antiquarians (cf. Goldsmith's *Citizen*) but were now out of favour. Why they are not being chosen as the master trends is extremely clear: having been limited, by their own choice, by rules that did not represent their specific characteristics, the artists and critics of England revolted against these self-imposed dispositions to show that they also had a distinguished and complex Olympus, albeit different from the Southern one.

All of this would never have happened without Joseph Addison and, although he has not produced a systematic work of philosophy, he has the right to be included in the empiricist tradition by merit of his study of the imagination and his consistent and well-defined theory, which Coleridge used without giving him his due. This is an *ante litteram* work of aesthetics that, as we have seen, did not exist at that time as a branch of studies of its own. Addison needs thus to be granted an outstanding place among the Fathers of the Enlightenment – the Masters of the Empiricist Tradition and their works: i.e. Bacon (1620), Locke (1690), Addison (1712), de Mandeville (1714) and, later, Hume (1739).[18] Furthermore, this claim rests also on Addison's role of divulger of the empiricist tradition in his journal *The Spectator*.

Indeed, in his analysis of the epistemology of the imagination, Addison confirms the common primary dispute of the empiricists, whose core was the effort to dismantle innatism and its implied design: the creationist theory championed by Descartes.[19] The empiricist considered it important to dismantle perceived truisms that had no truth behind them. We all have ideas that we take for granted, that we perceive as if we were born with them, which the Neoplatonists called common-sense ideas. Nevertheless, if rightly examined, we recognise that these are only the result of our space-time-specific education. It was therefore all too easy to link common sense with the idea that God created us with an innate foreknowledge. The theory, of course, upheld creationism but, more importantly, it upheld a principle of an authority external to man that humankind had to abide by, whether that of God or his representative on earth, the king, implicitly repeating a hierarchical cosmogony that kept people meek and acquiescent, either out of fear of retaliation or their expectation of a next-life reward.

Addison, undermining a finalistic reading of the world and evading the control that this system upheld, recognised, like the empiricists, an unprecedented position for the senses and the imagination, and he also assigned a subversive centrality to their pleasures. In Essay No. 413 of *The Pleasures*, disputing the causes of the pleasures connected to things "Great, New or Beautiful" (JA: 413, 63), Addison concludes – as the quote from Ovid, opening the essay, testifies: "*Causa latet: vis est notissima*" (Metam. IV, 287)[20] – that we must admit that it is impossible for us to assign clearly the "necessary and efficient cause of this Pleasure". In Aristotelian terms, this means that it is impossible for us to determine the agent of the causes and we can only reflect on the pleasures and displeasures caused "without by this meaning that the Final Causes" (or the final "why" for which a thing was produced) "lie more bare and open to our Observation". Nevertheless, he continues, "these, tho' they are not altogether so satisfactory, are generally more useful than the others, as they give us a greater Occasion of admiring the Goodness and Wisdom of the First Contriver" (JA: 413, 63) who "has so formed the Soul of Man, that nothing but himself can be its last, adequate, and proper Happiness", engaging us "to search into the Wonders of his Creation" (JA: 413, 64). What of course is missing here is an awareness that the cultural or perspectival standpoints from which one looks – the filters one applies – already determine the results: the choice of the epistemic stance, fatally guiding us towards certain findings, permits us only to see what we already know. If we look at nature, searching its beauty, we come to certain results; if we do the same through negative filters, we reach others, a point about the importance of one's perspective that Addison explained in Essay No. 411. These are the two opposites between which the creationist hypothesis was measured during the 18th century: creationism on one side, atheism on the other; and in the middle deists, freethinkers, scientists and sceptics. This is Addison's response to the issue, and what I interpret not as proof of his deism, the stance usually attributed to him, but as his unequivocal enlightened and sceptical answer to the theological rationalists:

> We are every where entertained with pleasing Shows and Apparitions, we discover *imaginary Glories in the Heaven*, and in the Earth, and see some of this *Visionary Beauty* poured out upon the whole Creation; *but what a rough unsightly Sketch of Nature should* we be entertained with, did *all her Colouring disappear*, and the several Distinctions of Light and Shade disappear? In short, *our Souls are* at present delightfully *lost and bewildered in a pleasing Delusion* (...) indeed the Ideas of Colours are so pleasing and beautiful in the Imagination (...) *as they are* at present by the different *Impressions of* the subtle *Matter on the Organ of Sight.* (...) *Light and Colours*, as apprehended by the Imagination, *are only Ideas in the Mind, and not Qualities that have an Existence in Matter*. (JA: 413, 64-65, emphasis added).

Addison is here referring to Locke's *Essay on Human Understanding*, Bk. 2, ch. VIII, and precisely to § 7, which I will quote in its entirety:

> §7. Ideas in the mind, qualities in bodies. To discover the nature of our ideas the better, and to, discourse of them intelligibly, it will be convenient to distinguish them as they are ideas or perceptions in our minds; and as they are modifications of matter in the bodies that cause such perceptions in us: that so we *may not* think (as perhaps usually is done) that they are exactly the images and *resemblances* of something inherent in the subject; most of those of sensation being in the mind no more the likeness of

> something existing without us, than the names that stand for them are the likeness of our ideas, which yet upon hearing they are apt to excite in us. (JL: Bk. 2, ch. 8, §7 p. 134)

As Addison says: "a pleasing Delusion". In Newton's words: "For the Rays to speak properly are not coloured. In them there is nothing else than a certain Power and Disposition to stir up a Sensation of this or that Colour."[21] He also refers to Newton's *Opticks* (1704), as did Locke, given that Newton's theories were well known before 1704 and that book, as Marjorie Hope Nicholson reminds us, "among the poets (...) was even more familiar than was the more famous work [*Principia* (1692)]" (1966: VII).

In his application of the empiricist theory of apprehension to aesthetics, Addison authorises an uncurbed and healthy[22] bodily knowledge that had previously been neglected: "Pleasures of the Fancy are more conducive to Health, than those of Understanding, which are worked out by Dint of Thinking, and attended with too violent a Labour of the Brain" (JA: 411, 58). To neglect the creationist hypothesis also meant ushering in atheism, and the absence of an outside authority that could be called in as a dogmatic system of reference for humankind, aimed at containing liberty and its free effects within the cage of morality.

Developing the empiricists' theories concerning the importance of the senses, seen as the only trustworthy antennae of the body that register and permit us to analyse reality, Addison launched his attack on the authority of the Ancients through his thoroughly new conception of the imagination, seen as a middle organ not so "gross (…) as sense, nor so refined as (…) understanding" (JA: 411, 57).[23] He is also careful to underline that "We cannot indeed have a single image in the fancy that did not make its first entrance through the sight; but we have the power of retaining, altering, and compounding those images (…) into all the Varieties of Picture and Vision that are most agreeable to the Imagination." Sight furnishes ideas that activate "the pleasures of the imagination, or fancy (which I shall use promiscuously)" (JA: 411, 56). Pleasure can be activated by visible objects "or when we call up their ideas into our minds by paintings, statues, descriptions, or any the like occasion". We can immediately be struck by the beauty of an object or associating thoughts of what the senses had previously experienced with newly acquired ones, or when inventing something anew, through wit, which is one of the ways through which the imagination works. Even on a first reading of Addison's papers, one quickly realises that his discussion of the pleasures of the imagination clearly enforces the primacy of the senses and the delight these might offer through their organs: sight, hearing, touch, smell, taste all being mentioned.[24]

It comes as no surprise, then, that Addison's empiricism was soon translated into a theory of the beautiful. Alexander Baumgarten, in his work *Aesthetica*, published in 1750, inaugurates a new science intended to analyse the psychological effects of the Beautiful, to which Edmund Burke would respond with his *On the Origin of the Idea of the Beautiful and the Sublime*, published in 1757, which incorporates the English or, as I propose to call it, the Northern aesthetics or Northern sublime.

By using the subjectively-connoted word "pleasures", Addison legitimises the opening of aesthetics to previously unknown territories, without the restraints and rules that had been prescribed until then. He echoes and promotes Locke's new epistemological theory to examine without a priori preconceptions the stages of apprehension of works of art and nature, both beautiful and ugly but still pleasurable. Addison needs thus to be considered Edmund Burke's precursor, particularly as far as the observation of the emotions that people feel and perceive in the presence of sublime scenes is concerned. Addison's opening to ugliness, which Burke in 1757 only repeated, remains historical:

> There may indeed, be something so terrible or offensive, that the Horrour or Loathsomeness of an Object may overbear the Pleasure which results from its 'Greatness', 'Novelty' or 'Beauty', but still there will be such a mixture of Delight in the very Disgust it gives us, as any of these three qualifications are most conspicuous and prevailing. (JA: 412, 59)

Joseph Addison thus authorises the indisputability and irrefutability of particularly personal reactions to art; feelings that could, at last and at least, be analysed, inaugurating for us – the reader will excuse the irony – aesthetic modernity before aesthetics as such was even born. Indeed, aesthetics, which at that time did not nominally exist as a science, was included in the rhetorical treatises of the Ancients, which prescribed rules. We see major examples in Plato's *Republic*, Bk. 10, and in Aristotle's *Poetics* (335 BCE), where Aristotle fixes the classical unity rules of action, time and place, concerning drama, all concurring to stave off passions through *catharsis*.

The point here, nevertheless, is not the choice between following imitatively the Ancients or defending the originality of the Moderns but to apply the word "beauty" to private feelings that were not before included in the territory of aesthetics. *The Pleasures of the Imagination* is a surprisingly innovative work that, though in line with the great English empiric tradition of Bacon and Locke and those that came afterwards, such as de Mandeville and Hume, surpasses even their claims. This Addison does with his genuinely new theory of the imagination.

The attention that Addison devoted to the faculty of the imagination is of major importance not only for the writers or poets of the 18th century but also for later generations, and specifically the Romantic poet Samuel Taylor Coleridge, who capitalise on the early but unequivocal affirmations of Addison without mentioning him, mainly "desynonymis[ing]", as he says, *fancy* and *imagination*.[25]

Coleridge thus reworks, in his *Biographia Literaria*, Addison's idea of primary and secondary imagination, i.e. imagination activated by the sight of beautiful scenes and art, and the autonomous creative capacity of the imagination. He qualifies Addison's *fancy* as a primary associative theory, as the philosopher David Hartley later affirmed, and restricts the properly creative theory that he calls "esemplastic" to the synthetic capacity of the secondary imagination to create inexistent forms, beings and fanciful unreal things:

> *Esemplastic*. The word is not in Johnson, nor have I met with it elsewhere. (…) I constructed it myself from the Greek words (…) i.e. to shape into one, because, having to convey a new sense, I thought that a new term would both aid the recollection of my meaning, and prevent its being confounded with the usual import of the word imagination. (STC: X, 91)
>
> The Primary Imagination I hold to be the living power and prime agent of all human perception, and as a repetition in the finite of the eternal act of creation of the infinite I AM. The Secondary I consider as an echo of the former, coexisting with the conscious will, yet still identical with the primary in the kind of its agency, and differing only in degree, and in the mode of its operation. (...) Fancy (...) has no other counters to play with but fixities and definites. The fancy is indeed no other than a mode or memory emancipated from the order of time and space, and modified by that empirical phenomenon of the will which we express by the word choice. (STC: XIII, 167)

Addison's words were as follows:

> [W]e have the Power of retaining, altering, and compounding those Images, which we have once received, into all the Varieties of Picture and Vision that are most agreeable to the Imagination (...). There are few words in the English language which are employed in a more loose and uncircumscribed sense than those of the *Fancy* and the *Imagination*. I therefore thought it necessary to fix and determine the Notion of these two Words (...) by the Pleasures of the Imagination, I mean only such Pleasures as arise originally from Sight, and that I divide these Pleasures into two Kinds: my Design being first of all to discourse of those Primary Pleasures of the Imagination, which entirely proceed from such objects as are before our eyes; and in the next place to speak of those Secondary Pleasures of the

> Imagination which flow from the Ideas of Visible Objects, when the Objects are not actually before the Eye, but are called up into our Memories, or formed into agreeable visions of Things that are either Absent or Fictitious. (JA: 57, 411)

In chapter XII of the *Biographia Literaria* (STC: XII, 160), Coleridge distinguishes and elevates this faculty of the mind as the highest ability possible: "imagination, or shaping or modifying power; (…) fancy, or the aggregative and associative power", taking a stance against Wordsworth, who thought the distinction "too general". Coleridge further specifies that "the aggregative and the associative, I continue to deny that it belongs at all to the imagination" (*ibid.*). Thus, as demonstrated by the latter part of the sentence, he directly recovers the definition of Fancy from the 18th-century theory of Addison, elaborated later, in 1749, in David Hartley's associationist theory,[26] a distinction even more precisely set in the quoted distinction between the primary and secondary imagination and fancy (STC: XIII, 167).

Addison's essays will thus promote everybody's right to imagine things creatively, not a guaranteed option in the 18th century if people did not see themselves as among those gifted by God. But this had another consequence: it signified that art no longer had to be confined within the frame of reference set by the Ancients and their imitative and prosodic cages. Accordingly, new and original topics, as well as matters, designs, forms, sensations and feelings, were all allowed to find a place in art and could be produced and considered as works of art. In this sense, it is not by chance that the battle for invention, creativity and, as derivatives, for autochthonousness and originality was fought in reviving, during the 18th century, the *Querelle des Anciens et des Moderne,* which had occupied the *Académie française* during the 1690s, with Boileau as the foremost champion of *des Ancients*. In England, champions of the Moderns were the editors Richard Bentley and the critic William Watton, followed in the 18th century by Addison and Edward Young, who opposed, amongst others, Jonathan Swift's defence of the Ancients in his work *The Battle of the Books* (1704).

Many of the champions of the Ancients believed that human nature was innate and universal in its standards, and thus unchangeable, asserting once and for all that its knowledge was inborn but then forgotten[27] rather than the result of an ongoing experiential, historical learning process, as Locke maintained. Consequently, they promoted the imitation of the Ancients as the best model, a principle to be pursued through the study of great works of the literature of the past that, in turn, were followed as the best examples for the creation of new ones. Homer was their most outstanding representative model. This static belief had severely limited creativity and not all artists complied with the *dicta* that prescribed simply the imitation of canonical forms. Artists felt they had something of their own to say that was underived from precedents.

The same point is being made by Addison in Essay No. 61, where he says that "the seeds of punning are in the minds of all men (...) and (...) will be very apt to shoot up in the greatest Genius *that is not broken and cultivated by the Rules of Art*" (JA: 61, 228, my emphasis), and when he affirms that the "first Race of Authors (…) excel greater Writers in Greatness of Genius" (JA: 61, 229), implying that they do not have to follow prescribed rules; he also calls them "the Masters of great Learning, but no Genius" (JA: 59, 220). Natural geniuses are those who work by "mere Strength of natural Parts and without any Assistance of Art or Learning" and "were never disciplined and broken by the Rules of Art" (JA: 160, 283).

In *The Spectator* No. 62, speaking of Locke, Addison defines the abilities of the imagination by separating them clearly from reason: "Wit lying most in the Assemblage of Ideas, and putting those together with Quickness and Variety, thereby to make up pleasant Pictures and agreeable Visions in the Fancy. Judgement, on the contrary, lies quite on the other Side. In separating carefully one from another, Ideas wherein can be found the least Difference, thereby to avoid being misled by Similitude, and by Affinity to take one thing for another." (JA: 62).

Democratically, like William Duff,[28] Addison sees imagination as a common-to-all faculty, present in each human being and there to be mined and used as a treasure that must be activated to render it productive in its creative function, i.e. to "esemplastically" change the world: a faculty able to proactively imagine new utopian solutions and changes. If, as Paul Hunter says,[29] the Counter-Reformation created the new readers, Addison's concept of the imagination, we can clearly state, created the utopian revolutionary, as Blake was later to testify with the imaginative creation of his own system. The new emphasis placed on the imagination was to shift the key for the interpretation of the world, and of one's place in it, from an outside authority: "the Sovereign of Nature" – God and his representatives on earth, the king and the clergy – to the internal authority of each person's imagination.

This subversive reading of the imagination corresponds exactly to what the empiricists asserted. All of them believe that geniality and ingeniousness are the results of an imagination improved through exercise, like reason, to produce "*complex ideas of mixed modes* (...) [b]y invention, or voluntary putting together of several simple ideas in our own minds" (JL: 265, Bk. 2, ch. XXII, § 9). So, too, it is for Addison.

The finality to which sensations may lead could well be a theological reading of the world but as Addison explains, this teleology cannot be considered the motor of the universe as, for example, Lord Shaftesbury believed. The same points were repeated and enforced by David Hume in his *A Treatise of Human Nature*, written in 1739 after Addison had written his *Pleasures,* where he affirms:

> For 'tis remarkable, that the present question concerning the precedency of our impressions or ideas, is the same with what has made so much noise in other terms, when it has been disputed whether there be any innate ideas, or whether all ideas be derived from sensation and reflexion. We may observe, that to prove the ideas of extension and colour not to be innate, philosophers do nothing but shew, that they are conveyed by our senses. To prove the ideas of passion and desire not to be innate, they observe that we have a preceding experience of these emotions in ourselves. Now if we carefully examine these arguments, we shall find that they prove nothing but that ideas are preceded by other more lively perceptions, from which they are derived, and which they represent.[30]

Also remarkable is the subtitle of Hume's Treatise: *Being an Attempt to introduce the Experimental Method of Reasoning into Moral Subjects,* a specification that clarifies his addressees, the Neoplatonists.

It is by positing the imagination as a faculty present in all human beings, even though in different quantities, that Addison undermines the theory of genius and ingeniousness as being an innate, or inborn, gift of the gods and therefore present only in some chosen people.

The new concept of imagination, seen as a faculty that all human beings possess and could improve through exercising it, represented a foray towards egalitarianism and democracy, unlike the conception of the visiting *daimon* – the intermediary between God and man – in Plato's *Timaeus*.

Without the dismantling of the theory of ingeniousness seen as a gift of God, no Romantic revolution would have occurred. The transformation of a gift bestowed on an elite by the gods into a faculty shared by everyone and that one only needed to exert it to become a genius oneself is indeed the foremost revolutionary move. It is comparable to the re-enactment of Prometheus's myth that Shelley, not by chance, rewrote in his *Prometheus Unbound* (1820) and which, in turn, revived the *non serviam* formula of Milton's Satan: "Better to reign in Hell than to serve in Heaven"[31] that represented the same possibility of freedom from fetters. Milton, accordingly, interpreted the fall of Eve and Adam as a *felix culpa*, providing them with tools that would become standard during the

Enlightenment: free will and free choice, representing autonomous reasoning and personal accountability.

This is also, in my interpretation, the hidden meaning of the symbolic cypher of the Miltonic serpent, present in Hogarth's etching *Variety* (1753).

William Hogarth, *Variety* (1753)
Image in the public domain

Hogarth, in putting this symbol of liberty, under a glass pyramid, the highly symbolic Masonic image of God, the Great Architect, reminds the initiate of the Order and of earth's hierarchies – symbolised by God's *presentia in absentia* on top. On the other hand, though, through the Miltonic serpent symbolism, he also reminds the initiates of the highly critical attitude they should exercise in order not to remain stuck in their rank and degree by their superiors' orders.

This was also Hogarth's way of testifying and paying homage to the complex relational and dialogical situation of the new social complexity of the 18th century. It is exemplified in the double, triple or infinite perspectives each beholder can choose for their epistemological interpretation of the historical vision.[32] Hogarth and Fielding, in their joint artistic project, pursued a mimetic focus set out in the *Manifesto* of the "new epic-comic-poem in prose", the novel. The 'Preface' to Fielding's *Joseph Andrews*[33] (1742) exemplifies this stance, and is to be read concomitantly with the etching *Characters & Caricaturas* (1743), the subscription ticket for *Marriage à la Mode* (1743-1745), where Hogarth and Fielding grin at each other in the lower middle part of the etching.

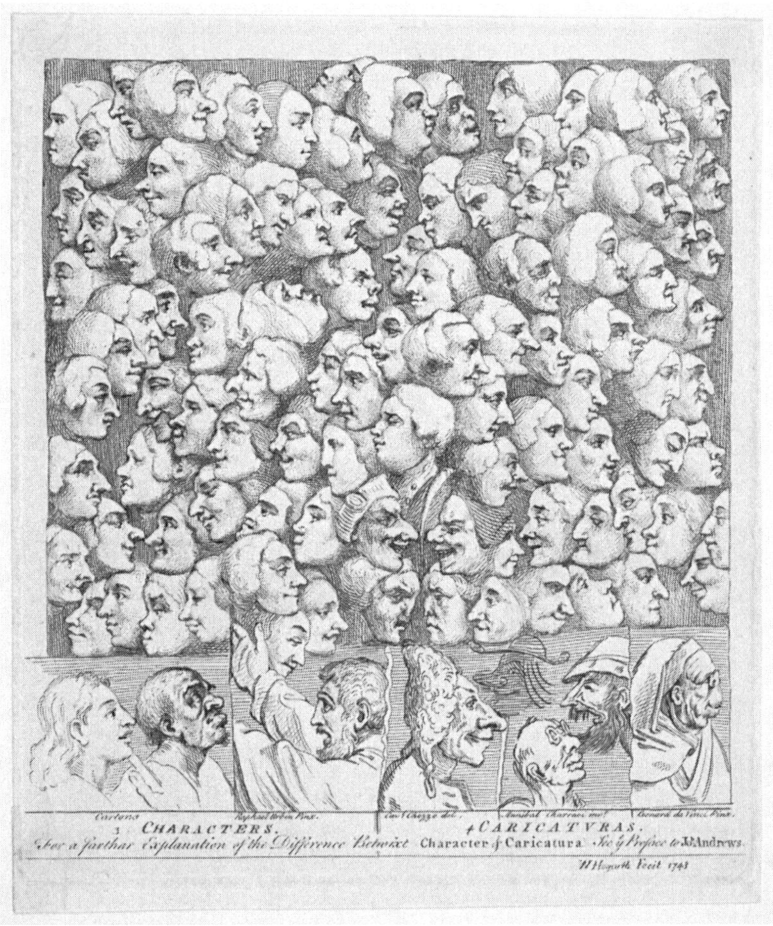

William Hogarth, *Characters & Caricaturas* (1743)
Subscription Ticket for *Marriage à la Mode* (1743-1745)
Image in the public domain
See centerfold for this image in colour

As it was after the fall of man, reality could once more be changed, made adherent to one's dreams and imagination. If everyone possessed the faculty of the imagination, then everyone could become an artist. The climax is indeed the capacity to romanticise the world in order to foster changes and actuate them, as the French Revolution would soon confirm.

Romanticism is indeed the victory of the idiosyncratic imagination and the difference of thoughts and ideals. The works produced during the Romantic age testify that Romanticism is the triumph of the imagination, and imagination is the triumph of the liberty of interpreting the world in a utopian way; the climax of free will, as one likes and intends to propound, without being taken to trial for it.

Addison introduced this tremendous revolution, the revolution of the free individual, making all human beings artists *in nuce*, granting to everyone, without any race, class, gender or difference restraints, the opportunity to read and interpret the world through the exercise of one's imagination. Addison's message should thus be considered the primary anti-biblical message of the age, giving back to man the option of choice, creation and interpretation without having to conform to ready-made created worlds. Disembodied forms had no power anymore and were substituted by the embodied imaginative and creative powers of people's minds.

In doing so, Addison not only undermined innatism, which was the milestone for the rationalists' theory of deduction (blind faith in reason as such), but also emancipated all people by rendering them accountable for making good use of their capacity to imagine the world anew. He gave everyone the chance to express new mythopoetic visions of life in utopian and revolutionary ways, capable of expressing personal and unconventional desires or ideals, a model that was later followed by science itself. In this sense, William Blake is, as we have seen, the epitome of Romanticism.

In his celebration of the power of the imagination and one's mind, Blake can be considered the climax of the considerations laid down by Addison. Romanticism, as a logical consequence, should be considered the triumph of the possibility of being "romantic" (read idiosyncratic), which develops into the plurality of views and interpretations that make up the complex and prismatic nature of English Romanticism. If we only think of Keats' return to the harmonious beauty of the South, of Shelley's atheism, of Wordsworth's celebration of nature as the place of contradictions, of Coleridge's inventions, of Byron's protesting stance, we can see that variety might eventually reign. All this testified to the alternative of adopting a Romantic subjective particularism, which, unfortunately, was soon enough curbed into the radical nationalisms of the single nation-states.

National states were quick in converting the newly-found anti-universal identity-characteristics of peoples into their own political agenda. Communities' identity issues and symbols were pared down into the formula of "the people as one", as Homi Bhabha aptly observes,[34] but conversely, the nation now considered their particular features to be non-reconcilable differences if compared with the features of those from without in order to exploit xenophobic issues.[35] These fictional constructions that hid "cultural liminality – within the nation" (HB:14) were created through the myths of shared land, language, folklore and invented traditions that provided the borders between those who shared them and those who did not.[36] According to Timothy Brennan, "[n]ations (…) are imaginary constructs that depend for their existence on an apparatus of cultural fictions in which imaginative literature plays a decisive role" (HB: 49). Accordingly, literary masterpieces should be interpreted, as Benedict Anderson states, as "national fetish[es] (...) part of the cultural wealth of particular nation-states (…) one of the factors in the development of 'imagined communities' of modern nation-states and their empire."[37] For Homi Bhabha, "nation" equates to and is the result of a "cultural elaboration" (HB: 3), literature being one of the vehicles for, and actively participating in, the construction of a "civil imaginary"[38] (HB: 147 et passim). Specially created "foundational fictions", as Simon During underlines, are nevertheless also important for minorities like ex-colonies (in his case, Australia) to form a "cultural nationalism", what I would call an essentialism of survival,[39] during which terms of "resistance" are applied to defend the minority group from "cultural and economic imperialism" (HB: 138).

This includes something that happened in the 18th century when English thinkers felt trapped in the cage of a Southern aesthetics that did not solely correspond to their characteristics. Rejecting this normative prison for an alternative mythology more adherent to their national characteristics gave them the opportunity to free themselves from the yoke of the South. They invented thus the Northern aesthetics.

To Hans Kohn's thesis of the origin of nationalism in England, which he linked to the Puritan revolution, I would only add my hypothesis of the mythologisation of origin through King Arthur. For Kohn, Puritanism exemplified Milton's request for liberty: "The affirmation of individual freedom from authority (...) the deliverance of man from the yoke of slavery and superstition (...) [which] culminated in the outcry: 'Give me the Liberty to know, to utter, and to argue freely, according to conscience, above all liberties'",[40] later echoed by Cromwell's plea for "Liberty of conscience and liberty of the subject (...) the 'Free Church' demanded a

'Free State'."[41] What Cromwell did not reach, the Glorious Revolution did. If we accept Malinowski's thesis that the function of myth "is to strengthen tradition and endow it with a greater value and prestige by tracing it back to a higher, better more supernatural reality of initial events",[42] then what was still needed to complete the picture was to root this liberty in a mythological past. The Arthurian myth, in the simplicity and directness of folklore, provided essential links with what the kingdom considered to be its elements of national pride: that of being the most advanced and modern nation in the world, where power was shared with the people, where liberty and a less authoritarian religion reigned, and where, through equity and the Common Law, the supremacy of law over authority had been established.

Even where this issue is concerned, Joseph Addison is again central; another essay in *The Pleasures of the Imagination*, No. 419, was to become the foundational essay of the new English mythology and aesthetics. Having theoretically emancipated the people and recast them into potential artists, Addison created the basis for a mythology of the Northern aesthetics. But let us proceed in order and focus on the essays and their architecture.

Essay No. 411 focuses on the senses, mainly on sight. Imagination and fancy activate primary pleasures originating from the sense of sight, and secondary ones by recalling objects in our mind. The imagination is then a faculty as powerful and as "transporting" as reason, and Addison recommends its use for good health, a healthiness psychologically covered by what we would ascribe to the Freudian *Ersatz Theorie.* This pleasure is distinguished from merely sensual, hedonistic pleasures.

Essay No. 412 defines the three sources that please the imagination: novelty or uncommonness, greatness and beauty, linking them to nature and its grandeur, made of a "rude kind of magnificence" and its "wide and undetermined prospect". Burke used these descriptions later for his definition of the natural sublime,[43] but they had also been used earlier in the deists' view of nature, as, for example, in Thomas Burnet's *Sacred Theory of the Earth* (Latin 1681; English 1684).[44] Horror is introduced, for the first time, as a tolerable feeling if delight ultimately prevails. Beauty is a concept Addison relates to the various species (animal and human); it is evoked by "a just mixture and concurrence" of "gaiety or variety of colours (...) symmetry and proportion" and in colours. To sight, he adds the other senses. A most important notation is being made here in that Addison clearly focuses on the nurture element connected with beauty, neglecting its Platonic and Neoplatonic innatism. He says: "There is not perhaps *any real beauty or deformity more in one piece of matter than another*, because we might have been so made, that whatsoever *now* appears loathsome to us, might have shown itself agreeable", implying that such judgement is only a matter of custom, education and "polite taste", i.e. a historical and cultural issue (No. 411, my emphasis).

Essay No. 413 speaks of the final and efficient causes of beauty that I have commented on – *Causa latet, vis est notissima*. Addison asks that we restrain ourselves from "reflect[ing] on (...) the necessary and efficient causes [the Agent that produces effects]" of the pleasure connected to what is "Great, New, and Beautiful", and to concentrate on the Final Cause [for Aristotle the finality or goal of the causes]. The hypothetical final causes "lie more bare (...) tho' they are not altogether so satisfactory" in that they only seem to provide us with the "Occasion of admiring the Goodness and Wisdom of the first Contriver" who "has so formed the Soul of Man, that nothing but himself can be its last, adequate, and proper Happiness." However, Addison offers this last explanation as a hypothesis and not as a certainty: "supernumerary ornaments to the universe", he says, have been added for us to "discover imaginary glories in the heavens and earth"; glories that subject us "in a pleasing delusion", able to produce – only delusionally – "ideas in the mind", like those of colours, which Newton explained scientifically and Locke "explained at large" (JA: 413, 64-65, emphasis added).

Essay No. 414 compares the "strokes of Nature" to the "Touches and Embellishments" of art since the latter is always inferior to the former. Works of nature are, nevertheless, the more pleasing as they resemble those of art, either originals or copies, that present "Design in what we call the Works of Chance". Chance is a word, I must underline, that a deist would not have used in this context, and art is most pleasing if it resembles the beauty of nature. For the first time, Addison mentions the climate element of clouds, which were to become a standard subject for Gainsborough in the 18th century and later in Constable's study and paintings up to the 19th century. In this essay, he also speaks about the English garden, expressing an opinion that later critics contested by overturning his argument completely: "Our English Gardens are not so entertaining to the Fancy as those in France and Italy, where we see a large Extent of Ground covered over with an agreeable Mixture of Garden and Forest, much more charming than the Neatness and Elegancy which we meet with in those of our Country. (...) Our British Gardeners (...) instead of humouring Nature, love to deviate from it as much as possible. Our Trees rise in Cones, Globes, and Pyramids. We see the Marks of Scissars upon every Plant and Bush (...) trimmed into a Mathematical Figure." This view was contested by Pope in his poem "Windsor Forest" (1713), where he refers to "order in variety" (v. 15). In Essay No. 477 (1712, JA: 4, 14-17), Addison, through the ploy of an admirer's letter, commented on his own garden, stating his preference for "a natural Wilderness", with "compositions (...) after the Pindarick Manner", that respects "the beautiful Wildness of Nature without affecting the nicer Elegancies of Art" (JA: 4, 16). This exactly matches the general praise that the English garden obtained.

Essay No. 415 examines architecture, the art "which has a more immediate Tendency, than any other, to produce (...) primary Pleasures of the Imagination." Its "Greatness" is, indeed, related to the "Bulk and Body (...) or to the Manner in which it is built". Regarding bulk and body, for Addison, the Ancients, amongst whom he mentions the Egyptians and the Chinese, are "infinitely superior to the Moderns". He then comments on geographical and climate issues, to which we shall return later, reverting to standard cultural readings speaking of the advantage that warm climates have in presenting "small Interruptions of Frost and Winters, which make the Northern Workmen lye half of the Year idle." Having studied Freart's *Parallel of the Ancient and the Modern in Architecture* and being initially a classicist, Addison admires the magnificence of the structures of the Ancients, which "open the Mind to vast Conceptions (...) because everything that is Majestic imprints (...) Awfulness and Reverence", which "strike[s] in with the Natural Greatness of the Soul." The greatness of manner, what we today would call style, is, he says, even more powerful. Whenever present, even if in a small building, style wins. To confirm his thesis, he compares the smallness of the Pantheon to a bigger but meaner "Gothick Cathedral", thus paying homage to the first, contrary to his later ideals. He quotes Freart's opinion that "ornaments divide and scatter (...) Sight", producing "Confusion". He then presents his ideas about the different control sight has on convex (lesser) or concave (greater) forms: in a concave form, like the inside of a dome, sight has central dominion over the whole circumference; arches, Addison says, are beloved for this reason. From the outside, sight can surround a dome but cannot dominate it with "one uniform idea"; the same happens with a "square pillar (...) and in a square concave". This would later be discussed by Hogarth in his *Analysis of Beauty* (1753), and was instrumental in the development of Hogarth's aesthetics of the "Line of Beauty", which comprises the antithetical union of the two visions, which we shall later comment on.

Essay No. 416 deals with the secondary pleasures of the imagination that the mind either activates on its own or are prompted by external visions or representations through the capacity of the imagination to see analogies and resemblances and its power to "enlarge, compound, and vary them at her own Pleasure". Addison speaks then of wit, and comments on ideas produced by words and their power, addressing also "Painting and Statuary". Words, he says, can produce more lively ideas than those activated by sight. Differences in the constructions of the imagination come from the different quality of perfection of each person's imagination, or from the different – culturally-shaped – meanings they affix to words: an interesting anticipation of Ferdinand De Saussure's semiotic theory.[45]

Essay No. 417 deals with the circumstances that may lead the imagination to a whole variety of images. This provides Addison with the opportunity to engage with Descartes regarding the structural and systemic processes of the mind. These work through traces activated in the mind by the "animal spirits", what we today call nerve reactions. Addison underlines that the imagination can and should be "formed" through exercise and cultivation so to "enlarge" it – a process everybody can undertake, as demonstrated by the man of taste, who, by his acquisition of standards, is one of the ideal exemplars of the age. He then praises the writers of the past through a garden metaphor: Homer's *Iliad* activates the imagination with what is "Great", connecting it with 'cold' qualities Burke would categorise as sublime: "it is like travelling through a Country uninhabited, where the Fancy is entertained with a thousand Savage Prospects of vast Desarts, wide uncultivated Marshes, huge Forests, misshapen Rocks and Precipices". Feelings of beauty, on the contrary, are stirred by Virgil's *Ænid*, which Addison describes as a "Beautiful" and "well ordered Garden". Ovid's *Metamorphoses*, for their part, evokes the "Strange", "inchanted Ground, and (...) Scenes of Magick." As Addison says: "In a word, *Homer* fills his Readers with Sublime *Ideas*" of heroes and gods and "God-like and Terrible" persons; Virgil admits beautiful persons and heroes; Ovid "describes a Miracle in every Story (...) and some new Creature at the end of it (...) something we never saw before, and shews Monster after Monster" (No. 417). Having set the holy trinity of the Southern aesthetics, he is now ready to conclude his argument by inserting Milton. He defines the poet as "a perfect Master in all these Arts". His *Paradise Lost* is so "Divine a Poem, in *English* (...) a stately Palace built of Brick, where one may see Architecture in as great a Perfection as in one of Marble, tho' the Materials are of a coarser Nature." He then enumerates "the Battle of the Angels" and the "*Creation of the world,* the several Metamorphoses of the Fallen Angel and the surprising Adventures their Leader meets with in his Search after Paradise", locating them in the artful but unreal realm of the "*Strange*".

In Essay No. 418, Addison deals with the Secondary Views of the

Imagination, which he widens to comprise – within the territory of the great, beautiful and strange – what is "Disagreeable (...) but pleases us", this being a "new Principle of Pleasure" that covers what Burke later categorised within the territory of the Sublime. These are, for Addison, smaller instances of a new territory that "may be properly called the Pleasure of Understanding", that please through an action of the mind – the mind compares the ideas that arise from words, or ideas created by the mind, with the real objects evoked by words, for example, the description of a dungeon. Descriptions of this kind comprise "what is Little, Common, or Deformed." An instance of this is Milton's Hell – even though most people would prefer Milton's Paradise, both are equally perfect in their description. These raise "a secret Ferment in the Reader", which works "with Violence, upon his Passions" (No. 418) and become thus tolerable in that they are only described and not witnessed. Thus, as Addison says, they become "more Universal, and in several ways qualified to entertain us" in our detachment. This is what Burke wrote in 1757: "When danger or pain press too nearly, they are incapable of giving any delight, and are simply terrible; but at certain distances, and with certain modifications, they may be, and they are, delightful, as we every day experience."[46] This "rational" distance is exactly what Kant would later interpret as the upper hand of reason, which makes it possible to check and direct what otherwise would be an authorisation for uncontrollable individualistic and subjective openings that Kant does not want to authorise. Nevertheless, the prominence Addison gave to the senses and the influence these exercised in Burke's treatise, as was to be expected, led, in its most extreme version, to an aesthetics of ugliness, such as the one produced in the 19th century by Karl Rosenkrantz,[47] an inadmissible result for the creator of the categorical imperative. Kant, indeed, takes great pains to rationalise and check this kind of possibility in his deontological system of ethics (*Kritik der praktischen Vernunft,* 1785).

Joseph Addison had already defined the two leading passions that could become universal: "Terror and Pity", and asked himself "how comes it to pass, that we should take delight in being terrified or dejected by a Description, when we find so much Uneasiness in the Fear or Grief which we receive from any other occasion?" His answer:

> If we consider (...) the Nature of this Pleasure, we shall find that it does not arise so properly from the Description of what is Terrible, as from the Reflection we make of ourselves at the time of reading it. When we look on such hideous Objects, we are not a little pleased to think we are in no Danger of them. We consider that the more frightful Appearance they make, the greater is the Pleasure we receive from the Sense of our own

> Safety. In short, we look upon the Terror of a Description, with the same Curiosity and Satisfaction that we survey a dead Monster.

In short, we look from the perspective of the triumph of rationality over evil, as Kant was to repeat in 1798.

The whole gamut of emotions inhabiting this spectrum is represented and literally depicted in the Gothic novel. They are also found, partly, in the a-religious Graveyard Poetry, which developed these issues though mainly to disparage, from an enlightened English standpoint those places of Europe (epitomised by Italy and France) where people could still believe in spirits and acquiesce to the fears of damnation that permitted religions (and Catholic kings) to control them in an authoritarian way. In a way, if Gothic Graveyard Poetry rationalises fears by seeing cemeteries as mere places where the dead lie, the Gothic novel ridicules those same fears and superstitions, downplaying them as rather silly irrational beliefs.

It is here, in the contraposition between Catholic and Protestant countries, that the dichotomy of North *vs.* South is identified: Italy and France, the lands of authority, mainly, against the Northern countries where Protestantism reigns: England, Germany and Holland (partly), where emphasis is laid on individualism. The dichotomy does not however recognise that this battle, fought through the Enlightenment's deconstruction of creationism and its related idea of destiny, can inherently deconstruct all religions altogether. The Gothic novel is thus a mock-heroic genre set against all kinds of supernatural beliefs, the result of the Enlightenment, which declares its war against *all religions* that proclaim obedience or reference to a higher authority beyond that of one's personal beliefs. It anticipates the stance of Romanticism in defending the imagination, free will and freedom of the new Prometheuses able to envisage by themselves new utopian worlds, as with Blake's *New Jerusalem* (1820-1827). Walter Pater absorbed all this and transposed it in his book *The Renaissance*, and thus it reached Oscar Wilde, who reworked it into his metamorphosis of Christ into an evolved human being in *The Ballad of Reading Gaol* (1898). Even these later instances, "Representations", as Addison says, can "teach us to set a just Value upon our Condition and make us prize our good Fortune, which exempts us from the like Calamities" or "to humour the Imagination in its own Notions, by mending and perfecting Nature where he [the artist] describes a Reality, and by adding greater Beauties than are put together in Nature, where he describes a Fiction. (...) In a Word, he [the artist] has the modelling of Nature in his own hands" (A: 418, 83).

To anticipate one of the hypotheses this book makes: Romanticism, assembling and collecting together the most varied stances and viewpoints but featuring no shared belief nor single philosophical stance, is a sort of transversal declaration of independence from tradition, asserting only the liberty and the opportunity for everyone to become the sole proprietor, and thus artist and moulder, of their own life, taking back the accountability of individual choice and free will.

Essay No. 419 which deals with the fairy way of writing, is discussed on its own in Ch. 2.2 of this work, this being the cornerstone of the invention of the English and, by extension, the Northern aesthetics.

Essay No. 420 deals with those writers who observe "Objects of a real Existence": "Historians, natural Philosophers, Travelers, Geographers, and, in a Word, all who describe visible Objects". Of the historian, Addison anticipates our topical historio*graphic* self-consciousness and conundrum when saying that they "shew more the Art than the Veracity of the Historian". The author also anticipates contemporary understanding of science, saying that nobody enlarges the imagination more than the authors of the new philosophy – science – who show us worlds hanging one above another, and the possibility of different species of living creatures, and in "discover[ing] in the smallest particle of this little World a new inexhausted Fund of Matter, capable of being spun out into another Universe", exactly what quantum physics claims today. He then posits the possibility that beings of a higher nature exist and the soul of man will be infinitely more perfect in the future when imagination will keep pace with understanding by creatively envisaging "in it self distinct Ideas of all the different Modes and Quantities of Space", i.e. imaginary worlds, that remind us of the leaps of creativity that make science progress, as Einstein demonstrated, in jumps rather than through the accumulation of information (cf. Kuhn: 1962).

Essay No. 421, the last of Addison's series, enlarges *The Pleasures of the Imagination* to address the linguistic arts of the "Polite Masters of Morality, Criticism and other Speculations abstracted from Matter", whose use of figurative speech: similitudes, metaphors, allegories and allusions that may affect the imagination, defines what we would call style, eristics and rhetoric. The concluding part of the essay, not by chance, marks the fact that what has been studied in the collection is also "the Influence that one Man has over the Fancy of another (...) to transport the Imagination with beautiful or glorious Visions (...) or haunt it with such ghastly Spectres and Apparitions [that can] ravish or torture the Soul (...) to make the whole Heaven or Hell of any finite Being"; this is a mastery often used to control humankind and, often, only for the controllers' personal ends.

2.2 The *Fairy Way of Writing*

Addison's Essay No. 419 deserves our detailed attention as it sets the cornerstone for connecting and rooting the political ideology of Northern aesthetics in the English medieval tradition of King Arthur and his knights, grounding Great Britain's emblematic legal tradition and politics in the symbolic world of the king and the knights, proxemically cyphered in their paratactic Round Table.[48] The autochthonous focus on inland tradition thus firmly roots the anti-Southern canon of English literature in the Celtic tradition, promoting the recovery of its literature and emphasising its autochthonous forgotten authors, that is, those who can be considered as the Northern classics: Chaucer, Spenser, Milton and Shakespeare.

This essay focuses on what Addison calls the fairy way of writing, a characteristic genre very familiar to the English since they are acquainted with it from childhood onwards as part of their folklore and memories. The fairy way of writing, from this essay onward, relates to other corollary characteristics that we have underlined as pertaining intrinsically to England's identity: the Saxon-Gothic, the Picturesque, as the specific quality of English nature and its sublime elements, the English garden, and the favouring of cold and dark elements in contrast to the solar and warm ones of the South. These factors contribute to the vogue for the Domestic Tour in the unusual Northern direction, in contrast to the continental Grand Tour. The nationalistic focus was soon deployed in the media: both in writing and in iconic representations, as an *anti litteram* advertisement of the new style of English politics, i.e. deployed as a symbol of democracy based on a social contract between stakeholders, a pact based on the modern model of a negotiated politics. Locke explains this in his *Two Treatises of Civil Government* (1689), in open contrast to Hobbes' absolutist stance expressed in the *Leviathan* (1651). Locke's sharing-of-power model, which he saw embodied in the English constitutional monarchy, would be repeatedly represented during the 18th century in the visually explicit icon of the varied and free English garden in contrast to the hypotactic French and Italian ones. This, let us call it, advertisement plan was, of course, also linked to the recovery of the diffuse tradition of King Arthur and the knights and the Celtic past. They served as an emblem of a jurisprudence based on Common Law and its ethical political style in which the community or the claimant could prevail on the law itself by means of the institution of equity[49] and against authority (king, judge, pope, whomever).[50] Aristotle's *epieikeia*[51] stood, indeed, in contrast with what happened on the continent and with what was happening in England during the Norman invasion.[52] And, as seen, the Round Table was another self-explicit and supporting emblem of a society, now, of equals, at least ideally.

Consequently, the various references to architecture would soon translate into favouring the Saxon-Gothic, the English architectonic style, as an emblematic and structural design-like applied reading of the literature of England, antique and autochthonous, evaluated on its own, Gothic, terms. Gilpin, Hughes, Hogarth, Percy, Hurd and Warton all defend the Saxon-Gothic in contrast to the continental and the Norman-Gothic. Consequently, Gothic authors are favoured, the autochthonous Northern canon is created, and the models of reference are critically elevated: Chaucer, Spenser, Milton and Shakespeare, admired for their use of Gothic – read Northern – forms and structures that did not comply with Southern classical norms.

But let us begin by analysing what Addison says of the fairy way of writing. Having to deal with "such persons as have many of them no existence but what he [the poet] bestows on them (...) fairies, witches, magicians, demons and departed spirits" (JA: 419),[53] Addison describes it as the most difficult form of writing in that there is no pattern to be followed and writers must rely only on their fancy. The writers should therefore be "superstitious" and conversant with "legends, fables and antiquated romances, and the tradition of nurses and old women" so as to make characters credible, evading having "fairies talk like people of his own species and not as other sets of beings" (JA: 419). This type of writing creates a "pleasing kind of horror", the pleasure that Burke would call sublime, due to the novelty and feeling of strangeness it creates. If men of "cold fancies" object to this type of literature, others will be pleased to give themselves up to so "agreeable an imposture". The Ancients, Addison points out, did not have much of this poetry – it belongs to a later age "when pious frauds were made use of to amuse mankind, and frighten them into a sense of their duty" (JA: 419). This remark points directly to the use religion makes of spirits, as control entities, so that a literature of spirits of the earth was felt necessary to exorcise spirits that religion wanted people to believe were real: "Our forefathers looked upon Nature with more reverence and horror, before the world was enlightened by learning and philosophy, and loved to astonish themselves with the apprehensions of witchcraft, prodigies, charms and enchantments" (JA: 419). The above-quoted passage goes beyond the merely literary notions expressed in that it clearly conveys that Addison does not believe in any kind of spirit, and he thinks his age is already enlightened so superstitions and fears have no more reason to exist. It had not been so in the past.

> There was not a village in England that had not a ghost in it, the churchyards were all haunted, every large common had a circle of fairies belonging to it, and there was scarce a shepherd to be met with who had not seen a spirit. Among all the poets of this kind our English are much the best, by what I have yet seen, whether it be that we abound with more stories of this nature, or that *the genius of our country is fitter for this sort of poetry*. For *the English are naturally fanciful*, and very often *disposed by that gloominess and melancholy of temper*, which is so frequent in our nation, to many wild notions and visions, to which others are not so liable. Among the English, *Shakespeare has incomparably excelled all others.* That *noble extravagance of fancy*, which he had in so great perfection, thoroughly *qualified him to touch this weak superstitious part* of his reader's imagination, and made him capable of succeeding, where *he had nothing to support him besides the strength of his own genius*. There is something so *wild and yet so solemn in the speeches of his ghosts, fairies, witches*, and the like imaginary persons, that we cannot forbear thinking them natural, though we have no rule by which to judge of them, and must confess, *if there are such beings in the world, it looks highly probable they should talk and act as he has represented them.* (JA: 419)

While the author connects this kind of magic poetry to the gloomy, melancholic predisposition of the English character, he also attributes more dignity to it by mentioning Ovid, who uses this type of writing in speaking of Envy, and Virgil, who did the same speaking of Fame; he then brings in Spenser and his use of "shadowy persons".

The locution "fairy kind of writing" comes, in reality, from Dryden and appears in the "Dedication of *King Arthur or The British Worthy* to Lord George Saville, Marquis of Halifax", as Addison states at the beginning of Essay No. 419, changing Dryden's *kind* into *way*.[54] Dryden, the outstanding, controversial Neoclassic literary critic of the second part of the 17th century, had a more balanced view than one would suppose or, at any rate, a more pliable view than that of Thomas Rymer.[55] Dryden shows a distinguished critical interest in Spenser (referring to him as "inimitable", and often praising his *Faerie Queene*),[56] as indeed he showed for Chaucer, Milton and Shakespeare. Of Shakespeare, as we know, he produced three adaptations.[57] Dryden commended his *Troilus and Cressida,* even though he rewrote it, admired Milton's *Paradise*, and was one of the first critics to exempt Shakespeare from the criticism of not respecting the classical unities. His work *King Arthur* (1691), originally meant for Charles II, who died before seeing it as Dryden himself tells us, had a prologue in the former ballad opera *Albion and Albanius* (1685)[58] that was performed only six times (as the theatre in which the performance was acted was closed when the Young Pretender, the Duke of Monmouth, landed in the west of England).[59]

Characters in the works pertaining to the fairy kind of writing, Dryden says, are "generally supernatural, as gods, as goddesses, and heroes", and the subject extends "beyond the limits of human nature", portraying the "marvellous (...) which is rejected in other plays" (JD:2, 153). He then says that this is "a modern invention", built on the foundations of an "ethnick worship" (JD: 2, 155), an interesting and dense definition we could today rewrite as the archetype or paradigm of folklore religion or belief of the English people.

In his other musical work, *King Arthur, the British Worthy*, Dryden avails himself of the music of Purcell, and when the play is staged today, it is staged rather for its music than for Dryden's content. Ironically, in his 'Preface' to Dryden's version of *King Arthur,* Walter Scott refers to Milton's unfulfilled intention to write an epic about King Arthur, leaving us with this implicitly inferior work by Dryden, who "was too much in the trammels of French criticism, to have ventured upon a style of composition allied to the Gothic romance".[60] But as we have pointed out, Dryden used his *King Arthur* for his own (political) ends. According to Scott, Milton would have transposed the "old romances" and their "Gothic incidents (...) the Ruinous Chapel, the Perilous Manor, the Forbidden Seat, the Dolorous Wound" in an invaluable way. Lamenting the uncertain use of the autochthonous tradition in Dryden, Scott finds the epic possibilities provided by Arthur and Merlin's myth belittled "into the prince and magician of a beautiful fairy tale (...) that might have been written by Madame d'Aulnoy (...) converting the Genii of the kingdom into the lighter and simpler device of airy and earthy spirits whose idea the Rosicrucian philosophy had long rendered popular and familiar",[61] devices that Pope also would use in his 1714 version of *The Rape of the Lock*. Nevertheless, what Scott fails to delineate is the fact that a recognisable Northern aesthetic was being created during the 18th century, in whose evolution he would contribute himself in the following century.

From our viewpoint, nevertheless, looking at the mythical origins of English national identity, Dryden's work acquires a historical interest linked with the recovery of what its author considers constitutes the British identity. King Arthur, as seen, has always been the symbol of a just and ethical jurisprudence, linked to the ancient Common Law, and to the autochthonous and elemental tradition of the land-and-earth-spirits that contested the aloofness of the Southern religious deities and kingly hierarchies.

In this sense, my claim is that Arthur, in its revival in the 18th century, provided a counter-tradition that contested both the religious and the political hierarchical paradigms typical of monotheistic religions and political absolutism, these being based on holistic and a hypotactic structuring. In contrast to this apical God and his angels, a dictatorial increase of the gods of Greece becoming now personified in one single God, Arthur pointed to the democratic ethical equivalence of parties, constantly defined with reference to the paratactic unity of Gothic architecture and the Round Table, and always directed towards shared positive values, neither less upright nor less moral than those introduced by monotheistic religions but also not based on the imposition of their laws and the threat of damnation, revenge and God's wrath as some of life's possible outcomes. The elemental creatures, provided by "the shore of old romances",[62] present a remarkable feature: in their completely earthly, grounded, terrestrial world, they cannot take over and guide humankind. Or, rather, they try to do so but are without real power to change humankind's free will; they cannot force anyone to do anything, as in Pope's *Rape of the Lock*, or only temporarily, as in *A Midsummer Night's Dream*. This is a key difference to standard religious credo and belief.

Of determining importance in King Arthur's myth is also the medieval Code of Honour: leaders gain their strategic leading position after demonstrating their valour, the "romantic idea of justice" to which Richard Hurd refers,[63] after showing their readiness to personally assume the weight of decisions, not merely giving orders or delegating combat to their troops but actively defending them rather than being defended by them. This is another significant plus of the ethical side of the chivalric world which is not based on a metaphysics of kingship that passes power over land and people simply by the right of descent. Knights did not have anyone above them; they were not anointed by God himself, as claimed by kings. The king was just one among them, the best in valour but not in an unquestioned way, and was not considered to be the vicar of God on earth. In short, knights were meant to govern on an ethical code of worth, the exact opposite of a code of theological, familial and dynastic kingship based on "political theology" (1958) in the words of Ernst H. Kantorowicz.[64] The premises on which kings' and chivalry's foundational codes might retain power were diametrically opposed, the one having set their values on earth and the other's in heaven. Whether the knights were upright or not makes no difference; and most probably they were not, or at least they were far from the idyllic picture outlined in romances or that I have outlined here. The proposed symbolic and enticing value system could, however, be underwritten and shared by everyone, and had still enough charm and power given the topical political and religious situations of the 18th century. It is therefore not by chance that this world of magic is reclaimed by the early Tudor political propaganda[65] that linked Henry VII's descent to the ancient kings of England of whom Geoffrey of Monmouth speaks in the *Historia Regum Britanniae* (1138). In this latter work, their ancestry is traced back to Brutus, the descendant of Æneas: "Henry VII's grandfather Owen Tudor came from an ancient family in Anglesey and could trace his descent via Llewellin ap Griffith to Cadwalader and, therefore, back to the Trojan founders of Britain" (Anglo: 19). Through this lineage, Henry VII affirms his Welsh genealogy. The story is well known but still worth repeating.

> The British History records the arrival of Brutus, grandson of the Trojan hero Aeneas, who conquered the giants then in possession of the land and built Trinovantum (London). The realm was divided at Brutus's death but subsequently descended in the line of his eldest son. Several of the later kings gained considerable victories on the Continent and even prevailed against the might of Rome. The Saxon invasions led to the prophecies of Merlin and to the vision conjured up before King Vortigern of a struggle between a red dragon, symbolising the British, and a white dragon symbolising the Saxons. At first, the white dragon is successful but is ultimately vanquished by the red thus was prophesied the final triumph of the British. The varied fortunes of the succeeding years are then narrated in the History which tells of mighty King Arthur who overthrew the Saxons, Picts and Scots, Ireland, Iceland, Sweden, the Orkneys, Norway, and Denmark, conquered Gaul and defeated a great Roman army which attempted to halt his advance. Finally, Arthur was preparing an assault upon Rome itself when news of rebellion forced him to return to Britain. He perished in the ensuing civil war and was succeeded by his nephew. Eventually the land was overcome by the Saxons, and Cadwalader, the last British king, his resources drained by famine and plague, was compelled to flee abroad and died at Rome. The book draws to its close again emphasising the prophecies made to Vortigern, though this time it was an angel who informed Cadwalader that the British would one day recover their land from the Saxons. (Anglo: 18)

These claims were repeated by the Stuarts[66] when dynastic issues became, once more, prominent and topical during Dryden's time. The day-to-day arena of politics was fought between king and parliament due to the Exclusion Crisis, the attempt of parliament to exempt James II from his claim to the throne. Going back to the mythical magic of Albion – the island conquered by Brutus, where, near the Thames, he had founded the city of New Troy (London) – they basked in the full glory later attained by Albion under the leadership of King Arthur and his knights. Brought up by Merlin, Arthur embodied a king raised in the Northern myth and values by local sages. Dryden's two plays, therefore, assume a clear intentionality: they form a *captatio benevolentiae* and a eulogy for the Stuart family via the explicit mythical references they deploy.

The fact is that the Stuart family traced their ancestry back to the Tudor derivation, from Arthur, and their Stuart lineage through the British prince, Llewellin, in continuation with the Tudor tradition of using British material to strengthen and popularise their claim to the throne.

As Sidney Anglo affirms, *Historia* brought together for the first time four elements: "The Trojan descent of the British kings; the prophecy to Cadwalader of an ultimate British triumph over the Saxon invaders; the greatness of King Arthur; and the British significance of the red dragon" (Anglo: 18). Since the Red Rose Lancastrian line of Henry VII appeared unsound to the Tudors, a solution was provided: "It was claimed through the Welsh princes, back to the primitive British Kings" (Anglo: 17).

Dryden, to authorise his reading, tells us that he came to the customs and rites of the heathen Saxons having consulted Bede, probably the *Historia ecclesiastica gentis Anglorum* (731), and Bochart (Bochartus), amidst other authors (JDS: 8, 118).[67] On this, Scott comments ironically: "We cannot trace the result of this study anywhere but in the song of the Saxon priests; and it did not surely require much reading to glean up the names of the Saxon deities, which are almost the only traits of national manners exhibited through the drama" (JDS: 8, 119). Nevertheless, notwithstanding Scott's comment, there are King Arthur, Merlin, Oswald (the Saxon magician), Philidel (an airy spirit) and Grimbald (an earthly elf). The story tells of the battle fought on St. George's day against the "heathen" Saxons, who are downplayed as a violent people, stabbing their enemies in the back, not in a face-to-face battle: "Revengeful, rugged and violently brave" (JDS: 8, 126). The war for the control of Britain is raised because Conon, Duke of Cornwall, has refused Oswald's marriage offer to his daughter Emmeline (now the blind wife of King Arthur). King Arthur is eulogised, portrayed as brave, magnanimous, merciful, serene and forgiving. Merlin advises him to fight against Oswald, the Saxon King of Kent, with his airy legions of spirits, confronting him with charms against charms, the cavalry of Oswald being a "beauteous horror" that provokes envy (JDS: 8, 128). The Saxons are shown to be violent and cruel, performing heathen sacrifices of animals "to Hell" (JDS: 8, 132) that are slaughtered in the names of their deities: Woden (Odin), Freya, his wife, Thor, the god of war (JDS: 8, 131) and Tanfan (JDS: 8, 133) are asked to enchant their enemies with Runick rites, drawing forecasts from the remaining entrails of the horses and human sacrifices. Philidel, the airy spirit of the Saxons, is described as composed of atoms, a being with silken wings. He is entrusted to produce a noisome mist of vapours and fog and breathe stench in the face of enemies. Sacrifice is justified to the victims by the – invariable – rhetoric of reward and honour, chanted by the chorus: "Of mortal cares you shall be eased, // Brave souls to be renowned in story. // Honour prizing, // Death despising, // Fame acquiring, // By expiring; // Die, and reap the fruit of glory, // Brave souls, to be renowned in story" (JDS: 8, 133). The battle is won by the Britons. Not having hurled the noisome fog on the Britons, Philidel is protected by Merlin, who will employ him in the knowledge that despite men battling for power, "the field is ours" (JDS: 8, 136). He commands Philidel to prevent Grimbald, "the cloven-footed fiend", dressed as a shepherd, to lead Arthur to the falls of a brook where he would die. Philidel succeeds in convincing them to follow him because nature and the trees behave as animated spirits to prevent them. Oswald and Arthur, who are said to have fought against the Picts together, meet on the field, and Arthur tells him he has wronged him because of love. Arthur proposes that Oswald share his kingdom with him if he restores Emmeline, his bride, who is his prisoner. She is wanted by both Osmond, the enchanter who produces an eternal winter heated only by love, and Oswald; Merlin and Arthur restore her sight but she cannot be freed. While the battle between the magicians continues, it is interesting to note that the good magician, Merlin, cannot overpower the bad one, Osborne. Arthur, meanwhile, must undergo the temptations of the Syrens, like Ulysses; later, Nymphs and Sylvaners appear from behind the trees but Arthur succeeds in his trial. Understanding that he is lost, Oswald proposes the one-to-one battle that he had previously rejected. Since the aim of Dryden's opera is Jacobite propaganda, Arthur responds by claiming the Stuarts' right to the throne: "As once Æneas, my famed ancestor, Betwixt the Trojan and Rutilian bands, fought for a crown, and bright Lavinia's bed, so will I meet thee, hand to hand opposed: My auguring mind assures the same success" (JDS: 8, 169). Arthur wins the final battle and spares Oswald's life with this command: "Lead back thy Saxons to the ancient Elbe" (JDS: 8, 170). Dryden also refers to Kent as the land that became "the gift" of Vortigern for Hengist's "ill-bought aid", reminding his audience that Vortigern, who, having asked Hengist (the Jute) to help him fight the Picts and the Scots, betrayed him: he and Horsa kill his son instead. Vortigern consequently loses Kent, "a land sacred to freedom and of its rights tenacious to the last" because "Britons brook no foreign power" (JDS: 8, 171). Merlin bestows on Arthur the prediction of fame and the title of the foremost of the three Christian worthies (Arthur, Charlemagne, Godfrey of Boulogne), thus enriching, implicitly, his title with that of *defensor fidei*, as would please the Jacobite Kings. As Scott explains in a note, the other "Worthies" were: "Three Pagans: Hector, Pompey and Alexander the Great; three Jews: Joshua, David, Judas Macabæus" (JDS: 8, 172). Furthermore, Arthur predicts that Saxons and Britons "shall be once one people; one common tongue, one common Faith shall bind our jarring bands, in a perpetual peace" (JDS: 8, 172). Britannia appears amidst windless air, calm and serene. It is interesting to note that another peace treaty seems to be signed with the coming on stage of Pan, the nymph Nereid, and Comus. Venus forsakes Cyprus for England, and all join in praise of Britannia in the dream of finding a solution in a double vision uniting Southern and Northern aesthetics, one that Shakespeare had already pursued in *A Midsummer's Night Dream*, where the two worlds vie for supremacy, and this bears detailed examination.

2.3 Shakespeare's *Fairy Way of Writing*

I must go seek some dewdrops here, and hang a pearl in every cowslip's ear.
—Shakespeare, *A Midsummer Night's Dream*

Shakespeare uses fairies and spirits in some of his most popular plays: *A Midsummer Night's Dream*, *Macbeth, Hamlet* and *The Tempest.*

Let us focus on *A Midsummer Night's Dream* (1595 ca., pub. 1600), where the rationale of the comic or romantic play, as it is usually defined, could not be clearer. Looked at from a structural viewpoint, the play begins in Athens, the city where classical aesthetics was born, here depicted as an enclosed, protected world where an initial, highly charged and significant legal issue, liberty, is being discussed. Once the law is passed, Athens is abandoned by all the main protagonists – only the representatives of the law, Theseus and Hippolyta, remain in the city. All other protagonists move to the Woods, a sort of country-underworld where anything might – and does – happen, a site where magic transformations overturn choices, free will and received categories, implying a state of lawlessness. Once transformations have taken place, the play ends with a final return to Athens but with all people involved forever changed by their experience.

The play could not be clearer in its conciseness, spatial indications and movements: Shakespeare is inviting both his audience and fellow playwrights to free themselves symbolically from the cage of the Ancients and their rules – which the Renaissance had fortified through university canons – and step into what Shakespeare considers to be the rich, autochthonous English literary tradition and its magic cultural environment. In Shakespeare's time, this was already an almost-forgotten cultural heritage that had to be recovered, a core that needed to be heeded, chosen and re-evaluated in its own right, an accomplishment towards which Spenser's *Faerie Queene* had led the way.

The play thus needs to be read side by side with the various contrapositions it presents (youth/maturity, fondness/love, rules/freedom,[68] Petrarchan love/eroticism,[69] aristocracy/artisans[70]), from a new hermeneutical, cultural and aesthetic viewpoint: the opposition between Athens and the Woods represents on a meta-theatrical level Shakespeare's statement about local and imported rules of playwriting.

In this play, Shakespeare clearly marks the clash between two aesthetics and two opposing worlds: Southern Athens, with its Arcadia and its classical rules, based on a rigid and strict authority – symbolised by laws on compulsory marriage – and the Northern Woods, presented as a world where magic fairies and humans, liberty and the imagination have free rein. The myths and rules of the two worlds clash when placed in direct contact and contrast.

Aesthetic liberty is symbolised most clearly in the anti-canonical comic improvisers of the play, the rude mechanicals who unknowingly also act as revolutionary and iconoclastic innovators. They do this, first, by making themselves seen and heard and by gaining respect. Second, the amateur actors acquire importance not only through Northrop Frye's hypothesis that Shakespeare inserts a low mimetic comic relief into a high mimetic structure[71] but also, most importantly, by claiming their place and thus coming to terms with their parodic acting; and, third, they reconcile the utterly colliding aesthetics (and social worlds): "How shall we find the concord of this discord?" (Act V, 1), the discord being, alongside that of classicism in opposition to the autochthonous English tradition, the contrast of both with the free and comic *carnivalesque* aesthetics of the mechanicals, providing the standard of freedom for all the others. Introducing the play to Theseus, Philostrates says:

> A play there is, my lord, some ten words long, // Which is as brief as I have known a play; // But by ten words, my lord, it is too long, // Which makes it tedious; for in all the play // There is not one word apt, one player fitted: // And tragical, my noble lord, it is; For Pyramus therein doth kill himself. // Which, when I saw rehearsed, I must confess //Made mine eyes water; but more merry tears // The passion of loud laughter never shed. (V, I, 60-65)

The fact that in the amateur play all rules of playwriting are despised – "in all the play, [t]here is not one word apt, one player fitted" – is extremely important in that the mechanicals provide the real moment of *carnivalesque* catharsis for the audience.[72] The mechanics dismantle all rules and borders between artistic forms and classes; rules are checked anew and erased; the sacred and the profane mingle. Indeed, many elements of the play clash violently, something critics have not failed to note.[73] Athens and the green, fertile and abundant world of the woods are diametrically opposed worlds, just like the spatial south and north, and an evidential material proof is the fact that it is not a generic north we are talking about here. The specific North depicted here is that of the English countryside, its floral species corresponding to the climate and environment of England, and this is underlined by the fact that in no other Shakespeare play is there as much nature on show. The countryside under the moonlight is precisely observed, another element in contrast with the radiance of the South:

> I know a bank where the wild thyme blows, where oxlips and the nodding violet grows, // Quite over-canopied with luscious woodbine, with sweet musk-roses and with eglantine. // There sleeps Titania sometime of the night, lulled in these flowers with dances and delight; // And there the snake throws her enamell'd skin // weed wide enough to wrap a fairy in. (Act II, 2, 248-56)

The two worlds could not be more distant from other points of view too: in one, authority and the law reign; in the other liberty and freedom: "if you yield not to your father's choice" (I, I, 69) "the law of Athens yields you up" (I, I, 119). This is the "unwished yoke" (I, I, 80) to which Hermia's soul does not consent "to give sovereignty" (I, I, 82). The same is true for Shakespeare if he is the champion of freedom, collapsing an aesthetics that is in contrast with the heritage of his intellectual fathers, his literary ancestors. Indeed, the quotes invite us to read it as a *double entendre* of Shakespeare's refusal to comply with the Aristotelian unities of the Greek drama. Hermia, if she does not accept the Greek symbolic order, is threatened with death or celibacy; Shakespeare was criticised by the critics of the period, who decried his innovations. The Duke bids Hermia "to fit your fancies to your father's will" (I, I, 118), a will he will later "overbear" (IV, I, 178),[74] just as critics would one day "overbear" Shakespeare's transgressions.

The two worlds are thus set in polarity. One is the free and magic Celtic world of fairies, the other the symbolic Greek world of laws (prosody, forms, unities) and its menaces: a polarity mirrored in the differences of the hierarchical structures of authority of the governing couples. The contrasts between the power and gender relationship of Oberon and Titania and that of Theseus and Hippolyta are striking. The playful light mood of the fairy world provides the setting for creative confusion while the Athenian court remains fraught with hierarchy and emotional suppression. Oberon and Titania are presented as a quarrelling couple of equals, who both want authority over the Indian boy. Oberon is incapable of prevailing over his wife if not through magic. Hippolyta, on the contrary, does not utter a single comment on Theseus' command, silently declaring complete submission to her husband's will, including his deadly menace to Hermia. The fairies who attend Titania respect her and she respects them; they are happy to assist her as Puck is happy to assist Oberon. Puck, as the fairies immediately notice, is also the embodiment of a character of English folklore that the Arden edition of the play[75] connects with a character in a treatise on demonology, where Robin Goodfellow is referred to as "the puckle" and "hob goblin, Hob being a common name for Robin."[76] For Walter Scott, "Robin Goodfellow, or Hobgoblin, possesses the frolicsome qualities of the French Lutin".[77] Scott,[78] in this instance, invites his readers to refer to another important work linked with the recovery of the Arthurian myth, the *Reliques of Ancient Poetry,* by Thomas Percy. Percy dedicated chapter 23 of volume 3 to Robin Goodfellow[79] while other chapters of his work are dedicated to King Arthur. He also set the origin of English literature in the productions of the bards of the "ancient Britons", connecting them to the "scalds or popular poets" of the "Gothic nations",[80] therefore the Goths.

A Midsummer Night's Dream is Shakespeare's ingenious way of presenting his audience with the overarching symbolic dichotomy between the authority and strictness of Greek *law* and the liberty and freedom connected to English *magic*.

Love is thus a symbol of unconditional liberty and free will, in stark contrast to the harsh otherness of Athenian laws that prompt Hermia and Lysander to leave the city and its rules behind. Shakespeare does the same with the Petrarchan love that he recasts in his *Sonnets* and their transgender eroticism. Love's force and power, and the ideal liberty it needs in order to flourish, are symbolised in love's blindness and its strong and vital erotic power.[81] The love between Theseus and Hippolyta is far from the polyamory that Oberon and Titania seem to practice without excessive jealousy, Oberon having spied on Hippolyta, Titania having fallen in love with Theseus (cf. II, I, 64-80), and both being fond of the Indian boy and competing for his affections. Puck's magic violet juice activates an uncontrollable and unfettered liberty that destabilises law and hierarchies, including class, gender, and even species borders. Given that a queen can be coupled to an artisan, Titania becomes the slave of Bottom, masked as an ass, provided he is, like Bottom, "a most lovely, gentlemanlike man" (I, ii, 74). By means of the juice, imagination reigns, just as it does through Prospero's magic wand in *The Tempest*. Once all has been upturned, things can be set right anew, the couples will remix as expected this time, Demetrius falling in love, eventually, with Helena, and Lysander again loving Helena. Both reigning couples are united again, though only because they have forgotten what has happened.

The audience, nevertheless, cannot forget what they have seen: they can judge the two worlds, the strict aesthetic and social laws of Athens undermined by the world of English magic. This world represents the intervention of the artist (or the judge) and his liberty to create a precedent, or a work of art following new laws, if the existing law and aesthetic order are alien to freedom and natural expression.

What I am saying is that Shakespeare applies libertarian Common Law[82] principles to debunk the strict rules of the unities of the ancient aesthetics and the rigidity of the Southern, in this case Athenian, laws to champion the liberty of the land of the fairies and their own hierarchies. In this, he indirectly pays homage to Queen Elizabeth and recovers the work of his fellow artist Edmund Spenser and his *Faerie Queene*, inaugurating its elevation to the central work for the Gothic canon.

The Tempest,[83] Shakespeare's final play, probably written in 1611, respects the unities of time, place and action, paying homage to the classical tradition. Nevertheless, the setting and magic elements in the subject and plot are typical of what we have defined as a Northern or Gothic play. We could extend what we said about *Midsummer* by saying that Shakespeare and Prospero, having broken the laws of Athens and Milan, live now in exile on their magic islands (rich in art and freedom).

The magic sorcerer, Prospero, the duke of Milan, usurped by his brother Gonzalo, flees to the magic island, where he lives with his daughter Miranda, Ariel, a spirit of the air, benevolent as a sylph, who controls nature, and Caliban, his negative, the monster.[84] Caliban has himself been usurped by Prospero (cf. I, II, vv. 336-45), who has taken the island from his mother, the now-dead witch Sycorax, and from him as her rightful heir: "The foul witch (...) who with age and envy // Was grown into a hoop" (cf. I, II, vv. 257-58) is the abused ghost of the play. After Prospero freed him from the hollow tree, where Sycorax had imprisoned him, Ariel, the spirit of the air, who flies on the back of bats, is now his servant. On Prospero's orders, he causes the tempest that will shipwreck Gonzalo.

Prospero can make himself invisible (cf. III, 3) and he alludes to his capacity to restore the dead to life (V, I, 48-49). As he had done with *A Midsummer Night's Dream*, Shakespeare, again, utilises popular lore concerning sorcerers and witches and the folklore revisions of the esoteric tradition present during his time. In John Dee,[85] or Burton's *Anatomie of Melancholy* (1621), tempests caused by spirits are mentioned, probably also to make people believe in the supernatural intervention in England's battle against the Spanish Armada.[86] Prospero, surely, reminded the people of the magus Merlin. His magic wand changes reality as Shakespeare's pen/art does. Prospero can conjure up worlds and change reality, and uses imagination for his own ends.

Shakespeare is here defending the liberty of art, liberty that cannot be fettered by reality. He is also championing the capacity to see through the "as if" lenses Immanuel Kant speaks of in his *Kritik der Urteilskraft,* capable of envisaging worlds that are 'inexistent', even if only for the time being. Shakespeare did not explain this capacity in the terms later provided by Addison, Kant, Coleridge, etc., but he did produce material proofs of what it was capable of.

According to Kant, it is through reflective (imaginative) judgement, which excludes the determinant one (connected with scientific truths and reality), that we can activate and are able to see, or even foresee, in creative terms. Kant explains reflective judgement as being organised on an *as-if* – or, in German, an *als-ob* imaginary reality-hypothesis – that functions like a metaphor used by the mind to see and explain reality in a new way: although it cannot be asserted to be truthful – reality necessitating the proof of the determinant (scientific) judgement – it can, nevertheless, in its freedom, provide a different view and thus envisage originality and change.[87] By means of this capacity to see the world in the *as-if* terms that magic and art can activate, and Prospero masters in *The Tempest*, Shakespeare focuses his audience's attention on his "farewell to the stage."[88] The fairies signify exactly this: Prospero's kingdom is made of the magic of art, the most powerful means to activate change and drive. I consider it extremely significant that Shakespeare once more, and in his last play, returned to the early English tradition of the fairy way of writing to set in order his earlier, now past, Southern allegiances (and kingdom), showing that he has now the undisputed power to make the Southern world comply with the rules of his island.

Shakespeare defends the early tradition of the English imagination. He treats it as the means of making people proactive, proposing literature and art as the key to humankind evolving into artists themselves,[89] as Prospero has done, choosing his magic library over the dukedom of Milan, preferring knowledge to power.

Though not a common feature, magic figures do appear in some other Shakespeare plays. In *Hamlet*[90] there is the ghost of Hamlet's father, and the witches in *Macbeth*. These can be interpreted as standard trigger-characters for that time; however, they do not, in my opinion, have a real overtone of Northern ancestry (leaving aside for the moment the Danish ancestry of Hamlet) or folklore, pertaining as they do to all cultures and civilizations in a transnational and geographical sense.

To conclude our examination of the fairies: White Latham's book, *The Elizabethan Fairies*, quotes Nathan Drake's *Dissertation on the Fairy Mythology, and on the Modifications which it Received from the Genius of Shakespeare* (1813), which delineates a popular tradition, extending from Gervase of Tilbury to William Warner. Both books point out the innovations that Shakespeare introduced into the previous fairy lore:

> Of the originality of Shakespeare in the delineation of this tribe of spirits, or Fairies, nothing more is required in proof, than a combination or grouping of the principal features; a picture which, when contrasted with the Scandick system and that which had been built upon it in England and Scotland previous to his own time, will sufficiently show with what grace, amenity, and beauty, and with what an exuberant store of novel imagery, he has decorated these phantoms of the Gothic mythology.[91]

The change from the initial outlook and behaviour of the Fairies[92] to their minimisation and positive attitude is attributed to Shakespeare's influence, also by Charles Lamb.[93]

Walter Scott, in his *Minstrelsy of the Scottish Border*[94] (1802), traces the origins of Shakespeare's fairies to the ancient Berg-Elfen, the elves of the mountains, or the gnomes of the Gothic and Finn tribes, saying that many poets of the 16th century used them, specifically "deserting the hackneyed fictions from Greece and Rome".[95] This confirms that there was an undercurrent of English writers who looked to the North for a different tradition, of which the Arthurian legend constitutes the core, to detach themselves from the classic Southern one.

Scott confirms that these writers "sought for machinery in the superstitions of their native country (...), the bard [Shakespeare] (...) improvising upon the popular belief assigned to them many of those fanciful attributes and occupations, which posterity have since associated with the name of fairy" (Scott: 1821, 305). According to Scott, the original fairies presented "the unamiable qualities, and diminutive size, of the Gothic elves" (Scott: 1821, 178) and they developed into small and benevolent creatures of the South of England only later due to Shakespeare, Drayton and Mennis. In contrast, in Scotland, they preserved a sharper and more impish character. Fairies, nevertheless, were threatened by Christianity, which has produced "the wreck of the Gothic mythology [of fairies]", so they "have preserved with difficulty their own characteristics, while at the same time they engrossed the mischievous attributes of several other classes of subordinate spirits, acknowledged by the nations of the north" (Scott: 1821, 266).

As Sir William Temple notes, in 1690, the fairy tradition was forbidden by "Ecclesiastical Commands",[96] and we can only surmise that this was done because it represented a counter tradition to the hierarchical monotheistic one, even though it was also used by the best classicists of the 18th century, most notably Dryden and Pope. Indeed, one of the most evident proofs is Pope's use of this tradition, in which he refers to the Count of Gabalis' work, through him to Hermes Trismegistus, and thus to the hermetic and initiatic tradition he refers to in his *Rape of the Lock* (1712, 1714), specifically in the 1714 edition where sylphs and gnomes are added. The *Lock,* could thus be read as a metaphor for the key steps leading to some form of esoteric knowledge, like that of the freemasons, where initiation rituals, tests and oaths secure progress. The offer to acquire a similar kind of higher level of religious knowledge is masterfully described in James Joyce's *A Portrait of the Artist as a Young Man*, a deal Stephen Dedalus rejects.

In Pope, Ariel is turned into a sylph and Belinda into a sort of nymph, later to be beset by the gnome Umbriel but only once her lock has been cut, signifying the loss of her innocence. Pope himself, as we have seen, links these elements to Rosicrucian lore[97]; nevertheless, we must be reminded that there was considerable reference to them in the folklore itself.

Fairies also appear in Ann Radcliffe's *The Mysteries of Udolpho*, and in her *Romance of the Forest*, a novel set in a northern mountainous countryside, where Adeline, the heroine, dreams and sings of fairies and aerial creatures that, as soon as the morning sets in, disappear.[98] Furthermore, in Shakespeare's time, fairies had appeared in Drayton's *Nimphidia*, in Lily's *Galathea*, in his comedy *Endymion*, and in Greene's *James IV*, where Oberon appears as the King of Fairies.[99]

Even Sir William Temple, allegedly thought to be the champion of the authority of the Ancients in the Battle of the Books, on closer scrutiny seems rather to examine things in a balanced way, acknowledging the variety of the English literary panorama, recognising the importance of fairies.[100] In this sense, Temple presents a rather controversial view of the Ancients. First, he historicises the concept of being an Ancient by unsettling the universality of the concept itself: "Thus much I thought might be allowed me to say, for the giving some Idea of what those Sages or Learned Men were, or may have been, who were Ancients to those that are Ancients to us" (p. 35); and, second, he presents a rather forward view of the Goths, seen as being poetically crucial before they were displaced by Christianity, and acknowledging their survival in the tradition of fairies:

> In the time of Boetius, who lived under Theodorick in Rome, we find the Latin Poetry smell rank of this Gothick Imitation, and the old vein quite seared up. (...) Out of this Quarry seem to have been raised all those Trophees of Enchantment that appear in the whole Fabrick of the old Spanish Romances, which were the Productions of the Gothick Wit among them during their Reign; and after the Conquests of Spain by the Saracens, they were applied to the long Wars between them and the Christians. From the same perhaps may be derived all the visionary Tribe of Faries, Elves, and Goblins, of Sprites and of Bui-beggars (…) At least, this belief prevailed so far among the Goths and their Races, that all sorts of Charms were not only Attributed to their Runes or Verses, but to their very Characters; so that, about the Eleventh Century, they were forbidden and abolished in Sweden, as they had been before in Spain, by Civil and Ecclesiastical Commands or Constitutions; and what has been since recovered of that Learning or Language has been fetcht as far as Ysland itself. How much of this Kind and of this Credulity remained even to our own Age may be observed by any Man that Reflects, so far as Thirty or Forty Years, how often Avouched, and how generally Credited, were the Stories of Fairies, Sprites, Witchcrafts, and Enchantments.[101] (p. 337, 344-45)

Notes

1 Joseph Addison, *The Pleasures of the Imagination*, in J. Addison, *The Spectator*, 4 vols. (1907 [1711-1714]), (ed.) G. Gregory Smith, (London: Dent), here vol. 3, pp. 54-96.

2 The idiosyncratic focus that Addison, with his papers, authorises could be seen as an anticipation of what we today could dub a seer-response criticism on the basis of Iser's formula of a reader-response criticism (W. Iser: 1976). Clarence DeWitt Thorpe, in his 'Addison's Theory of the Imagination as "Perceptive Response"', *Papers of the Michigan Academy of Science, Arts and Letters*, xxi, 1935, 509-30, focuses on Addison's perceptive response, which I would define as emphatic or affect-oriented.

3 In his emphasis on bodily sensations, he takes his place with the examiners of hedonism: cf. Walter Pater's theory of the multiplied consciousness and its critique in Oscar Wilde's *Dorian Gray*, Friedrich Nietzsche's Dionysian principle and, for the 18th century, also in De Sade's transgressive focus on sexuality. See also Susan Sontag (1967) 'The Pornographic Imagination', *The Partisan Review*,

Spring 1967, pp. 181-212.

[4] Cf. Hans-Robert Jauss (1982) *Toward an Aesthetic of Reception* (tr. Timothy Bahti) (Minneapolis: University of Minnesota Press), and Wolfgang Iser (1994 [1976]) *Der Akt des Lesens. Theorie ästhetischer Wirkung* (Stuttgart: UTB).

[5] Michael McKeon (1987) *The Origins of the English Novel, 1600-1740* (Baltimore: John Hopkins University Press), pp. 1-3.

[6] The mathematical calculus related to morality that Shaftesbury proposes in his *An Inquiry into the Originals of our Ideas of Beauty and Virtue; in Two Treatises* (1724), op. cit., brings us directly to his pupil Adam Smith and his work *Theory of Moral Sentiment* (1759), where reason is not deemed sufficient for moral fairness, and enthusiasm and feeling, inferred from religion, are called in as founding elements of the ethical dimension of economics.

[7] James E. Crimmins, 'Jeremy Bentham', *The Stanford Encyclopedia of Philosophy* (2015), Edward N. Zalta (ed.), https://plato.stanford.edu/archives/spr2015/entries/bentham/, retrieved Jan. 2017.

[8] Cf. Thomas Hobbes (1651) *Leviathan or the Matter, Forme, & Power of a Common-wealth Ecclesiasticall and Civill*, (London: Andrew Crooke), p. 45: "The passions that most of all cause the differences of wit are principally the more or less desire of power, of riches, of knowledge, and of honour. All which may be reduced to the first, that is, desire of power. For riches, knowledge and honour are but several sorts of power." Passions were thus the fuel of the "*bellum omnium contra omnes*", the war of all against all, dictated by envy, that promoted the *homo hominis lupus* understanding of humankind, as he affirms in his work *De Cive* (1651 [1642]) (London: R. Royston).

[9] The beginning of the debate is marked, in France, by Charles Perrault's 1687 attack on classicism with his 'Poème du siècle de Louis le Grande', (1692) in *Parallèle des anciens et des modernes en ce qui regarde les arts et les sciences, avec le Poème du siècle de Louis le Grand et une Epitre en vers sur le génie.* 4 vols. (Paris: Coignard). A work for the defence of the Ancients had, nevertheless, appeared previously, in the United Kingdom, by Henry Reynolds (1632, r. 1972), *Mythomystes, wherein a Short Survey is Taken of the Nature and Value of True Poesie, and Depth of the Ancients above our Moderne Poets* (Menston: Scholar Press), followed by another, later, important work, by Sir William Temple (1690) 'An Essay upon Ancient and Modern Learning', in *Miscellanea, Part II* (London: Simpson), reprinted (1909) in *On Ancient and Modern Learning and on Poetry*, ed. J.E. Spingarn (Oxford: Clarendon). In 1704, Jonathan Swift, who had been secretary to Temple, published *The Battle of the Books* (compl. 1697, r. 1901) (Dublin: E. Ponsonby). Works that need to be examined for this topic are: Dryden, (1668 r. 1982) *An Essay on Dramatic Poesy* (New York: Irvington) and for the background of the *querelle* A.E. Burlingame (1920, 1969) *The Battle of the Books in its Historical Setting* (New York: Bilo and Tannen). The resumption of the battle in the first half of the 18th century can be measured via the battle fought on how to interpret ingeniousness and originality, a fight that was, in the end, to attach

equal importance and dignity to the Moderns. Amongst the works that promote originality we find: Edward Young (1759) 'Conjectures on Original Composition in a Letter to the Author of Sir Charles Grandison', in Edmund D. Jones (ed.) (1922, 1934) *English Critical Essays, XVI-XVIII Centuries* (London: Oxford UP), pp. 315-64, and in William Duff (1767, 1994) *Essay on Original Genius* (London: Routledge/Thoemmes Press), a topic I have examined in depth in my book (2002) *Genio e immaginazione nel Settecento inglese* (Valdonega: Università di Verona). Recent studies on the topic are: Darrin McMahon (2013) *Divine Fury: A History of Genius* (Philadelphia: Basic Books), Penelope Murray (1989) (ed.) *Genius. The History of an Idea* (Oxford: Blackwell), Harold Bloom (2002) *Genius: A Mosaic of One Hundred Exemplary Creative Minds* (New York: Warner). See also Stephen Gill (1984) *William Wordsworth* (New York: Oxford University Press), Georg J. Buelow (1990) 'Originality, Genius, Plagiarism in English Criticism of the Eighteenth Century', *International Review of the Aesthetics and Sociology of Music*, 21, no. 2.

[10] Later repeated as "white paper, void of all characters", JL: 109, Bk. 2, ch. 1, § 2, p. 109.

[11] Francis Bacon (2000, [1620]) *The New Organon* (eds) Lisa Jardine, Michael Silverthorne (Cambridge: Cambridge University Press).

[12] For the theory concerning genius, see *The Spectator,* No. 160, for its relation to climate; for the imagination, as well as the essays in *The Pleasures of the Imagination* (411-421) see also Nos. 59, 61, 141, 160, 279, 590.

[13] Meyer H. Abrams (1953) *The Mirror and the Lamp. Romantic Theory and the Critical Tradition* (Oxford: Oxford University Press), p. 17. See also Abrams' other book (1971) *Natural Supernaturalism: Tradition and Revolution in Romantic Literature* (New York: Norton).

[14] Jean H. Hagstrum (1958, 1974) *The Sister Arts: The Tradition of Literary Pictorialism and English Poetry from Dryden to Gray* (Chicago: Chicago University Press), pp. 130-31; see also Richard Wendorf (1983) (ed.) *Articulate Images. The Sister Arts from Hogarth to Tennyson* (Minneapolis: University of Minnesota Press).

[15] Addison's thoughts on religion, besides those referred to in the quoted essay, are analysed in *The Spectator,* Nos. 213, 292, 356, 447, 459, 471, 483, 492, 574.

[16] John Locke (1997 [1690]) *An Essay Concerning Human Understanding* (London: Penguin), cf. Essay 2, ch. 1, § 2, and Essay 2, ch. 2, § 3. In Essay 2, ch. 11, § 2, he divides imagination from reason.

[17] See Addison, Essay No. 412: 62, where he speaks of the "different Stains of Light that shew themselves in Clouds of a different Situation."

[18] Dates, within parentheses, refer to the publication of their major works.

[19] Cf. Rene Descartes (1986) *Meditations on First Philosophy with Selections from the Objections and Replies*, tr. John Cottingham (Cambridge: Cambridge University Press); see also Gottfried Leibniz (1988) *Discourse on Metaphysics and Related Writings* (ed. tr.) R.N.D. Martin, Stuart Brown (Manchester: Manchester

University Press), and mostly in his *Theodicy.*
[20] "We do not know the cause, but the effects are evident", my translation.
[21] Newton, *Opticks*, Bk. I, part II, Proposition II, pp. 124-25.
[22] Addison believes in the healthiness of using the imagination and refers to Francis Bacon's *Essay Upon Health,* http://www.autshorama.com/essays-of-francis-bacon-31.html
[23] Until specific reference to another essay, all quotes refer to JA: 411.
[24] Cf JL: 609, Bk. 4, ch. XVIII, § 2, where the hypothesis of a sixth sense is contemplated, as in JL: 122 Bk. 2, ch. III, § 3.
[25] S.T. Coleridge (1956, 1817) *Biographia Literaria* (London: Dent), ch. IV, p. 50, hereafter referred in the text with STC: ch. and p. no.
[26] For David Hartley, in his (1749) *Observations in Man, his Frame, his Duty and his Expectations*, 2 vols (London: S. Richardson), complex thoughts are elementary sequences of sense impressions, derived from a cause-effect process.
[27] Innate knowledge had to be retrieved through an appropriate *aletheia* process, an act of disveiling and disclosure as Plato's philosophy of the Cave envisages, and, in Christianity, through the disclosing of the reading of created nature.
[28] William Duff (1994 [1767]) *Essay on Original Genius* (London: Routledge/Thoemmes) turns the concept of ingeniousness into that of invention, giving prominence to the imagination and, common to all, its ability to create and invent new original forms. Cf. Yvonne Bezrucka (2002) *Genio ed immaginazione nel Settecento inglese*, op. cit., pp. 25-54.
[29] J. Paul Hunter (1990) *Before Novels. The Cultural Contexts of the Eighteenth-Century English Fiction* (London: Norton).
[30] David Hume (1965 [1739]) *A Treatise of Human Nature: Being an Attempt to Introduce the Experimental Method of Reasoning into Moral Subjects* (ed.) L.A. Selby-Bigge (Oxford: Clarendon), p. 7, hereafter mentioned in the text as [DH: and p. no.]
[31] John Milton (2008 [1667]) *Paradise Lost* (eds) W. Kerrigan, Fallon J. Rumrich, M. Stephen. (New York: Modern Library), Bk. 1, vv. 262-64, p. 24. On Shelley cf. Kipperman, M. (1995) 'Macropolitcs of Utopia: Shelley's Hellas in Context'. In J. Arac, H. Ritvo (eds) (1995) *Macropolitics of Nineteenth-Century Literature* (Durham and London: Duke University Press), pp. 86-101.
[32] I have analysed perspective and cognition extensively through Calvino's *Palomar* and Virginia Woolf's works (cf. Bezrucka: 2010, Bezrucka: 2008d).
[33] Henry Fielding (1983 [1742]) *Joseph Andrews and Shamela* (London: Dent).
[34] Cf. H. Bhabha (ed.) (1990) *Nation and Narration* (London: Routledge), pp. 3, 299, 301. Hereafter referred to in the text with HB: and p. no.
[35] Cf. Michel de Certeau (1986) *Heterologies: Discourse on the Other* (Manchester: Manchester University Press).
[36] For the issue of identity and nation creation, see Benedict Anderson (1983) *Imagined Communities. Reflections on the Spread of Nationalism* (London: Verso), pp. 25-36, and Patrick Brantlinger (1996) *Fictions of State. Culture and*

Credit in Britain, 1694-1994 (Ithaca: Cornell University Press) and his (1988) *Rule of Darkness: British Literature and Imperialism 1830-1914* (Ithaca: Cornell University Press). For the relation of the novel to this issue, see: Patrick Parrinder (2006) *Nation & Novel. The English Novel from its Origin to the Present Day* (Oxford: Oxford University Press), Ruth Perry (2004) *Novel Relations: The Transformation of Kingship in English Literature and Culture, 1748-1818* (Cambridge: Cambridge University Press); on the Romantic Movement: David Duff (2013) *Romanticism and the Uses of Genre* (Oxford: Oxford University Press) and also D. Duff, C. Jones (2007) *Scotland, Ireland, and the Romantic Aesthetic* (Lewisburg: Bucknell University Press); Ina Ferris (2002) *The Romantic National Tale and the Question of Ireland* (Cambridge: Cambridge University Press); Gerard Carruthers, Alan Rawes (eds) (2003) *English Romanticism and the Celtic World* (Cambridge: Cambridge University Press); Leith Davis, Ian Duncan and Janet Sorensen (2006 [2004]) (eds) *Scotland and the Borders of Romanticism* (Cambridge: Cambridge University Press); Murray Pittock (2008) *Scottish and Irish Romanticism* (Oxford: Oxford University Press); Philip Connell, Nigel Leask (eds) (2009) *Romanticism and Popular Culture in Britain and Ireland*, (Cambridge: Cambridge University Press).

[37] As Benedict Anderson says, quoted in Patrick Brantlinger (1996) *Fictions of State. Culture and Credit in Britain, 1694-1994* (Ithaca: Cornell University Press), p. 4.

[38] S. During (1990) 'Literature – Nationalism's Other? The Case for Revision' In H. Bhabha (ed.) *Nation and Narration* (London: Routledge), pp. 138-53.

[39] Cf. my essay on the essentialism of South Pacific literature: Y. Bezrucka 'Albert Wendt's 'Flying-Fox in a Freedom Tree': Contagious Infection and 'Regional' Dissenting Bodies'. In A. Righetti (ed.) *Theory and Practice of the Short Story: Australia, New Zealand, The South Pacific*, Università di Verona, Valdonega, 2006, pp. 245-63.

[40] H. Kohn (1965) *Nationalism, its Meaning and History* (New York and Cincinnati: Van Nonstrand), p. 17.

[41] *ibid.*

[42] Bronislaw Malinowsky, (2013 [1935]) *Coral Gardens and Their Magic: A Study of the Method of Tilling the Soil* (Hamburg: Severus Verlag), p. 464.

[43] Cf. the recent relevant study on the early historical interpretation of the sublime by James I. Porter (2016) *The Sublime in Antiquity* (Cambridge: Cambridge University Press).

[44] T. Burnet (1684 [1681]) Telluris theoria sacra, *The Sacred Theory of the Earth* (London: R. Norton).

[45] Ferdinand De Saussure (1916, 1985) *Cours de linguistique générale* (eds) Charles Bally, Albert Séchehaye, Tullio De Mauro, Albert Riedlinger (University of California: Payot).

[46] Edmund Burke (1767 [1757]) *A Philosophical Enquiry into the Origin of Our Ideas of the Sublime and the Beautiful* (London: Dodsley), Part I, sect. VII, p. 60.

[47] Karl Rosenkrantz (1990 [1853]) *Ästhetik des Hässlichen* (Leipzig: Reclam). Nevertheless, it is not only the influence of Addison which is of relevance here but also the disharmony and the intricacy of Gilpin's pictureseque converge towards acceptance of non-normative forms of beauty.

[48] An important element of the Round Table is also the number of knights that can sit at it: designed by Merlin for Uther Pendragon, Arthur's father, in the various traditions the Round Table could sit from twelve up to one hundred and fifty knights, who shared the power as equals. For a historical examination of the myth of King Arthur, see Sharon Turner (1820 III ed. [1799-1805]) *Anglo-Saxons: Comprising the History of England, from the Earliest Period to the Norman Conquest* (London: Longman), 3 vols.

[49] On this concept cf. my article (2007) 'Law vs. Equity: Jarndyce vs. Jarndyce in Charles Dickens's "Bleak House"'. In Daniela Carpi (ed.) (2007) *The Concept of Equity. An Interdisciplinary Assessment* (Heidelberg: Winter), pp. 269-78.

[50] For an English attack on canonical law, see my article (2008) 'Representation and Truth: Law and Equity in Robert Browning's "The Ring and the Book"', *Pólemos*, Carocci, I/2008, pp. 21-34.

[51] Aristotle thus defines the aim of *epieikeia*: "all law is universal but about some things it is not possible to make a universal statement which shall be correct (…) this is the nature of the equitable, a correction of law where it is defective owing to its universality", Aristotle (1961) *The Nicomachean Ethics,* David Ross (tr.) (Oxford: Oxford UP), 133; Bk. 5, ch. 10.

[52] Even Tennyson's *Idylls of the King* (1885) can be taken as a statement on the justice of the law of the period in that the idylls champion the lost Arthurian equitable sense of justice present at the heart of the equity tradition, that of the Common Law and its jurisprudence based on the tradition of precedents.

[53] Sorcerers and demons were also present in King James VI of Scotland and I of England's (1603) *Demonology*, a treatise that attests his belief in white magic and his refusal of black spirits, that, seen from another standpoint, might be interpreted as an ingenious move to frighten people out of their wits to gather them into positive – for him – sanctity. Another important work on magic is that by Reginald Scot (1584) *The Discovery of Witchcraft* (London: William Brome), which also contains his 'Discours of Divels and Spirits', in ch. I, 4. Scot downplays the "miraculous actions (...) imputed to witches by witchmongers, papists and poets" – which Shakespeare was going to use for the delineation of Puck in his *A Midsummer's Night Dream* (1595/1596). See also Standish Henning (1969) 'The Fairies of *A Midsummer Night's Dream'*, *Shakespeare Quarterly*, Vol. 20, No. 4, 484-85; Howard, Earl of Northampton (1583) *Defensative against the Poyson of Supposed Prophecies* (London: Charlewood); James Mason (1612), *The Anatomy of Sorcery* (London: I. Legatte); Robert Burton (1883 [1617]) *Anatomie of Melancholy*, (Philadelphia: Claxton), op. cit., who writes: "Nero and Heliogabalus, Maxentius, and Julianus Apostata, were never so much addicted to magick of old, as some of our modern princes and popes themselves, are now-a-days.", p. 128.

Related to the topic of demonology see: Brian P. Levack (1995, 1987) *The Witch-Hunt in Early Modern Europe* (London: Longman).
[54] See the 'Dedication of *King Arthur or The British Worthy* to Lord George Saville, Marquis of Halifax', *The Critical and Miscellaneous Works of John Dryden*, (1800) (ed.) Edmund Malone (London: Baldwin and Son), vol. II, pp. 203-16, hereafter referred to in the text as JD, vol., and p. no., where Dryden makes reference to the "the airy and earthy spirits (...) that fairy kind of Writing", in JDW: 2, 214.
[55] René Wellek considered Thomas Rymer to be the most rigid Neoclassical critic, who did not accept Shakespeare's going against common sense and nature, the two foundation stones of the Neoplatonists. See P.A.W. Collins, 'Shakespeare Criticism', in B. Ford (ed.) (1984, 1982) *From Dryden to Johnson* (Harmondsworth: Penguin), pp. 378-80. T. Rymer (1693) in *A Short View of Tragedy; It's Original Excellency and Corruption with Some Views on Shakespear and Other Practitioners for the Stage* (London: Baldwin), ch. VII, speaking of Othello, goes beyond the proper borders of criticism by inserting some strong racial remarks that Shakespeare intented to undercut: "The Character of that State is to employ strangers in their Wars; But shall a Poet thence fancy that they will set a Negro to be their General; or trust a *Moor* to defend them against the *Turk*? With us a Black-amoor might rise to be a Trumpeter, but Shakespear would not have him less than a Lieutenant-General" (pp. 91-92); on the racial issue in *Othello,* see my article: 'Otello e la retorica visuale del Moro di Venezia', *Studi Culturali*, 3/2008, il Mulino, Bologna, 375-406.
[56] Albert Charles Hamilton (ed.) (1990) *The Spenser Encyclopaedia* (Toronto: Toronto University Press) refers to Dryden considering Spenser, with Homer, Virgil and Horace: "the top of all poetry and (...) one of his masters", p. 228.
[57] Dryden, champion and creator of the heroic play, undertook a systematic emendation and bowdlerization of those plays he thought were most to be commended and written by authors he admired. We therefore come across his corrections of Shakespeare, to be comprised and read within his debatable Neoclassicist agenda: "I undertook to remove that heap of rubbish, under which many excellent thoughts lay wholly buried", in 'Preface' (1679) to *Troilus and Cressida, or Truth Found too Late, a Tragedy* (London: J. Tonson, A. Swall), which is his adaptation of Shakespeare's *The Historie of Troylus and Cresseida*; another rewriting was his *All for Love, or the World Well Lost*, a moralistic adaptation of the, for him, too passionate *Anthony and Cleopatra*, and also his adaptation of Shakespeare's *Tempest* into *The Tempest, or the Enchanted Island* (1667 acted, 1670 pub.). Dryden also undertook a revision of Milton's *Paradise Lost*, transforming it into the opera *The State of Innocence and the Fall of Man* (1674). For his adaptations, see F.W. Kilburn (1910) *Alterations and Adaptations from Shakespeare* (Boston: Gerham) and James Vernon Lill (1954) *Dryden's Adaptations from Milton, Shakespeare, and Chaucer* (Urbana: University of Minnesota Press).

[58] The two protagonists are, respectively, King Charles II and his brother, the future King James II, Duke of York, a Catholic, who had publicly refused to submit to the Test Act – a disavowal of the transubstantiation – in 1673, resigning from his position as Lord High Admiral and having thus to leave the country. The play comments on the attempt to pass the Act of Exclusion (1678), for the fear of having, like in France, an absolute Catholic king, an outcome backed by the Tories and contested by the Whigs. The Lords eventually passed it, but with the exemption for the future King James II. This gave rise to an Exclusion crisis (1679-1681). Indeed, in 1679, again, to prevent the passing of the Act without exemptions, Charles II dissolved parliament; and did so again in 1680 and 1681. The Act, which would practically have excluded James II from his claim to the throne, prompted a group of politicians to support the claims of Charles's illegitimate, Protestant, son, the Duke of Monmouth, the Young Pretender. The issue, once James II produced a Catholic male heir, ended with the Glorious Revolution.

[59] Being an opera – we should be reminded that in music this is the age of the melodrama – to reach best results, Dryden says one has to learn from the Italians, and of this artistic form, he gives an account in his 'Preface'.

[60] Walter Scott (ed.) (1821) *The Works of Dryden*, 18 vols. (Edinburgh: Constable), vol. 8, p. 109, hereafter referred to in the text as JDS: vol. no. and page.

[61] *ibid.* p. 110.

[62] *ibid.* p. 109.

[63] Richard Hurd (1762) *Letters of Chivalry and Romance* (London: Millar, Thurlbourne, Woodyer), p. 13.

[64] Ernst H. Kantorowicz (1958) *The King's Two Bodies: A Study in Mediaeval Political Theology* (Princeton: Princeton University Press).

[65] Sidney Anglo (1961) 'The British History in Early Tudor Propaganda', *Bulletin of the John Rylands Library* 44, 1, 17-48, hereafter referred to as: Anglo and p. no.

[66] Vaughan Hart (1994) *Art and Magic in the Court of the Stuarts* (London: Routledge).

[67] Another work on King Arthur that appeared towards the end of the 17th century was Blackmore's *Prince Arthur*, a poem in 12 books, that the critic John Dennis severely criticised. Cf. Roberta Florence Brinkley (2015 [1932]) *Arthurian Legend in the Seventeenth Century* (London: Routledge), p. 87 and 166-69.

[68] Cf. Peter C. Herman (2014) 'Equity and the Problem of Theseus in *A Midsummer Night's Dream*: Or, the Ancient Constitution in Ancient Athens', *Journal for Early Modern Cultural Studies*, 14, 1, 2014, 4-31.

[69] Cf. Jan Kott (1998) 'Titania and the Ass's Head', in Kehler D. (ed.) *A Midsummer Night's Dream. Critical Essays* (New York: Garland), pp. 107-126.

[70] Louis Montrose 'A Kingdom of Shadows', in Kehler D. (1998) (ed.) *A Midsummer Night's Dream. Critical Essays* (New York: Garland), pp. 217-240.

[71] Northrop Frye (1971) *Anatomy of Criticism* (Princeton: Princeton University Press), see pp. 32-33. On page 151 he says: "[Romance] is best known to us, not

from the age of romance itself, but from later romanticizings: Comus, The Tempest, and the third book of The Faerie Queene in the Renaissance; Blake's songs of innocence and 'Beulah' imagery, Keats's *Endymion* and Shelley's *Epipsychidion* in the Romantic period proper."

[72] Cf. Mikhail Bakhtin (1941) *Rabelais and His World* (Bloomington: Indiana University Press); see also P. Stallybrass, A. White (1986) *The Politics and Poetics of Transgression* (London: Methuen).

[73] Cf. A. Shell (2015) 'Delusion in *A Midsummer Night's Dream*', in D. Loewenstein and M. Witmore (eds) *Shakespeare and Early Modern Religion* (Cambridge: Cambridge University Press), pp. 81-95; A.D. Nuttall (2000) '*A Midsummer Night's Dream*: Comedy as Apotrope of Myth', *Shakespeare Survey* 53, 49–59. See also P. Sabor and P.E. Yachnin (eds) (2008) *Shakespeare and the Eighteenth Century* (Aldershot: Ashgate).

[74] Cf. on this specific point: Peter C. Herman (2014) 'Equity', op. cit.

75 William Shakespeare (1993) *A Midsummer Night's Dream*, The Arden Shakespeare, ed. Harold F. Brooks, (London: Routledge).

76 *ibid.* p. 28, note on ll. 33-34 and pp. 146-49 referring to Reginald Scot (1584) *The Discoverie of Witchcraft*. People felt entitled to believe in witchcraft and spirits given the fact that it was no coincidence that James VI of Scotland, and I of England, had published his work *Demonology*, where spirits were testified as existing even though through a *via negativa*.

[77] Walter Scott says: "For his [Robin's] full character, the reader is referred to the *Reliques of Ancient Poetry* [by Thomas Percy]", cf. W. Scott (1802) *Minstrelsy of the Scottish Border* (Edinburgh: Black) vol. 2, p. 306.

[78] ibid.

[79] Thomas Percy (1765) *Reliques of Ancient English Poetry*, op. cit., 3 vols., vol. 2, ch. 24 dedicated to 'Robin Good-fellow' and Bk. 25 to the 'The Fairy Queen', pp. 181-86.

[80] Thomas Percy (1765) *Reliques of Ancient English Poetry*, 3 vols., op. cit., where, in vol. 1, Bk. 4: 'King Arthur's Death', pp. 68-77, and in Bk. 5: 'The Legend of King Arthur', pp. 77-82, the story of Sir Lancelot Du Lake is referred to through a translation taken from chapters CVIII, CIX, CX, of the first part of *Morthe Arthur*, as it stands in the 1634 edition (London: Dodsley), pp. 181-86. For the last quote see p. 534.

[81] Cf. H. Grady (2008) 'A "Midsummer Night's Dream" – Eros and the Aesthetic', *Shakespeare Quarterly*, 59, 3, 274-302.

[82] The Common Law, linked to equity, was based on Aristotle's *epieikeia*: "all law is universal but about some things it is not possible to make a universal statement which shall be correct (…) this is the nature of the equitable, a correction of law it is defective owing to its universality", Aristotle (1961) *The Nicomachean Ethics,* tr. David Ross (Oxford: Oxford UP), 133; Bk. 5, ch. 10. On the topic cf. Bezrucka: 2008b.

[83] William Shakespeare (1992) *The Tempest*, ed. Frank Kermode, *Arden*

Shakespeare, (London: Routledge).

[84] Recent postcolonial interpretations of the play read Caliban's figure as that of a usurped victim. They also refer to Montaigne's essay 'Of Cannibals' speaking of the Carib tribes. Explicit references are made to Bermuda (I. II. 229) as the location of the shipwreck of Gonzalo, see Francis Barker and Peter Hulme, 'Nymphs and Reapers Heavily Vanish: The Discursive Con-Texts of *The Tempest*'. In John Drakakis (ed.) (1985) *Alternative Shakespeares* (London: Methuen), pp. 191-205. See also the treatment of Caliban in Kevin Pask (2013) *The Fairy Way of Writing. Shakespeare to Tolkien*, (Baltimore: Johns Hopkins University Press), pp. 39-56, the only work I have been able to trace that develops the 'fairy way of writing' issue extensively, e.g. in *The Old Wives' Tale*, in Keats and in J.R.R. Tolkien.

[85]See Emile Grillot de Givry (1931) *Witchcraft Magic and Alchemy*, tr. J. Courtenay Locke (London: Harrap), p. 531, and Kurt Seligman (1948) *The Mirror of Magic* (New York: Pantheon); Davenport Adams, W.H. (1889) *Witch, Warlock, and Magician* (London: Chatto and Windus), p. 68. See also G. Gifford (ed.) B. White (1931) *A Dialogue Concerning Witches and Witchcrafts* (London: Oxford University Press).

[86] Robert Burton (1883 [1617]) *Anatomie of Melancholy* (Philadelphia: Claxton), Part 1, Sec. 2, Mem. 1, Subs. 3, p. 121.

[87]Immanuel Kant (1991 [1790]) *Kritik der Urteilskraft* (ed.) Gerhard Lehmann (Stuttgart: Reclam), § 67-68, pp. 345-56, where Kant speaks of the reflective judgement that organizes itself upon an 'as if' (Ger. *als ob*) hypothesis and uses an alternative, reflective organizing principle, which, nevertheless, cannot be used to assert facts about reality since reality necessitates the determinant (scientific) judgement.

[88] Cf. E.K. Chambers (1964) *Shakespeare: A Survey* (Harmondsworth: Penguin), p. 309.

[89] For the magic element, see Hewitt Alden (1934) 'The Fairy Lore of the Elizabethans', *The Elementary English Review*, 11, 1, 1-4.

[90] Hamlet is not by chance a Dane Prince, usurped by people with Latin names (Bezrucka: forthcoming).

[91] Minor White Latham (1930) *The Elizabethan Fairies: The Fairies of Folklore and the Fairies of Shakespeare* (New York: Colombia University Press), p. 4, quoting Nathan Drake (1838) *Shakespeare and His Times* (Paris: Baudry), p. 503.

[92] For the behaviour of fairies, see Robert Kirk (2008 [1893]) *The Secret Commonwealth of Elves, Fauns, and Fairies* (London: Dover).

[93] Latham: 1930, p. 3, quotes Halliwell-Philipps: "Charles Lamb, in a manuscript that I have seen, speaks of Shakespeare as having 'invented the fairies'; by which, I presume, he means that his refinement of the popular notion of them was sufficiently expansive to justify the strong epithet". See J.O. Halliwell-Philipps (1879) *Memoranda on the Midsummer Night's Dream*, p. 13.

[94] Walter Scott (1807 [1802]) 'Introduction to the Tale of Tamlane. On the Fairies

of Popular Superstitions' *Minstrelsy of the Scottish Border, Consisting of Historical And Romantic Ballads, collected in the Southern Counties of Scotland; with a Few of Modern Date, founded upon Local Tradition*, Vol. 2 (Edinburgh: Black), pp. 254-337, p. 305.

[95] *ibid.*

[96] William Temple (1709 [1690]) 'An Essay upon Ancient and Modern Learning' in *Miscellanea,* part II (London: Tonson).

[97] Pat Rogers (1993) 'Faery Lore and "The Rape of the Lock"', in Rogers P. *Essays on Pope* (Cambridge: Cambridge University Press), pp. 70–84.

[98] In Peter Sabor, Paul Edward Yachnin (eds) (2008) *Shakespeare and the Eighteenth Century* (Aldershot: Ashgate), Marcie Frank examines 'Fairie Times from Shakespeare to Scott', and speaks of the theatrical adaptations by Richard Leveridges and J.F. Lampe (p. 105), and the use of fairies in Ann Radcliffe's poetry, p. 105, that, interestingly, do not, like other mysteries of hers, receive a rational explanation. See also Jack Zipes (2000) *The Oxford Companion to Fairy Tales*, (Oxford: Oxford University Press). In Blake's painting *Oberon Titania and Puck with Fairies Dancing* (c. 1785) fairies are depicted as winged aerial creatures, incorporated in his cosmology. See also J. Chr. Smith, *The Fairies* (1755) and Chr. Dibdin's *Queen Mab*, Ben Johnson *Oberon: the Fairy Prince* 1611. Henry Purcell *The Fairy Queen* (1692), preceded the earliest collection of fairy tales in 1690.

[99] Floris Delattre (1912) *English Fairy Poetry: From the Origins to the Seventeenth Century* (London: Henry Frowde), see ch. I for the fairies in *MND*. See also Joseph Ritso (18751[831]) *Fairy Tales, Now First Collected: to which are prefixed Two Dissertations: 1. On Pygmies. I2. On Fairies* (London: F. & W. Kerslake).

[100] William Temple (1709 [1690]) 'An Essay upon Ancient and Modern Learning', in *Miscellanea,* part II (London: Tonson), p. 345.

[101] *ibid*, p. 337, pp. 344-45.

CHAPTER THREE

THE INVENTION OF THE NORTH

3.1 The 'Invention' of Northern Aesthetics

If we want to understand the apotheosis of subjectivity and sensibility that Romanticism represents and the Romantic idealism that characterises it, we cannot avoid studying the 18th century. Indeed, Romanticism constitutes no novelty for 18th-century scholars: the movement represents the full development of the cultural issues and topics discussed in the previous century. Romanticism, once seen from this perspective, can, indeed, be interpreted as the full flourishing of the empiric examination of how perception and the senses apprehend the world (Locke and Hartley's association theory of the mind); or, as a consequence of the dismissal of the genius theory and the related concentration on each human being's imagination in its creative capacity to change the world (Addison); or as the removal of outside authority to leave place for the internal, subjective one. With their common emphasis on personal accountability, the Commonwealth, the Enlightenment and, partly, also the Reformation in that it instituted the private reading of the Bible, indeed contributed to fostering a new confidence in all people's importance in the universe, which brought with it a progressive dismissal of outside authority, a move that the French Revolution was to repeat violently.

To be specific, we can state that in Great Britain, the new post-Renaissance 18th-century epistemic world-modelling – characterised by induction rather than deduction, and by Protestantism rather than Catholicism – would lead to the further step of a proud affirmation of an autochthonous aesthetics that would change the *Weltanschauung* and the cultural paradigms of the nation in promoting values and standards relative to the nation's specificity. In the 18th century, this focus led to the recovery and strenuous defence of the autochthonous artistic forms of Great Britain's past, its politics and its laws, an introspective attention that was soon followed by the other nations and countries of Europe. Vividly set in the categories that compose the Northern aesthetics, the new orientation emphasised the specific unique traits of a British artistic and literary production that was, at first, called Gothic but which later developed into the more comprehensive epistemic category covered by the term Romantic, the two terms often paired. The new adjective – Romantic – underlines the singularities of each nation as well as each individual, increasing thus the European spread of the various nationalistic strong regionalisms testified by the birth of Europe's national states.

As far as England is concerned, we can say that the birth of a characteristically English aesthetics – and by extension a Northern one, the result of the open antagonism to the Southern aesthetics – was backed by a philosophical, religious and political enlightened, i.e. anti-authoritarian, recovery of England's autochthonous prerogatives. This was a regional involutional emphasis that nevertheless launched the English Romantic Movement as well as the various European Romanticisms, with the German world following the English lead.[1]

Let us just mention the cultural shock that Goethe perceived in front of the Gothic dome in Strasbourg (13th and 14th centuries), designed by architect Erwin von Steinbach, that he describes in his essay *Von Deutscher Baukunst* (1772).[2] This architectural work enabled him to dismiss classicism and its classical beauty, the *edle Einfalt, und stille Größe* strenuously defended by Johann Joachim Winckelmann, making Goethe a champion, even though only for a while – his *Sturm und Drang* period, up to his going to Weimar (1775) – of the Gothic style. Interestingly enough, he defines Gothic as the German autochthonous style.

Indigenousness was to become a cultural catchword. If needed, a tradition could also be invented through the creation of *ad hoc* works of art to implement a certain mythic but scarce tradition on which the intelligentsia decided to focus. This is, for example, the case of the Celtic tradition and of the fake literary work *Poems of Ossian,* created by James Macpherson, a work that would make its fortune across the whole of Europe and be admired by all intellectuals of the period and, not by chance, even by Napoleon. In addition, we could also mention Thomas Chatterton's medieval manuscripts forged in the name of the monk Thomas Rowley, a Bristol poet of the 15th century, a fake poet that Thomas Warton included in his *History.*

An English autochthonous canon was therefore created through the archaeological *repêchage* of some exemplary but, at that time, forgotten authors: most often, artists whose decline had been influenced by the fact that due to their eccentricity and originality, they did not fit in the cage of the rules of the Southern aesthetics and its tradition. Artists of no secondary importance – we are here talking of some of the greatest masters of world literature: Chaucer, Spenser,[3] Milton and Shakespeare, who were thus granted a second chance and, let us say it, eternal fame. This new canon was set against the prevailing literary influence of the Greek and Roman classics, the columns of the Southern aesthetics (Homer, Virgil, Horace) imitated by the Neoclassicists, *in primis* Dryden and Pope.

Of fundamental importance in this complex aesthetic operation is the re-evaluation of the Gothic: it was appropriated and interpreted as an autochthonous Northern, non-French (Southern) style, and significantly renamed Saxon-Gothic[4] to differentiate it from the continental and the Norman-Gothic. The Saxon-Gothic was then applied and used, in its structural architectural matrix, to explain the autochthonous literature of England, as a visual paradigm in the interpretation of King Arthur's democratic – and thus anti-feudal – political power structure, and to defend the anti-classicist – and thus Gothic – design of Spenser's *Faerie Queene*. This was supported by a contemporary mythologisation of the island's Celtic origins and, from then on, its autochthonous Gothic poetry.

These concomitant actions clearly demonstrate the importance of the literary history of the 18th and 19th centuries in the creation and propagation of a strong regionalism: the idea of England as a country with an engrained unique artistic and philosophical identity. Of course, this identity was created as if England were, in its essence, a Northern country with defining characteristics of its own, determined by its natural prerogatives rather than as the result of a perspectival choice and its epistemic filter, targeted to focus only on its Northern qualities.

This would also favour and foster the first theorisation and defence of aesthetic regionalism and its 'characteristic beauty' – unequivocally claimed by Francis Grose (1788) – that asserted the right of each specific culture to fix its unique and peculiar aesthetic traits, i.e. to claim their own culturally determined aesthetics and rules. In these terms, aesthetic regionalism provides the final enfranchisement from the so-called universal aesthetics, creating a Romantic national beauty. English Romanticism, nevertheless, represented this same move applied to each individual artist, launching *de facto* the 'romantic' and unique beauty of every single individual and artist, which strong regionalism avoids seeing. This is also the link between Romanticism and nationalism, if uniqueness does not prevent the absorption of the one into the collective many, which, besides, is a crucial difference between German and English Romanticism. Indeed, under the heading 'Cultures', in the plural, and in contrast to Civilisation, aesthetic regionalism had also been defended by Gottfried Herder in Germany (1784). Nevertheless, defending his idea that each culture possesses unique characteristics, he defines them in essentialist terms, i.e. as if these characteristics were intrinsic, inherent (only) in this specific people. The concept was soon taken over by Fichte, who located this origin in the German language,[5] proposing it as the element that could unite Germany, which was still a politically subdivided land, thus transforming the concept of *Cultur* – the old German word for *Kultur* – into an overarching concept of language, seen as the shrine of German thought, then transformed into the epitome of German civilization. Herder himself, unfortunately, provided a collective glue with his insistence on a German common *Volksgeist* (the soul of the people): "Welches Volk der Erde ists [sic], das nicht eine eigene Cultur habe?"[6] This was a stance that could be and was taken up as the vehicle for transforming the one into the many.

In the field of aesthetics, the concepts used to philosophically authorise England's enfranchisement from the Southern aesthetics are Reverend William Gilpin's picturesque (later to be merged into Burke's sublime), the theorisation of the Saxon-Gothic and the Anglo-Saxon tradition used as a vehicle for an indirect criticism of religion through the pagan magic mythology of the fairies. The first two elements, being directly visible in natural scenery, became extremely persuasive for the spread of the new, anti-classical, theory of beauty on which the invention of the Northern aesthetics is naturally grounded.

But, as can clearly be seen, aesthetics is only an apparently neutral arena as it does not remain confined to issues concerning theories of beauty; it is applied and manipulated to become the vehicle for important societal issues and choices. In defending the enlightened outlook related to induction, science and the senses, aesthetics was linked to foster political and religious choices: to confirm via symbols the constitutional monarchy, to question both Catholicism and Protestantism, to spread tolerance and atheism. All of these entangled matters would find a place in the aesthetics that we have termed Northern.

Setting itself against the norms of the ancients and the Southern tradition, the love for Northern nature and the consequent flourishing of the Domestic – or Picturesque Tours, *à la* Gilpin – in antithesis to the ruling continental Grand Tour, ennobled England as a nation worthy of a unique, indigenous and regional aesthetics. This is of course in contrast to the classical, authoritarian Southern one. Of distinguished significance is also the 18th century's unconventional tours by scenery hunters and sentimental travellers going further north than the northern parts of the United Kingdom.[7] Among these, we can remember the journeys of Mary Wollstonecraft, Arthur Young, Samuel Johnson (1773), Thomas West and

Horace Walpole (1739-41), and later, in 1818, John Keats' *Northern Tour*, as well as the tours, sometime later, of Wordsworth in his move to the Lake District near the border with Scotland.[8]

These are all Northern tours[9] that champion a positive, picturesque reception of Northern barrenness: the harshness of a desolate rough world, not favourable to humankind and in contrast with the easy solar qualities of the harmonious South. These elements, which Gilpin had taught his readers to see, would later be transliterated in the theorisation of Burke's sublime (1757), and lead to the positive reception of all those anti-Southern non-cathartic forms: disharmony, the picturesque, particular instances and versions of the beautiful dictated by a personal taste – or what was thought to be personal – though most often, still, only the result of a cultural response; all effects that will be examined in the chapter devoted to Burke.

3.2 The Climate Hypothesis

Sir William Temple, in 1690, makes an interesting point linking variety among peoples with climate and customs, claiming their relevance as a factor influencing the production of literature:

> But as of most general Customs in a Country there is usually some Ground from the Nature of the People or the Clymat, so there may be amongst us for this Vein of our Stage, and a greater variety of Humor in the Picture, because there is a greater variety in the Life. This may proceed from the Native Plenty of our Soyl, the unequalness of our Clymat, as well as the Ease of our Government, and the Liberty of Professing Opinions and Factions, which perhaps our Neighbours may have about them, but are forced to disguise, and thereby they may come in time to be extinguish't.[10]

The point about climate was to be debunked, later in the century, by Isaac D'Israeli in his essay "On the Influence of Climate on the Human Mind", present in his work *Miscellanies or Literary Recreations* (1796), where he considers this theory to be one of the "follies of the wise" in his utterly modern belief in the supremacy of *nurture* above *nature*: "The human mind is indeed influenced not by climate, but by government; not by soils, but by customs; not by heat and cold, but by servitude and freedom."[11]

Milton, on the other hand, believed in the climate theory (cf. D'Israeli: 1796, 301-302) and so did Addison, who linked the fervid imagination of the Eastern Ancient ingenious authors with "the warmer Climates, who had most Heat and life in their Imagination" and, in contrast to them, he speaks of the *bienseance* "found out of latter Years (...) in the colder

Regions of the World; where we would make some Amends for our want of Force and Spirit, by a scrupulous Nicety and Exactness in our Compositions" (JA: 160, 284).

Oliver Goldsmith is extremely clear about what he thinks: "For a state to attain literary excellence (...) it is requisite, that the soil and climate should, as much as possible, conduce to happiness. The earth must supply man with the necessaries of life, before he has leisure, or inclination, to pursue its more refined enjoyments. The climate also must be equally indulgent, for, in too warm a region, the mind is relaxed into langours; and by the opposite excess is chilled into torpid inactivity."[12] Speaking of Sweden, he says: "They have, I am told, a language rude, but energetic; if so, it will bear a polish; they have also a jealous sense of liberty, and that strength of thinking, peculiar to northern climates, without its attendant ferocity" (OGE: 66).

Interestingly, in 1733, George Cheyne, in his *The English Malady*,[13] sees all these "nervous disorders" that we could group together under the term *melancholia* as being present "in any eminent Degree, especially in our Northern Climates" (GC: 16) where they "operate more" (GC: 19). The climate hypothesis became explicit. Cheyne, for example, tries to corroborate his theory with a whole series of physical descriptions and attending remedies: "Animal Food then, and Spirituous Liquors become more tolerable in *Northern Climates*, where the Want of sufficient *Sun* and the Moisture of the *Air*, makes the Solids of somewhat too loose and flabby a Nature, and so require a greater Proportion of Salts and Oils, needful to rouse and twitch them, than in more *Southern Climates*" (GC: 171). This state, he thinks, needs to be attributed to climatic conditions that physically interfere with what he calls the body: The *Animal Machin*e (GC: 201), an image he probably took from Descartes' *Traité de l'homme* (1660), and we find, later, elaborated in De La Mettrie's *L'Homme Machine* (1748); interestingly, Cheney – anticipating the empiricists – elaborates his observation in completely modern and *ante litteram* psychological terms:

> In the Southern Climates, as there is scarce any, at least few, Nervous Distempers of the lingering and chronical Kind, so there is very little Room for Exercise merely for Health: The Warmth and Action of the Sun keeping the Blood and Juices sufficiently fluid, the *Circulation* free, and all the Secretions in their due Degree and Plenty, so as to prevent Obstructions, to which the Thinness, Coolness, and Lightness of their almost Vegetable Diet contributes not a little. But in the more Northern and colder Climates, where the Food is more gross, higher and harder of Digestion, being mostly Animal; where the Perspiration is small, or scarce any at all, especially in Nervous or chronical Distemper, there is an

absolute Necessity of due Exercise and Labour to supply the Want of Sun and thin Air, and remedy these Defects: the Neglect of which, in our Climate ought to be, in Reason, reckon'd as absurd, ridiculous, and unnatural, as our using it appears *fantastical* to Orientals. The few Instances brought from Spain, Italy, Portugal, and even more Northern Countries, of People that live there to a great Age, and without Distempers, merely sitting still, are little to the Purpose, consider'd as a Rule for our Conduct (since, setting aside the above-mention'd Advantages which they enjoy in common with other Southern Countries, whereby Exercise becomes less necessary for them than for us) they are in a great measure excluded from the Benefit they might possibly reap from it, if it was necessary by its being impracticable in any high Degree: for it would be absurd to propose to them to take long continued Journies in their scorching Climate for the Cure of Distempers.

Melancholia was the English malady and, as all critics suggest, it is due to climate. Robert Burton, in his *Anatomie of Melancholy* (1621), says: "This melancholy extends itself not to men only, but even to vegetals and sensibles. I speak not of those creatures which are saturnine, melancholy by nature, as lead, and such like minerals, or those plants, rue, cypress, &c. and hellebore itself, of which Agrippa treats, fishes, birds, and beasts, hares, conies, dormice, &c., owls, bats, nightbirds, but that artificial, which is perceived in them all."[14]

Extremely significant, for the climate theory, are the words used by Anne Louise Germaine Necker, alias Madame de Staël, in her *à vol d'oiseau* panoramic view of European Romanticism. They knit together the climatic, cultural and libertarian issues on which her Northern vs. Southern – clear-cut, cultural and, at times, orientalist – distinction is being made, between these "two hemispheres of literature", clearly connecting place to "national character":

There are, it seems to me, two entirely different literatures, that coming from the South and that coming down from the North, that of which Homer is the main source and that of which Ossian is the origin. The Greeks, Latins, Italians, Spanish, and the French of the age of Louis XIV belong to that *genre* of literature that I shall call the literature of the South. English works, German works, and some Danish and Swedish writings should be classed in the literature of the North, which began with the Scottish bards, the Icelandic fables, and Scandinavian poetry. [...] The English poets, it may be said, are noteworthy for their philosophic spirit – it is displayed in all their works – [...] The shock to the imagination caused by the songs of Ossian dispose the mind to the most profound meditations. Melancholy poetry is the type of poetry most in accord with philosophy [...] We cannot in general decide between the two types of poetry of which we may consider Homer and Ossian the first models. All my feelings and all my ideas lead me to prefer the literature of the North. But what matters now is to examine in distinctive characteristics. [...] Climate is certainly one of the main causes of the differences between the images the North found congenial and those that people in the South preferred to summon up. [...] The vigorous nature that surrounds them arouses in them impulse rather than thought. I think it is wrong to say that the passions are more violent in the South than in the North. The South has a greater variety of concerns but less depth in any single one. And it is intensity that produces the miracles resulting from passion and will. The peoples of the North are less occupied with pleasures than with suffering, and their imagination is all the more fertile for it. The spectacle of nature powerfully affects them; and it makes them exactly like their climate: always dark and moody. Of course, the changing circumstances of life can change this disposition to melancholy, but it alone bears *the imprint of national character*. In a nation, as in a man, we need to find only the characteristic trait; all the others are the result of a thousand different accidents, but that one alone constitutes its being. *Northern poetry is much more suitable than Southern to the spirit of a free people.* The first known creators of the literature of the South, the Athenians, were more jealous of their independence than any other nation. But it was easier to reduce the Greek to slavery than the men of the North. *Independence was the main and unique food of fortune of the Northern peoples.* A certain pride of spirit, and indifference to life, generated by both the harshness of the soil and the gloom of the sky, were to make slavery unbearable. *And long before England knew wither the theory of constitutional government, the martial spirit that Irish and Scandinavian poetry sang with such enthusiasm gave man an extraordinary conception of his individual strength and the power of his will. Independence existed for each one before liberty was established for all.* At the time of the Renaissance, *philosophy began with the Northern nations, among whose religious customs reason had to struggle against fewer prejudices than among Southern peoples.* The Northern peoples, judging by traditions they have left to us and by Teutonic customs, had at all periods a respect for women that was unknown among the peoples of the South. In the North women enjoyed independence, whereas elsewhere they were condemned to slavery. This is another of the main causes of the sensibility that characterizes the literature of the North. [...] Finally, the Protestant religion, which almost all of the modern peoples of the North adopted, gave them a more philosophical spirit than those of the South had. The Reformation was the historical period that most effectively advanced the perfectibility of the human species. The Protestant religion harbours no active germ of superstition, yet lends virtue all the support that it can extract from sensibility. *In the countries where the Protestant religion is processed, it does not retard philosophical enquiry at all and effectively upholds morality.*[15]

The conclusion is an endorsement, nevertheless, not only of a climatic origin of character but also a cultural one, and is clearly linked to religion: "Might we not think, upon reading the writers of the North, *that they are of another nature*, with other bonds, in another world? The perfection of some of this poetry indeed proves the genius of its authors, but it is no less certain that in Italy the same men would not have written the same things even had they felt the same emotions" (MdS: 194-95). Literary works, she concludes, often express more of the general spirit of a nation than of the personal characters of their writers.

If emotions are the same, North and South present cultural – read religious – differences that mark their worlds with distinguished characteristics. Madame de Staël's assertions for claiming the differences between the two literatures are thus first cultural but then also climatic. She uses broad all-comprehensive geographical deictics, as we have done in this book, but, in our case, while qualifying them as inventions in their generalising and homogenising power.

This is an important difference in that Madame de Staël distinguishes the two literatures spatially and geographically, subsuming the religious differences of the Netherlands, England, Germany and the Scandinavian countries under her use of overarching, broad and homogenising adjectives. These include, for example, "Protestant" religion, without sufficiently qualifying the differences between the many variants of Protestantism in these countries, i.e. applying an undialectical reductionism. Nevertheless, she sees this cultural trait as being the main and determinant axiological demarcating border-line between cultures, as she clearly states in her introduction to the work we have just examined, *De la Littérature* (1800): "My purpose is to examine the influence of religion, custom, and law upon literature, and the influence of literature upon religion, custom and law" (MdS: 141). To de Staël's position we can add Hume's stance, in which he says: "The only observation, with regard to the difference of men in different climates, on which we can rest any weight, is the vulgar one, that people in the northern regions have a greater inclination to strong liquors, and those in the southern to love and women. Wine and distilled water warm the frozen blood in the colder climates (...) As the genial heat of the sun, in the countries exposed his beams, inflames the blood and exalts the passion between the sexes."[16] In the same essay, Hume considers "moral causes" and the characteristic of the human mind to be of a "very imitative nature" to exercise a propensity towards assuming a common national character: "[w]here a number of men are united into one political body (...) for defence, commerce, and government, that, together with the same speech or language, they must acquire a resemblance in their manners and have a common or national character, as well as a personal one, peculiar to each individual" (DNHC:2 48)

Religion, a cultural element, is, nevertheless, for de Staël the greatest hindrance to progress and freedom:

> The Spanish ought to have had a more noteworthy literature than that of the Italians. They should have united the imagination of the North with that of the South, the grandeur of chivalry with Oriental grandeur, the martial spirit continuous wars glorified with the poetry the beauty of the sun and climate inspired. But the royal power, supporting superstitions, smothered these happy germs of all kinds of glory. The subdivision of states which prevented Italy from becoming one nation, gave it at least enough freedom for the sciences and arts. But the unity of Spanish despotism, supporting the effective power of the Inquisition, left no living space to thought in any field, no means of escaping the yoke. (MdS: 189)

Hume is also very critical towards religion, partly confirming de Mandeville's position: he sees clergymen ("the majority") as characterised by "dissimulation", "driven by profit" and "feign[ing] more devotion than they are (...) possessed of"; they are people who "must promote the spirit of superstition by a continued grimace and hypocrisy" (DNHC: 248).

Furthermore, de Staël clearly refers to Montesquieu's theory when she says: "Melancholy, that fertile sentiment in works of genius, seems to belong almost exclusively to Northern climates. (...) The melancholy of Orientals is that of men happy in the enjoyment of nature; they reflected with regret only upon the rapid passing of prosperity, the brevity of life. The melancholy of the peoples of the North is the kind that arises out of the suffering of the soul, the emptiness that sensibility causes one to find in life, the meditation that constantly leads the mind from thoughts of the weariness of life to the mystery of death" (MdS: 191). She also adopts the same orientalist prejudice in judging philosophy: "No element of philosophy could develop in Spain, the invasions from the North brought only the martial spirit, and the Arabs were the enemies of philosophy"; a very debatable, if not even inconsistent, view (MdS: 190).[17]

However, what I want to underline is that these excerpts present the inherent peril of all broad categorisations. Organising thought according to homogenising traits is an important synthetic task. Nevertheless, one needs to keep in mind that there will always be other traits – variety being the panoply of reality, as Hogarth points out in his work – that undermine each encompassing holistic classification. The line of beauty needs thus to be found in the negotiated provisional points of contact of cultures rather than in their differences, otherwise, as Emily Brontë, Thomas Hardy and

Elizabeth Gaskell all show, havoc – and war – are the result.[18]

The clear-cut line de Staël sets between North and South is for her connected to the religious reformation in that she finds the cause for Protestantism having been initiated in the Northern countries. She cites how these people set greater value on personal virtue and civil progress and in being linked with a more democratic, freer, way of living and being.[19] These characteristics have influenced also the arts that can now, as she says, move freely, and within a territory, we could add – with the addition of the new natural and artistic categories of aesthetics – that has now a much bigger extension if compared with the previous one, which was limited to *la belle nature*.

De Staël, indeed, recognises the inclination of acquiescence to rules among French artists as a hindrance to the progress of the mind. She believes the German and the English, in their refusal to comply with these, were, on the contrary, fostering progress:

> The poetry of the North is far better suited than that of the South to the spirit of a free people (...). Independence was the first and unique source of happiness of northern people. A certain fierceness of the soul, a detachment from life born of a harsh land and melancholic sky, made servitude unbearable: long before England discovered the advantages of representative government, the war-like spirit that Erse and Scandinavian poets sung [sic] with such enthusiasm gave to man an extraordinary sense of his own individual strength, and of the power of his will. (MdS: 206)

Starting, on the one hand, with the climate theory to which Montesquieu had given lustre in his *Esprit des Lois* (1748),[20] de Staël underlines that pride of spirit needs to be connected to a harsh climate; on the other hand, she also points to cultural influences that bring one back, she says, either to Homer or to Ossian (whom she considers to be an original poet), i.e. to the South or to the North.

According to Montesquieu, the cold activates a contraction of the nerves whereas warmth produces their relaxation, leading to a very debatable theory: "Northern peoples are morally virtuous because their senses are dull, southern people are indolent and immoral because their passions are violent"; his conclusion being that institutions and the law in particular should therefore be adapted to these physiological reactions to climate in order to "be in accordance with their respective characters, tending in temperate climates to liberty and equality, in warm climates to tyranny and slavery."[21] The good legislator will, accordingly, try to stop vice and promote virtue. Nevertheless, Montesquieu also admits cultural and social influences and interferences when he says that climate has a stronger influence on the less-educated.

One of Montesquieu's detractors was David Hume, who claimed merely cultural rather than natural influences, saying that people change ideas and express different opinions, climate notwithstanding. The issue of the acculturation theory was repeated by James Dunbar in his work *Essays on the History of Mankind* (1780),[22] which insisted on acquired values being relative to a certain environment but depending on the free will of the person living in it. He thus eschewed both the innatist conundrums and the essentialist agenda.

As Frank Fletcher demonstrates, commenting on Montesquieu, the environment indeed has a relatively small effect on the people who have, through time, evolutionarily adapted themselves to their surroundings. He does, though, point out that climate still has important effects on the endocrine system of the body, i.e. on the thyroid and adrenal glands. Furthermore, studies on suicide rates point out an increased number of this kind of death in the darker regions of the North where the sun is scarce.[23]

3.3 Northern *vs.* Southern Perspective-Choices

The ideas of beauty that have become central in the Western world are often linked to theories connected with the sun. All the peoples of antiquity, particularly the Egyptian and Mesopotamian civilisations, included the sun in their mythologies to testify their homage to its enlivening energy, splendour and warmth but also, conversely, to its dangerous and vindictive power. Indeed, looking at the sun with the naked eye remains forbidden.

If the positive and negative magnetic powers of the sun are to be witnessed in all sectors of the cardinal points, by being naturally stronger in the South, near the equator, Greek and Roman mythologies connected the sun to their gods and goddesses. The sun became thus Helios for the Greeks and Sol for the Romans. Philosophers turned their attention to the sun. For example, Plato found beauty in sunrays.[24]

Southern regions, irradiated by the sun, are, concerning climate, commonly understood as more pleasant and healthier places to live. Poets, like Homer, thus speak of beauty and link it to the sun's luminescence and dazzling power. This last enticing element soon became a characteristic of beauty itself, which, it is said, has a power of its own that needs only to be seen to be perceived, *quod visum placet*. Aphrodite, the Greek goddess of beauty, possesses these powers in abundance. She represents love, eroticism and procreation. She is strictly linked to the sky by her father Zeus, the Father of the Sky, a sort of personification of the sun, who reigns over all gods in Olympus. In Roman mythology, Zeus is Jove and Aphrodite is Venus, and is linked to the planet homonymous with her.

It therefore comes as no surprise that famous Greek thinkers – Plato, Socrates, Aristotle, Homer and Hesiod – and Roman ones – Ovid, Horace, writing in Latin, and Longinus and Plotinus writing in Greek – attributed solar characteristics to the conceptualisations of beauty in their treatises. They collectively set fixed but Southern norms that became accepted in the whole of the Western world. These norms remain iconically visible in their architecture, paintings, music, statues, handicraft and in their written works, which all cultured people, across what we today call Europe, are encouraged to study and pay homage to. The same happened to Southern culture in general. Both the Trivium: grammar, logic and rhetoric, and the Quadrivium: astronomy, arithmetic, geometry and music, set the norms for European knowledge.

Regarding the prehistory of aesthetics, the Platonic tradition of beauty maintained its control over art and aesthetic matters up to and beyond the translation of Nicolas Boileau's *L'Art Poétique* (1674), which appeared in England in 1680, translated by Sir William Soame, with Dryden acting as a corrector. [25] In 1674, Boileau also translated Pseudo-Longinus' *Peri Hypsous* into French, calling it *Traité du Sublime ou du Merveilleux dans le Discours*. The translation of Longinus' *Peri Hypsous* had already appeared in Basel in 1554, in Venice in 1555, in Geneva in 1569 and in England in 1652. The latter version was translated by John Hall as *Peri Hypsous, or Dionysius Longinus' Of the Height of Eloquence*. However, the debate on sublimity started with the translation of Longinus' *Peri Hypsous* by John Pulteney, who used Boileau's French translation as his vehicle. Pulteney called it *A Treatise of the Loftiness or Elegancy of Speech* (1680), and it is in this version – i.e. via Boileau's text[26] – that Longinus' rhetorical sublime became known in England.

Boileau, the champion of the clear harmonious Neoclassical style and art,[27] had indeed confined Longinus' treatment of the sublime within stylistic matters, i.e. not emphasising enough the natural Sublime or the subjective inclination towards the sublime which appear in the *Peri Hypsous*. This issue was later to be treated extensively in the German world by Winckelmann, who saw absolute beauty only in Greek beauty, identifying it in Praxiteles' statues.

Boileau's harmonious sunny aesthetics conformed perfectly to the standards of Southern and Western European countries. Indeed, if rightly interpreted, it was the promotion of a thoroughly regional aesthetics, of Greek, and later Roman, imprint. Not by chance did the lands of the North, which did not relish the sun, or at least had less sun than the South, feel that somehow this aesthetics neither fully represented them nor adhered to the specific natures of their own countries.

During the 18th century, Great Britain and its intellectuals felt they somehow had to act in order not to be, so to say, digested by the continent. Whether this reaction to Southern aesthetics should be interpreted as a planned, concerted and rational move is rather difficult to ascertain. Nevertheless, what we witness happening during the 18th century is something that, in hindsight, we can term a sort of cultural revolution, a battle for independence being fought on the cultural level, with aesthetics as its battlefield. What we know for certain is that English intellectuals would win the war and a new, different, aesthetic tradition was born – the Northern aesthetics.

Nevertheless, we should underline the fact that in time, this aesthetics has been considered as setting standards of beauty that are accepted, as the old Southern ones were, in the whole Western world.

If we examine the history of the United Kingdom, both recent and past, to reach an understanding of this nation and its literary history from a cultural point of view, we will soon detect two major turning points. Although they happened early on in its history, both have had long-lasting consequences; indeed, cultural effects, in whose wake this nation still lives. The first one is connected to scholars like John Colet, Thomas Grocin, Thomas Linacre and Thomas More, who, during the 15th and 16th centuries – broadly, the Renaissance – established Greek and Latin study courses in Oxford. Indeed, it was this new Latin or classical orientation and canon that dimmed the previous strong Celtic, German and Scandinavian influences – broadly, the previous Northern cultural heritage of England.

The Latin, or Southern influence, with its rich, scholarly and complex mythology, was soon felt to be an element of cultural distinction that needed to be acquired by the knowledgeable men of England. In this way, the older heroic, fantastic and magic Celtic folklore mythology – the chthonic elemental tradition[28] – became implicitly disqualified and, in a second move, downplayed as being naïve, unsophisticated and, in sum, inferior. Its use in literary works was progressively neglected. Only uncontested artists, like Spenser, Shakespeare and Pope, later, used it in their works – nevertheless, mixed with a truthful respect for the Latin and classical topics. Indeed, rare works, like Shakespeare's *A Midsummer Night's Dream* (1590-1597) and *The Tempest* (1610-1611), placed the two traditions side by side in comparison, if not in direct antagonism. These works present the Northern magical, airy creatures: the sylphs and gnomes that we see appearing also, later, in *The Rape of the Lock* (1712-1714), which these artists recover from previous Anglo-Saxon sources, and from *The Faerie Queene*[29] (1590-1596) by Edmund Spenser.

These works testify to a rare return to this affectively[30] perceived tradition – i.e. perceived as if it was the original, essentialist core of England's literature – an origin connected with the pagan bardic lore of Ireland, Cornwall, Wales, the Isle of Man and Scotland: the Celtic tradition of England[31] and its language, which still survives today.[32] This connection of folk character, lore and language is often at the core of a strong regionalist agenda, which for the people who live in certain areas evokes an affectively connoted perception of place that is often turned into a highly charged homeland sentiment once this is seen as threatened by outside forces. Affective perception is then turned into easy-to-use psychological weapons by populistic movements, which resort to these non-rationalised drives eristically, i.e. in a strong rhetorical persuasive way, to promote their own ideological protectionist and separatist agendas.

As we know, it was the Latin, or the continental, tradition that became prominent and dominated the panorama of literary studies and its production up to the early 18th century. However, this orientation towards the Classics – Latin, Italian, French and Greek – and their aesthetics comes to an important halt during the 18th century, when the Northern elements reconquered a central place in no uncertain terms.

The English, or Northern, aesthetics is indeed the result of the attempt, promoted by the intelligentsia of 18th-century England, to emancipate their intellectuals and artists from the comprehensive influence that the Southern aesthetics had prescribed for them and for the Western world. How much this aesthetics was dominant is shown, without a doubt, by the fact that everybody perceived and recognized it as being *universal*.

The cultural engagement and promotion necessary to introduce the Northern change successfully was therefore shrewdly corroborated and validated by the material proof of the domestic, i.e. natural, landscape and environmental prerogatives of England. These were included as if they were engrained in the land and the country's regional characteristics: i.e. backing them with climate, folklore and essentialist theories that relied on the common-sense perception that the people born in one land were all the same and shared the same values.

On the one hand, this essentialist focus became an instrumental vehicle for the recovery of the Celtic elements and, on the other hand, through the ingenious creation of new stylistic and, semiotically-speaking, seemingly self-evident visual paradigms for the new Northern aesthetics. These elements were the picturesque, those of the cyphered interpretation of the structure and blueprint of the English garden, or that of the proxemically egalitarian Arthurian Round Table. Consequently, what was previously seen from the viewpoint of classical beauty and interpreted as insufficiently artistic, or as a work of no strong aesthetic appeal, was now turned, from the viewpoint of the Northern aesthetics, into a different but aesthetically attractive element – changing from a negative into a positive aesthetic value. We will follow, in due course, the evolution of this change in detail.

Let us first state that this change initiates the return to, and recovery of, the Celtic roots of England: an adjustment that takes root and is periodically rediscovered, and each time for national protective reasons. Its various reappearances, beginning in the 18th century, take place when a supposed, but affectively perceived, outside danger is felt as threatening the core identity of the nation, its Britishness. This was also the drive for the medievalism of the 19th century,[33] when industrialisation seemed to cancel the environment of the past altogether, or for the fantasy literature of the 20th and 21st centuries, when mechanisation and technology threaten to replace people or, more dangerously, when the social, demographic and economic conditions of the country change. But the same hazard was felt even before, particularly, in fact, in the 18th century, when the Southern aesthetics threatened to cancel the insular identity-characters of Great Britain, shading the English prerogatives connected with art, nature, environment and inhabitants. The same drive was also in the background of the recent Brexit referendum (April 2016), when, on the level of debate, European laws, based on the letter of the law of French jurisprudence, were felt to be a peril for English commercial and social life and perceived as menacing to English jurisprudence and its law system based on the equity principle and the precedent-tradition[34] while, on another level, debate featured the defence of the allegedly beleaguered English particularism, pandering to populist agitation[35] which seems to be becoming more widespread on a daily basis. In all these instances, we can say that the country reacts against an ever-different, but intensely felt, external Promethean enemy that intrudes into its – democratic – identity core.

The contrast between Northern and Southern lands, iconised in the opposition between darkness and light, have been used since Elizabethan times, and is well expressed in Queen Elizabeth I's painting, attributed to John Gower, celebrating the victory over the Spanish Armada that affirmed England as the chosen-by-God land. Their opposing religious stances, choices and orientations are marked as the gap existing between the sun and the moon, day and night, divided in the portrait by the imposing presence of Queen Elizabeth I, the Virgin Queen neglecting marriage to Philip II of Spain, as exemplified in John Gower's *Armada Portrait*:

Elizabeth I: Armada Portrait, attributed to John Gower, 1588
Image in the public domain
See centerfold for this image in colour

The same dichotomy is underlined in a poem by George Chapman, in 1594, *Hymnus in Cynthiam*, where Elizabeth is associated with the Roman deity of Diana but the English moon chases the warlike Southern sun of the King of Spain and his armada. The lines of the poem seem nearly a periphrasis or caption for the painting, ironically upturning the standard qualifications and values of light and darkness, depicting those southern lands as still languishing in darkness because of their total intolerance towards the progress of science:

> Set thy Christall and Imperiall throne, // (girt in the chast, and never-losing zone) // *'Gainst Europs Sunne directly opposit, //And give him darknesse, that doth threat thy light.*[36]

The anachronistic revival of the cult of the Protestant Elizabeth was clearly dictated by a militantly interventionist policy against Catholic Spain: "[b]ecause these values were increasingly found wanting at the court of England's Scottish King."[37]

Along with the recovery of the myth of King Arthur, Elizabeth is herself used as a symbol of the Celtic world, as *The Faerie Queene*, by Spenser in 1590, thus revitalising the chivalric values of King Arthur in a female body, as demonstrated at Tilbury on the 9th of August 1588 when she stirringly rallied soldiers preparing to give up their life to a win/lose battle against the Spanish Armada:

> My loving people, we have been persuaded by some, that are careful of our safety to take heed how we commit ourselves to armed multitudes for fear of treachery; but assure you, I do not desire to live to distrust my faithful, and loving people. Let tyrants fear, I have always so behaved myself, that, under God, I have placed my chiefest strength and safeguard in the loyal hearts and good-will of my subjects. And therefore I am come amongst you at this time, not as for my recreation or sport, but being resolved in the midst, and heat of the battle to live, or die amongst you all, to lay down for my God, and for my kingdom, and for my people, my honour and my blood, even in the dust. I know I have the body, but of a weak and feeble woman, but I have the heart and stomach of a king, and of a king of England too; and think foul scorn that Parma or Spain, or any Prince of Europe, should dare to invade the borders of my realms: to which, rather than any dishonour should grow by me, I myself will take up arms, I myself will be your general, judge, and rewarder of every one of your virtues in the field. (...) In the meantime, my lieutenant general shall be in my stead, (...) not doubting by your obedience to my general, (...) and your valour in the field, we shall shortly have a famous victory over those enemies of my God, of my kingdom, and of my people.[38]

This speech, and its recently transcoded film version, give us a clear idea about the contemporary increase of nationalistic overtones that we have already noted in the TV series *Game of Thrones*. The 2005 mini-series *Elizabeth I*, directed by Tom Hooper, particularly exploits all the nationalistic implications of this speech: Hooper directs Elizabeth walking through her troops, stooping before them to gather soil, which she slowly caresses in her hand as it falls slowly back to the ground, in contrast to the same scene in *Elizabeth* (1998), directed by Shekar Kapur, where the Queen addresses her soldiers, less impressively, only from the height of her stallion.

Notes

[1] The *Sturm und Drang* coterie, called *Geniezeit* as a period, was an organised and structured group that, around 1775, coalesced in a movement centred on Goethe. They promoted the elitist *Genie-Theorie,* that of the *Originalgenies,* i.e. of native, inborn geniuses, that the English had replaced, since 1712, with their democratic imagination theory. They move thus within the panorama of the old aesthetic framework, in contrast to Locke and Hume's imagination theory which foresaw that everyone could become an ingenious artist with or without having the gift of ingeniousness, which makes the remarkable non-elitist difference of English Romanticism.

[2] J.W. Goethe (1772) *Von deutscher Baukunst*, (Frankfurt am Main: Deinet).

[3] Cf. Charles Bowie Millican (2014 [1932]) *Spenser and the Table Round. A Study in the Contemporaneous Background for Spenser's Use of the Arthurian Legend* (Harvard: Harvard University Press).

[4] J. Wallis (1769) *The Natural History and Antiquities of Northumberland* (London: W. & W. Strahan) vol. 2, refers to the Saxon-Gothic, i.e. the architectural style of England present from the 5th century to the Norman Conquest (1066), and finds an example of this style in the Castle of the Duke and Duchess of Northumberland. The birth of the Continental Gothic style is usually, historically, linked to the reconstruction of Abbot Suger, who began the reconstruction of the Romanesque Abbey of Saint-Denis into a properly Gothic church between 1130 and 1140, to emphasise the element of light, interpreted as being directly linked to God.

[5] Cf. E. Hobsbawm (1990) *Nations and Nationalism since 1780: Programme, Myth, Reality* (Cambridge University Press), pp. 65-79.

[6] G. Herder, op. cit., 1784, p. 3: "What people on earth are they that do not possess a culture of their own?" (my tr.).

[7] How deictics are used in England is of extreme interest, particularly to foreigners: if from Cambridge, let us say, a person is meant to go to London, one is presumed to move "up" to London, clearly employing an axiological rationale which is not spatially correct, and favours an evaluative one, implying another type of assessment. For example, the deictic is inserted according to the importance of place rather than to spatial direction as such. All such linguistic forms are taken for granted by native speakers and ingrained in the *doxa,* common-sense linguistic forms that speakers use without thinking but that perpetrate the unheeded episteme of the *status quo.*

[8] Cf. M. Wollstonecraft (1970 [1796]) *Letters Written During a Short Residence in Sweden, Norway and Denmark* (Fontwell: Centaur); J. Boswell (1785) *The Journal of a Tour to the Hebrides with Samuel Johnson* (London: Henry Baldwin); A. Young (1770) *A Six Months Tour Through the North of England* (London: W. Strahan and W. Nicholl); Thomas West (2008 [1779]) *A Guide to the Lakes of Cumberland, Westmorland and Lancashire* (Cumbria: Unipress), Sarah Murray's (1799) *A Companion and Useful Guide to the Beauties of Scotland* (London:

George Nicol) sand Conti Camaiora I. (1993) *The Letters and Poems of John Keats' Northern Tour* (Europrint: Milano).

[9] Cf. Peter Fjagesund (2014) *The Dream of the North: A Cultural History to 1920* (Amsterdam: Rodopi). Fiagesund speaks of a Swedish scholar of the 17th century, Rudbeck, who, in 1681, wrote the first volume of his work *Atland*, dedicated to Olaus Verelius, who was then invited to the Royal Society of London (p. 109). Fiagesund's book presents a historical study of the Scandinavian region, and the book provides an important adjunct to my perspective.

[10] W. Temple (1690) *Miscellanea,* op. cit. p. 74. On page 16, he affirms: "Besides, I know no Circumstances like to Contribute more to the advancement of Knowledge and Learning among men than exact Temperance in their Races, great pureness of Air, and equality of Clymate, long Tranquility of Empire or Government".

[11] I. D'Israeli (1796) *Miscellanies; or, Literary Recreations* (London: Cadell And W. Davies). See his chapter 'On the Influence of Climate on the Human Mind', where with great irony he debunks Montesquieu's climate argument by paring all down to cultural causes (p. 288 and p. 307). In the work there is also a reference to Spenser: "If he is a writer, more elegant than profound, he delights in descriptive grandeur; in the touching narratives of suffering beauty, and persecuted virtue. If he possesses a romantic turn, his heroes are so many Arthurs, and the actions he records, put a modest adventurer into despair. No writers more than the historian, and the professed Romancer, so sedulously practice the artifice of awakening curiosity, and feasting that appetency of the mind, which turns from wholesome truth, to spirited fiction. We love not what we are, because it wants the grace of novelty; we are pleased with the wanderings of fancy, because they shoot far above the sober limit of nature", pp. 63-64. On page 320-21, he says "The madness of Orlando Furioso, though it wears, by its extravagance, a very original air, is only imitated from Sir Launcelot in the old Romance of Mort Arthur, with which the late Mr. Warton observes, it agrees in every leading circumstance."

[12] Oliver Goldsmith (1759) *An Enquiry into the State of Polite Learning in Europe* (London: Dodsley), hereafter referred to in the text as OGE: and p. no., here p. 15.

[13] George Cheyne (1733) *The English Malady or, a Treatise of Nervous Diseases of all Kinds; as Spleen, Vapours, Lowness of Spirits, Hypochondriacal, and Hysterical Distempers, Etc.*, 3 parts (London: G. Strahan).

[14] Robert Burton (1883 [1617]) *Anatomie of Melancholy* (Philadelphia: Claxton), p. 51.

[15] Morroe Berger (ed.) (1964) *Madame de Staël. On Politics Literature and National Character*, (New York: Doubleday), pp. 191-95, hereafter referred to in the text as MdS and page no.

[16] Cf. D. Hume (1881 [1748 Bodl. Ed. D]) 'Of National Characters' in *Essays Moral, Political and Literary* (eds) T.H. Greene, T.H. Grose (London: *sine ed.)*, vol. 1 of 2, p. 256. Hereafter referred to in the text as DHNC and page no.

[17] Let us just quote here the cultural importance of Ibn Sina (Avicenna) or Ahmad Ibn Rushd (Averroes).

[18] See on this Y. Bezrucka (2008) '"The Well-Beloved": Thomas Hardy's Manifesto of "Regional Aesthetics"', *Victorian Literature and Culture*, 36.1 (Cambridge: Cambridge University Press), 227-45. On the stylistic and thematic modernity of Thomas Hardy, cf. Maria Teresa Bindella (1979) *Scena e figura nella poesia di Thomas Hardy* (Pisa: Pacini).

[19] For the study of literature and authors, also Pope, in his *Essay on Criticism*, op. cit., insisted upon religion, giving to it the first place of topics of interest: "Religion, Country, Genius of the Age // Without all these at once before your eyes, // Cavil you may, but never criticise", vv. 121-23, p. 67.

[20] Charles-Louis de Secondat, Baron de La Brède et de Montesquieu (1748) *De l'Esprit des Lois* (Geneva: Barrillot).

[21] Quoted in Frank T.H. Fletcher (1934) 'Climate and Law. Influence of Montesquieu on British Writers', *Geography*, Vol. 19, No. 1, 29-36, p. 30.

[22] Cf. Dunbar James (1780) *Essays on the History of Mankind* (London: Strahan, Cadell, Carfour) Essay 6: 'Of the General Influence of Climate on National Objects', 7: 'Of the Farther Tendency of Local Circumstances to affect the Proceedings of Nations', and essay 9: 'Of the Relation of Man to the Surrounding Elements.'

[23] On this topic, see the mentioned study on the role of vitamin D as an antidepressant, unhappiness often linked to absence of light in the circadian cycle, a condition that triggers suicide rates: Michael Berk, Kerrie M. Sanders, Julie A. Pasco, Felice N. Jacka, Lana J. Williams, Amanda L. Hayles, Seetal Dodd (2007) 'Vitamin D deficiency may play a role in depression', *Medical Hypotheses,* 69, pp. 1316-19.

[24] See Plato (1950 [c. 360 B.C.E.]) *Republic*, 507b-509c, Bk. 6 (Harmondsworth: Penguin), where Socrates sees the sun as the son of Goodness, representing the illuminating element necessary for the apprehension of reality, as goodness is the element that illuminates reason with truth.

[25] Boileau's work was translated into English by Sir William Soames and John Dryden.

[26] Nicolas Boileau-Despréaux (1972 [1694, 1713]) *Preface to His Translation of Longinus and Critical Reflections on Longinus* (tr. John Ozell) (Sheffield: University of Sheffield).

[27] For an analysis of the influence of the concept of the sublime, see J.W. Draper, *Eighteenth-Century English Aesthetics: A Bibliography*, Heidelberg: Winter 1931, S.H. Monk, *The Sublime: A Study of Critical Theories in XVIII-Century England*, New York: Modern Language Association of America, 1935; John M. Aden (1953) 'Dryden and Boileau: The Question of Critical Influence', *Studies in Philology*, 50, 3, 491-509.

[28] Elemental creatures appear in Paracelsus' work *Liber de Nymphis, sylphis, pygmaeis et salamandris et de caeteris spiritibus* (post. 1566), as part of his

Philosophia Magna (s.d.). He theorizes the existence of these elemental creatures; they appear in another famous work, mentioned by Pope in his *Rape of the Lock*, De Montfaucon, N.P.H, Abbé de Villars (1670) *Le Comte de Gabalis, ou Entretiens sur les sciences secrètes* (Paris: Claude Barbin), a work which contributed to popularising these creatures. Anna M. Stoddart attributes the presence of these creature in Paracelsus to "the Teutonic realm of fairies"; see her *The Life of Paracelsus*, (London: Rider, 1915), p. 271, whereas Jacques-Albin-Simon, Collin de Plancy, (1863) *Dictionnaire Infernal* (Paris: Furne Jouvet), attributes the origin of gnomes to Lapland; see also 'Sylphs and Other Elemental Beings in French Literature', Edward D. Seeber, *PMLA*, 59, 1, Mar., 1944, pp. 71-83; here note 8 and 10, on p. 74.

[29] E. Spenser (1596) *The Faerie Queene* (London: Ponsobie), 12 Bks.

[30] This book is intended to rework and analyse essentialism through an affect theory: a theory of an empathically rich cognitive, and thus not entirely rational, perception of environmental and cultural elements that each micro-culture is faced with through its folklore, family, milieu, place and education. These cultural influences – that can be exported from place to place – are mistakenly perceived as if they were inherent and engrained characteristics of a national and geographical soil. Strong essentialism, thus, rather than rationally recognising custom-related behaviours and choices as the effect of cultural acquisition and cultural adaptation, instead ideologically roots them in a specific place with, as history testifies, terrific consequences, e.g. in the Nazi *Blut und Boden* ideology (Ger. blood and soil). Cultural traditions are, thus, in my opinion comparable to all other culturally-acquired common sense ideas. For example, we find specific inclinations for one type of food rather than another, whose non-appeal has only to be attributed to culture-specific acquired eating-notions, applicable, e.g. to entomophagy, creating disgust in people not used, culturally, to eating insects, which is completely unconnected to their real taste or gusto-value. In this sense, they can be maintained, changed or forgotten as long as they do not harm the new cultural environments into which they are exported.

[31] See C.W. Sullivan III (1989) *Welsh Celtic Myth in Modern Fantasy* (Westport: Greenwood Press); William Reese (1963) 'Survival of Ancient Celtic Customs in Medieval England'. In K. Jackson *et al.* (1963) (ed.) *Angles and Britons* (Cardiff: Wales University Press), pp. 148-68, Nora Chadwick (1964) 'The Celtic Background of Early Anglo-Saxon England'. In K. Jackson, P. Hunter Blair, B. Colgrave, B. Dickins, J. Taylor, H. Taylor, C. Brooke, N.K. Chadwick (eds) *Celt and Saxon. Studies in the Early British Border* (Cambridge: Cambridge University Press), pp. 323-52, see also her other book(1976) *The British Heroic Age: The Welsh and the Men of the North* (Cardiff: Wales University Press); Lucy Allen Platon (1960) *Studies in the Fairy Mythology in Arthurian Romance* (New York: Burt Franklin); see also Lady Charlotte Guest, *The Mabinogion,* op. cit., a series of stories collected by 12th- and 13th-century Welsh authors that are, probably, the earliest instances of prose literature of England.

[32] The Celtic languages are a group of languages in the Indo-European family; see Donald MacAulay (ed.) (1992) *The Celtic Languages: An Overview* in *the Celtic Languages* (Cambridge: Cambridge University Press) and D. MacAulay, (1992) 'The Celtic Languages: An Overview'. In D. MacAulay (ed.) *The Celtic Languages* (Cambridge: Cambridge University Press), pp. 1-8. The term "Celtic" was first used to describe this language group by Edward Lhuyd in 1707; see B.W. Cunliffe (2003) *The Celts. A Very Short Introduction* (Oxford: Oxford University Press), p. 48, following Paul-Yves Pezron, who had already made the explicit link between the Celts described by classical writers and the Welsh and Breton languages; cf. Alice Roberts (2015) *The Celts* (London: Heron Books). The Celtic family of languages is divided into two branches, the Insular Celtic languages and the Continental Celtic languages. The Continental branch includes Gaulish, Celtiberian and Lepontic languages, which were spoken in northern Italy, Spain, Switzerland and in a wide arc from Belgium to Turkey. The Insular Celtic languages were mostly those spoken on the islands of Britain, Ireland, the Isle of Man and part of France. They belong to one of two branches, the Goidelic and the Brythonic. The Goidelic languages are Irish Gaelic, Scottish Gaelic and Manx. The Brythonic languages form the other branch of the Insular Celtic languages. Welsh, Cornish, and Breton are Brythonic (cf. Martin J. Ball, James Fife (eds) *The Celtic Languages* (London and New York: Routledge, 1993). The SIL *Ethnologue* 2016 lists six "living" Celtic languages, of which four have retained a substantial number of native speakers. These are the Gaelic or Goidelica languages (i.e. the Irish language and Scottish Gaelic – both descended from Middle Irish), and the Brittonic languages (i.e. Welsh and Breton – both descended from Old Brittonic); see *https://www.ethnologue.com/.* The other two, Cornish (another Brittonic language) and Manx (a Goidelic language), died in modern times, with their presumed last native speakers, in 1777 and 1974, respectively. Revitalisation movements have led to the adoption of these languages by adults and children and produced some native speakers; see cf. John T. Koch (2006) *Celtic Culture: A Historical Encyclopedia*, (Oxford: ABC-CLIO), vol. 1, pp. 34, 365-366, 529, 973, 1053). Taken together, there were roughly one million native speakers of Celtic languages as of the 2000s (Cf. 'Celtic Languages' in *Ethnologue.* *https://www.ethnologue.com/subgroups/insular* retrieved 2016. In 2010, there were more than 1.4 million speakers of Celtic languages, cf. David Crystal (2010) *The Cambridge Encyclopaedia of Language* (Cambridge: Cambridge University Press). As the note demonstrates, the Celtic language is sometimes used as a demarcation line for inclusiveness and discriminatory traits.

[33] See, for example, the Pre-Raphaelite art that recovers an utterly medieval ambience, or Lord Tennyson's revival of King Arthur in his poem *The Idylls of the King*.

[34] For a 19th-century example, see my article 'Law vs. Equity: Jarndyce vs. Jarndyce in Charles Dickens's "Bleak House"'. In Daniela Carpi (2007) *The Concept of Equity. An Interdisciplinary Assessment* (Heidelberg: Winter), pp. 269-

78.

[35] Kirby Swales (2016) *Understanding the Leave Vote* (London: NatCen, 2016), p. 5, states: "By 2015 there was clear evidence that the UK was in a Eurosceptic mood, with two-thirds opposed to the UK's existing relationship with the EU. Twenty-two per cent said that we should leave the EU and 43% wanted a reduction in EU powers. It has been argued that Euroscepticism was not new but best seen as the intensification of a climate of opinion already present since the mid-1990s (in the wake of the EU export ban on British Beef). (...) On the face of it, people were weighing up the arguments and policies of the respective campaigns. For the Leave campaign, the key messages were mainly about 'taking back control' of borders, law-making, and the money Britain contributes to the EU budget. For the Remain side, the main arguments were about the economic benefits of membership and maintaining influence in the world." See the report for a well-balanced view of the topic. Important and interesting is that the Leave Agreement was set on the figure of 66% in the belief that "EU membership undermines Britain's independence" (p. 14).

[36] Louis Montrose (2006) *The Subject of Elizabeth. Authority, Gender, and Representation* (Chicago: University of Chicago Press), p. 147.

[37] John N. King (1990) 'Queen Elizabeth I: Representations of the Virgin Queen, in Renaissance Quarterly' Vol. 43, p. 67. For Elizabeth's portraits, cf. Daniela Carpi, Sidia Fiorato (2011) (eds) *Iconologia del potere. Rappresentazione della sovranità nel Rinascimento* (Verona: Ombre Corte).

[38] David Hume (1819) *The History of England from the Invasion of Julius Caesar, to the Revolution of 1688*, 6 vols. (London: Millar), vol. 2, pp. 374-75.

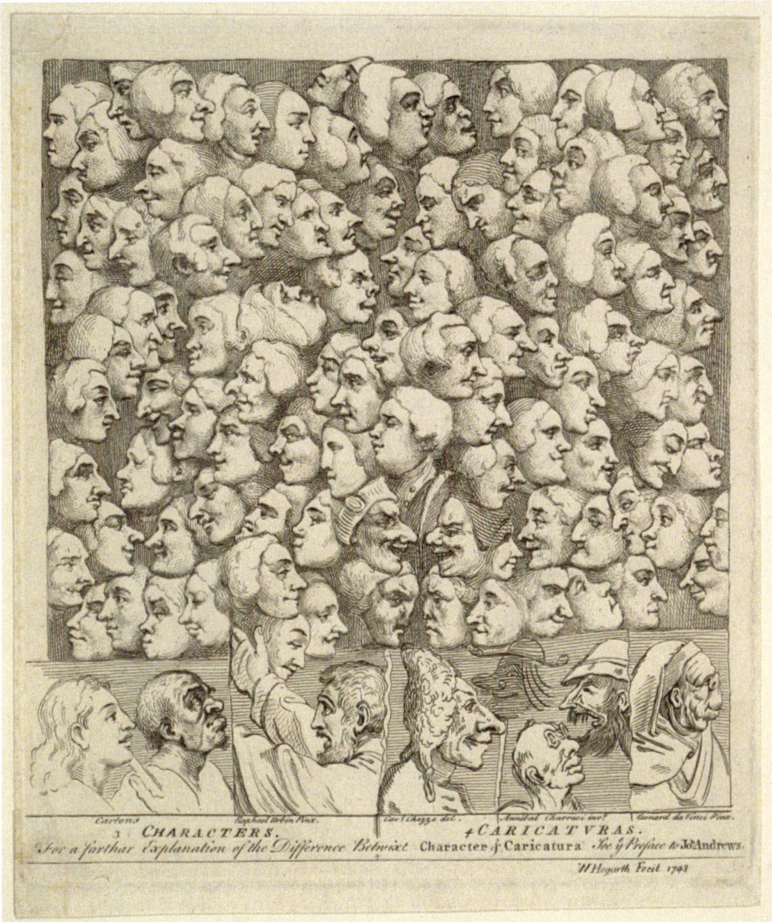

William Hogarth, *Characters & Caricaturas* (1743)
Subscription Ticket for *Marriage à la Mode* (1743-1745)
Image in the public domain

Elizabeth I: Armada Portrait, attributed to John Gower, 1588
Image in the public domain

CHAPTER FOUR

AESTHETICS APPLIED

4.1 William Gilpin's Picturesque (Domestic) Anti-Grand-Tour

The emancipation from the South took place through a systematic exaltation of a new, pre-Burkean nature, celebrated by Addison in *The Pleasures of the Imagination* (1712) for its irregular and uneven character: "[t]here is something more bold and masterly in the rough careless strokes of nature than in the nice touches and embellishments of art" (A: 414), features that Reverend William Gilpin would later define as "picturesque".[1]

The word "picturesque" appears for the first time in his work *A Dialogue Upon the Gardens of the Right Honourable the Lord Viscount Cobham, at Stow in Buckinghamshire* (1748).[2] Let us see under what conditions "Pleasure in the Imagination" occurs:

> Polipth.: I think the Ruin a great Addition to the Beauty of the Lake. There is something so vastly picturesque, and pleasing to the imagination in such Objects, that they are a great Addition to every Landskip. And yet perhaps it would be hard to assign a reason, why we are more taken with Prospects of this ruinous kind, than with Views of Plenty and Prosperity in their greatest Perfection: Benevolence and Good-nature, methinks, are more concerning in the latter kind.
>
> Calloph[ilus]: Our social Affections undoubtedly find their Enjoyment the most compleat when they contemplate, a Country smiling in the midst of Plenty, where Houses are well-built, Plantations regular, and every thing the most commodious and useful. But such Regularity and Exactness excites no manner of Pleasure in the Imagination, unless they are made use of to contrast with something of an opposite kind. The Fancy is struck by *Nature* alone; and if *Art* does any thing more than improve her, we think she grows impertinent, and wish she had left off a little sooner. Thus a regular Building perhaps gives us very little pleasure; and yet a fine Rock, beautifully set off in Claro-obscuro, and garnished with flourishing Bushes, Ivy, and dead Branches, may afford us a great deal; and a ragged Ruin, with venerable old Oaks, and Pines nodding over it, may perhaps please the Fancy yet more than either of the other two Objects.—Yon old

> Hermitage, situated in the midst of this delightful Wilderness, has an exceeding good Effect: it is of the romantick Kind; and Beauties of this sort, where a probable Nature is not exceeded, are generally pleasing. (Gilpin: 1748, 6-7)

The picturesque became the most characteristic natural element of the North, of a new taste and its related aesthetics: a way of seeing and describing directly connected with the valorisation of the characteristics of only a limited part of Britain. This geographical link is explicitly made by Polypthon: "As we are got into the North, I must confess I do not know any Part of the Kingdom that abounds more with elegant natural Views: Our well-cultivated Plains (…) are certainly not comparable to their rough Nature in point of Prospect" (Gilpin: 1748, 24).

Nevertheless, here we have to be very clear: The North, as a proxemic concept, is always an imaginary geographical point void of meaning if it is not set relative to something else. It does not correspond to a fixed space because, we should remember, what is considered to be North on a map is also the South to something more northerly than the place in question.

Nationalism, which is often directly implied in images (flags, military symbols and attire, characteristic places and objects), could count on an iconic tradition that had started with the religious images in churches, i.e. images used to exemplify their meaning even to illiterate people. One of its cyphered symbols, in the 18th century, is the blueprint of the garden, as we shall see.[3]

In the aforementioned *Dialogue*, Gilpin's character claims he is "more attracted to the sight of an ancient ruin than to the composed sights and to the prosperity in their most perfection", as well as to the "wild vastity […] of romantic kind",[4] a feature present in the park and symbolised by a Gothic building highly admired by visitors. For Gilpin, the concern is that of defending a non-artificial nature that denies both French symmetry and Italian formal, and non-Baroque, gardens, representing the classical world. To these, Gilpin counterpoints the British picturesque landscape and the English garden, this last read in political terms as the icon of their free and anti-authoritarian constitutional monarchy.[5]

Reverend Gilpin is thus the pivotal figure for the valorisation of the Northern nature and characteristics of the English environment. He *de facto*, more than any other, helped to increase and expand the attention of the English people to the autochthonous nature of their surroundings. In providing a new set of values, concentrated in the picturesque perspective, he enhanced the attractiveness for features that Burke would later, easily and without discussion, include in his theory of the sublime.

This new aesthetic paradigm was – let us be clear from the beginning – and still is, a new regional version of aesthetics, which overshadowed the aesthetics of the Beautiful, controlled by the Greek and Roman writers, prevalently stemming from Plato and Plotinus, that interpreted nature only according to the categories of the Beautiful, i.e. *la belle nature* as described by Batteux, which upheld its implicit theological reading of nature being God's work. This was an *aut-aut* reading that in turn created, without even the need to mention it, its binary counterpart: ugliness.

Gilpin taught the English people to look at things differently, providing them with a metaphorical new set of spectacles. As soon as his revolutionary positive focus on England's naturally wild and picturesque nature was accepted, British intellectuals felt authorised to proceed to a veritable retrospective invention[6] of a Northern aesthetics, which would, little by little, license the putting aside of the Southern classical Latin aesthetics, considered to be universal, and the associated Grand Tour and continental garden aesthetics. Let us now examine the role that the aesthetics of the picturesque played in revolutionising odeporics, or travel writing.

In his *Dialogue* (1749), as seen, Gilpin directed his readers towards the North, a place richer in natural and Romantic sights. Scotland, specifically, according to him, presented:

> the greatest Variety of garnished Rocks, shattered Precipices, rising Hills, ornamented with the finest Woods, thro' which are opened the most enchanting Views up and down the River, which winds itself in such a manner to shew its Banks to the best Advantage, which, together with very charming Prospects into the Country, terminated by the blue Hills at a Distance, make as fine a Piece of Nature, as perhaps can anywhere be met with. (Gilpin: 1748, 24)

In his study, *Three Essays: On Picturesque Beauty, On Picturesque Travel, and On Sketching Landscape* (1792),[7] Gilpin defines the picturesque as a characteristic, typical and seductive new kind of aesthetic emotion found in the English environment, which was pleasing, even though it did not present the appeasing qualities connected with beauty. Appeasing is a lemma that Gilpin does not employ but which well describes the lack in the picturesque of the classical cathartic effect of beauty. This type of environment can thus be defined as being *picturesque* or *wild*, whose activating drive will be that of "viewing the scenes of nature in a picturesque light" (Gilpin: 1792, IV). He says:

> I have several times been surprized at finding us ["picturesque people", he and his addressee: *William Lock, Esq of Norbury-Park*] represented, as supposing, *all beauty* to consist in *picturesque beauty*—and the face of nature to be examined *only by the rules of painting.* Whereas, in fact, we always speak a different language. We speak of the grand scenes of nature, tho uninteresting in a *picturesque light,* as having a strong effect on the imagination— often a stronger, than when they are properly disposed for the pencil. We every where make a distinction between scenes, that are *beautiful,* and *amusing;* and scenes that are *picturesque.* We examine, and admire both. Even artificial objects we admire, whether in a grand, or in a humble stile, tho unconnected with picturesque beauty—the palace, and the cottage—the improved garden-scene, and the neat homestall. (...) From scenes indeed of the *picturesque kind* we exclude the appendages of tillage, and in general the works of men; which too often introduce preciseness, and formality. (Gilpin: 1792, I-II, III)

The distinction "between such objects as are beautiful, and such as are picturesque—between those, which please the eye in their natural state; and those, which please from some quality, capable of being illustrated in painting" (Gilpin: 1792, 3) is, therefore, to be sought not in smoothness – the quality that Burke sees as the qualifying characteristic of beauty – but in what Gilpin calls:

> roughness [which] forms the most essential point of difference between the beautiful, and the picturesque; as it seems to be that particular quality, which makes objects chiefly pleasing in painting. – I use the general term roughness; but properly speaking roughness relates only to the surfaces of bodies: when we speak of their delineation, we use the word ruggedness. Both ideas however equally enter into the picturesque; and both are observable in the smaller, as well as in the larger parts of nature – in the outline, and bark of a tree, as in the rude summit, and craggy sides of a mountain. (Gilpin: 1792, 6-7)

The author then continues, extending his definition to art:

> A piece of Palladian architecture may be elegant in the last degree. The proportion of its parts—the propriety of its ornaments—and the symmetry of the whole, may be highly pleasing. But if we introduce it in a picture, it immediately becomes a formal object, and ceases to please. Should we wish to give it picturesque beauty, we must use the mallet, instead of the chissel: we must beat down one half of it, deface the other, and throw the mutilated members around in heaps. In short, from a *smooth* building we must turn it into a *rough* ruin. No painter, who had the choice of the two objects, would hesitate a moment. (Gilpin: 1792, 7-8)

To fully understand that what he means to defend is the autochthonous Saxon-Gothic architectural style and all that is entailed by it (Protestantism, the Enlightenment, the constitutional monarchy), we must go back to his first essay (1749), where all characteristics of the picturesque had already been laid out (and which Burke had exploited). Even in this first essay, Gilpin inserted an unequivocal observation about architecture which gave him the opportunity to point out the Celtic past of England, underlining its different mythology, religion, outlook. Let us quote it in its length:

> In several Parts of the Garden, I have had various Views of that old *Gothic* Building; we are now at last I hope moving towards it. I am so wonderfully pleased with its outward Appearance (Gilpin: 1749, 39).
>
> And in this Landskip there are as many beautiful Objects thrown off to a Distance as can well be imagined: That Variety of fine Wood; that bright Surface of Water, with the pointed Obelisk in the Midst of it; those two Pavilions upon the Banks of the Canal; and the still more distant View into the Country, are Objects which, in my Opinion, make no small Addition to the Beauty of your Landskip; or, to carry on your Allusion, may very well come in as a second Course in your Entertainment.— Our Attention, I think, in the next Place, is demanded by this venerable Assembly. That old Gentleman there sits with great Dignity: I like his Attitude extremely: If I understood the Runic Character, I might have known probably (for this Inscription I fancy would inform me) by what Title he is distinguished. But the Gracefulness of his Posture discovers him to have been nothing less than a Hero of the first Rank. He puts me in Mind of a *Roman Senator, sitting in his Curule Chair to receive the Gauls.*
>
> Calloph. Why, Sir, you have done him great Honour I must own; *but you have not yet honoured him* according to his Dignity: *He is nothing less*, Sir, I assure you, *than* the Representative of *a Saxon Deity*. You see here 'Thor and Woden fabled Gods—' with the whole System of your Ancestor's Theology. Walk round the Assembly, they will smile upon a true Briton, and try if you can acknowledge each by his distinct Symbol.
>
> Polypth. I must confess they do not to me seem accoutered like Gods: For my Part, I should rather suspect them to be *Statues of Heroes and Lawgivers, metamorphised into Divinities by the Courtesy of the Place:* I shall not however go about to dispute their Titles; but like my good Ancestors before me, acquiesce piously in what other People tell me.—Tho I cannot say but that Lady there, bearing the Sun (who represents I suppose Sunday) looks whimsical enough; and makes just such an Appearance as I could imagine the misled Conception of an enthusiastic Saxon might mould his Deities into. But in these other Figures I must own *I cannot see Superstition at all characterized*, which you may observe generally forms its Objects of Worship into the most mis-created things that can possibly enter the Imagination of Man.

> Calloph. Why, *Sir, amongst the Greeks and Romans, you may observe several very well-shaped Deities: The Hercules, the Apollo, and the Venus, are at this Day Standards of Beauty.*
>
> Polypth. Yes; but I am apt to attribute this rather to the Imagination of their Sculptors, than their Priests. *To shew Art, rather than to express Religion*, was the Point aimed at in these enchanting Pieces of Workmanship. - *But when Superstition acted without Controul*; when the fantastic Notions of Priests were put into the Hands of ordinary Workmen, even amongst the polite Greeks and Romans themselves, Lord! what misshapen Monsters crouded into Temples, and reared themselves aloft above Altars! Search other Countries likewise, Egypt and Africa. China and Japan, or any Place either ancient or modern, where Superstition prevails, and I dare engage in the whole Catalogue of their Deities you will scarce meet with one that bears any thing like the human Shape.
>
> Calloph. Why their Demi-Gods, or canonized Heroes, of which all pagan Nations had Abundance, were generally I fancy represented in the human Form. And *these Saxon Divinities, I suppose, pretend not to any superior Rank* — But however, as *no Degree of Veneration is exacted* from you, you may I think let them rest quietly upon their Pedestals, without any farther Molestation. (Gilpin: 1749, 41-44, emphasis added)

The reference to the Anglo-Saxon past of England is more than clear here: Southern deities are disparaged in contrast with the Lawgivers and Saxon Divinities that, as Gilpin underlines, do not claim any superiority of rank, implying that they do not claim the acquiescence of inferiors.

Specific Northern characteristics and what they stand for are analysed by the author by means of opposing criteria. Architectural ruins are set in an uneven, but natural, free and unconstrained landscape: irregularities and variety that Gilpin, as Warton later, finds well expressed in the Saxon-Gothic style and in the ruins of decayed castles and abbeys. Both Gilpin and, later, Warton underline the link between the picturesque ruins of time and the forgotten Saxon-Gothic system of values.

This is the beginning of a long-lasting connection that Ruskin returns to in *The Stones of Venice* (1851) where, in defining the *Gothicness* of the Gothic, he says: "There will be found something more than usually interesting in tracing out this grey, shadowy, many-pinnacled image of the Gothic spirit within us; and discerning what fellowship there is between it and our Northern hearts".[8] In the same work, he also justified the irregularity of the Gothic for its morality, connecting aesthetics with ethics, a move the art-for-art's-sake movement contested but that Ruskin proposed, in what I have called his aesthetics of the craftsman in opposition to that of the artist, aiming at man's essence and dignity:

> You can teach a man to draw a straight line, and to cut one, to strike a curved line, and to carve it; and to copy and carve any number of given lines or forms; and to copy and carve any number of given lines or forms, with admirable speed and perfect precision; and you find his work perfect of its kind: but if you ask him to think about any of those forms, to consider if he cannot find any better in his own head, he stops; his execution becomes hesitating; he thinks, and ten to one he thinks wrong; ten to one he makes a mistake in the first touch he gives to his work as a thinking being. But you have made a man of him for all that. He was only a machine before, an animated tool.[9]

Ethics was in Ruskin's view more important than aesthetics; this lesson was also taught by William Morris in his *Art and Crafts* movement and later absorbed by Roger Fry's Omega Workshop as the first step for the effective production of Morris' *Lesser Arts* (read English Design), but these are developments that will not be examined here.[10]

As can be seen, by linking nature and art, Gilpin indirectly provided an aesthetics that adhered to the English environment, in open contrast with the prevalent, but alien, Southern one. Gilpin's epistemic turn will, therefore, provide Burke with the opportunity to redefine Pseudo-Longinus' rhetorical and stylistic definition of the sublime[11] into a category detectable in nature itself, one capable of overtly contesting the cathartic quality of the Southern idea of beauty.

The defence and positive appraisal of the Northern and non-appeasing kind of nature were soon translated into a revolutionary upturn of the usual travel destinations, from being Southbound to being Northbound. In search of the picturesque, the 16th and 17th-century gentleman's *Grand Tour* was transformed into an inexpensive, democratic, inland journey. In direct antagonism to the upper classes' continental tours, the *Picturesque (Domestic) Anti-Grand-Tour* provided a new focus which inaugurated a strong wave of inland tourism, motivated by the search for picturesque places, something that changed the perception of the nation within the nation.[12]

A distinctly anti-exogenous and anti-exotic orientation in travel matters had already been expressed at the beginning of the 18th century when, in 1701, Robert Morden, a cartographer, in his *New Description and State of England*, gave voice to a shared feeling:

> The true knowledge of our Native Country concerns us much more than to be acquainted with the travels into foreign parts (...). Be not mistaken, England may Glory to be full of Natural Wonders, Rarities, and Excellencies as any Nation *under the Sun.* It becomes the Inhabitants not to be ignorant of them.[13] (my emphasis)

James Brome, in the 'Preface' to his *Travels over England and Wales*, published in 1700, had already underlined Great Britain's characteristics, taking a nationalistic stance: "There is not anything worth our wonder Abroad, whereof Nature hath not written a Copy in our Island (...). As Italy had Virgil's Grotto, so England had Ochy-Hole by Wells (...), the Pyramids at Stonehenge, Pearls of Asia in Cornwall, and Diamonds of India at St Vincent's Rock."[14]

But it was mainly after the publication of Gilpin's *Dialogue Upon the Gardens at Stow* (1748) that the Grand Tours decreased, due to the success of the Domestic Tour, or the Picturesque Travel phenomenon,[15] which exploited the aesthetics of the picturesque to aggrandise Great Britain's cultural value by providing a description of the kind of pleasures people really felt, via the positive assessment of the cold characteristics compared to the more immediately positive, solar ones. In short, the picturesque was the natural characteristic of the nation, as Gilpin repeated in his *Essay upon Prints* (1768).[16] Indeed, with its emphasis on the local beauties of England, it represented the vector for the nationalistic pride.

The *Picturesque Anti-Grand-Tour* phenomenon is one of the most interesting self-centred manifestations that can be connected to English Romanticism. As picturesque travels became important vehicles for cultural emancipation from the classicist yoke, Romantic subjectivism and its poetry neglected classicism's rules. Gilpin's picturesque perspective directed travel writing to focus on the complexity, intricacy and natural elaborateness of nature; as a result, for a while, it produced a decrease in interest in monuments or other ethnographic material. Interest in the classical country houses of the landed gentry was gradually replaced by the pleasure activated by nature. Introspective and emotional sentimental travellers begin to embody, paradoxically, the Romantic climax of attention to their senses and their reception capacity that the empiricist philosophers had promoted at the beginning of the century.

This tendency becomes most evident in Laurence Sterne's romantic and introspective book *A Sentimental Journey Through France and Italy* (1798), which represents the apotheosis of the senses-experience poetics on which the empiricists had focused. The journey is also a revision of the travel guides of the past: in its description of Yorick's sentimental inward journey of the mind, focused on feelings, affections, impressions, it leaves the comments on the monuments of Italy and France to the guides of the following century, the Baedekers.[17] Undoubtedly, some of these trips pursued the distinct inclination of the *Unendliche Reise,* the journey inside oneself, which is the final destination of the Romantic journey devoted to finding what one really is. This, moreover, is probably also the destination of the peripatetic walk within the English garden, which is a free walk directed by desires, without being constrained within a given path.

Grand Tours were, on the contrary, usually undertaken in the search of what one had previously studied or imagined; thus, they were expeditions in search of what one already knew, hence, again, a vision framed by previous aesthetics. Usually, the Grand Tour represented the final step in one's education, the final "live" course for students and cultured *connoisseurs*. Richard Lassels, "a tutor to several of the English Nobility and Gentry", in his text *An Italian Voyage* (1670) defined his task as: "To read to my country-men two profitable lessons. The first, to the profit of Travelling, the second, of travelling with profit."[18]

The trend of domestic tourism, with travel and relative odeporic production peaking between 1780-1790, dictated a new idiolect of taste to travel literature, a sort of travel diction, a poetical grammar derived from picturesque and sublime environments. It featured descriptions later used by Wordsworth and the Lake Poets (Coleridge, Southey, Lamb, Dorothy Wordsworth, De Quincey)[19] but which at that point are defined as Romantic, an instance of "a language of man speaking to man."[20]

The odeporics linked to the Picturesque Tour made frequent references, with the aim of ennobling itself, to its related sister arts, literature and painting, but also to architecture. Reception was being guided through references to the picturesque of Salvator Rosa, Claude Lorrain, Gaspard Dughet (dubbed Poussin, whom Nicolas Poussin made famous), or by referring to Piranesi and David Friedrich's sublime canvases capitalising on the pictorial picturesque heritage that contemporary guides quoted.[21] For example, Thomas West's *Guide* describes Coniston as a model for the "delicate touches of Claude", Windermere as a place of "the noble scenes of Poussin", and Derwent Water as an exemplification of the "stupendous romantic ideas of Salvator Rosa".[22] Describing Keswick, a small town in the lake region, John Brown stated:

> The full perfection of Keswick consists of three circumstances, Beauty, Horror and Immensity united [...]. But to give you a complete idea of these three perfections, as they are joined in Keswick, would require the united powers of Claude, Salvator, and Poussin. The first should throw his delicate sunshine over the cultivated vales. The second should dash out the horror of the rugged cliffs, the steeps, the hanging woods, and foaming waterfalls; while the grand pencil of Poussin should crown the whole with the majesty of the impending mountains.[23]

Horace Walpole, the creator of the Gothic novel, ironically, drew critical attention to the geographical paradox of the sister arts in that, despite being devoted to similar topics and themes, they were subject to different influences. Writing, he said, referred to the South, while painting was inspired by the Northern continental Alps: as a result, both forgot the British environment, to which the Domestic Tour was meanwhile paying homage: "As our poets warm their imaginations with sunny hills, or sigh after grottos and cooling breezes, our painters draw rocks and precipices and castellated mountains (...) Our ever-verdant lawns, rich vales, fields of hay-cocks, and hop-grounds, are neglected as homely and familiar objects".[24]

In Arthur Young's account, *A Six Months Tour Though the North of England*,[25] the word "picturesque" occurs thirty times and "romantic" twenty-four times, and they are mostly interrelated. The description of Lake Windermere, located between Lancashire and Westmoreland, seems to set the boundary and differences between classical (serene) beauty and the sublime (picturesque) one:

> Strain your imagination to command the idea of so noble an expanse of water thus gloriously environed; spotted with islands more beautiful than would have issued from the happiest painter. Picture the mountains rearing their majestic heads with native sublimity; the vast rocks boldly projecting their terrible craggy points: and in the path of beauty, the variegated inclosures of the most charming verdure, hanging to the eye in every picturesque form that can grace a landscape: with the most exquisite touches of la belle nature: if you raise your fancy to something infinitely beyond this assemblage of rural elegancies, you may have a faint notion of the unexampled beauties of this ravishing landscape. (Young: 188)

Berkshire Island, in the same way, features many attractive picturesque and romantic spots, creating "a variety that amazes the beholder".[26]

Another work that shows a distinguished propensity for the North, rather than for the hot South, is Samuel Johnson's *Journey to the Western Isles of Scotland* (1773). This is a diary of a Northern tour (83 days) that Johnson made with his future biographer and son-in-law James Boswell.[27] To his eyes, accustomed to beauty, the panorama seems awkward and unusual. Johnson is impressed by the harsh and hostile nature of the North: "naked of all vegetable decoration".[28] Breachaca Bay he defines as "horrible [...] if barrenness and danger could be so"; a formula, almost, for what the Gothic novel was attempting to create but not so appealing to the eyes of the classicist Johnson. He soon eschews descriptions of nature to comment on the social environment, praising, for example, Scottish universities for providing their students with the opportunity to graduate as doctors even at a very young age, unlike English ones. He also praises Scottish libraries, particularly that found in Aberdeen. He also notes the harshness of Cole Castle, which appositely reminds him of the Gothic and picturesque verses by Gray: "Huge windows that exclude the light. And passages that lead to nothing."[29]

Gray's rhymes remind us of the definition Johnson gives of the adjective 'romantick' in his *Dictionary* (1755): "1. Resembling the tales of romances; wild. [...] 2. improbable; false. [...] 3. fanciful; full of wild scenery";[30] wild sceneries that could be defined picturesque. This latter word strangely enough appears only juxtaposed to the adverb "graphically", signifying, he says: "in a picturesque manner".[31] The word Gothic appears neither in the first nor in the 1785 edition. It only appears, in fact, in later reprints, for example, in the edition of John Walker,[32] where "gothick" is thus defined: "Respecting the country or the manners of the Goths [...]. A particular kind of architecture, distinguished by the terms ancient and modern, the heavy or light [one] [....]. Rude, uncivilized" (JD: 434). Goths are defined as "the people in the northern parts of Europe first called Getes, afterwards Goths. [...] One not civilized; one deficient in general knowledge; a barbarian" (JD: 434). The term "picturesque" does eventually appear: "Expressing that peculiar kind of beauty which is agreeable in a picture, whether natural or artificial; striking the mind with great power or pleasure in representing objects of vision, and in painting to the imagination any circumstance or event as clearly as if delineated in a picture" (JD: 693).

Progress and urbanisation – phenomena that characterised many English areas in the 18th century and which accelerated from the beginning of the 19th century – would soon undermine previous positively empathic projections. While returning to rural pastoral settings in periods of acute social contrasts – via the myth of an idyllic countryside contrasted to a corrupted city – has been a standard milestone of the nostalgic dream for a hierarchically-ordered past and a conservative Old England,[33] these dreams had already been demolished at their first appearance. We see this, for example, in George Crabbe's poetry or in Goldsmith's *Deserted Village*.[34] Voices signal, before their time, the fact that the natural, social and the economic conditions of the natural world are rapidly changing.

Let us now focus on the anti-local counter-tendency, which brought people even further North. For example, *Letters Written during a Short Residence in Sweden, Norway, and Denmark* (1796), by Mary Wollstonecraft.[35] Disdaining the sublime setting of the Swiss Alps, but also for personal reasons, Wollstonecraft moved North and wrote of the excellent qualities of the Scandinavian countries. Southey said that this book "caused him to fall in love with the cold climate and the moonlight of the North". It was a book that "entered into the literary mythology of romanticism within a single generation."[36] To this work we can compare the oriental voyage of Lady Montagu and her shift of focus from the standard orientalist enframing – the one we find in Madame de Staël –[37] to the totally positive vision of the Turkish environment, in Montagu's *Turkish Embassy Letters*.[38]

As Karen R. Lawrence reminds us, even Margaret Cavendish described the North in her work *The Description of a New World, called the Blazing World*.[39] In this book the heroine goes as far as the North Pole, the destination the monster created by Viktor Frankenstein also reaches in Mary Shelley's *Frankenstein or the Modern Prometheus*. P.B. Shelley, Mary Godwin's husband, Wordsworth and Hazlitt all praised Shelley's novel, a book that Robert Louis Stevenson took with him to Samoa.

Additional, different versions of the Northern travels are represented by the Arctic explorations, which took place during the 19th century. In this case, it was the muscular-heroic Nordic conquering attitude which assumed a positive contrast to the supposedly enticing but enfeebling eroticism of the South. These can also be linked to the climbing ambitions of the recently founded Alpine Clubs, which promoted the vertical colonisation of heights as a heroic conquest-adventure, defining the Arctic sublime as the new extreme expansion target promoted by imperial propaganda.[40]

In sum, the 18th-century picturesque and epistemic revolution of empiricism reveals very well what would later develop into what we call Romanticism. Indeed, from an adjective depending from the beautiful, via Gilpin, the picturesque became an objectively recognisable aesthetic category, present all the way through to Uvedale Price,[41] though defined, at the end of the century, by R.P. Knight[42] as only the spectator's idiosyncratic projection. The latter, being produced by the observer's personal associative predisposition and not by an intrinsic quality of nature, presents thus a thoroughly Romantic outcome.

Price and Knight free the new aesthetic category of the picturesque even more than Gilpin did from the Neoclassical canons. As has already been seen, this new orientation would produce the Domestic Tours, devoted to the discovery of those characteristic and uniquely English places of the nation that went hand in hand with the mythology of its origin. The consequence of all this was the breaking of the aesthetic unity of the Western world, when the Sublime and the picturesque dismantled the primacy of the aesthetics of the beautiful.

In brief, space-politics operations, like the picturesque or imaginary ethnographic geography we are following here, confirm the primary role of literature and aesthetics in the creation of strong and lasting cultural values. The picturesque, in its revision of *la belle nature*, changed definitions long taken for granted, creating places of the mind and related identities, simply by proposing a different focus on natural elements that were invested with emotional significance – significance induced, initially, but soon acquired cultural emotions. By simply favouring irregularity instead of order, Gilpin successfully ennobled the English territory, making it an expression of both the intolerance of rules and the very liberty of its people.

Many people contributed to the creation of this new national feeling: Addison, Gilpin, Hogarth, Burke, Walpole, the Warton brothers, Hughes, Hurd, Percy and Scott, who, together, promoted a Romanticisation of the North. The dream of the North, notwithstanding the fact that it is a mere reversal of the binary South/North paradigm, was, on the one hand, to produce the aesthetic emancipation of the English nation and on the other to promote the spirit of independence that made the Romantic movement a unity of people driven only by their variously independent spirits, in complete antithesis to German Romanticism.

If interest in the North distracted people from the internal contrasts of the "imagined (United Kingdom) political community",[43] grouping differences into an un-organic whole, it also provided a common autochthonous and, most importantly, shareable origin by setting it in the nation's common Celtic past. Although people responded to the amplification and enlargement of England in positive terms, for some this constituted a problem. The panorama of the wild sceneries of Scotland and the people of its Highlands – now constitutionally part of Great Britain (1707) with the Acts of Union – glorified by Walter Scott [44] – were belittled by Dorothy Wordsworth, in very debatable terms, as she pronounced the new citizens inherently different: "savages of Britain's own internally colonized Celtic backyard",[45] one instance, even if it may be considered unacceptable for an antonymic to the prevalent reading of the Celtic issue.

English Romanticism – but also all European Romanticisms – demonstrates, paradoxically, an involution that culminates in the creation of national states but, at the same time, also an exogenous drive when those people united by a flag, for which they are asked to fight, discover – through this forced unity – that they are all unique and non-homogenising individuals: such are the darker, sometimes violent, energies at the heart of European Romanticism.

4.2 The English 'Picturesque' Garden and its Emblems

After the establishment of the constitutional monarchy (1689), the constitutionalists detected, in the form of the English garden, an emblem for the pride they felt in the democracy of their recently established political system. The garden represented visually the old Saxon liberties, previously expressed in the laws of King Alfred, in the *Magna Carta* and in the *Habeas Corpus* writ, elements now cyphered in this landscape-politics emblem. In the symbolic aesthetic reading of its cyphered blueprint, the garden became a metaphor for clearly defined political sidings. Chastised by Addison for its formal unnaturalness (JA: 414), the garden was championed by Pope for its liberty and freedom,[46] and by Gilpin for its picturesqueness – his vision of naturalness, wilderness and natural intricacy, and direct contrast to French rigour and the formality of the non-baroque Italian gardens, as we have seen. Where admired, the latter gardens focused on the element of water as a central feature, like Villa Lante, near Viterbo, or the Bomarzo garden, which focused on plant symbolism. The English interpretation of the garden aesthetics was entirely accepted by Kant, who, in his *Kritik der Urteilskraft,* promoted it, claiming that all that is rigidly ordered, as if it were mathematically produced, does not entertain for long, eventually producing "boredom".[47]

Such complex plexuses were deployed and used as cultural operations: the defence of the English garden aesthetics (Addison 1712, Pope 1732),[48] the theorisation of the picturesque (1747).[49] The aesthetics of the serpentine line enunciated in *The Analysis of Beauty* by William Hogarth (1753)[50] authorises the revision of the supposed universality and universal validity of the Greek-Roman beauty-concept, a point implicitly refuted in Burke's treatise on sublimity (1757). The latter can be considered the beginning of the demise of the idea of universal perfection.[51] Indeed, if we look at the history of aesthetics from an *à vol d'oiseau* perspective, Edmund Burke's authorisation of sublimity – philosophically the anti-canonical perception of both nature and reality – the outcome of aesthetic regionalism, unequivocally declared by Francis Grose in 1788, comes as no surprise in that Grose rewrites universalism in its contrary tendency, giving voice to the diverse aesthetics of the world. The further step towards a thoroughly personal understanding of beauty, epitomized in the second part the 18th century by taste, formed the counterpart of the creative idealism of the thoroughly Romantic "I", masterfully anticipated by William Blake's idiosyncratic, cosmogonic art.[52]

But let us analyse these garden issues in depth. The main feature of the English garden is that it has no fixed or marked path to follow. The Italian and the French gardens had a structure that was determined by paths. They presented a hierarchy that was immediately perceivable in their blueprints, whereas the English version left order to nature and was, resultantly, picturesque. Visitors were left to determine their own routes using their own senses. Sometimes people uttered the typical "Ha! Ha!" to signify they had reached the end of the garden, the from-afar-invisible ditch that marked the un/natural but thus unperceived border. Visitors were free to follow their own desire, which could be casual, determined by circumstances or an emotional inclination, without following an a priori plan.

This naturalness was mentioned in the 17th century by Sir William Temple, who promoted the freedom of the Chinese Sharawadgi:

> Among us, the Beauty of Building and Planting is placed chiefly in some certain Proportions, Symmetries, or Uniformities; our Walks and our Trees ranged so, as to answer one another, and at exact Distances. The Chinese scorn this way of Planting, and say a Boy that can tell an Hundred, may plant Walks of Trees in strait Lines, and over-against one another, and to what Length and Extent he pleases. But their greatest Reach of Imagination, is employed in contriving Figures, Order of Disposition of Parts, that shall be commonly or easily observ'd. And though we have hardly any Notion of this kind of Beauty, yet they have a word to express it; and where they find it hit their Eye at first Sight, they say the Sharawadgi is fine or is admirable, or any such Expression of Esteem.[53]

The same kind of freedom was promoted by Alexander Pope, who designed his garden at Twickenham on the river Thames, and spoke of gardens in his *Epistle IV to Lord Richard Boyle*, Earl of Burlington (1731).[54] Pope invites British architects to always consult "the Genius of the Place" (v. 57), asking architects to use that quality "previous even to Taste (…) Good Sense" (vv. 42-43), a quality that he sees lacking in Le Nôtre's gardens of Versailles (vv. 45-46), which, in their stiff geometry can be equated to "Timon's Villa" (cf. v. 99 et passim) and does not present any "pleasing Intricacies" nor "artful wildness to perplex the scene" (vv. 114-15). Rather, it is the exemplification of sterile order and a grammar made of symmetry, parallelism and artificiality, emphasised by its emblematic *ars topiaria*: "Grove nods at grove, each Alley has a brother, // And half the platform just reflects the other. // The suffering eye inverted Nature sees, Trees cut to Statues, Statues thick as trees, // With here a Fountain, never to be play'd" (vv. 117-121). Pope's "inverted Nature" of Versailles was at the utmost distance from "Nature to advantage dressed";[55] that the best architect of garden landscape uses to "gain all points" when the artist "pleasingly confounds, // Surprizes, varies, and conceals the Bounds." (vv. 55-56). Windsor Forest represented this ideal, and is a counter-French eulogy of the Stuart monarchy: "Here hills and ales, the woodland and the plain, // Here earth and water seem to strive again, // Not Chaos-like together crush'd and bruis'd, // But as the world, harmoniously confus'd: // Where order in variety we see, // And where, tho' all things, differ, all agree." (vv. 11-17).

The English architect who adopted the free landscape model of garden design is William Kent (1685-1748); he introduced a landscape style that Lancelot 'Capability' Brown (1716-1783) would go on to adopt. Further influence on English garden taste came from two works: *On Modern Gardening* (1771) by Horace Walpole,[56] and *The Dissertation on Oriental Gardening* (1772) by Sir William Chambers. Both were produced in the aftermath of Gilpin's picturesque[57] and, as with other licensing of Northern landscape and sublime perceptions, found favour.[58]

Walpole's study marks the confluence between aesthetics and politics in garden-reading, i.e. the garden blueprint understood as a political cypher of its proprietor. In his work, Walpole also praises the sunken fence, introduced by Bridgman, which got rid of the "too obvious (...) line of distinction between the neat and the rude" (HW: 81), the outside of the garden being thus included in the prospect. This move Walpole considered to be

> the capital stroke, the leading step to all that has followed, was [I believe the first thought was Bridgman's] the destruction of walls for boundaries, and the invention of fossés – an attempt then deemed so astonishing that the common people called them Ha! Ha's! to express their surprise at finding a sudden and unperceived check to their walk. (HW: 80)

One of the most famous garden quotes appears in this work and it refers to William Kent, the gardener Walpole considered a genius: "He leaped the fence, and saw that all nature was a garden" (HW: 81). Kent, working with "perspective, and light and shade" (HW: 81), "selecting favourite objects, and veiling deformities by screens of plantation, sometimes allowing the rudest waste to add its foil to the richest theatre (...) realised the compositions of the greatest masters in painting." (HW: 81). He also gave an *adieu* to fountains, the "last absurd magnificence of Italian and French villas (HW: 82) so that "[t]he gentle stream was taught to serpentize seemingly at its pleasure (...) A few trees scattered here and there on its edges", with the result that "[t]he living landscape was chastened or polished, not transformed" (HW: 82). Kent's ruling principle was his belief that "nature abhors a straight line" (HW: 85), which led to the excess of planting dead trees in Kensington-garden (HW: 85). Walpole also pays homage to Pope by saying that Kent learned how to go along with forms by using Pope's Twickenham garden as a model when designing the Prince of Wales' garden at Carlton House (HW: 83). John Dixon Hunt's 'Introduction' to Walpole's *Modern Gardening* underlines the fact that Walpole nationalistically remarks that the origin of the English garden is not related to the vogue for Chinese Sharawadgi applying their models to English deer parks.[59]

After the death of Kent, it was left to Capability Brown to naturalise the art of gardens to glorify English liberty, and thus to take its anti-symmetrical orientation and wildness even further.

The formality against which all English critics reacted is that of the Italian and French gardens. André Le Nôtre, the architect of Louis XIV, devised the Versailles Garden in adherence to an overarching hierarchical symmetry of this kind: a marked path, usually through parterres that lead through its fixed routes progressively toward the full magnificence of the king's castle. The castle was the identification object of the king, appositely created as an extension and symbol of the king's worth, power and aura to intimidate and create awe of his persona, expressing his mastery by dominating nature.[60] What it came to represent in Walpole's *Castle of the Otranto* was exactly a reification of power and authority, linked through the underground passage to the power of the Church.

The English garden, on the contrary, favoured freedom and was used to represent the mixed constitution of Lords and Commons, i.e. the constitutional monarchy. According to Michel Baridon, who notes that "after the second half of the 18th century the English garden favoured and promoted a landscape garden that either was or at least had to seem natural",[61] the ensuing garden symbolism conflated two slightly different myths, the Saxon and the Gothic. It was not by chance, then, that the libertarian yearning found its encrypted transcription in the plan of the naturalistic, but not natural, garden that was to become the English garden, as defined by Horace Walpole in his essay on modern gardening: "Enough has been done to establish such a school of landscape as cannot be found on the rest of the globe." (RW: 90)

In his reading of the English gardens, Michel Baridon connects the Saxon myth to King Alfred the Great. This is a reasonable hypothesis given that Alfred united the various identities that constituted England in the 9th century. Through law reform that conflated the Thora, the old pagan Anglo-Saxon law, and the early Christian one, the peoples of England could perhaps perceive themselves as represented by their new land's law. Nevertheless, my contention is that there was one previous king who could serve all masters and be a man for all seasons in his mythic existence only: it was King Arthur. In the 18th century, this was the king referred to for political propaganda on topical issues, often reified into his master symbol, the Round Table, this being the cypher image of a relational power politics and symbolic proxemics of decisions that belong, equally to all around the table, which the English would connect immediately with the ideology at work in the constitutional monarchy. This is also the situation of de Mandeville's beehive, where the emblematic hierarchy of the Leviathan is recast into a bottom-up cooperative hive.

Baridon, furthermore, links King Alfred to Gothic architecture. He interprets this link as a twofold myth, "subdivided into Saxon and Gothic proper" (MB: 384), a distinction he specifies by quoting William Warburton, who distinguished the two styles in a note for Pope: "Saxon should be applied to what we now call romanesque, while 'gothic' would be given the sense it now has" (MB: 384). Romanesque represents the persistence of the "Roman myth" representative of Latin classicism (see MB: 383-84), the Gothic being the bulky Saxon style. The distinction facilitated the use of the terms and their application, detectable in Swift's affirmation: "that the British Parliament was a gothic institution" (MB: 384).

This, we can add, was the exact opinion of the antiquarians, like Thomas Warton, who referred to the Saxon-Gothic as the style before the changes introduced under the "Norman yoke" (1066), the style of reference chosen by Warton.

It is, nevertheless, of interest to see how Baridon depicts King Alfred in the Saxon myth: "the king under whom the country had reached a state of almost perfect freedom (...) Saxon liberty in strict adherence to the principles of the *Witena Gemote* of the Germans" (MB: 384), a reference, he says, that would bring to our mind "the German model of Saxon liberty (...) described as a gathering that always took place in the woods" (MB: 384). The forest image with its vault of trees expresses "the asylum of British liberty" (MB: 384) that the author sees linked with Gothic temples. Baridon refers approvingly to William Stukeley, who, in 1723, wrote:

> The cloysters of this cathedral [Gloucester] are beautiful beyond anything I saw in the style of King's college Cambridge; nothing could ever have made me so much in love with Gothick architecture (as call'd) and I judg [sic] for a gallery, library and the like 'tis the best manner of building, because the idea of it is taken from a walk of trees, whose branching heads are curiously imitated by the roof." (MB: 386)

What I would like to underline, however, is that this quote conjures the image of the aisles of a perpendicular Gothic church – which did not exist during the 18th century. This style was the product of Pugin's 19th-century High Church attempt to recover Catholicism, later to be known as the 19th-century Gothic Revival.[62]

To Baridon's hypothesis I would add my design theory, based on the use of another symbol and the mythic King Arthur. King Arthur's Round Table came to represent the most condensed cypher for a shared, mediated and negotiated power that England needed to stop Catholic kings, in this case the Stuarts, who claimed their right to the throne only through blood lineage and hereditary descent. This lineage went against equality principles, defending itself through appeal to the divine right of kingship, via the usual link with religion and its interpretation of the anointed role of the king.[63] My claim is that the testimonial value of King Arthur, for constitutional propaganda, was far more persuasive than the image of the real King Alfred in that Arthur's myth provided, as its backbone support, a popular literary tradition that the people of England would know through folklore, which, though undoubtedly not real, possessed a common sense doxatic aura that could be taken for granted, both despite and because its historicity was unascertainable.

The link with architecture is furthermore applied as an emblem to fight back the imposition of the Southern aesthetics the English connected with absolutism: the order-and-degree rules and formula of medieval times represented by the religious and political *Scala Natura*;[64] or, in its hierarchical unity, perceived as a mystic whole, in Neoplatonist terms, emblematically represented in the symmetries, order and perceived perfection of the blueprint of the gardens of Versailles. We could add, on a minor scale, the Neoclassical frenzy of Palladian architecture, of which St. Paul's Cathedral, by Christopher Wren, is a fitting example. These were all unheeded iconically persuasive symbols intended to instil an undiscussed submission to authoritarian powers, powers built on imposed conformity to rules upon which Southern aesthetics – and specularly its art, religion and politics – insisted.

In this sense, garden design is explicit: the formal garden was usually associated with the Catholic religion, the prissy Dutch garden was its Protestant counterpart, and the English garden the emblem of Whig liberalism. This becomes patently obvious in another quote taken from Baridon:

> When the Goths had conquered Spain ... they struck out a new kind of architecture unknown to Greece and Rome; upon principles and ideas much nobler that what had given birth to classical magnificence. For this

> northern people having been accustomed, during the gloom of paganism to worship the deity in groves ... when their new religion required edifices they ingeniously projected to make them resemble groves as nearly as the distance of architecture would admit ... and with what skill and success they executed the project ... appears from hence, that no attentive person ever viewed a regular avenue of well-grown trees, intermixing their branches overhead, but it presently put him in mind of the long vista through a Gothic cathedral. (MB. 386)

Gibbon, in his *Decline and Fall of the Roman Empire* (1776-1788), wrote: "The most civilized nations of Europe issued from the woods of Germany and, in the ruse institutions of these barbarians we may still distinguish the original principles of our present laws and manners" (MB: 386). We have previously spoken of the Common Law of England but what is interesting to note is this evoked a muscular quality that was soon to be linked to architecture, through the architect Jeremy Vanbrugh (1664-1726). Speaking of one of his projects, Kimbolton Castle, with his commissioner, Lord Manchester, Vanbrugh invited him not to listen to "Italians" if they found fault in its style not being "Roman" enough – read classical – because the castle was something different, a statement that "will make a very Noble and masculine show". Here he uses the same arguments and analogy that literary critics had used to defend Spenser's *Faerie Queene* in their claim that it was a Gothic work of literature that needed to be read on its own Gothic terms (Hughes, Hurd, Warton). Vanbrugh, indeed, had not championed the masters of antiquity; he believed them to be foreign models for his country, and had rather dedicated himself to the "examples of medieval architecture that he could find in the north of England and in Scotland" (see MB: 380). His northward journey follows the same terms as the emerging domestic Picturesque Tours.

The Gothic was just another strong piece of the puzzle amidst the emblems of the Northern defence of originality, pragmatics of the senses, and the insights and ingeniousness of the imagination, i.e. the tradition of freedom and free will, connected to Milton's *non serviam* in his *Paradise Lost* or, better, willingly lost. This was the anti-normative, anti-Southern, "muscular" aesthetics of sublimity that the English intelligentsia set in binary contrast to the "feminine" aesthetics of the beautiful. For their coat-of-arms emblem, intellectuals elected their picturesque but democratic gardens, King Arthur and his negotiated politics, symbolised in the Round Table, their merely inductive, scientific sum of parts, as opposed to the metaphysical quiddities of deduction, and, finally, the architectural style of Arthur's times, strictly defined as Saxon-Gothic,[65] in this way appropriating the genesis of this European style. All in one, they covered nature, state, aesthetics and knowledge. They deployed these elements and set them up for their keen, subtle and finely intellectual image-fight: a symbolic iconic and iconoclastic battle for the new future aesthetic orientation of Europe and its Protestant Northern countries. Walpole, according to Baridon, kept a framed copy of the death warrant of Charles I at Strawberry Hill (MB: 387). He is also the first Gothic writer to poke fun – in an unheeded way – at the Italians, the people of Otranto (Apulia, Italy), who still lived under the yoke of the superstitions instilled by the Catholic religion, believing in spirits, moving statues and hyperbolic supernatural events: implicitly a disguised and removed critique of what was also happening at home.[66] In this sense, a revision of the Gothic novel that implements religion as one of its main issues is thus needed.[67] The Walpole indictment phase was soon followed by Mrs. Radcliffe's Gothic novels of rational explanation, and the Gothic novel of scientific apotheosis – Mary Shelley's *Frankenstein* (1818) –which thoroughly confirmed the empiricists' agenda.

The new Northern aesthetics bears its empiricist fruits in the non-unifying idiosyncratic variety of ideas and forms connected with the English Romantic artists, that, if they share anything, they share only the trust in their personal unique imagination.

Indeed, the Southern aesthetics and its strict rigid system of rules concerning the classical unities and the forms to be used in poetry allowed for no recognition of the best and most sublime artists of England, a tradition – that of Chaucer, Spenser, Milton, Shakespeare – that Addison, Hughes, Hurd, Young, Hogarth and Burke all undertook to defend and whom Thomas Warton institutionalised as the ground figures of the first English literature canon in his, and the first of its kind, *History of English Poetry*.

4.3 Hogarth's *Line of Beauty* (1753)

Another major assault set to undermine the Southern aesthetics, besides Gilpin's picturesque but before Burke's study on the sublime (1757), came via a direct attack perpetrated by the artist William Hogarth in his work *The Analysis of Beauty* (1753).[68] His siege was set against cathartic mechanical symmetry.

Hogarth's importance, notwithstanding the invaluable work produced by Ronald Paulson,[69] is still underestimated by critics, and as far as literature is concerned, I will provide one single example. Hogarth's engraving, *Characters & Caricaturas,* printed in April 1743,[70] exemplifies perfectly the rationale of the sister arts, *ekphrasis*[71] as well as intermediality,[72] connecting different multi-modal semiotic systems; in this case, language and images:

a literary work with an engraving, which condenses in one graphic work of art Henry Fielding's novel *The History of the Adventures of Joseph Andrews and of his Friend Mr. Abraham Adams* (1742).[73] The connection between the two works has been detailed by the author Henry Fielding himself, and at great length, in his 'Preface' to *Joseph Andrews*, which has, therefore, to be considered, for various reasons, a *manifesto* of the 18th century's newly emerging genre: the novel.[74]

If we examine one of the most widely read works of literary criticism that highlighted the canonical traits of the new genre, in whose wake we critics still work – Ian Watt's *Rise of the Novel*[75] – we come across a detailed description of all its characteristics. We learn, and this is its most prominent feature, that the new genre evades the classical settings of the romance and attempts to depict reality mimetically. Writers, nevertheless, will fall into what with hindsight we call the paradox of mimetic-delusion – believing that they are really portraying reality, without taking into consideration that they are only choosing some bits and pieces of it – as photographers do – choosing and freezing aspects they are interested in and use to attract our attention. Nevertheless, despite these implicit limits, the 18th-century attempt at realism was indeed the first historical attempt to historicise reality according to a space-time-specific logic to produce a realistic novel, the form that later, much later, led to the historio*graphic* novel.[76]

As Ian Watt says, characters in the new genre have actual names and surnames, and not merely emblematic ones like Innocence and Prudence; we find "here and now" settings; we encounter peculiar human beings who present idiosyncratic characteristics, and passions, that would not have found a place in previous literary genres (certainly not the romance, for instance). This is because, more than often, the focus of the new genre is the lower classes and their money problems, which are an all-pervading concern, and rightly so, the poor having to find money in order not to starve.

In the 'Preface' to *The History of the Adventures of Joseph Andrews and of his Friend Mr. Abraham Adams* (1742, FJ: 47-53), its author, Fielding, lays down the characteristics of the new genre, one he defines as: "comic romance (…) a comic epic poem in prose" (FJ: 47). Its rules are new, and, as he notes, he does not "remember to have seen hitherto attempted in our language" (FJ: 47). Fielding explains the new genre by providing explanations for his use of this oxymoronic definition, calling in the sister art of pictorial representation, to show the novelty and originality of the new type of prose, he points to the graphic artworks of his friend William Hogarth. Indeed, *Characters & Caricaturas*, Hogarth's 1743 engraving, is the iconic cypher of his and Fielding's common aesthetic project, and both works should be regarded – side by side – in reading Fielding's 'Preface' (FJ: 47-53). Fielding distinguishes here between the comic and the burlesque, saying that the comic always remains confined "strictly to nature" whereas the burlesque "is ever the exhibition of what is monstrous and unnatural" (FJ: 48), and he qualifies his claim with a reference to the sister arts:

> But to illustrate all this by another science, in which, perhaps, we shall see the distinction more clearly and plainly, let us examine the works of a comic history painter, with those performances which the Italians call Caricatura, where we shall find the true excellence of the former to consist in the exactest copying of nature; insomuch that a judicious eye instantly rejects anything *outré*, any liberty which the painter hath taken with the features of that *alma mater*; whereas in the Caricatura we allow all licence—its aim is to exhibit monsters, not men; and all distortions and exaggerations whatever are within its proper province. Now, *what Caricatura is in painting, Burlesque is in writing*; and in the same manner the comic writer and painter correlate to each other. And here I shall observe, that, as in the former the painter seems to have the advantage; so it is in the latter infinitely on the side of the writer; for the Monstrous is much easier to paint than describe, and the Ridiculous to describe than paint. And though perhaps this latter species doth not in either science so strongly affect and agitate the muscles as the other; yet it will be owned, I believe, that a more rational and useful pleasure arises to us from it. *He who should call the ingenious Hogarth a burlesque painter, would, in my opinion, do him very little honour*; for sure it is much easier, much less the subject of admiration, to paint a man with a nose, or any other feature, of a preposterous size, or to expose him in some absurd or monstrous attitude, than to express the affections of men on canvas. It hath been thought a vast commendation of a painter to say his figures seem to breathe; but surely it is a much greater and nobler applause, that they appear to think. (JF: 49, my emphasis)

This was exactly the aim of the new art(s) and genre, which were both to dedicate themselves to depicting people as they really are – neither ridiculing them through the excesses of a *caricatura* nor universalising or aggrandising them (as had been done in romances) – and not making them more beautiful than they were in reality but instead representing them in their variety and in their dignity as *characters*, exactly like the varied humanity of London, which included even ugly people, like those encircling Hogarth and Fielding in the engraving. This was their common aesthetic project "hitherto unattempted in our language" (JF: 52) and never attempted before in art, on which, the two artists, laughing at each other in the etching, commented and implemented in their respective art media, engraving and writing. Ugliness was finally given a place in art. It had never had one before, and with it, came a chance for the revision of belittling categories.

Let us now focus on what kind of aesthetic changes Hogarth is aiming at in his treatise on Beauty. In the 'Preface' to his work, which, on the title page reproduces his engraving *Variety* (1743, cf. the present study, p. 43) he explains the use of the symbol of the serpent in the glass pyramid by referring to the advice Michelangelo gave the painter Marco da Siena, as reported in Lomazzo, to make a figure always: "Pyramidall, Serpentlike and multiplied by one two or three" (WH: 2-3); to express "motion" like the cone of a flame, aspiring "to reach its proper sphere", therefore highlighting 'change' and development and not stasis. Nevertheless, in the caption of the image on the frontispiece of his book, he clearly refers to Milton's Satan: "So vary'd he, and of his tortuous train // Curl'd many a wanton wreath, in sight of Eve, // to lure her Eyes". Now, Milton's work does not present a direct indictment of Eve's sin from his authorial point of view, but only expresses pity for the couple suffering God's punishment and their subsequent expulsion from the garden. In this, the poet connects the sin committed – choosing not to respect God's will – with the *felix culpa* issue that inaugurates free will for humanity. In this sense, a positive reading and symbolism are linked not to Satan and evil themselves but to the opening, through sin, to free will and freedom: "Better to reign in Hell than serve in Heaven" is his *dictum*, the serpent embodying *par excellence* the anti-authoritarian angel and man.

Soon after (WH: XX), Hogarth qualifies how the triangular form of the glass, the pyramid, and the serpent within it, act as a symbol of this line: "the two most expressive figures that can be thought of to signify not only beauty and grace, but the *whole order of form.*" Given Hogarth's Rosicrucian and Freemasonry knowledge, which he also passed on to Fielding, this might also mean the height of hermetic and esoteric knowledge. Indeed, it could be considered conducive to the Light of a Protestant and the rule-free ethics (and aesthetics) of "grace" (WH: 3).[77]

Hogarth connects this image to the line of beauty he elaborates in his *Analysis of Beauty* (1753). The line of beauty iconises, through the movement of the serpent and its continuous changing of sides, adaptability to new situations, changing contexts and new realities: an icon of "Variety". Variety reflects the space-time-specific provisional solutions that should, according to him, substitute the irrevocably prescriptive *dicta* of the past. In contrast, choices should be measured out, each time, according to the specific situation, just as the square-and-compass symbol of freemasonry, used by architects and masons to measure out spaces, was intended to indicate. The line of beauty, guided by the serpent's symbolism of free will and free choice, signifies the capacity of renewal, evoked through the shedding of the skin of the serpent and its changing motions. This new epistemological turn I have termed the "aesthetics of the shell",[78] recovering Hogarth's definition in the *Analysis of Beauty* (1753). Hogarth focuses on the coexistence of a vision from within, and a vision from without, separated only by the thin shell that also unites them. He uses this as a metaphor for the double and multiple perspectival points one can adopt when looking at reality. The title of the etching – Variety – reminds us clearly not to look for a single and once-and-for-all truth but rather for provisional truth; truth adapted to specific situations and the changes needed to comply with varied circumstances. In this, and in the highly emblematic way Hogarth uses images, a symbol also of the pliability of Common Law might be recognised.

The attack on Southern aesthetics and its religion is then crucially set through the words of Roger De Piles but in the terms of Northern grace: "Grace and beauty are two different things; beauty pleases by the rules, and grace without them" (WH: VII). Hogarth speaks of the serpentine line as one that is avoided by the Italians and the French, although "some artists use it" (WH: VIII-IX). Albrecht Dürer, another genius but "fettered in his rules of proportion", as Hogarth says, did not. He then refers to the caption of another of his works from the same years (1745) as the frontispiece of his engraved works, "in which I drew a serpentine line lying on a painter's pallet with these words under it, THE LINE OF BEAUTY" (WH: XI, referring to his 1745 self-portrait *The Painter and his Pug*). He found the line explained in Michelangelo but, at that point, Hogarth prefers to find his own voice, looking for "words as would best answer my own ideas", the result of which is *The Analysis of Beauty* (WH: XXV). If variety is ugliness, as we have hinted before, art should accept it because reality is not always beautiful, and this offers one possible answer to the meaning of "motion" as a change from the old – beautiful – artistic subjects.

It would need a book of its own to comment on the various points Hogarth makes in his *Analysis*; I therefore just analyse what I think to be his most interesting point about aesthetics, which I have already termed the aesthetics of the shell, which complies with both his request for variety and his use of the serpentine line. In the *Analysis*, he says:

> [L]et every object under our consideration, be imagined to have its inward contents scooped out so nicely, as to have nothing of it left but a thin shell,

> exactly corresponding, both in its inner and outer surface, to the shape of the object itself: and let us likewise suppose this thin shell to be made up of very fine threads, closely connected together, and equally perceptible, whether the eye is supposed to observe them from without, or within; and we shall find the ideas of the two surfaces of this shell will naturally coincide. The very word, shell, makes us seem to see both surfaces alike. (…) [T]hink[ing] of objects in this shell-like manner (…) the imagination will naturally enter into the vacant space within this shell, and there at once, as from a centre, view the whole form within, and mark the opposite corresponding parts so strongly, as to retain the idea of the whole, and make us masters of the meaning of every view of the object, as we walk round it, and view it from without.

In essay No. 415 of *The Pleasures of the Imagination*, Addison compared the different mastery sight has on concave and convex form. In a concave form, like the inside of a dome, sight dominates the form, being the centre "that collects and gathers into it the Lines of the whole Circumference" (JA: 415, 557); while with a convex form, like seeing a dome from the outside, or a square pillar or a concave square, sight "does not take in one uniform Idea, but several Ideas of the same kind" (JA: 415, 557) so it cannot dominate it in a single glance.

Hogarth's *Line of Beauty* is linked to the same issues but it subverts the anxiety of total spatial dominance that Addison betrays in his treatment of the convex and concave forms. Cyphered in the serpentine line, and read as the line of beauty, the new epistemic vision defined by Hogarth, via the aesthetics of the shell, was to present the subversive dismantling of dualism, and of all dualistic binary thought, favouring rather the points of union that can be found through a third point of view, a vision able to upset the Manichean discriminatory logic of life and aesthetics. This vision institutes, on the contrary, an emphasis on variety and the places where miscegenation takes place or is created. The same subversive space-dominance was used, much later, for example, by Cézanne and Virginia Woolf.[79] This new vision is characterised by the simultaneous presence of multiple perspectives, which completely upturns Leon Battista Alberti's strictly geometrical and mathematical domineering perspectival box or cage, depending on one's viewpoint.[80] According to Hogarth's new spatial syntax, two simultaneously coexisting opposite visions – one from within and one from without – can only be provisionally united, via dialogical and negotiated points of contact that cannot be fixed once and for all, and that need to be continuously revised. External doxatic sight cannot be relied on for these types of operations whereas only the imagination will be able to conflate "the opposite corresponding parts so strongly (...) as to retain the idea of the whole" (WH: 42-43),[81] beating a rationality that would only see one or other, the inside or the outside. The whole proves to be more than the mere sum of its parts.

The line of beauty that also features in Hogarth's self-portrait, *The Painter and His Pug* (1745) at the Tate Gallery in London is the line signifying variety. Variety (of viewpoints, of opinions, of epistemic interpretations of the world) that is constantly changing is not regarded by Hogarth as relativism; indeed, he clearly specifies that the two visions are to be kept united because the one is conducive to the other in such a way that they form a single line that represents them both. It is, in this sense, the line of mediation where conflicting parties might avoid war. It seems therefore that the aesthetic "of two curves contrasting" could be defined as the cypher of the negotiated ethics of modernity, where opposite parties come together, dialogically, to mediate between positions and, provisionally and for the time being only, form some unity. In the moment of unity, there remains the possibility and imminence of fluidity, change and a departure from the present position to a new one. This new, and symbolic, theory of vision "may be of use (...) in shewing (...) a mechanical way of gaining the opposite points in its surface, which never can be seen in one and the same view" (WH: 45). And why was there the need to do so? Because life presents alternate interpretations, visions and ways of thinking: "In the common way of taking the view of any opake object, that part of its surface, which fronts the eye, is apt to occupy the mind alone, and the opposite, nay even every other part of it whatever, is left unthought of at that time: and the least motion we make to reconnoitre any other side of the object, confounds our first idea, for want of the connexion of the two ideas, which the complete knowledge of the whole would naturally have given us, if we had considered it in the other way before" (WH: 43-44). What I argue is that Hogarth, here, is presenting the symbol of a new, relational dialogic ethics where different positions are examined, discussed and negotiated to find provisional solutions to problems, leaving behind the old search for an eternal, once-and-for-all ahistorical, atemporal answer. This concept is always marked by his desire for a double vision, well represented in his aesthetics of the shell. Reality had to be considered in its *phenomena*, *noumena* not yet, being a given: this is a clear attack on Plato's idea that only this higher knowledge was the one worth pursuing. For Hogarth, there was only reality and it was not a fixed entity. As a result, he connects the serpentine line to Lomazzo and Michelangelo and condenses its finality with the adjective "Motion" (WH: V), an extremely modern way of indicating constant development and negotiation in opposition to *stasis*:

> the waving line, or line of beauty, varying still more, being composed of two curves contrasted, (...) the serpentine line, by its waving and winding at the same time different ways, leads the eye in a pleasing manner along the continuity of its variety (...) and which by its twisting so many different ways, may be said to enclose (though but a single line) varied contents; and therefore all its variety cannot be expressed on paper by one continued line, without the assistance of the imagination, or the help of figure; (...) where that sort of proportioned winding line, which will hereafter be called the precise serpentine line, or line of grace, is represented by a fine wire properly twisted round the elegant and varied figure of a cone. (WH: 83-84)

The non-normative aesthetics that Hogarth devised reproduced the anti-heroic variety that London presented to the world exactly: a mixture of humanity, which, according to the classical canon, did not merit aesthetic representation; a mosaic of people that, Hogarth, notwithstanding, decides to depict in one of his most exemplary mimetic works of art, *Characters & Caricaturas* (1743). He refuses to depict these new anti-exemplary characters as *caricaturas*, i.e. via exaggeration, limiting himself to reproducing them mimetically, exactly as Fielding's characters will be "confine[d] (…) strictly to nature", and not be depicted as "burlesque (…) [which] is ever the exhibition of what is monstrous and unnatural" (JF: 48-49).

Ronald Paulson tells us that the first draft of the 'Preface' to the *Analysis* was "polished" by Hogarth's friends (Benjamin Hoadly, James Ralph, Thomas Morell, James Townley).[82] Quoting from the original text, Paulson points out that Hogarth, with his art, wanted to correct "the Power of habit and custom" that the "natural philosophers" – presumably the Neoplatonists Shaftesbury and Francis Hutcheson – were championing:

> who by their extended contemplation, on universal beauty, as to the harmony and order of things, were naturally led, into 'the wide Roads' of uniformity, and regularity; which they unexpectedly found 'cros'd and interupted', by many other openings Relating to a kind of beauty, differing from those they were so well acquainted with, they then for a while travers'd these, seeming to them, 'contradictory paths', till they found themselves bewilder'd in the 'Labarinth of variety'.[83]

The "labarinth" of the changed reality required motion because different situations, types and realities had a claim on the artist's attention, requiring to be seen and examined and – what for those times was revolutionary – they could not be excluded from the arts anymore. This was despite attempts by the "grand theory of beauty", as Tatarkiewicz[84] calls it, to promote only perfection, a concept that will progressively fade from the panorama of the arts. What was always shunned, constituting a non-normative and thus an eccentric exception that needed to be controlled, had now found, through Hogarth and Fielding, a right to a place in the arts, like the non-beautiful characters of London, Hogarth's etchings and the prostitutes and thieves in Defoe's books. These were the types that Shaftesbury asked the artist to avoid:

> Now the Variety of Nature is such as to distinguish every thing she forms, by a peculiar original Character; which, if strictly observ'd, will make the Subject appear unlike to any thing extant in the World besides. But this Effect the good Poet and Painter seek industriously to prevent. They hate Minuteness, and are afraid of Singularity; which wou'd make their Images, or Characters, appear capricious and fantastical. The mere Face-Painter, indeed, has little in common with the Poet; but, like the mere Historian, [145] copys what he sees, and minutely traces every Feature, and odd Mark. 'Tis otherwise with the Men of Invention and Design. 'Tis from the many Objects of Nature, and not from a particular-one, that those Genius's form the Idea of their Work. Thus the best Artists are said to have been indefatigable in studying the best Statues: as esteeming them a better Rule, than the perfectest human Bodys cou'd afford. And thus some considerable Wits have recommended the best Poems, as preferable to the best of Historys; and better teaching the Truth of Characters, and Nature of Mankind.[85]

This was also the position of the late Neoclassicist Sir Joshua Reynolds, the watchdog of classicism, who directed the Royal Academy of Art in London from 1769 to 1797, in the name of the "Grand Style", and who, in his opening address to the academic year on 16 Oct. 1780, in *Discourse IX*, said:

> The Art which we profess has beauty for its object; this it is our business to discover and to express; the beauty of which we are in quest is general and intellectual; it is an idea that subsists only in the mind; the sight never beheld it, nor has the hand expressed it: it is an idea residing in the breast of the artist (…) and which, by a succession of art, may be (…) among the means of bestowing on whole nations refinement of taste: which, if it does not lead directly to purity of manners, obviates at least their greatest depravation, by disentangling the mind from appetite, and conducting the thoughts through successive states of excellence, till that contemplation of universal rectitude and harmony which began by Taste, may, as it is exalted and refined, conclude in Virtue.[86]

Thus, strictly avoiding "blemishes", the aim of the "great style" (JR: 105) should be devoted to eschewing all that was not comprised in the beautiful. The real artist had thus an

> eye (...) enabled to distinguish the accidental deficiencies, excrescences, and deformities of things, from their general figures" so that "he makes out an abstract idea of their forms more perfect than any one original. (...) This idea of the perfect state of Nature, which the Artist call the Ideal Beauty, is the great leading principle by which works of genius are conducted.

This is the Grand Style that Hogarth makes fun of in his preliminary sketch for *Boys Peeping at Nature.*[87]

4.4 Burke's *Sublime*: Northern Elements in 18th-century Literature

Light is more pleasing than darkness.
Summer, when the earth is clad in green,
when the heavens are serene and bright,
is more agreeable than winter,
when everything makes a different appearance.

— Burke, *A Philosophical Enquiry into the Origin of our Ideas of the Sublime and the Beautiful* (1757)

The love for Northern nature revolutionised the travel rationale of the aristocratic travellers of the century. Indeed, the blueprint provided by the Picturesque Travels, *à la* Gilpin,[88] brought about a change connected with the effort Reverend Gilpin took to ennoble England from an aesthetic point of view. He pursued this aim by concentrating on the English landscape and inventing for it a particular and superimposed, geo-political dimension. This pseudo-political reading of landscape was, starting with Addison, also to be linked to an *ante litteram* ecological focus dedicated to keeping English nature – seen as a mirror of the English character – freer and more natural in its garden forms than those on the continent. The media operation was based both on verbal texts (travel literature reports), and non-verbal iconic representations, for example, the political cypher of freedom read in the plan of an English garden, contrasted with the formality of the French gardens by Le Nôtre at Versailles or Vaux-Le-Vicomte. Travel writers gave English nature a unique distinctiveness, worthy of an aesthetic identity of its own, condensed in picturesque sites, an aesthetics that Burke, soon after, renamed as the aesthetics of the natural Sublime.[89] It is a complex aesthetics, constructed upon theoretical statements grounded in nature, founded on the reference and power of the intermedia sister arts and on the ethos of freedom. This aesthetics, for its distinguishing traits, I term Northern, in consonance with what it was meant to be.

Gilpin's *Picturesque* (1737), and his appreciation of intricacy in nature – preceded by Joseph Addison's praise of the characteristics of the English environment (1712) – were soon to be adapted into Edmund Burke's theory of the sublime in 1757, which represented a repositioning of the merely rhetorical literary sublime style of Longinus.

A natural Sublime had already been developing in England since the late 17th century, condensing the appeal that travellers felt after seeing the great vast Alps in their continental Grand Tours. A climax of this interest is represented by the extraordinary ambivalence of Thomas Burnet, in *The Sacred Theory of the Earth* (Latin, 1681; English, 1684), a book that on the one hand condemned mountains as monstrosities, the "ruins of a broken World," and on the other responded to their majesty emotionally, which makes Marjorie Hope Nicholson conclude that in England a "natural Sublime" preceded a "rhetorical Sublime."[90]

Indeed, the concept of sublimity existed before this;[91] it was no English invention as Samuel Monk points out. Previously sublimity was linked merely to the rhetorical domain, and a strong impulse to separate the rhetorical and the natural sublime came only from the publication of the *Peri Hypsous*, attributed to the Greek theorist Pseudo-Longinus, translated by Boileau in 1674 into French and, only later, in 1739, into English by William Smith.[92] Longinus developed his theory of the rhetorical sublime as a style of writing, an entirely different concept from the sublime experience a viewer might perceive in the presence of nature and art that Burke was to examine in detail.

Edmund Burke's treatise *On the Origin of the Ideas of the Sublime and the Beautiful* (1757) will, on the one hand, provide a justification for the positive reception of those irregular traits that had been ousted by the pitiless dichotomous Manichean logic of the Beautiful. In this, it inaugurates a new aesthetic panorama founded on the new category, the sublime, as the *tertium quid* between beauty and ugliness; but, on the other hand, it authorises the demise of the idea of perfection (of beauty as the only aesthetic category to be aimed at), which is my point.[93] The new category was to dismantle the metaphysics of the beautiful and the universal aesthetics connected with it. Consequently, non-cathartic disharmony, characteristic beauty and empathic taste would eventually be given a place in the newly-developed discipline of aesthetics.[94] Via Burke, aesthetics came to cover personal sensual taste and culturally determined standards of taste. As taste is connected to the senses, to their liberty and freedom,[95] critics were prompted to call this literary period "The Age of Sensibility".[96] I think we should call it "The Age of Sensibility and Imagination", to pay due tribute to Addison's 1712 essay sequence, *The Pleasures of the Imagination*. The central role Addison gave to the senses and to this creative, revolutionary, utopian faculty of the mind, in his manifesto dismantled the elitist theory of ingeniousness: shared imagination replacing the innately present ingeniousness of the gifted-by-God *genii* and *vates*.[97]

Burke's theory of the sublime authorised, in this way, a key change in aesthetics to comprise, for the first time, personal, emphatic, and endogenous emotional responses in aesthetic perception and evaluation. In this sense, the sublime is an extension and the direct consequence of the absorption of the empirical stance applied to aesthetics. Indeed, sublimity, linked to personal fears and emotions, needed the perusal and consideration of utterly subjective feelings on which aesthetic judgements of a work of art started from then on to depend. The sublime broadened and opened an entirely new panorama that admitted the inclusion, into the former bastions of beauty, of sentiments, passions and pleasures. These could even be ethically debatable elements in that they followed utterly subjective and therefore also passion-driven criteria, the criteria of the body, the ever-neglected ghost of aesthetics.

In claiming the pleasurable empirical feelings of pain, terror and fear, Burke enlarged the panorama of the old normative aesthetics of the beautiful to the personal, emotional reactions of the sentient Seers and Viewers, besides those of the arts' beneficiaries that, in turn, were asked to reflect on their reception. People were now prompted to examine their responses to nature and works of art in complete freedom. Furthermore, in focusing on the specifically aesthetic reaction of each human being, Burke claimed back the viewers' active collaboration in perception and thus widened, once and for all, the panorama of art. The gamut was no longer, at this stage, solely confined to Charles Batteux's *la belle nature*, the chosen, beautiful nature, that required artists "*à faire un choix des plus belles parties de la nature pour en former en tout exquis, qui fût plus parfait que la nature elle-même, sans cependant cesser, d'être naturel*",[98] which was linked to testifying to God's perfect architectural design.

It is not surprising, therefore, that all-natural anti-solar elements merge, in 1757, into Burke's sublime. These elements were foreseen in Addison's attention to the "different Stains of Light that shew themselves in Clouds of a different Situation" (A: 412, 62), present in the hues of nature described in James Thomson's *Seasons* (1726-1730), in Gainsborough's studies of clouds,[99] and in the pleasure that William Gilpin perceived in looking at the picturesque intricacies of nature, later to be confirmed in Burke's revolutionary discarding of beauty in favour of the definition of natural sublimity, in Constable's paintings of clouds and in Turner's modernity of art in the next century.[100]

Let us now, therefore, focus on Burke's revolutionary definition of sublimity. Burke, in his treatise, considers darkness, obscurity, night and blackness. In section VI, he connects darkness to vacuity, solitude and silence, seeing the common denominator of these elements in "Privation." Darkness is for him "more productive of sublime ideas than light," and he quotes Milton, who envisages Deity wrapped in a "majesty of darkness" (*Paradise Lost*, Bk. 2, v. 263). Furthermore, darkness and gloominess produce, according to Burke, sublimity in architecture (sect. XV), a quality well observable in Gothic churches. Darkness, in contrast to Locke's claims, is in Burke's view always terrifying, even without the help of superstitious associations, because obscurity has a "powerful dominion over the passions" (sect. IV). In the dark, passions take the upper hand and dominate rationality, producing fear: "Everyone will be sensible of this, who considers how greatly night adds to our dread, in all cases of danger". Danger and darkness are sublime precisely because they produce fear. Literature makes good use of this and works on the combination. Gray, Young, Parnell, Blair and Collins, in their major concentration on Death, the ultimate Unknown Mystery, apply these literary elements to poetry, standard material which soon passes over into the Gothic novel.

Thomson's lead was soon to be followed by the Graveyard or Melancholy poets: Thomas Warton's *The Pleasures of Melancholy*, *Night-Thoughts* by Edward Young (1742-45), and *Elegy Written in a Country Churchyard*, by Thomas Gray (1751) can all be considered instances of this, together with Thomas Parnell's *A Night-Piece on Death* (1721) and Hugh Blair's *The Grave* (1743). The Southern values, represented by the sunny pacifying pastoral and bucolic poetry, are undermined by Goldsmith in *The Deserted Village* (1770). The same happened with the vogue for Picturesque Tours as opposed to the Continental Grand Tour.

Even as far as colours are concerned, the darker ones seem more intense to Burke, thus instituting a hierarchical palette for the sublimity of Northern lands: "Among colours, such as are soft or cheerful (except perhaps a strong red, which is cheerful) are unfit to produce grand images. An immense mountain covered with a shining green turf, is nothing, in this respect, to one dark and gloomy; the cloudy sky is more grand than the blue; and night more sublime and solemn than day" (sect. XVI). Night and silence also prevent attention from being dissipated (sect. XVIII). Darkness, and by extension night, for their capacity to engender fear become in the treatise an unconditional element of sublimity:

> We have considered darkness as a cause of the sublime; and we have all along considered the sublime as depending on some modification of pain or terror: so that if darkness be no way painful or terrible to any, who have not had their minds early tainted with superstitions, it can be no source of the sublime to them. But, with all deference to such an authority, it seems to me, that an association of a more general nature, an association which takes in all mankind, may make darkness terrible; for in utter darkness it is impossible to know in what degree of safety we stand. (sect. XIV)

As an example of idiosyncratic Graveyard poetry, we can take Edward Young's *Complaint: or, Night-Thoughts on Life, Death, and Immortality*, published in London, 1742-1745. In this poem, the night brings about silence and darkness, and with it a sense of loneliness and deprivation for the recent loss of the poet's wife and daughter, describing utter epistemic trauma, symbolised in the poet's puzzlement and disorientation, an attitude not generally found in the gamut of expected' feelings.[101] Nevertheless, if night is the synonym of death and absence, it is also the only link the poet finds with his beloved shades, day becoming meaningless and night the only respite.

Lilian R. Furst, in her study of the night in European Romanticism, interprets the night – and Romanticism – as the rejection of "the belief system that inspired their predecessors, the exponent of the Enlightenment",[102] i.e. of empiricism. In my opinion, the night represents not only a tribute to the sublime but, foremost and paradoxically, it is the objective correlative of the Enlightenment, used by the Graveyard poets to justify exactly the non-superstitious aesthetics of the North, rationally eschewing the standard frightful nightly presences such as ghosts and spirits.

The night is indeed one of the four important *topoi* of the Northern aesthetics, along with its misty and gloomy atmospheres, northern panoramas, and the intricacies of nature being the others. These elements had been used as the distinctive features of the poetry of the Warton brothers and, in particular, of Thomas Warton and his 1777 collection.[103] Furthermore, they also appear as constitutional elements of Thomson's *Seasons* (1726-1730) and in Thomas Warton's most important work and the first English attempt to write a history of literature, *The History of English Poetry, from the Close of the Eleventh to the Commencement of the Eighteenth Century* (1774-1781), a work that promoted a new poetics while setting the first English poetical canon and, by focusing on the characteristics of contemporary anti-classicist poetry, succeeded in changing the course of English literature altogether.

Thomas Warton was indeed an early model for the Graveyard poets in providing a new anti-classical poetry prior to Burke's study of the sublime (1757), and this since the appearance of his poem *The Pleasures of Melancholy* (1745), whose title is a direct homage to Addison and to Robert Burton's *Anatomy of Melancholy* (1621). The poem is highly relevant for Northern aesthetics in that it can be read as a coded farewell to the aesthetics of the South.

Contemplation is, indeed, invoked in the poem to help the poet leave sunny Tenerife to reach a different place and atmosphere [England]:

> "O, *lead me*, queen sublime, *to solemn glooms // Congenial with my soul; to cheerless shades*, // To ruin'd seats, to twilight cells and bowers, // Where thoughtful Melancholy loves to muse // Her favourite midnight haunts. (ll. 17-21)

The atmosphere was soon linked to the night, which figures prominently in this poem, and that becomes the most important *topos* of the poetry of melancholy, being conducive to pensive thoughts, probably of the manic-depressive kind,[104] a melancholic state that makes the poet desire the more "congenial" Northern environment:

> But let the sacred Genius of *the night* // Such mystic visions send, *as Spenser saw*, // When thro' bewild'ring *Fancy's magic maze*, // To the fell house of Busyrane, he led // Th' unshaken *Britomart*; or *Milton* knew, // When in abstracted thought he first conceiv'd // All heav'n in tumult, and the Seraphim // Come tow'ring, arm'd in adamant and gold. // *Let others love soft Summer's evening* smiles, (70) // As listening to the distant waterfall, // They mark the blushes of the streaky west; // *I choose the pale December's foggy glooms*. // Then, when the sullen shades of evening close, // Where through the room a blindly-glimmering gleam // They dying embers scatter, far remote // From Mirth's mad shouts, that through th' illumined roof // Resound with festive echo, let me sit, // Blest with the lowly cricket's drowsy dirge. (ll. 62-79)
>
> When azure noontide cheers the daedal globe, // And the blest regent of the golden day // Rejoices in his bright meridian tower, // *How oft my wishes ask the night's return*, (110) // *That best befriends the melancholy mind! // Hail, sacred Night!* thou too shalt share my song! Sister of ebon-scepter'd Hecate, hail! // Whether *in congregated clouds thou wrapp'st //Thy viewless chariot, or with silver crown // Thy beaming head encirclest,* ever hail! What though *beneath thy gloom the sorceress train,* // Far *in obscured haunt of Lapland moors*, // With rhymes uncouth the bloody caldron bless; // Though Murder wan beneath thy shrouding shade (120) // Summons her slow-eyed votaries to devise // Of secret slaughter, while by

one blue lamp // In hideous conference sits the listening band, // And start at each low wind, or wakeful sound; // What though *thy stay the pilgrim curseth oft*, // As all-benighted in Arabian wastes // He hears *the wilderness around him howl // With roaming monsters,* while on his hoar head // The black-descending *tempest ceaseless beats*; // *Yet more delightful to my pensive mind (130) // Is thy return, than blooming morn's approach*, // *E'en then*, in youthful pride of opening May, // When from the portals of the saffron east // She sheds fresh roses, and ambrosial dews. // Yet not ungrateful is the morn's approach, // *When dropping wet she comes, and clad in clouds*, // While through the damp air scowls the lowering south, // *Blackening the landscape's face, that grove and hill // In formless vapours undistinguish'd swim:* // Th' afflicted of the sadden'd groves (140) // Hail not the sullen gloom; the waving elms // That, hoar through time, and ranged in thick array, // Enclose with stately row some rural hall, // Are mute, nor echo with the clamours hoarse // Of rooks rejoicing on their airy; boughs // While to the shed the dripping poultry crowd, // A mournful train: secure the village hind // Hangs o'er the crackling blaze, nor tempts the storm; // Fix'd in unfinish'd furrow rests the plough: // Rings not the high wood with enliven'd shouts (150) Of early hunter: all is silence drear; // *And deepest sadness wraps the face of things.* (ll. 107-52)

Or let me sit // Far in sequester'd aisles of the deep dome, // There lonesome listen to the sacred sounds, // Which, as they lengthen *through the Gothic vaults*, // In hollow murmurs reach my ravish'd ear. // *Nor when the lamps expiring yield to night, And solitude returns,* would I forsake // The solemn mansion, but attentive mark // The due clock swinging slow with sweepy sway, // Measuring Time's flight with momentary sound.[105] (emphases added)

The poem seems almost to be a literary anticipation of his *History of Poetry*: his invitation to abandon Southern aesthetics, the celebration of England's Northern atmospheres – as ever itemised in contrast to Southern lures – the desire for the magic rather than the religious element, the direct mention of both Spenser and Milton, authors recovered, with Chaucer and Shakespeare[106] as the canonical authors of English literature, and the Gothic, better the Saxon-Gothic architecture, with its hidden political and religious link to the rhetoric of chivalry embodied in King Arthur, in whose honour, Thomas Warton produced a series of poems: "The Grave of King Arthur", "Sonnet on Stonehenge", "On King Arthur's Roundtable at Winchester".[107]

The religious element was fundamental. As was the case in the poetry connected to King Arthur, Thomas Warton always mentioned the polytheistic religion of the Druids, and critics of the age distinguished between the Saxon-Gothic (pre-Norman invasion) and the Gothic (post-Norman invasion), demarcating the difference between the persistence of a polytheistic creed and the affirmation of a monotheistic one.

Furthermore, if William Gilpin taught a nation to see their environment through new eyes, Burke philosophically authorised a breach of the fortress of the Beautiful. He extended the limits of aesthetics. Indeed, this is his grandeur and glory, to include what was previously simply dismissed under the label of ugliness. Burke, that is, adopted the lexical semantic families of Thomas Warton's poetry and the formal terminology that Gilpin [108] used to describe the picturesque: irregularity and disproportion, combined with the acceptance of the fearful but sublime emotions that, in the excitement and pleasure they produced, had nothing to share with Aristotelian catharsis or "the Platonic theory of fitness and aptitude".[109] In doing so, the unutterable side of a difficult aesthetic category became at least analysable.[110] Fear, terror, uneasiness and emotions, somehow capable of producing a strange pleasure, were eventually admitted in the panorama of holy aesthetics.[111] This brought with it further changes connected with a whole set of different pleasures.[112]

In due course, sublimity also legitimised personal and even idiosyncratic and non-normative perceptions: we have to remember that this is also the first age of an overt sexual revolution, the age of the Marquis De Sade's disrespectful attitude towards standard morality (and religion).[113] It was an opening that led to the age's notorious erotic literature (John Cleland, Eliza Haywood, Herbert Croft) and, later, to the first aesthetics of ugliness, with Karl Rosenkrantz's *Aesthetik des Hässlichen* (1853).

Fear is exploited in enhancing the mysterious nature of the death of people, in the dark atmospheres of country churchyards, in haunting ghosts, aptly created by writers who exploit gullibility and superstition. Of course, this is done with such blatant, and sometimes even ironic excess (e.g. *The Castle of Otranto* with the helmet dropping from the sky and killing Conrad), that in the end one perceives that the genre was created with the precise intention of undermining such beliefs – or the esoteric groups that upheld such beliefs – to reinstate the lost light of rationality (Walpole, Radcliffe and Jane Austen). If Walpole's novel left room for any doubt, then this was done on purpose. Why otherwise transpose the scene in Italy, in Apulia to be precise, with *The Castle of Otranto* (1764), if not to underline the fact that such beliefs could only be entertained by the people of this country, one of the strongholds of Catholicism? Enlightenment and its rational scientific attitude was, at that time, at its height in England. On the other hand, there were also emotions and superstitions, fed up to that point and in an ongoing way by religions, which still claimed a fideistic reliance on belief to maintain an authoritative power that was external to man, securing acquiescence, submission and obedience.

The same enlightened focus was confirmed in the novel genre, not only in the realistic novels of action by Defoe, Fielding and Smollett, or in the introspective tradition inaugurated by Richardson, but also in the Gothic novel. The Gothic novel adhered to other priorities intended to dismantle the authoritarian requests of submission, deference and meekness that the religious hierarchies still demanded. This was symbolised in the darkness of the Gothic churches and castles, where hidden and disquieting places hinted at the secrets and torture of the Inquisition. Two Gothic novels exemplify this indictment against religion: *The Castle of Otranto* and *The Monk*, both clearly connected to the evaluation of the rationality of the English and, again, by extension their Northern characteristics.

Gothic literature, often from a safe spatial removal (Italy, Switzerland, France), in its higher works constantly hints at and discusses religious issues, and, whether directly or indirectly, is always related to religious matters in order to deconstruct superstitions and belief.[114] The hierarchical systems of religion, and also its related beliefs in unsubstantial manifestations such as ghosts and supernatural events, were often criticised if not downright ridiculed for their implausibility, and downplayed as exaggerations that only Italians and other Catholic continental peoples (Spain, for example) could still believe in. Lewis's *The Monk* was indeed a paradigmatic work of this genre, comprising in its descriptions the torture of the Counter-Reformers and the Inquisition. *The Castle of Otranto,* though indirectly, poked fun at and derided those peoples who were still gullible enough to believe in a whole series of absurd, unrealistic and improbable events, such as being fearful of supernatural acts of revenge that could assume the forms of retribution depicted in the novel: i.e. fear emblematising the system of terror (in life and afterlife) that religions still uphold to keep people submissive, meek and acquiescent.

Let us now put these elements into a synoptic, taxonomic and dichotomous table, to be read via Hogarth's shell logic, i.e. placing ourselves in the mediatory border "line of beauty" to see it through Hogarth's logic of variety:

Southern *vs.* Northern Characteristics

Sun *vs.* Moon, Clouds (Gainsborough, Constable)
Day *vs.* Night (Graveyard Poetry)
Beauty *vs.* Sublimity (E. Burke)
Harmony *vs.* Intricacy (W. Gilpin)

Classicism *vs.* Gothic Literature and Architecture (Duff, Warton, Gray, Hughes, Walpole, Hurd)
Symmetry *vs.* Line of Beauty (W. Hogarth)
French Garden *vs.* English Garden (J. Addison, Pope, Gilpin, Kemp, Brown, Price)
Order and Harmony *vs.* Picturesque (W. Gilpin)
Grand Tour *vs.* Picturesque (Domestic) Anti-Grand-Tour (W. Gilpin, W. Kemp, L. Brown, U. Price)
Outbound Tourism *vs.* Inland Tourism and National Heritage
Heroes *vs.* Real characters (Defoe, Fielding, Hogarth)
Believers *vs.* Enlightened Sceptics
Universal Aesthetics (Eurocentric assumption) *vs.* Aesthetic Regionalism (F. Grose)[115]

Historical Table of Works Linked to the Northern Aesthetics

Joseph Addison, *The Pleasures of the Imagination* (1712)
Joseph Addison, *Fairy Way of Writing* (1712)
John Hughes, 'Preface' to *The Faerie Queene* (1715)
James Thomson, *Seasons* (1726-1730)
James Macpherson, *Ossian Poems* (1739)
Thomas Warton, *The Pleasures of Melancholy* (1745)
William Gilpin, *A Dialogue upon the Gardens at Stow* (1748)
William Hogarth, *The Analysis of Beauty* (1753)
Thomas Warton, *Observations on the Faerie Queene* (1754)
Edmund Burke, *A Philosophical Enquiry into the Origin of our Ideas of our Ideas the Sublime and the Beautiful* (1757)
Thomas Gray, *The Bard. A Pindaric Ode* (1757)
Richard Hurd, *Letters on Chivalry and Romance* (1762)
An Essay on Original Genius, William Duff (1767)
Horace Walpole, *The Castle of Otranto* (1764)
Thomas Percy, *Reliques* (1765)
William Duff, *Essay on Original Genius* (1767)
Horace Walpole, *Anecdotes of Painting in England:* "On Modern Gardening" (1771)
Thomas Warton, *History of English Poetry* (1774, 1778, 1781)
Francis Grose, *Rules for Drawing Caricaturas: with an Essay on Comic Painting* (1788)
Thomas Gray, *The Bard. A Pindaric Ode* (1757)
Oliver Goldsmith, *An Enquiry into the Present State of Learning* (1759)
Richard Hurd, *Letters on Chivalry and Romance* (1762)

The table exemplifies the features that were emphasised to ennoble and progressively emancipate the North and its peculiar aesthetic, religious and political dimensions, which shows that a massive attack was launched against the sunny South and its classical aesthetics, which had, up to then, dominated the Western world from a Eurocentric perspective in its claim to universality, and its monotheistic religion and authoritarian politics.

That this was the issue becomes patently obvious if one reads what Thomas Warton says in respect to this in his *History of English Poetry* (1774):

> The genius for romance and of popery was the same; and both were strengthened by the reciprocation of a similar spirit of credulity. The dragons and the castles of the one were of a piece with the visions and pretended miracles of the other. The ridiculous theories of false and unsolid science (...) were surely more likely to be advanced under the influence of a religion founded on deception, than in consequences of Luther's reformed system, which aimed at purity and truth (...) Many of the absurdities of the Catholic worship were perhaps (...) in some degree necessary in the early ages of the church (...) But when the world became wiser those mummeries should have been abolished (...) in a cultivated age, abounding with every species of knowledge, they continue to retain those fooleries which were calculated only for Christians in a condition of barbarism, and of which the use no longer subsists. (TW: vol. 3, XVI-XVII)

Northern aesthetics can thus be claimed to be, if not the direct result of an atheistic outlook, at least the outcome of an agnostic or enlightened orientation. This was testified to by the variety of declensions and nuances of the liberty of thought that the Romantic poets, at the end of the century, exemplified in their totally different personal attitudes and stances: Blake a dreamer, Wordsworth a believer, Coleridge inclining to be one, Shelley an atheist, Keats a nostalgic reactionary classicist, Byron a sublime individualist, all testifying to their personal freedom and liberty. Indeed, they are Romantic not because they share a belief in a school like the German *Sturm und Drang* poets but precisely because they stoutly defend personal liberty and their free, idiosyncratic imagination and, foremost, the possibility of believing whatever they like. Romanticism and the defence of taste rather than the rules of aesthetics were only consequences of the freedom that each mind was entitled to follow in its sentimental, idealistic or imaginative, subjective reception of reality, creating unique, and thus Romantic, artistic individuals.

Accordingly, Romanticism can be interpreted as the result and climax of the empiricists' requirement to pay attention to the reactions and responses of one's senses. This is particularly well represented by the sentimental, idealistic, personal and unique re-definition of taste – a keyword for the 18th century – that downgrades the older definition of taste as the knowledge of artistic standards into its modern definition as a thoroughly subjective inclination for certain qualities of the objects of beauty rather than qualities adherent to the previously normative and discriminatory aesthetic standards. This is exactly how Wordsworth defined it, seeing it as a thoroughly subjective, anarchic and non-normative predisposition, comparable to the preference, for example, one feels for sherry rather than for whisky.[116]

Demarcation lines were set in the imaginary, but also all too real, geography produced by the Gothic novel. Two 19th-century women writers deconstructed their premises: Mary Shelley's *Frankenstein, or the Modern Prometheus,* and Charlotte Brontë's Romantic novel *Wuthering Heights*, as we shall see, incorporate all the above-mentioned characteristics in their works but, in focusing on the consequences these demarcation lines and imaginary geographical borders produce, they overturn their premises.

Northern nature was overtly used demagogically and ideologically by Walpole, who made it the cypher of English freedom, encrypted, as he saw it, in the landscape politics of the free-to-move-about English garden design, an iconic proof that visually bespeaks and denotes the liberty of English politics. The horizontal constitutional monarchy was then played against the vertical and radial hierarchy of the absolute monarchy of France that Pope, for example, sees perfectly expressed by the fixed and guided symmetries of the paths pointing to the King's palace in Le Nôtre's French gardens at Versailles. A later, but similar, visual iconic statement was made by de Mandeville: as we have seen, he reconfigured the body politics of the beehive-chest of the monarch over which the head of the king presides in the frontispiece of Hobbes's *Leviathan* by A. Bosse (1651) into the image of the beehive where the queen is herself part of the hive, where roles are respected because they are mutually agreed upon (1724).[117]

Religion, as de Mandeville,[118] who agrees with Locke,[119] underlines, cannot be rationally demonstrated, therefore it cannot be claimed to justify ethical or spiritual choices that are always utterly cultural, i.e. space-and time-specific to their environment.

Consequently, Northern aesthetics gives rises to a debate as to whether nature should be read in the terms of a *Natura Naturata* (given once and for all and remaining the same throughout time and forever); or as the created nature of the deists and its derivative Romantic outcome that adopted what M.H. Abrams aptly called "Natural Supernaturalism" and that tried "to save the (...) cardinal values of (...) religious heritage" (Abrams 1953: 66); or as a biologically changing *Natura Naturans*. The *Natura Naturata* stance adopts the deistic stance and its double standard (connecting religion and science), based on the secularisation of inherited theological ideas that constituted "a displaced and reconstituted theology", with an aim to "sustain the inherited cultural order".[120] Indeed, Enlightenment is mentioned but not fully taken into consideration by Abrams. Not everybody was prepared for a thoroughly scientific outlook, i.e. the acceptance of a constantly changing environment. The rivalry was still that of a *Natura Naturans* – a nature constantly in the making – rather than having been set in stone once and for all, as the *Natura Naturata* concept asserts. It needed Darwin to become accepted but sublimity undoubtedly influenced and boosted the new outlook.

Northern aesthetics, underlining the disharmonic elements of nature that did not comply with the theological and teleological reading of the deists, promoted an understanding of nature that did not exactly fit into the creationist view. In this sense, Northern aesthetics needs to be linked and set amongst the various cultural operations aimed at the promotion of the Enlightenment, a conclusion that, later, Madame de Staël would reach.

Northern aesthetics went hand in hand with the attack that the Fathers of the English Enlightenment, Bacon, Locke, de Mandeville and later Hume, were launching on the religious interpretation of nature and human beings. These philosophers were fully aware of the fact that the epistemic stronghold of the theological reading of world and nature was inherent to the issue of innatism.[121]

Nature, indeed, often produced terrible manifestations: earthquakes, erupting volcanoes, avalanches, floods and sea storms that could not be easily taken as evidence or as material proof of nature's theological Design theory, as Leibniz had suggested, with his belief that we live in the best world possible.[122] Natural manifestations led to rational doubts about the Design theory, and brought with them the threat of atheism, which would undermine the existence of a governing God behind nature, nature having always been taken as God's cypher, his *Codex (Dei)*. Meanwhile, the undermining of the genius theory, which meant the dismantling of innatism, led to Shelley's atheism as its most rational outcome.

Once English intellectuals ascertained, through aesthetics, that they had to emancipate themselves from the yoke of the classical models that under- or mis-represented them, they started to evaluate their environment in a different way. The confirmation of what they considered to be the unique identity of the English nation at this point, proceeded through the recovery and mythologisation of their past supposed origin and roots detected in the island's Celtic tradition.

4.5 Francis Grose and Aesthetic Regionalism

The reception of art and nature, during the 18th century and after the appearance of Gilpin and Burke's treatises, was often characterised by the fascination exercised by the Northern traits of the English territory and its cultural Celtic and Gothic identity traits. This response was, unequivocally, championed by the theorist and antiquarian Francis Grose. This was done in 1788 by means of his defence of an aesthetic cultural relativism or, better, regionalism. Regionalism was not limited to its English branch. Grose's reading is neutral and measured, equipoised and restrained from any quality evaluation. He defines aesthetic regionalism in a meta-critical way: he does not assess whether one version is better than another; he consistently defends only the possibility of there being plural versions of culturally-characterised aesthetics, which, though diverse, are all equally valuable in expressing their peculiar cultural context.

Frances Grose, indeed, debunks aesthetic holism – the universally applied notion of Greek beauty on which the hierarchic reading of aesthetics was based – once and for all, defending the liberty for a plurality of aesthetic choices defined by the standards set by the environment or culture in which they appear.[123] Aesthetic regionalism – the space-time-specific aesthetics – which he envisages, through his defence of a cultural relativism, unconditionally justifies the liberty of each nation, region or cultural environment to set its own standards of beauty, *de facto* anticipating utterly postmodernist positions (Bezrucka: 1995, 85-111).[124] This was, unequivocally, to lead to romantic individualism, personal sensibility and empathic inclinations that would take the place vacated by normative taste – based on the application of standards[125] – but also provide, *a posteriori,* an explanation for the already-developed Northern regionalism.

Northern aesthetics was thus to embody the autochthonous forms and aesthetic qualities of English territory, perceived as being English because of its attributed Northern qualities. The English Northern aesthetics (using generic Nordic qualities), as we have seen, brought with it, nevertheless, another axiological determinant which consisted of the light of empiricism and freedom.

A truly conscious embarrassment, and thoroughly rational understanding of the cultural relativity of all aesthetic choices and ideas, was, nevertheless, to be reached towards the end of the 19th century with the work of a regionalist novelist, Thomas Hardy, who indisputably launched aesthetic postmodernity in his last novel, *The Well-Beloved*.[126] As far as aesthetics is concerned, this work constitutes the manifesto of a final battle against the ever-resurgent dictatorship of the ahistorical metaphysics of Beauty.

Aesthetic regionalism was undeniably the result of Francis Grose's farsightedness. Grose was an antiquarian and early *critical regionalist*[127] – open to new and outside influences but not prone to accepting them *in toto* just because they were new or exotic. Grose asserted his critical capacity to also assess and ennoble inside cultural heritage, conscious of the identity issues connected to it. In this, he was, unconsciously, an *ante litteram* culturalist: he downgraded the universality claims of the Southern aesthetics (Greek and Latin) in a work he published anonymously in 1788 on the aesthetics of caricature. Even though contingent to the topic of caricature that he was studying, his observations are the earliest on the regionalist topic and the most precise that I could trace. He says:

> To obtain this art [caricature], the student should begin to draw the human head, from one of those drawing-books where the forms and proportions, constituting beauty, according to the European idea, are laid down.[128]

What is interesting, and revolutionary is his description of the space-and-time-specific, i.e. the cultural characteristics of what he means by the "European idea" in a long footnote that defines the specific definitions of beauty and ugliness related to this region; it is worth quoting in its entirety:

> The features of the human face, and the form and proportions of the body and limbs, are in particular countries subject to certain peculiarities; and agreement with, or material deviation from which, constitutes the local idea of beauty or deformity: I say local, because it does not appear that there are any fixed or positive ideas of either; if there were, they must necessarily be the same everywhere, which is by no means the fact; for they differ so greatly in different places, that what is esteemed a perfection in one country, is in another pronounced a deformity.
>
> In China and Morocco, excessive corpulence is esteemed a beauty; and among the valleys of the Alps, the natives return thanks to God for his partiality to them in decorating their necks with the comely goiter or craw, here lately shewn as an object of the most shocking deformity.
>
> Great eyes and small ones, that it is recorded as a circumstance of the great beauty of a woman in the seraglio of Tamerlane, that she was entirely without a nose, having no mark of that feature, except two small apertures through which she drew her breath. The sculptors of ancient Greece seem to have diligently observed the forms and proportions constituting the

> European ideas of beauty; and upon them to have formed their statues. These measures are to be met with many drawing-books; a slight deviation from them, by predominancy of any feature constitutes what is called Character, and serves to discriminate the owner thereof, and to fix the idea of identity. This deviation, or peculiarity, aggravated, forms Caricatura.
>
> On a slight investigation, it would seem almost impossible, considering the small number of features composing the human face, and their general singularity, to furnish a sufficient number of characterising distinctions to discriminate one man from another; but when it is seen what an amazing alteration is produced by enlarging one feature, diminishing another, increasing or lessening their distance, or by any ways varying their proportion, the power of combination will appear infinite. Caricaturists should be careful not to overcharge the peculiarities of their subjects, as they would thereby become hideous instead of ridiculous, and instead of laughter excite horror. It is therefore always best to keep within the bounds of probability. Ugliness, according to our local idea, may be divided into genteel and vulgar. The difference between these kinds of ugliness seems to be, that the former is positive or redundant, the latter wanting or negative. Convex faces, prominent features, and large aquiline noses, though differing much from beauty, still give an air of dignity to their owners; whereas concave faces, flat, snub, or broken noses, always stamp a meanness or vulgarity. The one seems to have passed through the limits of beauty, the other never to have arrived at them: the straighter right-lined face, which was nearly the Grecian character of beauty, being a medium between the negative of vulgar, and the redundancy of genteel ugliness. Perhaps this idea may arise from our early impressions received from the portraits of the famous men of antiquity, most of whom, except Socrates, are depicted with prominent features or aquiline noses. The portraits of the twelve Cæsars have caused the aquiline nose to be styled Roman. (FG: 4-6)

Grose then inserts a series of tables exemplifying drawing-examples and detailed rules on how to emphasise the peculiar physiognomic characters that would lead to the creation of a caricature. My contention is that this essay, which constitutes a *unicum* in its European footnote, deserves to be quoted in all books on aesthetics for its anticipation of both Romantic and postmodern aesthetic relativism and provisionality, a stance in whose theoretical wake many theorists are still working today while others still look to and need to cling, as usual, onto certainties. It is interesting that my copy of this work is printed in a copy of Hogarth's *Analysis of Beauty* which is *sine data*, but which in the British Museum Catalogue appears edited, under this editor, in 1791, Hogarth having died in 1764. Nevertheless, as Ronald Paulson testifies, Hogarth had, in the second draft of his work, jotted down an "analysis of the ridiculous" that was to be set in parallel to the "analysis of beauty" (Paulson 1993: 64). The, *a posteriori,* editor of the 1791 edition of Hogarth's *Analysis*, Samuel Bagster, has at least set things right by publishing, in the absence of the treatise on the ridiculous by Hogarth, Francis Grose's *Rules for Drawing Caricaturas: with an Essay on Comic Painting* (FG: 1-24) to go with it.

From the point of view of its influence, we can read Grose's implicit affirmation of variety as a defence of the autochthonous cultural elements of a region. Grose's aesthetic regionalism contributed greatly to the work of other unknown regionalists and antiquarians who worked to free themselves from the yoke of the so-called universal aesthetics, for which read Greek and Roman, and create their own national heritage. Grose's extremely concise work deserves thus to be connected with those other well-known champions of a national aesthetics we have focused on: Addison, Gilpin, Hogarth and Fielding, Burke, the Warton brothers, Horace Walpole, Gainsborough and Constable, these latter being *par excellence* Northern painters.

Another man aware of the complexity of the cultural systems of each nation/culture was Oliver Goldsmith. He exemplified his views in his masterpiece *A Citizen of the World* (1762), as well as in his previous work, *An Enquiry into the Present State of Polite Learning in Europe* (1759),[129] whose title already circumscribed (Greek) universality to Europe, signalling his awareness the he lived in a much greater world, exactly as Grose would do later. In the essay focused on criticism, having absorbed the empirical tradition, he marks cultural differences in apprehending the same objects and says:

> ALL objects affect us with pleasure in one of these two ways, either by immediately gratifying the senses with pleasing sensations, or by being thought in a secondary manner capable of making other objects contribute to this effect. The pleasures of immediate sensation are coeval with our senses, and, perhaps, most vivid in infancy; the secondary source of pleasure results from experience only, from considering the analogy of nature, or the capacity a part has to unite to a whole. The pleasures of the first sort, are derived from the beauty of the object, those of the second, from a consideration of its use. The first are natural, no art can increase them without mending the organ which was to give them admission. The second are artificial, and continually altering, as whim, climate, or seasons direct. To illustrate my meaning. The beauty of a guinea, for instance, its regular figure, and shining colour, are equally obvious to the senses in every country and climate, these qualities please the wildest savage as much as the most polished European; as far as it affects the senses, the pleasure a guinea gives is therefore in every country the same. BUT the consideration of the uses it can be turned to, are another source of pleasure,

which is different in different countries. A native of Madagascar prefers to it a glass bead; a native of Holland prefers it to every thing else. The pleasure then of its sensible qualities are every where the same; those of its secondary qualities every where different. He, whom nature has furnished with the most vivid perceptions of beauty, and to whom experience has suggested the greatest number of uses, in the contemplation of any object, may be said to receive the greatest pleasure that object is capable of affording. Thus the Barbarian finds some small pleasure in the contemplation of a guinea; the enlightened European who is acquainted with its uses, still more than him; the chymist, who besides this, knows the peculiar fixedness and malleability of the metal, most of all. This capacity of receiving pleasure, may be called Taste in the objects of nature. The polite arts in all their variety are only an imitation of nature. He then must excel in them, who is capable of inspiring us at once with the most vivid perceptions of beauty, and with the greatest number of experimental uses in any object described. But as the artist, to give vivid perceptions must be perspicuous and concise, and yet to exhibit usefulness requires minuteness; here are two opposite qualities required in the writer, in one of which his imagination, in the other his reasoning faculty is every moment liable to offend; what has he in this case to guide him? *Taste is, perhaps, his only director. Taste in writing, is the exhibition of the greatest quantity of beauty and of use, that may be admitted into any description without counteracting each other.* The perfection of taste therefore proceeds from a knowledge of what is beautiful and useful. Criticism professes to increase our taste. But our taste cannot be increased with regard to beauty, because, as has been shewn, our perceptions of this kind cannot be increased, but are most vivid in infancy. *Criticism then can only improve our taste in the useful. But this, as was observed, is different in every climate and country;* what is useful in one climate being often noxious in another; therefore criticism must understand the nature of the climate and country, &c. before it gives rules to direct Taste. **In other words, every country should have a national system of criticism. In fact, nothing can be more absurd than rules to direct the taste of one country drawn from the manners of another.** There may be some general marks in nature, by which all writers are to proceed; these, however, are obvious and might as well have never been pointed out, but to trace the sources of our passions, to mark the evanescent boundaries between satiety and disgust, and how far elegance differs from finery, requires a thorough knowledge of the people to whom the criticism is directed. IF, for instance, the English be a people who look upon death as an incident no way terrible, but sometimes fly to it for refuge from the calamities of life, why should a Frenchman be disgusted at our bloody stage? there is nothing hideous in the representation to one of us, whatever there might be to him. **We have long been characteriz'd as a nation of spleen, and our rivals on the continent as a land of levity.** Ought they to be offended at the melancholly air which many of our modern poets assume, or ought we to be displeased with them for all their

> harmless trifling upon pincushions, parrots, and pretty faces. **What is rational with us, becomes with them formality;** and what is fancy, at Paris, is at London, phantastical. **Critics should, therefore, imitate physicians, and consider every country as having a peculiar constitution, and consequently requiring a peculiar regimen.** (pp. 90-98, emphases added)

Recovering the body politics metaphor and applying it to the nations of Europe, Goldsmith, in his view of nations as bodies that for survival reasons cannot be dissected, anticipates the exportation of the concept of regionalism from criticism to society, *de facto* anticipating the demagogic use of the body propaganda of Nazism and the reactionary view of a strong regionalism – defending inherent geographical and territorial characteristics – like the Nazis, who directly linked *Blut und Boden* – blood and soil. Most certainly, Goldsmith does not work in this direction, restraining himself, like Grose, from the assessing attitude that would introduce the hierarchic rationale in placing the most civilised nations of the world in a prime position to impose their own values on the "less civilised", an attitude that imperialist nations assumed in the 19th and 20th centuries.

Strong regionalism capitalised on the confusion between *Cultur* and *Zivilisation*: *Cultur* represents the variety of cultures in the world as well as the subcultures within a nation, and *Zivilisation* provides a demagogically chosen climax of the nation's values. It does this, however, at the price of erasing the plurality of those subcultures of which it is formed, as Gottfried Herder was to exemplify in his *Ideas on the Philosophy of the History of Mankind* (1784-1791).[130] In this work, Herder, using the dangerous medieval body politics metaphor, states that each *Cultur* [read *Kultur*] has its own *Volks*geist (my emphasis, tr. soul of the people). It was left to Johann Gottlieb Fichte in his *Wissenschaftslehre* (1794) to base his nationalism on the German language, which for him symbolised the essence and intrinsic superiority of German values (recovering Tacitus' view)[131] in comparison to the other European languages (and their relative country-spirit). F.D.E. Schleiermacher, the father of modern theology, endorsed this reading: "Only one language is firmly implanted in an individual (...) For every language is a particular mode of thought and what is cogitated in one language can never be repeated in the same way in another (...) Language, thus, just like the church or the state is an expression of a peculiar life which contains within it and develops through it a common body of language."[132]

Raymond Williams would say:

> In his [Herder's] unfinished *Ideas on the Philosophy of the History of Mankind* (1784-91) he wrote of Cultur [the old German word for Kultur]: 'nothing is more indeterminate than this word, and nothing more deceptive than its application to all nations and periods'. He attacked the assumption of the universal histories that 'civilization' or 'culture' - the historical self-development of humanity - was what we would now call a unilinear process, leading to the high and dominant point of C18 European culture. Indeed, he attacked what he called European subjugation and domination of the four quarters of the globe, and wrote: "Men of all the quarters of the globe, who have perished over the ages, you have not lived solely to manure the earth with your ashes, so that at the end of time your posterity should be made happy by European culture. The very thought of a superior European culture is a blatant insult to the majesty of Nature." It is then necessary, he argued, in a decisive innovation, to speak of 'cultures' in the plural: the specific and variable cultures of different nations and periods, but also the specific and variable cultures of social and economic groups within a nation. This sense was widely developed, in the Romantic movement, as an alternative to the orthodox and dominant 'civilization'. It was first used to emphasize national and traditional cultures, including the new concept of folk-culture (...). It was later used to attack what was seen as the MECHANICAL' (q.v.) character of the new civilization then emerging: both for its abstract rationalism and for the 'inhumanity' of current industrial development. It was used to distinguish between 'human' and 'material' development. (RW: 89)

Oswald Spengler[133] was again to use the usual body-metaphor for cultures, as if they had a life cycle, to promote the pessimistic nationalist rhetoric, repeated recently about Europe, that, as seen, led to the recent reactionary involutional move.

We can nevertheless conclude that ethnic groups, formed by individual identities, are often demagogically but crucially united by cultural elements that need best be hypostasised only in the past, as Frederick Barth states:

> What is the unit whose continuity in time is depicted in such studies [ethnohistories]? Paradoxically, it must include cultures in the past which would clearly be excluded in the present because of differences in form – differences of precisely the kind that are diagnostic in synchronic differentiation of ethnic units. The interconnection between 'ethnic group' and 'culture' is certainly not clarified through this confusion."[134]

This is something that Patrick J. Geary (2003) has convincingly confirmed, speaking of the peoples' histories being the result of the "amnesia of the processes of ethnogenesis and migrations".[135]

To testify how much history is historiography, we can quote Ernest Renan, who, ahead of his time, in a *Lecture at the Sorbonne* in 1882, said:

> Forgetting, I would even go so far as to say historical error, is a crucial factor in the creation of a nation, which is why progress in historical studies often constitutes a danger for [the principle] of nationality. Indeed, historical enquiry brings to light deeds of violence which took place at the origin of all political formations, even of those whose consequences have been altogether beneficial. Unity is always effected by means of brutality. [...] the essence of a nation is that all individuals have many things in common, and also that they have forgotten many things. [...] A nation is a soul, a spiritual principle. Two things [...] constitute this soul or spiritual principle. [...] A heroic past [...] a common will in the present [...] It presupposes a past; it is summarized, however, in the present by a tangible fact, namely, consent [...] a daily plebiscite.[136]

Nevertheless, the attention that the 18th century devoted to the unique individual – no longer subsumable under universal principles and categories – as a being who lives in precise space and time categories that determine his or her identity led to a change of perspective that Michael McKeon linked to the ascendancy of individualism.[137] Nevertheless, it very soon resulted in a nationalistic reconfiguration. This was due to the necessity to characterise the reasons for which a person is unique as well as why one felt English rather than, e.g., French. Napoleon's presence on the international scene, in this sense, and the danger he represented for national conglomerations gave nations a tremendous boost for their reconfiguration as national states. We therefore witness the appearance of taxonomical reclassifications, at first through the creation of national types. Hume defined "natural character" as depending on "fixed *moral causes*" the result of "acquire[d] resemblance of manners" (DHNC: 249) or a "contagion of manners" due to the imitative character of the mind that was the result of:

1. a long-lasting government;
2. the presence of small and contiguous governments that nevertheless show people as having a different character and thus tend to acquire differences of manners "as the most distant nations" (DHNC: 249);
3. a national character that commonly follows boundaries (and which do not follow air) and depends rather on "battles, negotiations, and marriages" (DHNC: 249);
4. a national character does not only depend on physical boundaries of a nation: the Jews' aterritoriality testifies that though "scattered (...] [they]

maintain a close society (...) and have but little in common with the nations amongst whom they live" (DHNC: 250);

5. a different language or a different religion within the same boundaries preserves a "distinct and even opposite set of manners", the opposite being also true as in:

6. the "same manners will follow a nation (...) over the whole globe";

7. the manners of nations change according to alterations of government, mixtures of new people, or "by inconstancy of human affairs" (DHNC: 250), which provides Hume with the opportunity to praise his nation's attitude in matters of religion, testifying tolerance:

> Not to insist upon the great difference between the present possessors of BRITAIN, and those before the ROMAN conquest; we may observe that our ancestors, a few centuries ago, were sunk into the most abject superstition, last century they were inflamed with the most furious enthusiasm, and are now settled into the most cool indifference with regard to religious matters, that is to be found in any nation of the world. (DHNC: 251);

8. if there is close communication between nations due to policy, commerce or travelling, similar manners are acquired; all these points lead then to his last point.

9. Hume, having presented national characteristics pertaining to other countries, can now conclude with strong national pride, in a paean, that England, with its republican attitude, which fosters liberty and protects variety, presents a "wonderful mixture of manners and characters in the same nation" notwithstanding climate, or physical causes, this being confirmed by the fact that "all these causes take place in the neighbouring country of SCOTLAND, without having the same effect" (*ibid.*), probably then a result of its government: "a mixture of monarchy, aristocracy, and democracy (...) All sorts of religion are to be found among them (...) Hence the English, of any people in the universe, have the least of a national character" (DHNC: 252). Finding this last trait positive, he signals also the acceptance, as underlined through his hint to Scotland, of the different, not-so-homogenous amalgam of regional and marginal cultures or minorities.

Likewise, Murray G.H. Pittock (1997) in his study of "the four nations [England, Scotland, Ireland and Wales] and many regions that make up these islands" underlines the necessity of "viewing differing groups in their own terms [to] allow the uncertainty and provisionality of British identity in the period to emerge", a fact which confirms "the invention of the modern British state in the 1685-1714 period, and the nature of resistance to it".[138]

The next reconfiguration, leading to a racist drift, proceeded via race, to which the grand minds of the age also gave their imprimatur: Hume, in the same above-quoted essay, hypothesising the inferiority of coloured people[139] and Kant[140] subdividing people along clear-cut aesthetic categories: the English, Spanish and Germans embody the sublime; the French and Italians the beautiful. He also repeats the negative connotation against coloured people, taking up Hume's opinion to endorse his own.[141]

The nation had already metamorphised into race issues via the human taxonomy adopted in the classifications of Linnaeus (who speaks of variety), Buffon (who uses the term "race") and Blumenbach, who, in his *De generis humani varietate nativa* (1775), subdivided humanity into five "national varieties (...) Caucasian, Mongolian, Ethiopian, American and Malay" as Nicholas Hudson affirms, "invest[ing] traditional folk prejudice with (...) intellectual authority":

> over the period of a century, 'race' gradually mutated from its original sense of a people or single nation, linked by origin, to its later sense of a biological subdivision of the human species. These changes (…) derived in part from the rise of a new science of human taxonomy.[142]

Hierarchical assessment would, in due course, be demagogically used and exploited to back the nationalist, then imperialist, propaganda of the 19th century. Discriminative differences were defined through hypostatised assessments, pseudo-sciences (Bezrucka: 2011) and apt criteria to perform racial quality assessments and create borders and discrimination. This was soon done, imperialistically, by adopting Spencer's time-arrow progressive evolution. This was in fact a misreading of Darwin's *On the Origin of the Species* (1857) which had presented evolution as a merely sometimes positive, but at times also regressive adaptation-process to a given environment. Adaptation was thus confused with anthropological genetics.[143] As Nicholas Hudson rightly states:

> The reunion of 'race' and 'nation' had such important consequences because of the way these terms had been redefined during the Enlightenment. 'Race' now meant more than just a 'lineage' or even a variation of the human species induced by climate or custom. It meant an innate and fixed disparity in the physical and intellectual make-up of different peoples. 'Nation', in turn, was more than a group of people living under the same government. It was the very 'soul' of personal identity, the very lifeblood churning through an individual speaking a particular dialect in one of Europe's innumerable regions. From the often violent coupling of 'race' and 'nation', refashioned in these new forms, were spawned the

> most virulent forms of nineteenth-century racism, and finally the political barbarities of our own century. (H: 259)

A "'racialising' of peoples – the subjection of populations to scientifically invalid forms of classification based on an arbitrary selection of phenotypical or genetic differences (...) [to relegate] to the dustbin of dangerous and useless terms" (H: 259). Indeed, it created the logic of supposed primitive cultures feeding the agenda of imperialism with the idea that some nations needed to educate them, with the justification that this was the "white man's burden".[144]

History, as can clearly be seen, is linked to a space-politics that tends to forget its own history of prevarication and conquest. Nevertheless, it is not only major and terrible events that create horrors; even apparently simple aesthetic assessments used insensitively – "I think it's beautiful", "I do not like it, it's ugly" – do not consider that even simply judging cultural or national forms of art as primitive implies that there are more evolved ones (implying that the latter are better).[145]

Notes

[1] See Malcolm Andrews (1989) *The Search for the Picturesque: Landscape Aesthetics and Tourism in Britain, 1760-1800* (Stanford: Stanford University Press) and his (1994) *The Picturesque. Literary Sources and Documents* (Mountfield: Helm) 2 vols.; Christopher Hussey (1967) *The Picturesque. Studies in a Point of View* (London: Frank Cass & Co); W.J. Hipple Jr. (1957) *The Beautiful, The Sublime, and The Picturesque in Eighteenth-Century British Aesthetic Theory* (Carbondale: Southern Illinois University Press). Cf. William Gilpin (1972 [anastatic copy of the 1792's first edition by R. Blamire]) *Three Essays: on Picturesque Beauty; on Picturesque Travel; and on Sketching Landscape to which is Added a Poem, on Landscape Painting* (Farnborough: Gregg).
[2] William Gilpin (1748) *A Dialogue upon the Gardens of the Right Honourable the Lord Viscount Cobham at Stowe in Buckinghamshire* (Buckingham: Seleey).
[3] Copley Stephen, Garside Peter (eds) (1994) *The Politics of the Picturesque* (Cambridge: University Press).
[4] Cf. William Gilpin (1748) *A Dialogue upon the Gardens,* op. cit. On the role of women in gardening, cf. Stephen Bending (2013) *Green Retreats: Women, Gardens and Eighteenth-Century Culture* (Cambridge: Cambridge University Press), and P. Bicknell (1981) *Beauty, Horror and Immensity: Picturesque Landscape in Britain: 1750-1850* (Cambridge: Cambridge University Press).
[5] Cf. my observations on the English garden in (2002) *Genio e immaginazione*, op. cit., pp. 60-63 and 123-27.
[6] I am here using the term "invention" in Eric Hobsbawm and Terence Ranger's

sense (eds) (1983) *The Invention of Tradition* (Cambridge: University Press).
[7] W. Gilpin ([1972 1794 [1792]), *Three Essays,* op. cit.
[8] J. Ruskin (1903-1912) *The Works of John Ruskin*, ed. E. T. Cook and A. Wedderburn, 39 vols, *The Stones of Venice* vol. IX Bk. 2, ch. VI, § 3 182, emphasis added. In the same work, Ruskin affirms: "[t]here is, however, a marked distinction between the imaginations of the Western and Eastern races [...] the Western, or Gothic, delighting most in the representation of facts, and the Eastern (Arabian, Persian, and Chinese) in the harmony of colours and forms" cf. *ibid.* Bk. 2, ch. VI, III, § 41, p. 215.
[9] Cf. Bezrucka, Y. (1993) *Virginia Woolf's Artists: The Influence on Her Work of the Aesthetics of Roger Fry and Clive Bell*, PhD, Royal Holloway Bedford New College, University of London, p. 16, quoted from J. Ruskin (1903-1912) *The Works of John Ruskin*, (eds) E. T. Cook and A. Wedderburn, 39 vols, *The Stones of Venice* vol. IX, Bk. 2, ch. VI, sect. I, § 12, p. 193.
[10] Cf. *ibid.*
[11] Cf. *Peri hypsous, or Dionysius Longinus of the height of eloquence* (1652). Rendred out of the Originall by J. H. Esq, (London: Roger Daniel for Francis Eaglesfield).
[12] For the classic attractions of the Picturesque Tours cf. Ian Ousby (1990) *The Englishman's England. Taste, Travel and the Rise of Tourism* (Cambridge: Cambridge University Press).
[13] R. Morden (1701) 'New Description and State of England', in J. Brewer (1997) *The Pleasure of the Imagination. English Culture in the Eighteenth Century* (Bath: Harper Collins), pp. 632-33 (my emphasis).
[14] J. Brome, *Travels over England and Wales*, II ed., (London: Goslin) (1707 [1700]), 'Introduction', s.p., quoted in R. Morden, *New Description*, op. cit. p. 633.
[15] The Domestic Tour, or Picturesque Tour, notwithstanding its importance for the Northern aesthetics, has not yet been given its due place in recent travel writing studies either: P. Hulme and T. Youngs [2002] (2013) *The Cambridge Companion to Travel Writing* (Cambridge, New York: Cambridge University Press); T. Youngs (2013) *Cambridge Introduction to Travel Writing* (Cambridge, New York: Cambridge University Press); Carl Thompson (2011) *Travel Writing* (Abingdon, UK: Routledge).
[16] W. Gilpin (1768) *Essay Upon Prints: Containing Remarks upon the Principles of Picturesque Beauty; the Different Kinds of Prints; and the Characters of the Most Noted Masters: Illustrated by Criticisms upon Particular Pieces: to which are added, some Cautions that may be Useful in Collecting Prints* (London: G. Scott).
[17] Baedeker's guides were published from 1827 and became the prototype for every future guide; they defined places and their peculiar beauty and provided travellers with useful advice on logistics and food.
[18] R. Lassels, 'Introduction', *An Italian Voyage, or A Compleat Journey through Italy*, Paris, Du Moutier, 1670, p. iii.

[19] W. Hazlitt connected the Romantic poets to nature, defining them as Lake Poets in G. Keynes (ed.) (2004) *Selected Essays of William Hazlitt: 1778 to 1830* (Whitefish: Kessinger Publishing), p. 187, where he quotes Wordsworth, Coleridge and Southey as poets pertaining to the Lake School.

[20] Cf. 'Preface' to Wordsworth and Coleridge's *Lyrical Ballads* (1801, called the '1800 edition').

[21] Cf., for example, P. Luckombe, *The Beauties of England* (London, Davis and C. Reymers, 1769), and the works quoted and mentioned in this study.

[22] Thomas West, quoted in K. Thomas (1983) *Man and the Natural World. Changing Attitudes in England 1500-1800* (London: Penguin), p. 266. These painters (Gaspard Dughet is often called Poussin because he was Nicolas Poussin's brother-in-law) were instrumental in teaching the English public to appreciate the informal landscape gardens upon which the picturesque capitalised.

[23] Cf. P. Bicknell (1981) *Beauty, Horror and Immensity: Picturesque Landscape in Britain, 1750-1850* (Cambridge: Cambridge University Press). pp. X e 1-2.

[24] H. Walpole (1798 [1762-65]) *Anecdotes of Painting in England* (1762-1765), vol. III (London: Robinson), p. 450, also quoted in J. Barrell (1980) *The Dark Side of the Landscape* (Cambridge: Cambridge University Press), p. 7.

[25] A. Young (1770) *A Six Months Tour Through the North of England*, vol. III, (London: W. Strahan, W. Nicholl).

[26] *ibid.* cf. on p. 184 "One inclosure in particular breaks into the wood in the most picturesque manner imaginable. This end of the lake is bounded by the noble hills of cultivated inclosures (…) which are viewed from hence to much advantage; they rise from the shore with great magnificence. To the left a ridge of hanging woods, spread, over wild romantic ground, that breaks into bold projections, contracting the elegance of the opposite shore in the finest manner."

[27] See: http://www.online-literature.com/samuel-johnson/journey-to-scotland/1 where he asserts: "I had desired to visit the Hebrides, or Western Islands of Scotland, so long, that I scarcely remember how the wish was originally excited; and was in the Autumn of the year 1773 induced to undertake the journey, by finding in Mr. Boswell a companion, whose acuteness would help my inquiry, and whose gaiety of conversation and civility of manners are sufficient to counteract the inconveniences of travel, in countries less hospitable than we have passed."

[28] Cf. http://www.online-literature.com/view.php/journey-to-scotland/5

[29] J. Boswell (1785) *The Journal of a Tour to the Hebrides with Samuel Johnson*, (London: Henry Baldwin), p. 742.

[30] S. Johnson (1755) *A Dictionary of the English Language*, 2 vols. (London: W. Strahan), vol. 2, p. 1717.

[31] *ibid.* vol. 1, p. 931.

[32] *Johnson's English Dictionary as improved by Todd and Abridged by Chalmers with Walker's Pronouncing Dictionary* (1835) (Boston: Nathan Hale), hereafter referred to in the text with JD: and p. no.

[33] Cf. R. Williams (1973) *The Country and the City* (London: Chatto & Windus).

[34] Cf. 'The Village', 1783.
[35] M. Wollstonecraft (1970 [1796]) *Letters Written During a Short Residence in Sweden, Norway and Denmark* (Fontwell: Centaur).
[36] Cf. P. Nyström (1980) *Mary Wollstonecraft's Scandinavian Journey* (Göteborg: Kungl. Vetenskaps-och Vitterhets Samha¨ llet), p. 76.
[37] For the ethnic visions of the Orient, cf. E.W. Said, (1995 [1978]) *Orientalism. Western Conceptions of the Orient* (London: Penguin).
[38] Lady Mary Wortley Montagu (2004 [1716-1718] *Turkish Embassy Letters* (London: Virago).
[39] K.R. Lawrence (1994) *Penelope Voyages: Women and Travel in the British Literary Tradition* (Ithaca, NY: Cornell University Press), p. 45.
[40] Cf. Loomis, C. '*The Arctic Sublime*' in U.C. Knoepflmacher, G.B. Tennyson (eds) *Nature and the Victorian Imagination* (Berkeley, Los Angeles, California University Press), pp. 95-112, who claims that even Coleridge's *The Rime of the Ancient Mariner* was influenced by an Arctic expedition (pp. 98-99).
[41] U. Price (1971) [1796-1798]) *An Essay on the Picturesque, as Compared with the Sublime and the Beautiful, and on the Use of Studying Pictures, for the Purpose of Improving Real Landscape* (London: D. Walker for J. Robson), 2 vols., reprint (Farnborough: Gregg) from the 3-volume edition of 1810 [1794].
[42] Cf. R.P. Knight (1972 [1805]) *An Analytical Enquiry into the Principles of Taste* (Farnborough: Gregg); see also his work (1972 [1795]) *The Landscape. A Didactic Poem in Three Books Addressed to Uvedale Price* (Farnborough: Gregg).
[43] Cf. B. Anderson (1983) *Imagined Communities. Reflections on the Spread of Nationalism* (London: Verso).
[44] Cf. W. Scott (1995 [1871]) *Rob Roy* (London: Penguin).
[45] Quoted in A. Gilroy (ed.) (2000) 'Introduction'. In *Romantic Geographies: Discourses of Travel, 1775-1844*, Manchester, (Manchester: University Press), p. 3. See also A. Gilroy (ed.) (2004) *Green and Pleasant Land: English Culture and the Romantic Countryside* (Leuven: Peeters).
[46] Alexander Pope shows great interest in garden aesthetics. He created his own garden in Twickenham, on the river Thames, and theorizes upon it in the *Epistle IV* to Lord Richard Boyle, Earl of Burlington (1731) in *Windsor Forest.* See Herbert Davies, *Pope. Complete Poetical Works*, (Oxford: Oxford University Press) (1983 [1966]), pp. 314-21, pp. 21-50.
[47] Immanuel Kant (1991 [1790]) *Kritik der Urteilskraft*, ed. Gerhard Lehmann (Stuttgart: Reclam), pp. 102, 130-131, here p. 131.
[48] See Addison's Essay No. 419 of *The Pleasures of the Imagination* (1712).
[49] W. Gilpin (1724-1804), the first theorist of the natural, non-pictorial, picturesque, defines its characteristics in *A Dialogue upon the Gardens at Stow* (1993 [1748]) (New York: Ams). On page 24, Polypthon says: "As we are got into the North, I must confess I do not know any Part of the Kingdom that abounds more with elegant natural Views: Our well-cultivated Plains (…) are certainly not comparable to their rough Nature in point of Prospect."

[50] William Hogarth (s.d. 1791 [1753]) *The Analysis of Beauty* (London: Bagster).
[51] Edmund Burke (1828 [1757]) *A Philosophical Enquiry into the Origin of our Ideas of the Sublime and the Beautiful* (London: Dove).
[52] For the paradigmatic change from holism to particularism, cf. my book (2002) *Genio e immaginazione*, op. cit., pp. 79-132.
[53] William Temple (1709 [1690]) 'An Essay upon Ancient and Modern Learning', in *Miscellanea,* part II (London: Tonson), pp. 129-30.
[54] Alexander Pope *Complete Poetical Works*, op. cit., pp. 314-21, e pp. 37-50.
[55] A. Pope (1709), 'An Essay on Criticism' in *Complete Poetical Works*, op. cit., v. 297, p. 72.
[56]Horace Walpole (1888 [1780]) 'On Modern Gardening', in *Anecdotes of Painting in England: With Some Account of the Principal Artists* (London: Hazell, Watson & Viney), vol. 3, pp. 63-92, referred to hereafter in the text as HW and page number. The essay was, nevertheless, first published in 1771, when it appeared at the end of the fourth volume of 'Anecdotes of Painting in England' under the title: 'The Modern Taste in Gardening'.
[57] W. Gilpin (1993 [1748]) *A Dialogue upon the Gardens of the Right Honourable the Lord Viscount Cobham at Stow in Buckinghamshire* (New York: Ams) see p. 48.
[58] Cf. Sir William Temple (1982 [1718]) 'Upon the Gardens of Epicurus', 1685, in *Works*, op. cit., I vol.; Stephen Switzer, *Iconographia Rustica or the Nobleman, Gentleman and Gardener's Recreation* (New York: Garland), being an attack against the Dutch taste imported by William of Orange exemplified by the Het Loo garden, ad Apeldoorn, in the Netherlands. Cf. also Batty Langley (1972 [1728]) *New Principles of Gardening* (New York: Garland), another work championing a more 'natural' garden design to contrast the 'formal' Italian and French ones.
[59] John Dixon Hunt (ed.) (1995 [1780]) *The History of the Modern Taste in Gardening* (New York: Ursus), Dixon Hunt just renames the essay 'On Modern Gardening'.
[60] Less aristocratic gardens and lawns, specifically, were often used by their owners as considerable markers of wealth in that they could choose whether to cultivate land for crops. For a modern treatment of the garden theme, cf. D. Carpi (1993) 'Il giardino come metafora e metamorfosi in 'The Virgin in the Garden' di A.S. Byatt.' In D. Carpi, G. Franci, G. Silvani (eds) (1993) *Raccontare i giardini* (Milano: Guerini), pp. 117-130.
[61]Michel Baridon (1989) 'History, Myth, and the English Garden'. In *The Fashioning and Functioning of the British Country House* (eds) Gervase Jackson-Stops, *et al.*, National Gallery of Art, Washington (London, Hanover: New England University Press), pp. 373-91.
[62] Cf. K. Clark (1964 [1928]) *The Gothic Revival* (Harmondsworth: Penguin).
[63] What Kantorowicz has aptly disveiled in its ideological manoeuver and termed a political theology, cf. Ernst H. Kantorowicz (1958) *The King's Two Bodies: A Study in Mediaeval Political Theology* (Princeton: Princeton University Press).

[64] Cf. my article (2016) 'Beehive-Images and Politics in Bernard de Mandeville's *The Fable of The Bees:* Empiricism *vs* Innatism', op. cit., pp. 1-26.
[65] The Saxon-Gothic refers to the Anglo-Saxon-Gothic style, typical of the turriform churches built form the 5th up to the 11th-c. Norman invasion. Cf. J. Wallis (1769) *The Natural History and Antiquities of Northumberland*, (London: W. and W. Strahand). Continental Gothic style refers, usually, to the aftermath instances of Gothic churches that follow the renovation of the Romanesque church of Saint-Denis, brought forth under the direction of Abbot Suger, between 1130 and 1140, who changed the old church to give prominence to light (the light of God).
[66] A case in point study of the novel is Toni Wein's (2002) *British Identities, Heroic Nationalisms, and the Gothic Novel: 1764-1824* (Gordonsville VA: Palgrave), see pp. 49-69.
[67] An essential work in this sense is that by Diane Long Hoeveler (2014) *The Gothic Ideology: Religious Hysteria and Anti-Catholicism in British Popular Fiction, 1780-1880* (Cardiff: University of Wales Press).
[68] Cf. W. Hogarth (s.d., prob. 1791 [1753]) *The Analysis of Beauty* (London: Bagster), hereafter referred to in the text with WH and page no.
[69] Cf. Ronald Paulson (1991) *Hogarth: 'The Modern Moral Subject' 1697-1732*, vol. I (New Brunswick and London: Rutgers University Press); (1992) *Hogarth: High Art and Low 1732-1750,* vol. II (New Brunswick: Rutgers University Press), (1993) *Hogarth: Art and Politics 1750-1764*, vol. III (Cambridge: Lutterworth).
[70] I have already hinted at the importance of the links between these two works in my books (2002) *Genio ed immaginazione,* op. cit., pp. 3 and 110-11 and (2016 [2015]) *A Synopsis of English Literature* (Verona: QuiEdit), pp. 170-71. For perfect reproductions of Hogarth's etchings, cf. Sean Shesgreen (1973) *Engravings by Hogarth*; see, for example, Plate 49 'Characters Caricaturas' (Toronto: General Publishing Company).
[71] Cf. Jean H. Hagstrum (1958) *The Sister Arts: The Tradition of Literary Pictorialism and English Poetry from Dryden to Gray* (Chicago: Chicago University Press); and Ulrich Weisstein (1993) 'Literature and the (Visual) Arts. Intertextuality and Mutual Illumination'. In Ingeborg Hoesterey and Ulrich Weisstein (eds) (1993) *Intertextuality: German Literature and Visual Art from Renaissance to the Twentieth Century* (Columbia Chicago: Camden House Press).
[72] I use intermediality in the sense attributed to it by Dick Higgins, describing works "in which the materials of various more established art forms are 'conceptually fused' rather than merely juxtaposed", cf. Eric Vos (1997) 'The Eternal Network. Mail Art, Intermedia Semiotics, Interarts Studies', p. 325. In Ulla-Britta Lagerroth, Hans Lund and Erik Hedling (eds), *Interart Poetics. Essays on the Interrelations of the Arts and Media* (Amsterdam, Atlanta: Rodopi).
[73] Henry Fielding (1983 [1742]) *Joseph Andrews and Shamela* (London: Dent), subsequently referred to parentetically in the text as FJ and page no.
[74] In an earlier examination of the 18th century, I have used two engravings by

Hogarth – that I consider figuratively vivid icons and thus emblematic in providing a synthetic but highly symbolic visual understanding of the whole century – the manifesto of the novel, seen above, *Characters and Caricaturas* (1743) and *Variety* (1753), both reproduced here, because they best express the new – Northern and enlightened – line of beauty. The two works iconically express the modernity of the 18th century exemplifying the decline and transformation of the holistic paradigm into a regionalist one (Bezrucka: 2002: 2, 16, 78, 120-21, 129, 136 *et passim*). An earlier visual iconic statement was made also by de Mandeville, who revised with his literary *Fable of the Bees* the frontispiece of Hobbes's *Leviathan* by A. Bosse (1651). The beehive-chest of the monarch, on which the head of the king presides, is by him rewritten into the image of a beehive where the queen is herself kept as a sort of prisoner, an animal society where everybody has a sense only if roles are respected but are also mutually agreed upon (1724). This icon can be considered the visual transposition of the attack on innatism – a shorthand for authoritarianism – which is the strongest intellectual assault the empiricists set on kingship and religion (Bezrucka: 2016).

[75] Cf. Ian Watt, *The Rise of the Novel. Studies in Defoe, Richardson and Fielding*, op. cit. More recent critical studies on the novel are those of Michael McKeon (1987) *The Origins of the English Novel: 1600-1740* (London: Johns Hopkins University Press), who finds in the "questions of truth and questions of virtue", and the separation of "thought and experience", and between "'self' and 'society'", the major issues of the new genre that he sees coincidentally growing with the rise of individualism, p. 419; see also chapters 2 and 3, and pp. 65-128. Cf. also (1983) Lennard J. Davies, *Factual Fictions. The Origins of the English Novel* (New York: Columbia University Press); John J. Richetti (1969), *Popular Fiction Before Richardson, Narrative Patterns 1700-1739* (Oxford: Clarendon), and J. Paul Hunter (1990) *Before Novels. The Cultural Contexts of the Eighteenth-Century English Fiction* (London: Norton).

[76] The term historio*graphic* novel reminds us of the ideological, chosen focus, of history-representations that are always mediated by the historiographers who, instead of providing us a paratactic list of dates and happenings, typical of the chronicle, present us rather their hypotactic interpretation. This self-consciousness has led to the questioning of the truthfulness of the accounts of history writing and their demystification as historio*graphy*, underlining their axiologically mediated observer's account. In so doing, historians present things ideologically filtered, or, in the terms used by Walter Benjamin, "the history written by the winners" or, as we would say today, the stakeholders (cf. W. Benjamin (1962 [1955] *Angelus Novus. Saggi e frammenti* (Torino: Einaudi), p. 78.

[77] On the subversive use of the masonic references in Hogarth to signify the superiority of the "Protestant Englishness" and his "anti papism", see Elisabeth Soulier-Détis (2010) *'Guess at the Rest'. Cracking the Hogarth Code* (Cambridge: Lutterworth), p. 201. For an application of this code on Fielding's *Tom Jones* and its original results, see Luigi D'Agnone (2017) *A Triple-Faced Janus: Tom Jones*

as Bastard, Pretender, and Cowan (unpublished PhD Thesis, University of Verona).

[78] Y. Bezrucka (2002) *Genio,* op. cit., p. 96.

[79] See Y. Bezrucka (1995b) 'Il postmodernismo: l'accettazione ironica del doppio senso'. In Y. Bezrucka (ed.), *Tra passato e futuro. Assaggi di teoria dell'architettura*, (Trento: Autem), pp. 85-111, and Y. Bezrucka (1994) 'Assenza, violenza, proliferazione dei sensi in 'Between the Acts' di Virginia Woolf', *Quaderni del Dipartimento di Letterature Straniere Moderne dell'Università di Verona*, 19, 1994, 97-107.

[80] See Y. Bezrucka (2010) 'Regimi scopici e tassonomie visuali: da Virginia Woolf a Italo Calvino' In Chiara Battisti (ed.) (2010), *Parola e visione*, Verona: Ombre Corte), pp. 92-104.

[81] I have commented on this point in my (2002) *Genio e immaginazione*, op. cit., pp. 96-97.

[82] Cf. Ronald Paulson (1992) *Hogarth: High Art and Low 1732-1750,* vol. II (New Brunswick: Rutgers University Press), p. 59.

[83] *ibid.* p. 66.

[84] W. Tatarkiewicz (1974 [1962-67]) (ed.) tr. D. Petsch, *History of Aesthetics* (Berlin: de Gruyter).

[85] Anthony Ashley Cooper, 3rd Earl of Shaftesbury, (ed.) Douglas Den Uyl (2001 [1732]) *Characteristicks of Men, Manners, Opinions and Times* (Indianapolis: Liberty Fund), 3 vols., vol. 1, sect. 3.

[86] (Sir) Joshua Reynolds 1992 [1797] *Discourses* (Harmondsworth: Penguin), pp. 230-31, hereafter referred to as JR and page no.

[87] S. Shesgreen (1973) *Engravings by Hogarth* (New York: Dover), no. 17.

[88] See W. Gilpin (1972, 1794 [1792]) *Three Essays,* op. cit.

[89] Edmund Burke (1827 [1757]) *Philosophical Inquiry into the Origin of our Ideas of the Sublime and the Beautiful* (London: Dove), hereafter referred to in the text as *Sublime.*

[90] Cf. Marjorie Hope Nicholson (1997 [1959]) *Mountain Gloom and Mountain Glory: The Development of the Aesthetics of the Infinite,* (Washington: Washington University Press).

[91] Pseudo-Longinus, in his work on rhetoric, *On the Sublime*, or *Perì hýpsous*, fixed a stylistic, not a natural, sublimity as the highest aim of literature. The work was translated into French in 1764 by Boileau. Cf. Samuel Monk (1935) *The Sublime: A Study of Critical Theories in Eighteenth-Century England* (New York: MLA) who lists all the editorial versions of the work. See also Karl Axelsson (2007) *The Sublime: Precursors and British Eighteenth-Century Conceptions* (Bern: Peter Lang).

[92] Dionysius Longinus (1735) *On the Sublime*, tr. ed. William Smith (London: J. Watts). Cf. Caroline A. Van Eck, Stijn Bussles, Marten Delbeke, Jürgen Pieters (eds) (2012) *The Early Modern Reception and Dissemination of Longinus' 'Perì Hupsous*' (Leiden: Brill). Smith's edition, according to W. Vaughan, "concentrated

on the Protestant culture, which was seen as providing the basis for free enquiry (...) set against (...) the forces of conservatism and repression, embodied by continental Catholic cultures, in particular in France." See William Vaughan (1999) *British Painting: The Golden Age from Hogarth to Turner* (New York: Thames and Hudson), p. 11, quoted in A. van Eck, op. cit*.*, p. 209.

[93] Burke dedicated the III part, section 9, of his *Inquiry*, significantly entitled 'Perfection not the Cause of Beauty', to demolishing the idea "that perfection is the constituent cause of beauty". Cf. E. Burke, *Philosophical Inquiry into the Origin of our Ideas of the Sublime and the Beautiful*, op. cit., p. 105.

[94] In 1750, A.G. Baumgarten published his work (1961 [1750]) *Aesthetica* (Hildesheim: Olms), defining aesthetics as a new philosophical science.

[95] See my treatment of taste in Bezrucka: 2002, 113-16.

[96] Cf. Northrop Frye (1956) 'Towards Defining an Age of Sensibility', *English Literary History*, 23, 2, 144-52.

[97] Cf. Y. Bezrucka, *Genio*, op. cit., pp. 17-77.

[98] Charles Batteux, *Les Beaux Arts*, Bk. 1, part 1, as quoted in A. Toscano (1991) 'Charles Batteux: les quatre poétiques', *Rivista di Estetica*, XXI/3, pp. 67-78.

[99] Thomas Gainsborough's studies of clouds are remarkable for the impressionistic devotion he shows to painting those slight variations of colour changes of the sky, an intent that already includes a sort of strictly formal and nearly abstract colour-oriented drive. See as an example his *Landscape in Suffolk*, (c 1746-50), present at the Kunsthistorisches Museum, Vienna. J.M.W. Turner's interest in skies and clouds is often linked to his works depicting the storms at sea, or nature in its prime colours such as in *The Fighting Téméraire. Tugged to her Last Berth to be Broken Up*, Exh. R.A. 1839, National Gallery London, or in his *Dolbadarn Castle*, 1799, pencil and watercolor, Tate Gallery, London.

[100] See, for example, his painting *Cloud Study* (1822), presently in the Tate Gallery.

[101] Something similar happens in Thomas Warton (1777) *Poems*, op. cit., in his poem 'The Suicide', pp. 146-55.

[102] Lilian R. Furst (2005) 'Lighting Up Night'. In Michael Ferber (ed.) *A Companion to European Romanticism* (Oxford: Blackwell)p. 506 (pp. 505-21).

[103] Thomas Warton senior (1688-1745), professor of poetry at Oxford, and his two sons Thomas, Jr. (1728-1790), the author of *The History of English Poetry* and *Poems* (1777), and Joseph (1722-1800), a poet and academic himself, authored works that embody the revolution of the age. Joseph, famous for his poem *The Enthusiast* (1744), devises a poem that comprises rich classical allusions with distinguished English elements: Versailles' gardens and its fountains are compared to the pine-topped precipices that, abrupt and shaggy, are near a foamy stream or some bleak heath (vv. 25-30); free English nature is then compared to artificial French nature. Reference to the Northern climate could not be clearer than in the mention of Boreas, the, ironically, Greek god of the North wind, who brings forth hollow winds near the sea where "wild Tempests swallow up the Plains, and

Boreas Blasts, big Hail, and Rains combine To shake the Grove and Mountains" (vv. 148-151), places where the poet likes to sit and watch, and where "The little Fayes that dance in neighbouring Dales, Sipping the Night-dew, while they laugh and love, Shall charm me with aërial notes" (vv. 173-75).

[104] Cf. Heinrich von Ofterdingen, a.k.a. Novalis ([1800] 1951*) Hymnen an die Nacht. Die Christenheit oder Europa* (Wiesbaden: Insel).

[105] Retrieved from: http://loki.stockton.edu/~kinsellt/projects/pom/pom.html 03.03.2017, ll. 201-10, my emphasis.

[106] For the instrumental role covered by T. Warton in the Elizabethan revival, see Earl R. Wasserman (1939) 'Henry Headley and the Elizabethan Revival', *Studies in Philology* (University of North Carolina Press), Vol. 36, No. 3 (July 1939), pp. 491-502.

[107] Cf. note 13, ch. 1 in this book.

[108] Burke takes care not to mention the sublime picturesque elements directly in his work. The only occurrence of the lemma appears in connection with the pictorial and descriptive understanding of the word, referring to the mental image (hypotyposis) that Virgil's description of the Cyclops at work, though sublime, fails to evoke, whereas it works in the description of the "fatal beauty" of Helena, cf. E. Burke, *Sublime*, op. cit., Section V, 5, 'Examples That Words May Affect Without Raising Images'.

[109] Cf. E. Burke, *Sublime*, Part 3, Section IV, 'Proportion Not the Cause of Beauty in the Human Species'.

[110] It took much longer to study ugliness on its own terms and this was done in the following century, when Karl Rosenkrantz proceeded to examine it in his work: (1990 [1853]) *Ästhetik des Hässlichen* (Leipzig: Reclam), but the book is mainly structured on a mere binary Manichaean overturning of the classical qualities of the beautiful reverted into disharmony, therefore the sublime comprises further and more important hues of the aesthetics of difficult interpretation.

[111] Holy because it is always linked to the numinous, being, for the Platonic aesthetics, condensed in the dictum: "Beauty is Goodness, and Goodness is Truth", which is God's extension and manifestation.

[112] It is not by chance this is also the century in which the Marquis De Sade's works appear. Cf. François Ost (2005) *Sade et la loi* (Paris: Odile Jacob).

[113] Let us only mention, to illustrate this, Manfred's attraction to his son's intended, Isabella, as an instance of a hidden element of pedophilia, in Horace Walpole's *The Castle of Otranto* (1764), or the copious erotic literature of the age, e.g. Cleland and Haywood, as canonically accepted testimonials.

[114] Cf. Matthew Gregory Lewis's devilish behaviour of the atheist Ambrose, the eponymous protagonist of *The Monk* (1795). See also David Punter (2001) *A Companion to the Gothic* (Hoboken: Wiley-Blackwell) and Wendy Jones (1990) 'Stories of Desire in the Monk', *ELH*, Vol. 57, No. 1, pp. 129-50.

[115] For the single elements, see my essays in my edited books on the topic where I have analysed this concept and its importance in various literary works: cf.

Bezrucka: 1995a 1995b, Bezrucka 1997, Bezrucka 1999a, 1999b, partly in Bezrucka: 2002.

[116] Cf. 'Taste' in Raymond Williams (1976) *Keywords. A Vocabulary of Culture and Society* (London: Fontana), pp. 313-15.

[117] See Y. Bezrucka (2016) 'Beehive-Images', op. cit.

[118] *ibid.*

[119] Locke, writing his *Letters Concerning Toleration* (1689–92), formulated a theory of religious tolerance to prevent religious wars. Three arguments are central: (1) Earthly judges, the State in particular, and human beings generally, cannot reliably evaluate the truth-claims of competing religious standpoints; (2) Even if they could, enforcing a single "true religion" would not have the desired effect because belief cannot be compelled by violence; (3) Coercing religious uniformity would lead to more social disorder rather than allowing diversity.

[120] Cf. Meyer H. Abrams (1971) *Natural Supernaturalism: Tradition and Revolution in Romantic Literature* (New York: Norton), p. 12, p. 65, 68.

[121] I consider the attack on innatism as the major and revolutionary move of the empiricist philosophers of England against the preceding systems of authority (Bezrucka: 2016).

[122] Cf. Gottfried Wilhelm Leibniz (1710) *Essais de Théodicée sur la bonté de Dieu, la liberté de l'homme et l'origine du mal*, En. tr.: *Essays of Theodicy on the Goodness of God, the Freedom of Man and the Origin of Evil.* Leibniz's treatise is intended to answer the question of whether a God exists or not, given that evil is present both in nature and in Man. He adopted an optimistic answer, directly taken over by Alexander Pope in the ending lapidary apothegm of his *Essay on Man:* "whatever is, is right". Leibniz's idea is that we are in the best world possible, even if – or just because – we can neither foresee nor participate in God's holistic eternal knowledge that always prevents further evil than that happening right now. Indeed, even Leibniz's *New Essays on Human Understanding,* written in 1704 but pub. posth. in 1764, cf. (1996 2nd ed.) (eds) Peter Remnant and Jonathan Bennett (New York: Cambridge University Press), is Leibniz's further attempt to defend innatism – the stronghold of the Design theory of the world, i.e. creationism – at the expense of John Locke's theory of the *tabula rasa* and the primacy of reason and experience, in his (1609) *An Essay Concerning Human Understanding*, op. cit.

[123] Cf. Bezrucka: 2002, pp. 118-23.

[124] 'Il postmodernismo: l'accettazione ironica del doppio senso' in Y. Bezrucka (ed.), *Tra passato e futuro. Assaggi di teoria dell'architettura*, Autem, Trento 1995, pp. 85-111.

[125] Not surprisingly, Lord Shaftesbury, in the early 18th century, had strongly insisted on the necessity of standards for matters concerning taste, intent as he was in defending the *status quo* of beauty, that he, with all Neoplatonists, considered an innate standard. See his (1714) *Miscellaneous Reflections*, III, 1.

[126] I have developed this 19th-century version of aesthetic regionalism in Y. Bezrucka, '"The Well-Beloved": Thomas Hardy's Manifesto of "Regional

Aesthetics"', *Victorian Literature and Culture*, 36.1, 2008, pp. 227-45.
[127] On this concept and its importance in various literary works: cf. Bezrucka: 1995a, 1995b, 1997, 1999a 1999b, and extensively in 2008a. See also R.M. Dainotto (2000) *Place in Literature. Regions, Cultures, Communities* (Ithaca, London: Cornell University Press) who reads regionalism as a new form of nationalism (p. 173).
[128] Francis Grose, 'Rules for Drawing Caricaturas: with an Essay on Comic Painting', in W. Hogarth, *The Analysis of Beauty*, Bagster, London s.d. (1791? [1753]), pp. 1-24, hereafter referred to as FG and p. no. Grose's work had appeared previously but anonymously in 1788, for the editors H. Grant and S. Hooper with the title *Rules for Drawing Caricaturas*.
[129] Oliver Goldsmith (1759) *An Enquiry into the State of Polite Learning in Europe* (London: Dodsley).
[130] J.G. Herder (1784) *Ideen zur Philofophie der Geschichte der Menschheit* (Riga, Leipzig: Kartknoch). See also R. Williams (1988 [1976]) *Keywords. A Vocabulary of Culture and Society* (London: Oxford University Press), pp. 87-93. See also Franco De Faveri 'Per una filosofia della sociologia. 'Gemeinschaft' und 'Gesellschaft' in prospettiva', in Y. Bezrucka (ed.) (1999) *Forme e caratteri del regionalismo*, op. cit., pp. 9-87; cf. also Tönnies Ferdinand (1969 [1887]) *Gemeinschaft und Gesellschaft. Grundbegriffe der reinen Soziologie* (Darmstadt: Wissenschaftliche Buchgesellschaft).
[131] Cornelius Tacitus (1894) *Tacitus The Agricola and Germania* (ed.) R.B. Townshend (London: Methuen & Co.).
[132] See Elie Kedourie (1960) *Nationalism* (Essex: Anchor Press), p. 63, a statement that would back up the translator/traitor theory; but in this case language is seen in essentialist terms, that is in a sort of nominalistic way, the way Swift makes fun of in his *Gulliver's Travels*.
[133] Oswald Spengler (1991 [1918]) *The Decline of the West* (eds) A. Helps, Helmut Werner (or. title: Der Untergang des Abendlandes, tr. C.F. Atkinson) (New York: Oxford University Press).
[134] Frederick Barth (ed.) (1969) *Ethnic Groups and Boundaries: The Social Organization of Cultural Difference* (Oslo, Tromso: Universitetsvorlaget), p. 12.
[135]Patrick J. Geary (2003) *The Myth of Nations: The Medieval Origins of Europe* (Princeton: Princeton University Press), hereafter referred to in the text as GP and p. no.
[136] Ernest Renan (1882) 'What is a Nation?' in H. Bhabha (ed.) (1990) *Nation and Narration* (London: Routledge), pp. 8-22, here 11, 19.
[137] Cf. M. McKeon (1987) *The Origins of the English Novel, 1600-1740* (Baltimore: John Hopkins University Press), p. 419.
[138] See Murray G.H. Pittock (1997) *Inventing and Resisting Britain. Cultural Identities in Britain and Ireland, 1685-1789* (London: Macmillan), p. 2, 6.
[139] Cf. D. Hume (1818 [1748 Bodl. edit. D]) 'Of National Characters' in *Essays Moral, Political and Literary* (eds) T.H. Greene, T.H. Grose (London: *sine ed.*),

vol. 1 of 2. He rather surprisingly hypothesises that "Such a uniform and constant difference could not happen, in so many countries and ages, *if nature had not made an original distinction* between these breeds of men" and his idea that "I am apt to suspect the negroes to be naturally inferior to the whites. There scarcely ever was a civilized nation of that complexion, nor even any individual eminent either in action or speculation. No ingenious manufactures amongst them, no arts, no sciences." (footnote 10 on I. XXI. 20). Nevertheless, we have also to underline that he opposed slavery strongly, as can be seen in vol. 2, in his essay 'Of the Populousness of Ancient Nations'.

[140] I. Kant (1991 [1764]) 'Of National Characteristics, so far as They Depend upon the Distinct Feeling of the Beautiful and Sublime', in *Observations on the Feeling of the Beautiful and Sublime* (tr. ed. John T. Goldthwait) (Berkeley: California University Press), pp. 97-116.

[141] *ibid.* pp. 110-111, where, in enraging terms, he claims that: "The Negroes of Africa have by nature no feeling that rises above the trifling. Mr. Hume challenges anyone to cite a single example in which a Negro has shown talents. (...) So fundamental is the difference between these two races [white/black] of man, and it appears to be as great in regard to mental capacities as in color."

[142] Nicholas Hudson (1996) 'From 'Nation' to 'Race': The Origin of Racial Classification in Eighteenth-Century Thought', *Eighteenth-Century Studies*, 29, 3, 247-264, hereafter referred to in the text with H: and p. no., p. 258.

[143] See my article, Y. Bezrucka (2011) 'Bio-Ethics Avant la Lettre: Nineteenth-Century Instances in Post-Darwinian Literature'. In D. Carpi (ed.) *Bioethics and Biolaw through Literature* (De Gruyter, Berlin), pp. 188-202, and Bezrucka (2008a).

[144] Cf. R. Kipling's poem (1899) 'The White Man's Burden: The United States and the Philippine Islands', *McClure's Magazine*, 12, 4, 290-91.

[145] Let us only be reminded of the classifications important institutions, such as, for example, the Musée de l'Homme in Paris, adopted in grading art according to debatable criteria and captions that presented works of art as "primitive" forms of art, definitions which presuppose that there are more "advanced" art forms that are holistically seen along an evolutionary scale. Having adopted an embarassing, to say the least, rationale of classification, the Musée was closed and has only recently been reopened: its ethnographic art works are now present in the Musée du Quai Branly, which follows a completely different master-logic.

CHAPTER FIVE

MYTHOLOGISING ORIGINS

5.1 Welsh Bards and the Saxon-Gothic

In 1740, the Warton brothers decided to reform English poetry and, to this end, published a series of poems that was to become exemplary for a new kind of taste. The titles of the poems are self-evident: *The Enthusiast, or The Lover of Nature* (published in 1744 and reviewed in 1748), *Ode to Fancy* (published in 1746 and reviewed in 1748) written by Joseph Warton, and *The Pleasures of Melancholy* (published in 1747 and reviewed in 1755) written by Thomas Warton. With their unquestionable *ante litteram* emphasis on personal reception and emotions, they signal a marked attention to feelings, nature, and the British past, features that would later be called Romantic.

The Wartons promoted a distinguished brand of 18th-century aesthetics, freed from the previous Neoclassical fetters, that focused attention on characteristic local elements in England, e.g. Stonehenge. They wanted poetry to express precisely this Gothic regional character, aiming to facilitate the emancipation from the Greek and Roman aesthetics that they felt inadequate for the British environment and not representative of English libertarian prerogatives. These issues are, indeed, given an unprecedented emphasis in the first *History of English Poetry* (4 vols.),[1] published from 1774 to 1781 by Thomas Warton, where the author defines what English poetry should be. This was the first history of poetry ever written in England, which bore witness to a perceived need to study the past to fix its evolution and envisage its distinct cultural heritage for the present and the future. Because of this, it is deserving of close study, since it can be considered the first attempt at creating an English canon. Marking the Elizabethan age as the "most Poetical age of these annals" (TW: III, 490), Thomas Warton wanted English poetry to resume "the predominancy of fable, of fiction, and fancy, and a predilection for interesting adventures and pathetic events" (TW: III, 491), elements he saw, in their anti-classical features, capable of exciting the mind with a wealth of possibilities rather than pacifying it, a capacity that should not be overshadowed by the reverence exercised by the best models. These are emotions Thomas Warton considered to also be neglected by the new enlightened scientific orientation that, if it had abolished popish "impostures" in taking away "the mantle of mystery" from religion (TW: III, 491),[2] it had also taken it away from poetry. He therefore highlights, in the early medieval imaginative poetry inspired by chivalric and folklore elements, a use of the imagination, which was later confirmed through the oriental influences this literature absorbed after the Saracen, Arabian, invasion in Spain (8th c.):

> That peculiar and arbitrary species of Fiction which we commonly call Romantic, was entirely unknown to the writers of Greek and Rome. It appears to have been imported into Europe by a people, whose modes of thinking, and habits of invention, are not natural to that country. It is generally supposed to have been borrowed from the Arabians. But this origin has not been hitherto perhaps examined or ascertained with a sufficient degree of accuracy. It is my present design, by a more distinct and extended inquiry than has yet been applied to the subject, to trace the manner and the period of its introduction into the popular belief, the oral poetry, and the literature of the Europeans. It is an established maxim of modern criticism, that the fictions of Arabian imagination were communicated to the western world by means of the crusades. Undoubtedly those expeditions greatly contributed to propagate this mode of fabling in Europe. But it is evident, although a circumstance which certainly makes no material difference as to the principles here established that these fancies were introduced at a much earlier period. (TW: I, 1-2)

The earlier literature, before the Orient-inflected one Warton refers to, is the Romantic chivalric literature of England, produced by the Celtic bards of Cornwall and Wales, regions united by their common Welsh language, peoples who established themselves in "Armorica of Basse Bretagne, now Brittany" (TW: I, 3) in the 4th century to escape the "Roman yoke".

Warton sees these bards as poets belonging to the mythical Court of King Arthur, implanted in Armorica by their chiefs, Maximus and the Prince of Meiriadoc. To support his point, he quotes Milton attesting the same tradition: "What resounds // In fable or romance, of Uther's son [King Arthur] // Begirt with BRITISH and ARMORIC knights" (TW: I, 4). In a note to his text, Warton states:

> The secession of the Welsh, at so critical a period, was extremely natural, into a neighbouring maritime country, with which they had constantly trafficked, and which, like themselves, had disclaimed the Roman yoke. It is not related in any Greek or Roman historian. But their silence is by no means a sufficient warrant for us to reject the numerous testimonies of the

> old British writers concerning this event. It is mentioned, in particular, by Llywarchen, a famous bard, who lived only one hundred and fifty years afterwards. Many of his poems are still extant, in which he celebrates his twenty-four sons who wore gold chains, and were all killed in battles against the Saxons. (TW: I, 4)

From the information provided, we understand that Warton sees Arthur as being a Welsh or Cornish Briton, a member of the people living in Britain before the arrival of the Romans and the Saxons, thus as being a Celt.

Warton is very modern in his approach to this issue because, as we shall see, he tries to interpret history in a non-static, non-foundational way, avoiding, as far as he is able, using the grand myths of history. Consequently, he revises the whole question of origins under the almost unascertainable complicated results of the scattered migration and diaspora that cannot be grouped in the usual national histories.[3] This perspective, besides Rinaker's claim that Warton was the initiator of "historical criticism",[4] makes him also a culturalist in the true sense of the term, in that he favours migration-of-cultures theories over single-nation foundational ones:[5]

> Nor will it prove less necessary to our purpose to observe, that the Cornish Britons, whose language was another dialect of the antient British, from the fourth or fifth century downwards, maintained a no less intimate correspondence with the natives of Armorica: intermarrying with them, and perpetually resorting thither for the education of their children, for advice, for procuring troops against the Saxons, for the purposes of traffick, and various other occasions. This connection was so strongly kept up, that an ingenious French antiquary supposes, that the communications of the Armoricans with the Cornish had chiefly contributed to give a roughness or rather hardness to the romance or French language in some of the provinces, towards the eleventh century, which was not before discernible. (TW: I, 4-5)[6]

He then continues:

> And this intercourse will appear more natural, if we consider, that not only Armorica, a maritime province of Gaul, never much frequented by the Romans, and now totally deserted by them, was still in some measure a Celtic nation; but that also the inhabitants of Cornwall, together with those of Devonshire and of the adjoining parts of Somersetshire, intermixing in a very slight degree with the Romans, and having suffered fewer important alterations in their original constitution and customs from the imperial laws and police than any other province of this island, long preserved their genuine manners and British character: and forming a sort of separate

> principality under the government of a succession of powerful chieftains, usually denominated princes or dukes of Cornwall, remained partly in a state of independence during the Saxon heptarchy, and were not entirely reduced till the Norman conquest. Cornwall, in particular, retained its old Celtic dialect till the reign of Elizabeth. (TW: I, 5)

The close relationship between Wales and Cornwall is upheld by facts: "their languages, customs and alliances (...) were the same (...) Cornwall is frequently styled as West-Wales by the British writers. (...) We find the Welsh and Cornish, as one people, often uniting themselves as in a national cause against the Saxons." (TW: I, 6)

Warton, therefore, conjectures that the Welsh "fictions (…) literally found in the tales and chronicles of the elder Welsh bards" (TW: I, 6) were passed over from England into the French romances and not the other way around. This he bases on the fact that Cornwall and Wales figure so prominently in the French romances: "Cornwall (...) is made the scene of so many romantic adventures" (TW: I, 6), which would also explain the tradition of "*romantic* castles, rocks, rivers, and caves" (TW: I, 7), *par excellence* anti-classical elements, that they brought to France:

> It is difficult to ascertain exactly the period at which our translator's original romance may probably be supposed to have been compiled. (...). I am inclined to think that the work consists of fables thrown out by different rhapsodists at different times, which afterwards were collected and digested into an entire history, and perhaps with new decorations of fancy added by the compiler, who most probably was one of the professed bards, or rather a poetical historian, of Armorica or Basse Bretagne. In this state, and under this form, I suppose it to have fallen into the hands of Geoffrey of Monmouth. If the hypothesis hereafter advanced concerning the particular species of fiction on which this narrative is founded, should be granted, it cannot, from what I have already proved, be more antient than the eighth century: and we may reasonably conclude, that it was composed much later, as some considerable length of time must have been necessary for the propagation and establishment of that species of fiction. The simple subject of this chronicle, divested of its romantic embellishments, is a deduction of the Welsh princes from the Trojan Brutus to Cadwallader, who reigned in the seventh century. This notion of their extraction from the Trojans had so infatuated the Welsh, that even so late as the year 1284, archbishop Peckham, in his injunctions to the diocese of St. Asaph, orders the people to abstain from giving credit to idle dreams and visions, a superstition which they had contracted from their belief in the dream of their founder Brutus, in the temple of Diana, concerning his arrival in Britain. The archbishop very seriously advises them to boast no more of their relation to the conquered and fugitive Trojans, but to glory in the victorious cross of Christ. (TW: I, 9)

Warton's hypothetical *stemma codicum* also explains why from Armorica, in the year 1100, Gualter, archdeacon of Oxford, brings back to England the *Bruty-Brenhined*, or *The History of the Kings of Britain,*[7] handing it over, written in "British or Armorican language", to the Benedictine monk Geoffrey of Monmouth, who would later translate it into Latin as the *Historia Regum Britanniae,* which, according to Warton, he finished in the year 1138 (TW: I, 7-8), a date confirmed by recent research.[8] The genealogical derivation of the Welsh princes from the Trojan Brutus to Cadwallader rests thus on this work and was used by the House of Stuart for their claim to the throne.

Warton, as seen, fully conscious of the difficulty to ascertain the hypotext of the chronicle, takes into consideration other genetic theories. He appears aware of the possibility that these can be used and manipulated as dangerous identity proofs, what we today would call "invented traditions" *à la* Hobsbawm.[9] At first, given that Geoffrey of Monmouth refers to Hengist's burial as having been carried out in "the manner of the SOLDANS (...) partly an argument that our romance was composed about the time of the crusades" (TW: 1, 13), he seems inclined to think that the "chronicle, supposed to contain the ideas of the Welsh bards, entirely consists of Arabian inventions" (TW: I, 13). This would lead to the claim that the chronicle had been written between the 9th and the 11th centuries, and not before, but some elements that appear to have a derivation from the 11th century are rejected for being "an artful interpolation of the translator, who was an ecclesiastic" (TW: I, 11).

The complexity of the origin of the chronicle seems to tell us that Warton, a Whig, is trying to impede the Stuart family's claim to the throne – and that of Catholics in general – which had seen a resurgence in the 1715 and 1745 Jacobite Risings, ending with the Battle of Culloden (1746). Indeed, Stuart propaganda claimed their right to the throne through their descent from the just and fair King Arthur and his presumed ancestry from the Roman Brutus and from Brutus linking back to Æneas. Focusing on the use that Stuart artists made of this myth, V. Hart says: "Arthurian mythology and the magical feats of Merlin were represented as foretelling the virtues of Stuart rulers and their accord with the harmony of the heavens",[10] creating what Hart (1994:33) defines as a veritable "Arthurian Neoplatonism". Furthermore, they confirm the union of Neoplatonism and the Church. But the fact is that the Whigs were doing the same, using the myth for their own ends, as Warton confirms, in establishing for King Arthur a merely Celtic tradition used to change the history of English literature and to find a Celtic origin for the Constitutional Monarchy. This was done notwithstanding the acceptance of an Arabian engrafting: "the native vein of British fabling had been tinctured by (...) fairy tales which the Arabian had propagated in Armorica, and which the Welsh had received from the connection with that province of Gaul" (TW: I, 63), tales which in the most ancient Welsh bards do not appear.[11] These "wonders of oriental fiction" being continuously reworked "by troubadours and minstrels (...) centred about the eleventh century in the ideal stories of Turpin and Geoffrey of Monmouth, which record the supposititious achievements of Charlemagne and King Arthur, where they formed the ground-work of that species of fabulous narrative called romance", that were later used by the Italian poets and "their disciple Spenser" (TW: I, 72).

Thomas Warton, therefore, claims a new English *stemma codicum* both for the romances both of England and France, deriving the French tradition of the romances from the "fictions, literally found in the tales and chronicles of the elder Welsh bards" (TW: I, 6), and not vice versa. In so doing, Warton supports the counter-tradition of the chthonic, magical and non-assertive link to the home*land* Celtic tradition – which, as we have seen, implied the constitutional, lawful monarchy.[12] He then uses the recently published Percy's *Reliques of Ancient Poetry* (1767) to his advantage:[13] "[a late ingenious critic [T. Percy][14] has advanced an hypothesis, which assigns a new source, and a much earlier to these fictions. (...) 'Our old romances of chivalry may be derived in a LINEAL DESCENT from the ancient historical songs of the Gothic bards and scalds (...) of the north'" (TW: I, 22).

Not only that; quoting Percy, he says: "[m]any of those songs are still preserved in the north, which exhibit all the seeds of chivalry before it became a solemn institution" (*ibid.*). He adds that even the common arbitrary fictions of romance were familiar to these ancient scalds, long before the oriental influence established itself at the time of the crusades: "They believed the existence of giants and dwarfs, they had some notion of fairies, they were strongly possessed with the belief of spells and inchantment, and were fond of inventing combats with dragons and monsters" (*ibid.*). This is a tradition that Warton says is confirmed by the French critic Mallet in his introduction to the *Histoire de Danemarc*:[15]

> Can we not explain from the Gothic religion (...) how, even to the present age, the people are still infatuated with a belief of the power of magicians, witches, spirits, and genii, concealed under the earth or in the waters? Do we not discover in these religious opinions, that source of the marvellous with which our ancestors filled their romances; in which we see dwarfs and giants, fairies and demons, &c. (...) The fortresses of the Goths were only rude castles situated on the summits of rocks, and rendered inaccessible by

> thick misshapen walls. As these walls ran winding round the castles, they often called them by a name which signified SERPENTS or DRAGONS; and in these they usually secured the women and young virgins of distinction, who were seldom safe at a time when so many enterprising heroes were rambling up and down in search of adventures. It was this custom which gave occasion to antient romancers, who knew not how to describe any thing simply, to invent so many fables concerning princesses of great beauty guarded by dragons, and afterwards delivered by invincible champions. (TW: I, 23).

Warton, thus, points out the similarities of the Eastern and Northern traditions of the imagination, deconstructing clear-cut oppositions (civility/barbarity) concluding with the supposition that, due to migrations and diaspora, "all Europe was originally peopled from the east" (TW: I, 28), and by remarking that our ideas of Odin's Goths' barbarism is only due to "prejudices [that] have hastily formed concerning the character of all rude nations" (TW: I, 29), having brought to Scandinavia a poetry rich in heroes, pagan superstitions, capricious spirits of extravagance and bold eccentric conceptions "which so strongly distinguish the old northern poetry" (TW: I, 29).

Warton then comments on dichotomies, using the Orientalists' language against Orientalist thought, as if he were applying Said's categories and his critique before its time (Said 1976). Quoting what Hugh Blair says in his *Dissertation on Ossian*: "A most ingenious critic observes, that what we have been long accustomed to call the ORIENTAL VEIN of poetry, because some of the EARLIEST poetical productions have come to us from the east, is probably no more ORIENTAL than OCCIDENTAL."[16] He then continues:

> But all the LATER oriental writers through all ages have been particularly distinguished for this VEIN. Hence it is here characteristical of a country not of an age. I will allow, on this writer's very just and penetrating principles, that an early northern ode shall be as sublime as an eastern one. Yet the sublimity of the latter shall have a different character; it will be more inflated and gigantic. Nor is this fantastic imagery, the only mark of Asiaticism which appears in the Runic odes. They have a certain sublime and figurative cast of diction, which is indeed one of their predominant characteristics. (TW: I, 30)

The Goths "might have added a darker shade and a more savage complexion to their former fictions and superstitions; and that the formidable objects of nature to which they became familiarised in those northern solitudes, the piny precipices, the frozen mountains, and the gloomy forests, acted on their imaginations, and gave a tincture of horror to their imagery" (TW: I, 31).

This provides Warton the opportunity to set the Northern genealogy for the English tradition besides that of "Britain (...) originally peopled from Gaul, a nation of the Celts" (TW: I, 33), "through an hypothesis equally rational, and not altogether destitute of historical evidence" that "many colonies from the northern parts of Europe were afterwards successively planted in Britain and the neighbouring islands" *(ibid.)*, a hypothesis he considers to be confirmed by the fact that the Picts and Scutes, peoples from Norway, had conquered Scotland and Ireland (*ibid.*), thus completing his theory of the northerly origin of Arthur's myth.

The catalogue of images on which Thomas Warton focuses is that of Gothic poetry, of the fairy way of writing, of the Gothic novel, and in general that of the northern tour. He concludes that the medieval age that finds its cypher in the Gothic should not be considered barbaric but only different (read Northern) and, conversely, that Northern elements have a right to an aesthetics of their own.

These characteristics are then linked to the Gothic architectural style, the anti-classical style. As critics have noted, the Warton brothers' poetry, and I am not referring to the poems directly dedicated to King Arthur, would all, in their revisions, become more Gothic and, by extension, more Northern, indicative of the direction Thomas Warton wanted poetry to go. Indeed, the Elizabethan Age is for Warton one of transition, characterised by the fusion of imagination and reason.[17] It evolved into the more rational poetry of the 18th century, which, despite its Romantic tendency, is still not Romantic enough. Warton promotes further Romanticisation, changes he had already adopted in his poetry, years before writing *The History of English Poetry*. A. Fenner writes:

> Between the editions of 1744 and 1748 'The Enthusiast' is altered significantly in nine places. Joseph Warton has inserted "ruin'd tops of Gothic battlements" into the wild landscape he contrasts with the gardens of Versailles; and he has added considerable detail to a picture of the noble savages in the new world, where he longs to go and live (36-37, 236-241) (...) The goddess Contemplation, to whom the poet speaks throughout, has moved in the revision from a mansion to a grotto. A sacred tower becomes a wasted tower, fabled banks become winding marge; embroider'd meads are altered to ye broider'd (...) and painted landscapes to daedal (2, 37, 256, 27, 248). The gothic grotto and wasted tower, here, would seem to speak for themselves, as clearly as does the Augustan favourite, painted, which the poet discarded.[18]

Compared to the 1747 version, the 1755 edition of *The Pleasures of*

Melancholy has, as its characterising trait, a "sensationally gothic" atmosphere, clearly aiming at "romanticiz[ing] his poem".[19]

Warton's pre-Burkean poems provide us with the opportunity to follow the change from a classical, mechanical, pastoral and clichéd reception of nature to the private interpretation of nature seen in the melancholic intensity of "the Eye of the Beholder", as Addison, with his ingenious paraphrase, indicated. The discriminatory element is the emphasis that is now set on the specific difference of the English environment. Topographically, these peculiarities were later to be identified in the Gothic architecture, in the picturesque, and in the sublime disquieting natural elements such as tempests and storms, manifestations that outweigh rationality, events that in eschewing immediate recognition, make people, for the time being, concentrate on their immediate sense perception. What would, however, be constantly underlined is the beholder's focus on that sensual perception promoted by Locke and Addison. As we have seen, it is the mark of the modern emancipation from models and fetters that led to those 'romantic' shifts in literature, fostered by, and parallel to what, the empiricist outlook had produced in philosophy: the necessity of grounding theories on material proofs. Gilpin's picturesque and Burke's sublime, in leaving to autonomous and private definition what these emotions were, followed suit: inviting the percipients to analyse their own sensory-experiences in such a way as to become more aware of their surroundings and of themselves. The Domestic Tour, such as, for example, Tobias George Smollett's fictional version in his *The Expedition of Humphry Clinker* (1771) with its devotion to people and places, and Laurence Sterne's revision of the Grand Tour in *A Sentimental Journey through France and Italy* (1768) devoted only to people, represent the literary climax of two different sensory-experiences.

Also, Warton's need for "pathetic events" (TW: III, 491) is far from the formal, restrained and contained subjects and styles of Neoclassicism as they were pursued at the beginning of the century, and which would progressively be shunned by the emotional and even pathetic apperceptions, or by what we today would define affective, enigmatic emotions, capable of subjugating the spirit with surprise, disquiet, wonder and curiosity rather than the final catharsis, harmony and equilibrium typical of the comforting aesthetics of beauty. These different emotions are not reassuring confirmations that the *status quo*, if properly checked, contained and repressed, still works as common-sense *stasis* would have. Indeed, Warton, who translates this attitude into literary terms, finds that the "inundation of classical pedantry [which was coming from the translations of the classics rather than the originals] soon infected (...)

poetry (...) producing extravagancies (...) pursued to a blameable excess" (TW: III, 494).

In fact, it was exactly the contrary that followed, in that it was the need for "real life and manners" provided by the Italian tales of Boiardo, Ariosto and Tasso that eventually usurped "the place of legends and chronicles" as these were tailored for "a more discerning and curious age" (TW: III, 495-96), so much so that also the "rugged features of the original Gothic romance were softened (...) engrafted on the feudal manners in Sydney's *Arcadia*" (TW: III, 496). If science requested realism, religion and the Reformation, on the other hand, still exerted an influence, upholding the system of the spirits. Science

> had not yet destroyed every delusion, nor disenchanted all the strong holds of superstition (...) Every goblin of ignorance did not vanish at the first glimmerings of the morning of science. Reason suffered a few demons still to linger, which she chose to retain in her service under the guidance of poetry. Men believed or were willing to believe, that spirits were yet hovering around (...) that fairies imprinted mysterious circles on the turf by moonlight. (...) Prospero had not yet broken and buried his staff (TW: III, 496).

A thoroughly rational outlook, he admits, would not have allowed an artist like Shakespeare: "The Shakespeare of a more instructed and polished age, would not have given us a magician darkening the sun at noon, the Sabbath of the witches and the cauldron of incantation" (TW: III, 496).

Speaking of the Gothic romance, Warton sees it maintaining its ground, notwithstanding the onslaught of classical fictions, the tales of Boccaccio and Bandello and the daring "machineries of giants, dragons, and enchanted castles, borrowed by the magic storehouse of Boiardo, Ariosto and Tasso, [that] began to be employed by the epic muse"; these were machineries "censured by the bigotry of precise and servile critics (...) abounding in whimsical absurdities and unwarrantable deviations from the practice of Homer and Virgil" (TW: III, 497).

Warton therefore justifies magic – the utopian *'as if'* world of the imagination – connecting it with the original classics: the floating of Spenser's Lady of the Lake reminds him of Neptune, Ariel makes him imagine a sea-nymph and the witches of Macbeth conjure Hecate. He concludes that masques and pageantries formed a "national taste for allegory", which in the *Fairy Queene* is wrought upon chivalry (TW: III, 498), producing a moralising effect. In contrast to these elements:

> the old historical songs of the minstrels contained much bold adventure, heroic enterprise, and strong touches of rude delineation, yet they failed in

> that multiplication and disposition of circumstances and in that description of character and events approaching nearer to truth and reality which where demanded by a more discerning and curious age. (TW: III, 495-96)

As we have seen so far, Warton's literary history discredits the prejudice regarding the supposed barbarity of the Northern peoples, in particular, of Odin's Goths in Scandinavia, contradicted – so he observes – by their rich, different and unusual poetical production, and influenced by their environment rich in Gothic elements (TW: I, 24-26). Referring to their "circus" tradition, Warton underlines the fact that "judiciary combats [judicial duels], and proofs by the ordeal" have astonishingly passed into the legislature of Europe (TW: I, 23), which bespeaks negatively only of the countries that admitted it, besides being a shorthand reference to Warton's contemporaries that would remind people of the *autodafé* trials and verdicts of the Inquisition. Having pointed out the abuses of religion for the elimination of enemies, he then makes his point about what aspects of the "Runic theology" have "to this day [been] retained" (TW: I, 35) and what has persisted as superstitions about spectres and spirits and of the Gothic religion in the northern lands: "even to the present age, the people are still infatuated with a belief of the power of magicians, witches, spirits, and genii, concealed under the earth or in the waters (...) Do we not discover in these religious opinions, that source of the marvellous with which our ancestors filled their romances, in which we see dwarfs and giants, fairies and demons" (TW: I, 23). To the judiciary combats of German origins he also links the "amphitheatrical circus of rude stones", and the Northern and Gothic anti-classical architectural artefacts (TW: I, 23 n.). These bespoke a style that was appropriated and cyphered by the antiquarians of the age, in the Saxon-Gothic mode, and set, as we have seen in Gilpin, side by side with the proudly national, free English environment and garden style.

Warton then looks at the genealogy of the peoples of the island:

> That Britain was originally peopled from Gaul, a nation of the Celts, is allowed: but that many colonies from the northern parts of Europe were afterwards successively planted in Britain and neighbouring islands, is an hypothesis equally rational, and not altogether destitute of historical evidence. Nor was any nation more likely that the Scandinavian Goths (...) to make descents on Britain (...) As to Scotland and Ireland, there is the highest probability, that the Scutes, who conquered both those countries, and possessed them under the names of Albin Scutes and Irin Scutes, were a people of Norway. The Caledonians are expressly called by many judicious antiquaries a Scandinavian colony. The names of places and persons, over all that part of Scotland which the Picts inhabited are of

> Scandinavian extraction. A simple catalogue of them only, would immediately convince us, that they are not of Celtic, or British origin. (TW: I, 33)

All this being "obscure and complicated" (TW: I, 33-34), the author adopts, wisely, a migration standpoint that focuses on the regionalist identities present in the non-organic nation.

It is now time to look at these apparently merely cultural operations from another point of view. To use the past for scientific ends is one thing, but to use and invent and claim one specific descent rather than another is something entirely different. It is important to bear in mind the fact that the synergy against what felt like a foreign intrusion was fostered by aestheticians and literary writers who wanted to recover their freedom to create whatever work of art they wished, without having to pay homage to the acquired Southern tradition. Nevertheless, the appeal created by the lure of a mythical origin for one's derivation as a people soon made itself felt and politicians saw advantage in using it, as we have seen, particularly the Stuart family, which claimed their Arthurian origin and in the 18th century still insisted that they were kings anointed by God.

We can now set the panorama we have been forming so far into its proper frame and perspective. Real origins and mythological ones are difficult to trace and, being set in the past, can easily be interpolated (Ossian's textual history *docet*).[20] It is therefore useful to quote a scholar who has studied the topic thoroughly. Patrick J. Geary, in his book *The Myth of Nations*,[21] speaking of the pseudo-history on which nationalism – and, we could add, literary nationalism – is founded, writes:

> A historian (...) who listens to the rhetoric of nationalist leaders, and who reads the scholarship produced by official or quasi official historians, is immediately struck by how central the interpretation of the period from circa 400-1000 is to this debate. Suddenly, the history of Europe over a millennium ago is anything but academic: the interpretation of the period of the dissolution of the Roman Empire and the barbarian migration has become the fulcrum of political discourse across much Europe. (GP: 7)

The demagogic manipulation of history by politicians or historians – a retrospective, selective and fully eristic manoeuvre – is thus often based on the voluntary amnesia of the processes of ethnogenesis and migrations, which, as Patrick J. Geary says – and as our reading of Warton's *History of English Poetry* has demonstrated – are "easy prey for ethnic nationalist propaganda" (GP: 9).[22]

Ethnic issues, nevertheless, if seen rightly, are only the result of waves of migrations: engrafting of peoples on peoples to produce new peoples.

Keeping this in mind, "conscious nationalism and racism" can only be disdained. Pseudo-history, choosing one single perspective amidst the variety of possible ones, assumes,

> first, that the peoples of Europe are distinct, stable and objectively identifiable social and cultural units and the they are distinguished by language, religion, custom, and national character, which are unambiguous and immutable. These peoples were supposedly formed either in some impossibly remote moment of prehistory, or else the process of ethnogenesis took place at some moment during the Middle Ages, but then ended for all time. (...) Implicit in these claims is that there was a moment of "primary acquisition" (...) which established once and for all the geographical limits of legitimate ownership of land. (GP: 11-12)

Cultural appropriation was systematically pursued in England in the 18th century when a distinguished English tradition, an Anglo-Saxonism that marginalised the Welsh and the Irish, was created – a tradition that is nowadays received – and was helped in its establishment by literature, and this is our particular contention, through the King Arthur myth: used both by the Stuart kings and their Whig opponents, who, in the end, via the Glorious Revolution and the constitutional monarchy, were able to prevail and oust the Catholic family from kingship. Indeed, a 'French' Revolution had already taken place in England with the Commonwealth and the beheading of Charles I.

As Patrick Geary demonstrates, Europeans proudly trace their national identities to some peoples of the past (Celts, Franks, Gauls, Goths, Huns or Serbs), or to some other imaginary ethnic core, without acknowledging that the idea of a national character, fixed once and for all in a distant past, is a historical misinterpretation of the truth, which is more typically a story of simple displacement, dislocation, miscegenation and successive engrafting of peoples and their cultural characters.

Geary dismantles nationalist myths when looking at the history of Europe's transformation during the period of the grand migrations, these being the real drive, as is still true today, behind their 'histories':

> The Celts, another Indo-European people (...) spreading from what is today Czechoslovakia, Austria, and southern Germany and Switzerland to Ireland in the sixth century B.C.E., pushing back, absorbing, or eradicating the indigenous European population until the only survivors were the Basques of southern France and northern Spain. From the first century B.C.E., Germanic peoples began pushing the Celts from the east to the Rhine, but they and the Celts confronted a different invader, the expanding Roman Empire which conquered and Romanized much of Europe as it did Asia

> Minor and North Africa. New migrations of Germanic and Central Asian peoples began in the third century, eventually replacing the Roman imperial system with a mosaic of separate kingdoms. In the East, bands of Slavs filtered into the Alps, the Carpathian Basin, the Balkans and Greece. The last major population influxes of the first millennium were the arrival of the Magyars in the Danubian plain and the Scandinavians in Normandy and Northern England. (PG: 10)

Ultimately, Geary concludes, the actual formation of European peoples is an extended and ongoing process that began in antiquity and continues, unceasingly, in the present. If rightly understood, this perspective undermines all attempts to reduce the complexities of many centuries to a single, eternal, foundational moment that can cancel out history and regionalisms. Nevertheless, this is exactly what had happened in 18th-century Great Britain, as we have detailed in its consequences,[23] and which is still happening even nowadays in many European countries.

5.2 *The Faerie Queene*, King Arthur and the Celtic Tradition: Hughes, Thomas Warton, Hurd, Walpole and Percy

The counter-move to Southern aesthetics found one of its privileged means and vehicles in the celebration of the architectural (and literary) Gothic tradition. The attack proceeded systematically via the ennoblement of the harsher, bulky, muscular styles of the North that were in formal terms interpreted as visual symbols of democracy, in open contrast to the rigidity of Neoclassical symmetrical architecture. The attack was pursued, as far as I can ascertain for the first time in history, by applying the formal elements of Saxon-Gothic architecture for the interpretation of the sister art of literature.

This was not the only means: another important onslaught, although not highlighted enough among the established traditions of the 18th century, against the Southern aesthetics,[24] is the presence of a distinguished literary Celtic counter-tradition. This tradition goes hand in hand with a political Whig one (Anglo: 1961, Hart: 1994) established, as we have already seen, in Addison's defence of the fairy way of writing and in the recovery of Spenser's *Faerie Queene*.

In this chapter, we will thus examine how literary critics, scholars and antiquarians applied the Saxon-Gothic architectural style – the English pre-Norman architecture – to interpret the sublime structural unity of Spenser's *Faerie Queene,* a work that assumes an instrumental role for the recovery and creation of an autochthonous English tradition. Indeed, if examined through the lenses of the Southern aesthetics, *The Faerie Queene,* along with Shakespeare's plays, had been belittled and disparaged despite its originality.

Along with Thomas Warton's *History of English Poetry* (1774-1781), which can be read as an *a posteriori* justification for the Gothic elements he used in his poem *The Pleasures of Melancholy* (1747), we need first to examine the philosophical defence of the Gothic architectural style present in *An Essay on Original Genius* (1767), written by William Duff.[25]

In this work, Duff justifies the "uncommon design" and the "stupendous Gothic structures" (WD: 256, 257) by matching to them the characteristics Burke had ascribed to the sublime, i.e. presenting an: "[a]wful, though irregular grandeur, which elevates the mind, and produces the most pleasing astonishment" (WD: 257).[26] Justifying irregularity, he also endorses the formulation of Gilpin's theory of the picturesque.

In 1762, five years before Duff's study, some relevant works on Gothic architecture had already appeared: Horace Walpole's *Anecdotes of Painting in England* (1662-1771),[27] and before that, in 1754, the *Observations on the Faerie Queene* by Thomas Warton, which offers a partial critique of the *gothicness* of the work.[28] The essays on the Gothic in *Anecdotes*, in addition to making Walpole the central figure of the medievalism of that century, are considered to be the first British attempt to also outline the aesthetics of the literary Gothic that, one would presume, he also applied in his novel *The Castle of Otranto* (1764). In a chapter dedicated to architecture and architects, Walpole first qualifies his critical stance towards the Ancients: "Rules prevent faults but they prevent improvement also" (HW5: 159), then championing Gothic architecture for "the gloom, ornaments, magic of the hardiness of the building", which he prefers to "the simplicity of the Grecian" (HW5: 159), and for their reference "to old knights, crusades, the wars of York or Lancaster, &c" (HW5: 158).

Hardiness and the knights are considered in relation to the Gothic, balanced by Walpole's ironic reference to the use the church makes of the style: "Mr. Chute thinks gothic buildings were designed by bishops and monks, who from observing the effect of the gloom of their convents, applied it to churches" (HW5: 160). The Gothic is thus defined as pliable, meaning it is "different in every country, which shows it formed itself in each, and was not imported from any peculiar country" (HW5: 160). It is therefore the result of space-time-specific cultures, a claim made as if to prevent the French from saying that the English have adopted theirs. Furthermore, the Gothic is, in his view, masculine; it becomes feminine, according to his debatable gendered parameters, only in comparison with the Elizabethan manors, whose style was only defensive: "To that style succeeded the richness and delicacy of the Gothic."[29]

Warton, Walpole and Thomas Gray make 1762 the *annus mirabilis* for the beginning of the Gothic Revival, being scholars and poets cited by Kenneth Clark as the founders of the Gothic Revival that would flourish with the Gothic perpendicular of the 19th century, promoted by architect A.W.N. Pugin.[30] Nevertheless, there is an important distinction to be drawn here: the recovery of the Saxon-Gothic in the 18th century has to be necessarily linked to its reference to the Druids and the Celtic tradition, whereas Pugin's aim was to link an already established English tradition to a High Church Catholic revival, i.e. an attempted, and successful, religious re-appropriation.

This gives us the opportunity to clarify the complicated relationship between a) Gothic architecture – read and used by antiquarians as the original pre-Norman, Saxon or better Anglo-Saxon architectural style of England; b) the Gothic novel as the vehicle of an anti-Catholic and, in general, anti-authoritarian and anti-monotheistic standpoint; and c) the Gothic Revival, which represented the authoritarian response of the High Church of England.

Mark Canuel, a scholar who has concentrated his attention on the topic of religion in Gothic novels,[31] has widely demonstrated that the Gothic novel represents a *topos* for the discussion of religion in literature, which he analyses in Ann Radcliff's novels. We have already analysed the attack on religion in de Mandeville's *magnus opum* (Bezrucka: 2016), but we could also add Bentham's *Church of Englandism and its Catechism Examined* (1818),[32] which underlines the fact that "the demand for religious uniformity either eliminated persons from any political or civil identity whatsoever, or produced the 'mendacity and insincerity' that religious uniformity purported to avoid (Bentham XXI)" (Canuel 1995: 511). To this we could add the reference to Richard Prices's belief in the "importance of religious belief in the consolidation of all nations" (Canuel 1995: 511). But Thomas Warton also has clear anti-Catholic traits when, for example, he speaks of "the barbarism of the Catholic worship, and the doctrines of scholastic theology" (TW3: 495) at the shows for Anne Boleyn's coronation, or when he directly links papal authority to the persistence of superstition (TW: 1, 287-308, in part. 295, 308).

Coming back to the *Fairie Queene*, to the works already mentioned we must add Richard Hurd's *Letters on Chivalry and Romance* (1762).[33] Hurd's work applies the Gothic design to literature, using architecture and its form as a reference for poetic structure, drawing an analogy that had already been used by another scholar, John Hughes.

Since Richard Hurd's analysis is more detailed, let us start with him. Hurd admired Spenser's *The Faerie Queene* and decided to defend it as a work of art, which in his view had been unjustly forgotten. Hurd defines *The Faerie Queene* as a "Gothic poem" (RH: viii, 320), explicitly asserting that classicism cannot give directions to the chivalric romance in that this form presents aesthetic laws of its own; he defended thus the liberty to change the rules of aesthetics and claimed the Gothic as the style with which to judge this poem, one that authorises us to define this style as the distinctly English one:

> When an architect examines a Gothic structure by Grecian rules, he finds nothing but deformity. But the Gothic architecture has its own rules, by which when it comes to be examined, it is seen to have its merit, as well as the Grecian. The question is not, which of the two is conducted in the simplest or truest taste: but whether there be not sense and design in both, when scrutinized by the laws on which each is projected. The same observation holds of the two sorts of poetry. Judge the *Faerie Queene* by the classic models, and you are shocked with its disorder: consider it with an eye to its Gothic original, and you find it regular. The unity and simplicity of the former are more complete: but the latter has that sort of unity and simplicity which results from its nature. (RH: viii, 319-20)

Therefore, assessing these works with classical interpretation schemes will produce critical errors: "Under this idea then of a Gothic, not classical poem, *The Faerie Queene* is to be read and criticised" (RH: vii, 317). "Gothic manners" are superior in Hurd's opinion because, although passions, spirit and violence are the same in the Classical and the Gothic, the Gothic includes "magnificence" and more "variety" (RH: vi, 313). Furthermore, the fancies of the British bards are more sublime, terrible and alarming than those of the "classic fablers (...) the *manners* they paint, and the *superstitions* they adopt, are the more poetical for being Gothic" (RH: vi, 316). Therefore, these works should be interpreted, like *The Faerie Queene*, "on these principles" to set their merits, not on those "hitherto attempted" because "classic ideas of unity [...] have no place here" (RH: viii, 321). He therefore claims the use of a new unity: "of design and not of action" (RH: viii, 322). To explain his point, he uses the metaphor of the Gothic garden design, establishing a radial centrifugal image, a sort of radial sun, where every knight is free to move as he wishes, guided by the common centre, which could be the moral ideal that they share with their king or queen:

> A wood or grove cut out into many separate avenues or glades was amongst the most favourite of the works of art, which our fathers

> attempted in this species of cultivation. These *walks were distinct from each other had each their several destinations*, and *terminated on their own proper objects. Yet the whole was brought together* and considered under one view by *the relation which these various openings had*, not to each other, but *to their common and concurrent centre*. (RH: viii, 322, my emphasis.)

The Faerie Queene, which in Spenser's original project was divided into twelve adventures, offered the emblematic symbol of the proxemic Round Table to resolve the problem of relationships between equal stakeholders. This form exemplified exactly the paratactic, non-hierarchical, negotiated unity of equals where nobody presides over the others. Spenser tries thus to unify the individual parts, "intertwisting several actions" (RH: viii, 323). If equality produces "disorder" (RH: viii, 324) – since the knights are at liberty to go where they wish – Hurd ethically justifies this Gothic element as the result of freedom and liberty. The classical element – that of hierarchy – is forcedly introduced by Spenser due to the "violence of classic prejudices" (RH: viii, 323-24). The fact that he does not completely dismiss the classical model forces him to adopt two other types of unities to tie his subjects closer together. One is of his own invention: "interrupt[ing] the proper story of each book, by dispersing it into several (...) [then] intertwisting the several actions together to give something like the appearance of one action to his twelve adventures"; and the other is the classical (hypotactic) expedient of introducing an internal hierarchy, establishing the superiority of "Prince Arthur" (RH: viii, 323). Indeed, King Arthur, "though inferior to each [knight] [i]n [h]is [o]wn specific virtue [...] is superior to all by uniting the whole circle of [t]heir virtues in himself" (RH: viii, 325) through his magnanimity (magnificence).

Hurd considers this attempt to be an artificial "appearance of unity [...] in contradiction to His Gothic system", based structurally on the equality of the knights (RH: viii, 325). The result is "confusion" (RH: viii, 325). The confusion Hurd perceives is indeed that of putting together British liberty and classical hierarchy: "two things in nature incompatible, the Gothic, and the classical unity" (RH: viii, 324). He therefore concludes that the submission to hierarchies is "the proper, and only considerable, defect of this extraordinary poem" (*ibid.*). The superimposed hierarchical unity, in fact, undermines the structural, egalitarian, paratactic design and ethical scope of the poem, emblematically signifying the freedom and democracy so admired by Hurd.

From the metaphorical reading, Hurd focuses on the formalistic visual language of architecture applied to *The Faerie Queene*. We might say that, like other formalists, i.e. the garden formalists, he defends the political image of the constitutional monarchy, particularly in his admiration for the ethics of chivalry that presupposed the voluntary acceptance of the authority of what might be termed a better equal (Arthur). Hurd's implicit critique of Spenser's hypotaxis (hierarchy) seems rather to speak of the critic's emblematic readiness to dismiss hierarchy (read the monarchy) altogether, rather than being a real critique of Arthur's control over the knights.

Furthermore, Hurd also illustrates his point through the garden design metaphor, pointing to William Kent's landscape gardens as his examples. The supreme art of nature, and Kent's, who respects it, consists of the ability "of disposing his ground and objects into an entire landscape [...] in so easy a manner, that the careless observer [...] discovers no art in the combination" (RH: viii, 322). He concludes that the purpose of the work is an artificial naturalness, exactly like the one proposed in the model of de Mandeville's beehive, a naturalness that can oust even the queen if that is what is needed for the wellness of the hive.

Addison also adopted architecture, but with a different and classical *penchant*, as a reference for literature in his essays on wit in *The Spectator,* 1711 (JA: 58-63, 215-42), where he says: "Poets who want this strength of genius to give that majestic simplicity to nature, which we so much admire in the works of the ancients, are forced to hunt after foreign ornaments, and not to let any piece of wit of what kind so ever escape them. I look upon these writers as Goths in poetry, who, like those in architecture, not being able to come up to the beautiful simplicity of the old Greeks and Romans, have endeavoured to supply its place with all the extravagancies of an irregular fancy" (see JA: I:62, 235-36). This fancy, though irregular, was admired as being majestic by others, like Hurd. In his essay in *The Spectator,* Addison does not speak much of Spenser, whom he does not celebrate, although he does mention him in one of the essays in *The Pleasures of the Imagination*, No. 419 (JA: III: 419, 87), so that it was left to Steele to write in praise of this poet (JA: IV, 540, 245-48). Addison describes Spenser as an allegorist, and allegorists he did not like (JA: II: 297, 175), being unable, or unwilling, to see the formal structure of the work that other critics praised.

Thomas Warton, in his *Observations on the Faerie Queene,*[34] chastises Spenser's "weak and undiscerning judgement", referring to his choice of Ariosto as his model rather than Tasso (TWO: 3). In contrast to his opinion, this choice confirmed the result of the decree that the Academia della Crusca had passed, assessing Ariosto's *Orlando Furioso* to be superior to Tasso's *Gerusalemme Liberata*. Warton also comments on this fact by pointing out Spenser's acquiescence in the aesthetic laws of the

Continent: "For Italy, in the age of Queen Elizabeth, gave laws to our island in all matters of taste, as France has done ever since" (TWO: 3). He then judges the twelve-day feast organised by the Queen to be the guiding plan of the work.[35] He sets Prince Arthur as the principal knight and general hero of the poem, representing magnificence and magnanimity (TWO: 4), a hero in search of Gloriana (Glory). Nevertheless, if there is consciousness of the importance "for the hero and his design", of a unity of action "by which this design should be properly accomplished", this classical unity has not properly been respected (TWO: 4). Arthur, having not been made "the principal agent in the redress of each particular wrong", was not made in the perfect pattern of the Knights; he assists them in the "service of all the twelve virtues" and only in this limited sense does he complete "the proposed grand end, viz. the attainment of Glory" (TWO: 5). But Warton, missing the point that Spenser does not want to make Arthur superior to his knights, goes on to chastise the poet for making of Arthur "only a subordinate, or rather accessory character; the difficulties and obstacles which he should have surmounted in order to gain the proposed end, are done to his hand, and removed by others" (TWO: 5). This shows precisely what Spenser wanted, i.e. to show that he is here talking of a society of equals in which Arthur does not want to outshine his fellows "with a steady and superior lustre" (TWO: 5-6). Warton wished to see precisely this quality in the hero, and therefore concludes by saying: "No poet ever shewed more imagination with less judgement, than the author of the Faerie Queene" (TWO: 159). Not by chance, Warton uses the metaphor of the Gothic architectural style to praise Milton in the same work:

> Impressions made in earliest youth, are ever afterwards most strongly felt; and I am inclin'd to think, that Milton was first affected with, and often indulg'd the pensive pleasure, which the awful solemnity of a Gothic church conveys to the mind, and which is here so feelingly describ'd, while he was a schoolboy at St. Paul's. The church was then in its original Gothic state, and one of the noblest patterns of that kind of architecture. (TWO: 247)

If Richard Hurd expressed his praise for the choice of making each of the twelve books a book *per se*, Warton defines it as a failure of the poem (7). According to him, Spenser, in completing each book *per se* – applying the principle of parataxis without privileging a holistic hypotaxis – "has remarkably failed in endeavouring to represent all the virtues completed in the character of one" (8); that is, by not making of Arthur the superior leader. Warton rebukes Spenser for not imposing on the poem a single, grand and unifying structure, which was the reprimand of all Neoclassicists, including, for this specific instance, Addison. Henry Morley, in his introduction to his edition of *The Spectator*,[36] points out the Neoclassical attitude of Addison, in the year 1694, at 23 years of age:

> [Addison] was so far under the influence of French critical authority, as accepted by most cultivators of polite literature at Oxford (...) that from 'An Account of the Greatest English Poets' he omitted Shakespeare. Of Chaucer, he then knew no better than to say, what might have been said in France, that '- age has rusted what the Poet writ, // Worn out his language, and obscured his wit: // In vain he jests in his unpolish'd strain, // And tries to make his readers laugh in vain. // Old Spenser next, warm'd with poetic rage, // In ancient tales amused a barb'rous age; // But now the mystic tale, that pleased of yore, // Can charm an understanding age no more.' (TWS: xi)

Warton, eventually, assumes a contrary position, conceding that the poem, even though not formally classical, can be judged positively for the pleasure it produces when reading it:

> Though the FAERIE QUEENE does not exhibit that economy of plan, and exact arrangement of parts which Epic severity requires, yet we scarcely regret the loss of these, while their place is so amply supplied, by something which more powerfully attracts us: he has remarkably failed in endeavouring to represent all the virtues completed in the character of one. The poet must either have established TWELVE KNIGHTS without an ARTHUR, or an ARTHUR without TWELVE KNIGHTS, as it engages the affection of the heart, rather than the applause of the head; and if there be any poem whose graces please, because they are situated beyond the reach of art, and where the faculties of creative imagination delight us, because they are unassisted and unrestrained by those of deliberate judgment, it is in this of which we are now speaking. To sum up all in a few words; tho' in the FAERIE QUEENE we are not satisfied as critics, yet we are transported as readers. (TWS: 12-13)

The element that Warton praises is the recovery of the English past connected with King Arthur via the use of romance:

> Among others, there is one romance which Spenser seems more particularly to have made use of: It is entitled MORTE ARTHUR, The Lyf of Kyng Arthur, of his noble Knyghtes of the round table, and in thende the dolorous deth of them all. This was translated into English from the French, by one Sir Thomas Maleory, Knight, and printed by W. Caxton, 1484. From this fabulous history, our author has borrow'd many of his names, viz. Sir Tristram, Placidas, Pelleas, Pellenore, Percivall, and others.

> As to Sir Tristram, he has copied from this book the circumstances of his birth and education with much exactness. Spenser informs us that Sir Tristram was born in Cornwall, &c. And Tristram is my name, the only heire // Of good king Meliogras, which did raigne // In Cornewaile. (15)

Having himself studied the philological *stemma codicum* of Arthur's story, Warton praises Spenser's knowledge of the sources:

> Drayton [in his *Polyolbion]*, in these lines, manifestly alludes to a passage in Geoffrey of Monmouth; who informs us, that a Spanish giant, named Ritho, having forcibly conveyed away from her guard Helena the niece of duke Hoel, possessed himself of St. Michael's Mount in Cornwall, from whence he made frequent sallies, and committed various outrages; that, at last, king Arthur conquered this giant, and took from him a certain coat, which he had been composing of the beards of kings, a vacant place being left for king Arthur's beard. Spenser has copied many other fictions from MORTE ARTHUR, I apprehend that he drew this from thence, and not from Geoffrey of Monmouth; not to mention, that Spenser's circumstances tally more exactly with those in the romance. (20)

These erudite pieces of information provide Warton with the opportunity to comment on sources and characters: Merlin, the Holy Grail, Lancelot, begirt by British and Armoric Knights (27). He then comments on Spenser's genealogy and origin of fairies: "As to Spenser's original and genealogy of the Fairy nation, I am induc'd to believe, that part of it was supply'd by his own inexhaustible imagination, and part by some fabulous history":

> He tells us, B. ii. c. 10. S. 70. that man, as first made by Prometheus, was called ELFE, who wandring through the world, at last arriv'd at the gardens of Adonis, where he found a female, whom he called FAY; that the issue of these two were called Fairies, who soon grew to be a mighty people, and conquer'd all nations. That their eldest son Elfin govern'd America, and the next to him, named Elfinan, founded the city of Cleopolis, which was enclos'd with a golden wall by Elfiline. That his son Elfine overcome the Gobbelines; but that, of all Fairies, Elfant was most renowned, who built Panthea of Crystall. — To these succeeded Elfar, who kill'd two brethren-giants; and to him Elfinor, who built a bridge of glass over the sea, the sound of which was like thunder. At length Elficleos rul'd the Fairy land with much wisdom, and highly encreas'd its honour: he left two sons, the eldest of which, fair Elferon, died an immature death, and whose place was supply'd by the mighty Oberon, whose wide memorial (continues our author) still remains, and who dying, left Tanaquil to succeed him by will, who is likewise called Glorian, or GLORIANA. (39)

All in all, Thomas Warton's essay on the Gothic structure of the *Faerie Queene* (1754) defends both Spenser's purpose in becoming a Romantic poet[37] and, in his subsequent first English study of the kind, the *History of English Poetry* (1774, 1778, 1781), the recovery of the older tradition of the island to move away from the enslavement of Latin prosody and classical and Neoclassical metres and subjects.

Warton's essay also applies architectural design to understand the sister art of writing. If Warton defines Spenser as a Romantic, as Rinaker explains, to mean "in imitation of the medieval *romance*",[38] this was also surely due to the appeal he sought for "feelings [and] imagination" rather than "intellect [and] reason" (CR: 45). To compare Spenser's poem to the models of antiquity, Warton says, it "wou'd be like drawing a Parallel between the Roman and the Gothick architecture" (CR: 41), its interest lying not in "proportion, but variety of detail" (CR: 45), qualifying execution with invention. Spenser, Warton says, had mingled "reality and romance", "truth and fiction to adorn his 'fairy structure'", producing a "formlessness and a richness which he thought preferable, in a 'romantic' poem, to exactness" (CR: 45). Warton deploys Addison's categories of the creative imagination to emphasise the originality of the poem. In comparison to Ariosto's 'fancy' (associative power), Spenser's imagination creates thoroughly original "images" (TW: II, 323).

Speaking of Elizabethan poetry in his *History*, Thomas Warton says: "I shall class and consider the poets of this reign, under the general heads, or divisions, of SATIRE, SONNET, PASTORAL, and MISCELLANEOUS poetry. Spenser will stand alone, without a class, and without a rival" (TW: IV, sect. XLIV, 2). This went exactly against the remarks Dryden made of Spenser's work, chastising Spenser's disrespectful rejection of hierarchy:

> For there is no uniformity in the design of Spenser: he aims at the accomplishment of no one action; he raises up a hero for every one of his adventures; and endows each of them with some particular moral virtue, which renders them all equal, without subordination, or preference. Every one is most valiant in his own legend: only we must do him that justice to observe, that magnanimity, which is the character of Prince Arthur, shines throughout the whole poem; and succours the rest, when they are in distress.[39]

And, as we know, the representation of a society of peers was to become the standard interpretation of the Arthurian legend and its major ideological passport to the 18th century.

But the most original interpretation of the poem was provided by John

Hughes, in his very early edition of the *Faerie Queene*, published in 1715. He is the first critic to apply the structural metaphor of architecture and the Gothic architectural style to explain its formal – literary – design. Hughes makes a very interesting point, and one which was to be repeated by all literary critics to come who wanted to defend Spenser's recovery of the Arthurian world and defend it against the attacks of the classicists:

> To compare it [The Faerie Queene] (...) with the models of Antiquity would be like drawing a parallel between the Roman and the Gothick architecture. In the first there is, doubtless, a more natural grandeur and simplicity; in the latter, we find great mixtures of beauty and barbarism, yet assisted by the invention of inferior ornaments; and though the former is more majestick in the whole, the latter may be very surprising and agreeable in its parts.[40]

Warton's *dicta* on subjects and emotions were espoused and followed to the letter, as we have seen, by the Sepulchral Graveyard poets who, in also taking over the claims of the antiquarians, adopted in their poems the dark nights and gloomy atmospheres of the (by now assumed) autochthonous, bulky Saxon-Gothic architectural elements. These dark architectural elements also figured in Horace Walpole's Gothic story, *The Castle of Otranto* (1764), but they were used ironically to poke fun at those who believed in the paradoxical events happening in Otranto, backed up as his work was by the previous appearance of James Macpherson's dark atmospheres of the, fake, Ossian poems: *Fingal* 1761 and *Temora* 1763.[41]

Other critics and antiquarians would pursue the recovery of the past and the early history of English literature. An important figure among them is Thomas Percy, with his collection of older poetry: *Reliques of Ancient English Poetry* (1765).[42] This was a first collection with a bards and minstrels' *corpus*, in rivalry with publications of other competing identity strands: Welsh, Runic, and Erse poems that produced an increase, comprehensible from the analysis we have produced so far, of the regionalisms within the nation, to which the poems of Ossian gave prominence, producing research in rival traditions such as the Cambrio-British Wales and the Milesian-Ireland bardic past, as Philip Connell, convincingly, points out.[43] Unfortunately, as Connell says, the Gothic genealogy of English Literature was diminished by the political commitment to other topics, such as the divisive ancient constitutionalism that prevented literary Gothic scholarship from becoming an effective vehicle for "patriotism" (PC: 264), instead becoming one central point of the attack on the Catholic religion and thus on the Stuart kings. Indeed, as we have seen, there were at least four regionalist groups involved in the panorama of 18th-century history: the English, the Scots, the Irish and the Welsh, all pursuing their different literary traditions, all remaining motivated by their own identity issues, trying to prevent themselves from being subsumed by another prevailing group.

Toni Wein, who examines the implications between the Gothic novel and nationalism, sees "the Gothic Novel as the best and earliest resting-place for a nationalist ideology",[44] for the celebratory use it makes of feudal and chivalric codes that safeguarded the medieval order and degree, and the power connected with these, but also as a vehicle for an *avant la lettre* dissemination and advertisement of a cohesive group identity to which the Gothic provides a mythical coherence. This, according to Wein, is a form of nationalism that cannot simply be dismissed as political paradigms based on leaders' impositions on the people, because such a stance does not properly take into consideration the cultural elements that promote nationalism from the bottom up, rather than the other way around. As we have seen, literature and aesthetics play a distinguished role in the construction of political paradigms, and not only indirectly but also patently and clearly so, even if, unfortunately, they often pass unnoticed and are absorbed in an unperceived way.[45]

The 18th-century changes we have outlined are therefore direct evidence of the construction/invention of the imaginary Northern geographical paradigm and its ideological and cultural background. Northern identity is created as if it were in its essence 'Northern', through a mere reversal of paradigms (South/North into North/South), a move that Jacques Derrida defined as a "white mythology" (Bezrucka: 1995b). Created by an easy dualistic epistemic filter, rather than being the result of the contact points of a variety of viewpoints, as Hogarth would have it, these *foci* were localised in a supposed imaginary geography whose essence was made to coincide with certain characteristics of a Northern style, e.g. the old Gothic architecture.[46]

The features of the style, nevertheless, were iconised in its democratic symbols: the freedom of the English garden, Arthur's Round Table and his emblematic political style, the intricacies of the picturesque and the sublime, all clear examples of how aesthetics, far from being disinterested, as Kant saw it, is often demagogically used as an indirect but still political emblem and cypher.

It is left to Blake to combine the national values in his famous sentence: "Liberty is the Goddess of Britannia".[47] The emphasis on national characters, of course, was a European phenomenon but in Great Britain it was ahead of its time. As a case in point, we have already mentioned Goethe's flash in seeing the Dome of Strasbourg (XIII-XIV century), which made him a champion of the Gothic. Not surprisingly, even for Goethe, the defence of the Gothic passes through the defence of new and original literary forms and the non-imitation of the classics. The Gothic style was claimed as their "native" style by many European countries before the defence of the peculiar, national originality was relativised by the Romantics to endorse the unique traits of every single artist.[48]

The defence of the Moderns is then the *recto* of the anti-classicist coin, whose *verso* is the return to a British foundational past that the intelligentsia set in Anglo-Saxon times; it is a past that the Antiquarian Society also studied, devoted as they were to the reconstruction of "Bryttish antiquitys."[49]

The contribution to Gothic scholarship provided in *The Antiquities of England and Wales* (1773-1787) by the antiquary Francis Grose[50] is also of great importance. Grose offered an overview of the regional Saxon and Gothic works and, as I have already claimed (Bezrucka: 2002), he should be considered the first theorist of an anti-universal regionalist aesthetics, being posited as a firm believer in the existence of a long line enacting the relativity of beauty.[51] The anti-universality of beauty was strongly reaffirmed during the 19th century, Walter Pater starting his major work, *The Renaissance*, with the peremptory statement: "Beauty is relative."

Medieval Gothic architecture provided locations and places suitable for those sublime feelings, such as fear, horror and the non-cathartic directives of the sublime that Gothic literature, inspired by Horace Walpole's *The Castle of Otranto* (1764), exploited, features on which Burke's aesthetic treatise had insisted (1757). Moreover, the Gothic was also perceived as a Northern style by J.H. Füssli (1741-1825), who will find in it completely different argumentations: "We are more impressed by Gothic than by Greek mythology because the bonds are not yet rent which tie us to its magic: he has a powerful hold on us, who holds us by our superstition or by a theory of honour".[52]

In the 18th century, the instrumental role in claiming the Celtic tradition to be the genuine native origin of English poetry was taken over by the Warton brothers, or better, by Thomas Warton, who proceeded to enhance this supposed local artistic model and promote it through an *ad hoc* creation of an indigenous, autochthonous tradition. Soon after, he would transform it into the English canon. We must not forget that he was an Oxford Fellow who became Poet Laureate from 1785-1790: he spent time exploring the archaeological *repêchage* of the roots of the Arthurian Legend and revising its *stemma codicum,* giving priority to those authors who had used the tradition of magic and fairies.

This is the core of a, likely, "invented tradition" which created a native, forgotten English foundational origin for King Arthur's myth, a tradition that Warton thought needed to be recovered. He, therefore reattributed the origin of the Arthurian legend and the chivalry tradition to migrant Welsh and Cornish bards, who "had thrown off (…) dependence on the Romans" (TW: I, 4) and moved to Brittany, specifically to Low Armorica. He backs up this theory through Milton, who refers to "the knights of Wales and Armorica as the customary retinue of King Arthur" (TW: I, 4). Once there, the transfer of the English bard tradition took place as it was adopted by the French in their *Chanson de geste* and the *Cycle de Charlemagne*. The canon Thomas Warton created was formed with authors who recovered that original tradition (Chaucer, Spenser, Milton, Shakespeare), or forged similar ones (cf. Macpherson's *Ossian*).

In addition, the Warton brothers would diffusely refer to a tradition of "romantic castles, rocks, rivers, and caves" (TW, I: 7), instrumental for their recovery and evaluation of the English Gothic style, Old-Gothic or Saxon-Gothic, interpreted as a Northern and not a continental style.

These are all cultural and promotional moves, proving that the literary history of the 18th century implies an ideological manipulation, a sort of advertising campaign for the diffusion of cultural constructs aimed at political propaganda. And what exactly was propagated? The idea of an autochthonous Englishness, corresponding to this invented England's national core identity, characterised in essentialist Northern terms, to emancipate themselves, once and for all, from the dominant Southern artistic rules. The interesting point is, nevertheless, that they themselves adopt a space focus that does not enable them to see beyond to what, despite this, is also there.

When Francis Grose comes on the scene, towards the end of the 18th century (1788), he makes a strong claim for the implicit cultural regionalism of all ideas of beauty,[53] and thus cancels any possible nationalist or essentialist *penchant* from any aesthetic categorisation. That is, he limits the truth value of all assertions about beauty to their specific culture. Nevertheless, there would be philosophers who feared this regional downgrade of aesthetics as too strong an emblem of liberty and freedom. One of them was Immanuel Kant, who again, as forcefully as possible, insisted on the universality of the Beautiful (1798), recovering precisely Plato's homology of Beauty, Truth and Goodness.

Why, however, does this happen? Because detractors knew perfectly that it would set art free from the yoke of morality and all that was related to it, starting from the social control that aesthetics exerted on all cultural issues, without this being entirely realised by the people. Indeed, Kant knew perfectly well that this disregard for rules would be the key to the emancipation of individuals from every kind of outside authority, and from every kind of collectivism, besides that of national states; it would open the door to what he considered uncontrollable individualism, or Romanticism, as it would later be called. This, a dreaded outcome, would indeed come to pass.

People knew better: the road to emancipation and personal accountability, though it still had a long way to go, was now open so that, at a certain stage, nobody was entitled to set fixed rules to achieve beauty, neither the Ancients nor the Moderns.[54] Harmony, symmetry and the beautiful were no longer the only aesthetic guidelines. Each culture, as Francis Grose pointed out, had different standards and the right to see beauty wherever and however it wanted to see it; any community had the right to produce its own aesthetic rules. Aesthetic regionalism and the liberty linked to it were thus born, along with the right to be original, which goes hand in hand with it.[55]

The new orientation favoured, on the one hand, the 19th-century nationalistic trend and the birth of the European national states but, on the other, with the defence of an aesthetic cultural regionalism, it also unequivocally supported liberty, as called for by the theorist Francis Grose in his *Rules for Drawing Caricaturas* (1788) so that it might inaugurate the artistic creations of what was called the sentimental, affective, or even idealistic, Romantic ego.

In the 'Preface' he wrote for his *History of English Poetry*,[56] Thomas Warton expressed the hope that he might be thanked by the antiquarians of his age "for enriching the stock of our early literature by these new accessions [ancient manuscript poems never printed before] (...) and I trust I shall gratify the reader of taste, in having so frequently rescued from oblivion the "rude inventions and irregular beauties of the heroic tale, or the romantic legend" (TW: I, viii), a "national poetry" found and recovered "from a rude origin and obscure beginnings" (TW: I, ii). Exactly as Percy claimed in his title, Warton also invited the reader's appreciation for a "set of textual relics, precariously salvaged from historical oblivion" (Connell, 2006: 163).

This reference to "rude inventions and irregular beauties" takes us immediately out of the borders of classical beauty to move into what Warton defined as "the most picturesque and expressive representations of manners" (TW: I, iii) of the early ages. Warton uses language that the people of England would immediately associate with the "picturesque" Gilpin had acquainted them with. The poetry he is referring to is that written after the Norman accession because Saxon poetry – dismissed by

Warton as "little more than religious rhapsodies" – is not illustrative of their original "pagan state" (TW: I, vi), and therefore he chose the later Norman period: from that era, he explains, "our national character began to dawn" (TW: I, vi).

Special analysis is reserved, in book one, for *Brut of England*, *Regnorum Chronica*, tales of *Chivalry and Romance*, *English Minstrels*, metrical romances, *La Mort Arthure*, *Pierce Plowman's Vision*, and *Geoffrey Chaucer*, to whom seven sections are dedicated.

It is in "Dissertation 1" that Warton sets down the roots of what he calls "Of the Origin of Romantic Fiction in Europe" (TW: I, 1-72). To sum up: the work starts with a clear Northern incipit "[t]hat peculiar and arbitrary species of Fiction which we commonly call Romantic, was entirely unknown to the writers of Greece and Rome" (TW: I, 1),[57] and indeed, as we have seen, he claims a Celtic origin for King Arthur's myth (4th century). This "mode of fabling" (TW: I, 2) was then propagated during the Crusades (11th-13th c.), but he claims to correct this tradition through a "more distinct and extended inquiry", importation being, for him, linked to a "much earlier period" (*ibid.*), exactly when the "Saracens, or Arabians" coming from the northern coasts of Africa around the 8th century effected a complete conquest of Spain, establishing their royal seat in Cordoba. The Spaniards were soon captivated by their "extravagant inventions" and their "romantic and creative genius" (TW: I, 2). Though retaining Europe as the centre of reference, this gives to the Romantic tradition an Eastern origin and, through later migration, a Southern one. Furthermore, another proxemic, i.e. spatial, connection is proposed for meteorological and climate reasons: "The ideal tales of these eastern invaders, recommended by a brilliancy of invention hitherto unknown and unfamiliar to the cold and barren conceptions of a western climate, were eagerly caught up and universally diffused. From Spain (…) they soon passed into France and Italy" (TW: I, 2, my emphasis). This specification enriches the issue of the merely deictic and proxemic geographical location of a supposed northernness even more, translating mere space-politics into Edward W. Soja's "spatialized ontology", the product of the often forgotten "social dynamics of spatialization".[58] Setting it apart from a merely cartographical and geometrical cardinal-point spatial-logic, artistic production is for Warton directly connected with a place-specific environmental and cultural cause: climate and its influence on people but also with a sociological and anthropological one: migration and its social outcome.

It is at this point that Warton's "Dissertation 1" takes an unexpected turn, in his reading of the Armorica region as a Welsh colony, where

Welsh bards migrated during the fourth century, fleeing from England due to the Roman invasion. He also adds that no other region of France can boast "so great a number of ancient romances", as those produced by the Armorica bards of Arthur's retinue (TW: I, 3). Warton testifies with evidence taken from manuscripts preserved in the British Museum, where the "autient BRITUN corteis" that "firent *le lai*" (TW: I, 3) are often mentioned,[59] and from the frequent references to them in Father Lobineau's *History of Basse Bretagne* (1707).[60]

Thomas Warton sees these bards as led by a secessionist and revolutionary Roman general, Maximus, who had considerable interest in Wales, having married Ellena, the daughter of Eudda, a powerful chieftain of North-Wales, and by Conau, the lord of Meiriadoc or Denbigh-land. Defeated by the Romans, Maximus and Conau had to retire with their army and bards to Brittany where there was a people who had thrown off the Roman yoke.

Warton, admitting that there are no Greek or Roman sources, refers to the testimony of the Bard Llywarchen (TW: 1, 4). He also quotes Milton's *Epitaphium Damonis*: "Et tandem Armoricos Britonum sub lege colonos",[61] bearing witness to the acceptance of the Armorican people of the laws of the Britons; and to give further evidence he quotes *Paradise Lost* (PL, I, 579): "What resounds in fable or romance, of Uther's son [Arthur] begirt with British and Armoric knights" (TW: I, 4).[62] In Charles Symmons's notes to Milton's text, *Epitaphium Damonis,* in which the history of Arturo (King Arthur) is related, we read: "In the fabulous history of Britain, Brutus, the grandson of Æneas, leads a colony of Trojans to this island, which he conquers and civilizes. He had previously married Imogen, the daughter of some Greek King called Pandrasus. Rutupium is Richborough on the coast of Kent. Armorica (or Bretagne) in France was conquered and occupied by the Britons, as is generally supposed, when they were pressed by the Romans. But we have no certain account of this emigration and conquest. Uther Pendragon being changed by the magic of Merlin into the likeness of Gorlois, Prince of Cornwall, got possession of his wife, Jögerne's bed, and Arthur was the offspring of the trespass."[63]

This was Warton's view of Arthur's chivalric romance, which he saw as the blending of the chthonic deities of the Welsh and the Gothic Scalds, later connected with the tradition of magic that came from Arabia.

But let us now see what one of the most outstanding, and debated, scholars of the psychological understanding of Celtic folklore, Walter Evans-Wentz,[64] referring once more to the climactic theory, in 1911, says:

> The natural aspects of Celtic countries, much more than those of most non-Celtic countries, impress man and awaken in him some unfamiliar part of himself – call it the Subconscious Self, the Subliminal Self, the Ego, or what you will – which gives him an unusual power to know and to feel invisible, or psychical, influences. What is there, for example, in London, or Paris, or Berlin, or New York to awaken the intuitive power of man, that sub-consciousness deep-hidden in him, equal to the solitude of those magical environments of Nature which the Celts enjoy and love? (XXI)

Evans-Wentz organises thus his understanding of Celtic folklore under the "naturalistic", which I would rename environmental or chthonic tradition:

> The belief in fairies often anthropomorphically reflects the natural environment as well as the social condition of the people who hold the belief. For example, amid the beautiful low-lying green hills and gentle dells of Connemara (Ireland), the 'good people' are just as beautiful, just as gentle, and just as happy as their environment; while amid the dark-rising mountains and in the mysterious cloud-shadowed lakes of the Scotch Highlands there are fiercer kinds of fairies and terrible water-kelpies, and in the Western Hebrides there is the much-dreaded 'spirit-host' moving through the air at night. The Naturalistic Theory shows accurately enough that natural phenomena and environment have given direction to the anthropomorphising of gods, spirits, or fairies, but after explaining this external aspect of the Fairy-Faith it cannot logically go any further. (XXI-XXII)

The result of this would also explain Pythagoras' and Plato's understanding of all external nature as being "animated throughout and controlled in its phenomena by daemons acting by the will of gods", which is to men "nothing more than the visible effects of an unseen world of causes" (XXII).[65] The Druid theory,[66] being related to the fairies and based on an anthropomorphic hypothesis, he dismisses as "altogether inadequate" (XXIII).

The "mythological theory" explains "fairy faith" (XXIII) for Wentz as being "the diminished figures of the old pagan divinities of the early Celts; and many modern authorities on Celtic mythology and folk-lore hold it" (XXIII). His theory is that the fairy faith is the folk-religion of the Celts, based on a sympathetic, responsive and direct contact with nature, uncorrupted by civilization, comparable to that of the Australian Arunta and the American Red Man (XXV). Therefore, Celtic Studies are for him the "germ of much of our European religions and philosophies, customs, and institutions" (XXVII), and interestingly, he foresees a period when "the mythology of the Celts will be held in very high esteem" (XXVIII). Maybe this period has come once again but, unfortunately, interest is not only due to a cultural revival but also to issues of populistic exclusion, rather than inclusion, working towards closed-society models and, therefore, as scholars, it merits our greatest attention as a phenomenon pursued via an acritical strong regionalist attitude rather than a critical and strategic one.[67]

Evans-Wentz refers then to the revolution that took place in religion when Christianity took over the magic and effectively deleted it under the spell of belief in the Bible. He reports that it was on the hill of Tara that the battle between the pagans and the Christian religion was fought, and won by St. Patrick, who now dwarfs the Liath Stone beside it, as at Carnac where the Christian Cross overshadows dolmens and menhirs (W: 14). This battle marks the victory of the "new" magic of St. Patrick that prevailed over the magic of the Druids, when the old and the new religions met in warfare, in the presence of the high king of Ireland and his court (W: 513).

Evans-Wentz mingles a rational and partly psychological understanding about these creatures that he sees as being intermedial elements, nearer to human beings than God is, imagined and created by the people to understand the strange and unexpected manifestations of nature so as to come to terms with them.[68]

But, as we have demonstrated, by being so connected with the natural environment, in the 18th century, these polytheistic magic entities became a strong vehicle for a nationalistic mythology, used and linked to King Arthur's chivalric romance and all that went with it. Elements such as the lineage of kings, the ousting of kings, the Glorious Revolution, and the model parliament that was linked to the knights' Round Table, were parables of a new religion, that of politics. This made strong use of mythological issues with strong consequences for the people of England, who were united but also divided by them, as power politics requires.

5.3 Invention and Rootedness at War, Culture *vs.* Essentialism

Besides studying literature from a close reading and strictly rhetorical and stylistic point of view – i.e. analysing the work in depth, its place in the canon, its culture, within its genre – literature needs to be studied comprehensively, in a holistic way: works should be studied from an intermedial, eristic, historic and broadly cultural point of view because they participate powerfully in the creation of their culture, i.e. in the creation of the axiological values of a society. In this sense, even minor forms of literature, particularly best-sellers, read by millions of people, citizens and voters, who usually pass unheeded by academia, should be carefully analysed. Not everyone has the privilege of attending universities, where literary production is studied and sifted exactly to investigate which values are being passed on to the reader; meanwhile, best-sellers spread their message worldwide, and sometimes the message is not a democratic one.[69]

Literature, as with all media, participates strongly in debating and creating common sense views, new epistemic understandings and cultural *Weltanschauungen*. It can create new perspectives or defend old ones, but although it is a truism that literary works are one of the mediums through which our societies are shaped, everyone needs to pay attention to the messages that are circulated at all levels.

As a starting point in this section, I would like, speculatively, to put together the positions of some of the most distinguished theorists of nation-creation theories,[70] to examine the 18th-century national and nationalistic imaginative construction of English identity, because this will also be the core element of the transmutation of the Northern aesthetics into a literary and political process rich in identity consequences. To Benedict Anderson's imaginative communities and to Patrick Brantlinger's examination of the 19th-century role of the empire, we should add the concept of the invention of tradition by Eric Hobsbawm and Terence Rangers. Indeed, their specification of how a nation is created finds a whole series of material proofs in the Northern aesthetics that fully endorse their hypothesis:

> It is clear that plenty of political institutions, ideological movements and groups – not least in nationalism – were so unprecedented that even historic continuity had to be invented, for example by creating an ancient past beyond effective historical continuity either by semi-fiction (Boadicea, Vercingetorix, Arminius the Cheruscan) or by forgery (Ossian, the Czech medieval manuscripts). It is also clear that entirely new symbols and devices came into existence (…) such as the national anthem (of which the British in 1740 seems to be the earliest) the national flag (still largely a variation of the French revolutionary tricolour, evolved 1790-4) or the personification of 'the nation' in symbol or image either official as with Marianne and Germania, or unofficial, as in the cartoon stereotypes of John Bull, the lean Yankee Uncle Sam and the 'German Michel'.[71]

Identity manoeuvres consist of the creation of a mythological past, in constructions that for Timothy Brennan are backed by the decisive role of literature, which provides the necessary "apparatus of cultural fictions"[72] to create national states.

The mythic past of England was partly recovered and partly created by the Warton brothers, who focused on the Celtic origins of the English nation to contrast the continental tradition and free themselves from the models and yoke the classics had set on the rules of literary creation. The Celtic origins, and the recovery of the mythical figure of King Arthur, were invoked also because they were far enough in the past to be difficult to trace. Thomas Warton's theory of the origin of English literature, presented as Northern literature, connected with his vision of its romanticisation, focused people's attention on the peculiarities of the regional nature, styles and history of England. The history of how he privileged certain forms has been delineated in the previous chapters.

The Celtic elements of Britain move around distinguished traditions which cover four geographical zones where the Celtic language is still sometimes spoken by the people: in Wales, where it persists as Welsh language, in Cornwall were this variety is called Cornish, in Ireland where it is called Gaelic, and in Scotland. Why go back to this mythic past? Because one starts out belonging somewhere, one becomes part of an autochthonous clan or community, one shares a knowledge made of traditions, folklore and values, and one eschews being an outsider.

Prys Morgan, writing about the Celts, says that it is exactly during the 18th century that a revival of the Celtic origin started to appear in Wales. Catholic culture waned in the 16th century and was not replaced by a Protestant one, a decline fortified during the 17th century, which by the 18th was perceived as a "loss of history".[73] This was marked by the loss of indigenous language and music. The result was the creation of a past "which never existed".[74]

The same happened with Scotland. Hugh Trevor-Hoper traced the invention of the Highland past of Scotland.[75] Based on the recovery of the Caledonian past, this population was thought to have resisted the Roman armies, an old legend refuted in 1729 by the Jacobite antiquary Thomas Innes, but interestingly recovered in 1739 by James Macpherson – linked to the Ossian poems – and Reverend John Macpherson, who, in concert, created an "indigenous literature of Celtic Scotland and, as a necessary support to it, a history. Both this literature and this history, in so far as it had any connection with reality, had been stolen from the Irish."[76] As Trevor-Roper hypothesises, Macpherson had only taken up Irish ballads and reconverted them into the *Ossian* epic, a forgery admired in all Europe. The cultural and political manoeuvre was then backed by the Reverend, who wrote a critical dissertation placing Irish-speaking Celts in Scotland four centuries before their arrival, dismissing genuine ballads in favour of the fake ones. He then contended that the native Irish literature had been stolen from the Scots. On top of that, James Macpherson wrote an "Introduction to the History of Great Britain and Ireland" in 1771, which endorsed this 'history'. Walter Scott himself tried to clear this fake tradition by contesting its truthfulness.[77]

The same nationalistic issue reappears later, in the 19th century, in the critical attention devoted to ancient elements present in the island by the Pre-Raphaelite artists Matthew Arnold[78] and, later, William Butler Yeats.[79] Yeats recovered the political element of this tradition, as Joseph Addison had done at the beginning of the 18th century, by insisting on the cyphered political interpretation of the English nature.

5.4 Emily Brontë's *Wuthering Heights:* "This North Wind that Chills *Me*"

Wuthering Heights, published by Emily Brontë in 1847, under the *nom de plum* of Acton Bell,[80] is the novel where the contrasts between the Northern and Southern aesthetics are best epitomised and acted out, one against the other, through the vector of a rich, metaphorical, spatial and geographical perspective. The underlying dichotomous Manichean logic behind this archi-semic aesthetic contrast is deployed in the novel on various levels: in terms of characters, environment, landscape, settings and architecture, but all masterfully extended by Brontë to comprise the implied racial *niveau*.

The activator of the sharp differences between this geographical opposition is, as would later happen in novels by Thomas Hardy, Elizabeth Gaskell and George Eliot, an intruder who arrives unexpectedly into a formerly closed and apparently peaceful regional community, bringing both novelty and upheaval. The intruder is Heathcliff. It is his powerful and unsettling presence that transforms what might seem to be a love story into a topical novel of wide-ranging international identity politics. These issues are artfully discussed and brought to the fore by the novel.

My contention is that *Wuthering Heights* upscales the previous 18th-century aesthetic issues – issues that it seemed could be kept safely within the, apparently neutral, cultural limits of choosing between a Northern or a Southern aesthetics. Pointing out clearly the consequences of an essentialist geographical regionalism, brought forth on the broader social level, the novel shows us that aesthetic neutrality is an unrealistic dream.[81] Once the aesthetic agenda of the Northern beauty, formerly applied only to works of art, is extended to human beings and society at large, the rationale at work behind it and the dramatic consequences it can produce are unveiled. The novel warns us about using an imaginary geographical border-ratio in that, as Brontë demonstrates, it creates real boundaries that discriminate against people, i.e. drawing frontlines, even metaphorical ones, means creating them, with consequences; a *dystopia* rather than a *utopia* might be the unwanted result.

Brontë focuses on the consequences of such irrational discriminations, too easily drawn and, as she shows us, effectively at work in the novel. These produce Catherine's ghost, who, like Hamlet's father, is there to testify to her unsolved tragic destiny and the terrible events connected with her story: a story in which uncritical common sense, hatred, *ressentiment*, revenge and persecution prevail over freedom, peaceful inclusion and goodness. Brontë, that is, hints at the consequences that a racist, non-inclusive society might produce and the damage and trauma this might cause.[82]

The depiction of the consequences of this essentialist orientation is the most effective and best-developed theme of the novel (Meyer, 1996). From the central and topical race issue, the book revises other discriminatory realms of class and gender demarcations: class being rewritten into Nelly's agency and its enormous importance in the book; gender issues, upheld by the unwritten, but not less strict law, that symbolically forbids Catherine's marriage to Heathcliff because they would end up being "beggars" (WH: 8, 31); class downfall preventing a marriage of true minds, Catherine being fully conscious that Heathcliff and Linton are "as different as a moonbeam from lightening or frost from fire" (WH: 8, 30). Much of the book's undiminishing appeal to all generations and cultures lies precisely in the revolutionary message it proposes, which is that of undermining discriminatory hindrances set against the miscegenation of people Brontë felt were rising and spreading during her time: "My great miseries in this world have been Heathcliff's miseries, and I watched and felt each from the beginning; my great thought in living is himself. If all else perished, and *he* remained, *I* should still continue to be. (...) I *am* Heathcliff!" (WH: 9: 81). The tragic destiny of Catherine and Heathcliff, like Romeo and Juliet earlier, indeed did not remain a private tragedy; it spread and affected the whole community, which, in its primary metaphorical geography, is a symbol of the extended nation. In this sense, parallels can be drawn between the contrasts within England, taking England and Scotland as the symbols of other (Welsh and Irish) regionalisms within the nation.

The fictional strategy used by the author to make her points consists of setting two different milieus, two opposed microcosms within one spatial world, and deploying them one against the other as space-specific cultures with their own different values and rules.

Opposing contrasts are introduced through the master metaphor of the two mansions, where the two families, to which the story relates, live. Respectively set as opposed geographical poles – like nations on a map – the two houses, although belonging to the same region represent its two antipodean poles as the signpost on the Yorkshire Moors signals: "W.H. cut on its north side, on the east, G., and on the south-west, T.G. The signpost serves as a guide-post to posit the Grange, the Heights, and [Gammerton] village" (WH: 10, 101) on the community map. Most importantly for the Northern aesthetics, the two houses have remarkable architectural differences: one is a mansion built in the classicist, probably Palladian tradition, surrounded by a two-mile park (cf. WH: 3, 41), thus a country mansion of the landed gentry; the other is "in a situation and residence so much inferior" (cf. WH: 4, 43), clearly reminding us of a stout and dark Saxon-Gothic architecture, with all the nationalistic implications the style brings with it. A symbolic North where economy lingers. This is how Wuthering Heights appears to Dr Lockwood, described as a Gothic church with the usual architectural paraphernalia:

> Wuthering Heights is the name of Mr. Heathcliff's dwelling. 'Wuthering' being a significant provincial adjective, descriptive of the atmospheric tumult to which its station is exposed in stormy weather. Pure, bracing ventilation they must have up there at all times, indeed; one may guess the power of the north wind blowing over the edge, by the excessive slant of a few stunted firs at the end of the house; and by a range of gaunt thorns all stretching their limbs one way, as if craving alms of the sun. Happily, the architect had foresight to build it strong: the narrow windows are deeply set in the wall, and the corners defended with large jutting stones.
>
> Before passing the threshold, I paused to admire a quantity of grotesque carving lavished over the front, and especially about the principal door; above which, among a wilderness of crumbling griffins and shameless little boys, I detected the date '1500', and the name 'Hareton Earnshaw.' I would have made a few comments, and requested a short history of the place from the surly owner; but his attitude at the door appeared to demand my speedy entrance, or complete departure, and I had no desire to aggravate his impatience previous to inspecting the penetralium. (WH: 1, 20)

Not by chance, the two mansions are bought by the Southerner, Heathcliff, who, having been excluded by both houses, assumes a coloniser's attitude of conquest, treating the two households as if they were war booty. In so doing, he, nevertheless, is able to destroy the fictitious borders between them, homogenising them into a single faction, exactly as happens at the end of a war.

Wuthering Heights, the place where Catherine Earnshaw and Heathcliff belong, and Trushcross Grange, the property of the Lintons, are the opposed, alternating micro-universes of the novel. In the first one, the Heights, Northern elements prevail: the "north wind" of the moors, the "gaunt thorns" and the "fir trees" characterise its space; in the other, the Grange, Southern elements are strategically distributed, such as the blue-bells that surround its turf steps, the brightness and harmonious elegance of the house, the thorough absence of Northern vegetation and its related wind. The wind in the novel, to which Heathcliff refers, becomes the metaphor of the uprising racism he is a victim of: "this North wind that chills *me*" (WH: 241,).

There is, nevertheless, a third element. It relates to a neutral natural setting: the moors. This is the liminal border between North and South, a Hogarthian line of beauty which, if seen as a border separating the concave and convex of the shell aesthetics, it is also, in the double vision proposed by Hogarth, the only place where the two opposing sides merge, cancelling the border and all its discriminations and biases, leaving merely the unrestrictive equality of the physical materiality of the body, providing to the northerner Catherine and the southerner Heathcliff the possibility of sharing, for once, a non-polarised space and place. The moors and their marshes are depicted as being a space still unexplored, underlined by the fact that in this no-man's territory even locals lose their way, having no more maps to guide them (cf. WH, 2:26). Brontë points out clearly that the border is the free space where the usual cognitive and epistemic-dividing matrix and logic of maps do not function, being swallowed by the variety of the territory itself. This, as we have seen, had been anticipated in Hogarth's shell aesthetics, which included the subversive deconstruction of dualism and all binary thought. In keeping the two foci of a double vision within a single whole, Brontë, like Hogarth, is able to debunk a single stable perspective, creating a space where miscegenation and variety can coexist without being subject to an exclusion logic, a space where events and emotions overflow the narrators' necessity to order the narrative according to the strict common-sense logic of choice. This pluralistic point of view is also confirmed by the constantly underlined partiality of the various frames that try to contain the reading of the novel through a controlling narrative. Neither Lockwood nor Nelly, both acting as possible filters for understanding the novel, are convincing, focusing on the impossibility of pinpointing the novel in a neat, all-encompassing design or, in our metaphorical sense, in a geographical map: the novel, and the moors in particular, eschewing maps and borders, remain an untameable territory or, in J. Hillis Miller's words, an "uncanny" text.[83]

Borders are, as recent history demonstrates, non-lieux, unmarked and non-categorisable spaces where people remain anonymous, places where people are anthropologically undefined.[84] This is, in sum, a heterotopic place (Foucault: 1967)[85] where Cathy and Heathcliff can ramble freely because here they are one and undifferentiated, testifying that a no-man's land is possible. It is the place of liberty from norms, doxa, common sense and codified behaviours, Marc Augé's non-anthropological space, where the private body, not set in society's role, can, eventually, be itself. The moors comprise the two poles within their larger natural spatial unit, materialising the line of beauty of Hogarth's aesthetics of the shell[86] – where *within* and *without* freely coexist and, eventually, merge. It is only here that Hogarth's variety eventually has a chance, this being the place where odd ends meet and one side is nothing without its mating and different counterpart: a border place where borderlines are cancelled, where Catherine and Heathcliff can be "rude as savages" (WH: 6, 52). People from the two houses move about freely in this space because here borders are eventually erased and, just for the time being, people are protected by a finally productive matching *limen*, where neither convex and concave exist as such anymore because they coexist, united. Civilized, but discriminative, urban laws, or community country values, do not exist anymore here. Within this eternally varied but immutable nature – the same for everyone – all are equals and unite freely, as we have witnessed in the metaphoric Shakespearian woods in *A Midsummer Night's Dream.* The latter describes a sort of parallel blueprint for this novel – outside the woods, characters are divided by an impending and questionable civilization, read unwritten law, which, like the law of Athens, does not fully comply with this free place.

The moors represent nature itself, without a North or a South, that remains outside and is thus also a powerful metaphor for the planet, the place whose good and bad manifestations we all share: the doctor from the city risking his life whilst arriving at night during a snow storm. In this extended meaning, Brontë is also remarking that nature has no borders, being humanity's common *kepos*, our – only – garden. Therefore, as a spatial entity, nature is also set against the urban environment of both London and Liverpool, the two cities mentioned in the book. It is also the place haunted by Cathy's ghost, who loses her way there herself and, not finding peace even in death, begs to enter her house once more. The "outside", beyond the moors, is represented and brought into the regional setting of Yorkshire not only by Lockwood but also by Heathcliff, himself an outsider and thus a foreigner according to insiders' values.

The actors of the book are not many but they all have distinct roles that colour the canvas of Brontë's novel so as to permit her to disclose her deeper meaning and her final concerned message: "This north wind that chills *me*" being the wind of nationalism, autochthonousness and essentialism, of borders and regionalisms of all sorts, that does not recognise the *non-lieu* of the moors where freedom reigns.

Lockwood, the doctor from London, is there to witness, testify and provide material proof that such a place really exists in that he can relate the "magic" that takes place there: a space where ghosts might appear, something that he would not have believed even if someone had told him; but that he, in person, cannot but witness in its material proof and truth value, that through him we, as readers, are asked to believe. His function is that of a rational witness who has seen Catherine, knocking on the windowpane to get into Wuthering Heights, with her blood running.

Let us therefore start with these two very important characters. Dr Lockwood, the doctor from London and external visitor, is the narratee of Nelly Dean's story, who is an implied but unreliable narrator,[87] and the other is Heathcliff, the young boy Earnshaw, Catherine's father, brings back from a trip to Liverpool. The city was, during those times, one of the capital slave-ship ports in England: "In 1769, the year in which Mr. Earnshaw found Heathcliff in the Liverpool streets, the city was England's largest slave-trading port, conducting seventy to eighty-five percent of the English slave trade along the Liverpool Triangle, exchanging manufactured goods from the Mersey region for West African slaves, who were exchanged for plantation crops in the American and the Spanish American colonies" (Susan Meyer: 1996, 98).[88] Lockwood is a very perceptive man as one of his notations makes clear: "It is strange how custom can mould our tastes and ideas: many could not imagine the existence of happiness in a life of such complete exile from the world as you spend, Mr. Heathcliff" (WH: 2, 26-27), clearly perceiving that Heathcliff's obsession with the moors is due to Cathy's presence in them.

The story is related in hindsight by Nelly, a servant of the Earnshaw family, to Dr Lockwood. Interestingly, the first comments the reader gets on Heathcliff, now an adult man, come from Lockwood, another class-outsider, who is surprised by the man's unexpected, out-of-context phenotypical physical appearance: "A dark-skinned gipsy in aspect, in dress and manners a gentleman", significantly remarking that he is not exactly the sort of man one would expect there. Indeed, as Lockwood specifies, he is not the expected "northern farmer" type (WH1: 21). Similarly, Cathy's daughter, also, Catherine second, appears to Lockwood different from the people in her environment: "That pretty girl-widow, I should like to know her history: whether she be a native of the country, or, as is more probable, an exotic that the surly *indigenæ* will not recognise for kin" (WH: 4, 42), a thought prompted by Nelly's remark reminding Lockwood that he is in a place where borders matter: "We don't in general take to foreigners here" (WH: 6, 51).

Heathcliff's body is always read by the people around him through the invented pseudoscience of physiognomy (Bezrucka: 2011), the minor sister of racism, that connects space-and-time beauty values to goodness, and its opposite, i.e. inferred ugliness to evil. His traits have caused him trouble with the Lintons, the neighbours living at the Grange, who scrutinise and cast him out from their Palladian sort of manor for his skin colour. Heathcliff experiences a rejection there he will never forget. His identity portrait as "little Lascar, or (…) American or Spanish castaway" (WH: 6, 55) is decided on mere matters of physical aesthetics, on the fact that he is a lad "who looks an out-and-outer" (WH: 6, 55). Slipping from his appearances to her inconsistent physiognomic reading, Mrs Linton, out of the blue, and without him having said a word, judges him to be "a wicked boy (…) quite unfit for a decent house!" (WH: 6, 55).

Heathcliff is also the target of the envy, neglect and hate of Catherine's brother Hindley, who, jealous of his father's attention to him, neither befriends him nor considers him to be a genuine member of the family, a fiendish attitude Catherine always opposes. In Hindley's view, he is simply an "interloper", wheedling to his father, an "imp of Satan" (WH: 4, 47); for Nelly, he is what he is: "a sullen, patient child: hardened (…) by ill-treatment" (WH: 4, 46). This is the result of people's inclination to read only by what is already known, exactly as Cathy's strong, masculine attitude is not approved by her father: "I cannot love thee, thou'rt worse than thy brother" (WH: 5, 49), so that "being repulsed continually hardened her" (WH: 5, 50) a trait she shares with Heathcliff. The experience that both Catherine and Heathcliff endure is also parallel to that of the Creature assembled by Victor Frankenstein in Mary Shelley's novel *Frankenstein; or The Modern Prometheus* (1818), written prior to *Wuthering Heights*. Exactly in the same way as the Monster does, Heathcliff soon turns his initial trust in society into hatred, mirroring and interiorising people's attitude, i.e. becoming what others project onto him, a double-binding relation with outside society as that between Iago and Othello (Bezrucka: 2008c). Like Mary Shelley, who uses her monster to back up the empiricist theories of the *tabula rasa* promoted by Locke and Hume, Brontë makes Heathcliff into an instance of the same theories. Neglected by Hindley, who, as soon as his father dies, turns him outside the house to work with the servants, depriving him of the education formerly imparted, Heathcliff starts to hate him. Only as long as Cathy keeps him up to date with lessons can Heathcliff bear "his degradation" (WH: 6, 52). Together they are still completely free to roam on the moors: an experience of liberty and friendship that stops soon after the incident at the Linton's house, which causes Catherine's shock in understanding that he is not perceived or conceived to be a member of 'their' society. Like Frankenstein's Creature, Heathcliff's rage changes him and, as if he wanted to show them what a real rascal does, he internalises the inappropriateness and unfitness his environment projects on him, and *ressentiment* will dictate his revenge.[89]

Catherine, who had considered Heathcliff to be her equal and her natural 'manly' mirror, testified by her outspoken affirmation: "Heathcliff is me", has, despite this, eventually interiorised the *idola* and values of her society and has married Linton (as Heathcliff later interiorises outside values becoming the monster they see in him). The Lintons have exercised their beauty fascination on her: appearing as a better society and milieu than hers at the Heights, she has agreed to be assimilated by them. The new shiny world has mesmerised her, and once back from her stay at the Grange, Catherine has new manners and standards, being now "a little lady", a change she is to pay for by her death and unhappiness. This, indeed, distances her from Heathcliff, who, broken, exiles himself from the moors for three years. Heathcliff returning now an affluent man, who has probably worked hard to become rich to be accepted by this society and to show Catherine that they would not necessarily be beggars, once he discovers she is married, he becomes a lost man, who starts his revenge against an insiders' society that has unjustly made an outcast of him.

Identity inequality is most clearly played out in his *ressentiment*: Heathcliff being ruthless against everyone as they were with him. He is instrumental in Hindley's catastrophe, he buys the Heights, and exercises his revenge on the Lintons by marrying Isabella, a widow with a child, Hareton, only because she is Catherine's sister-in-law. She will bear him a feeble child, Linton. Catherine, herself the mother of Cathy, pays for the distance she has put between herself and Heathcliff with her life – her unhappiness leading to a self-inflicted malaise that will kill her. This could be compared to an indirect suicide: Heathcliff remaining her elective/neglected man, forever. Her ghost, her presence *in absentia*, will thus haunt the free-land of the Moors and she will not be granted peace, having herself accepted and applied the racist logic of transforming merely aesthetic, cultural issues, into values that she has accepted as being natural and innate. This transforms her ghost into the ghost of English civilization, a civilization that does not accept beggars. In reverting the empiricists' agenda completely, Catherine, paradoxically, has returned to Platonic belief, taking for granted that those outward signs – physiognomics – correspond to inborn traits, i.e. misjudging the outward elegance and beauty of the Lintons as being exactly what she wants, a belief destroyed by Heathcliff's return at the Grange:

> He took a seat opposite Catherine, who kept her gaze fixed on him as if she feared he would vanish were she to remove it. He did not raise his to her often: a quick glance now and then sufficed; but it flashed back, each time more confidently, the undisguised delight he drank from hers. They were too much absorbed in their mutual joy to suffer embarrassment. Not so Mr. Edgar: he grew pale with pure annoyance: a feeling that reached its climax when his lady rose, and stepping across the rug, seized Heathcliff's hands again, and laughed like one beside herself. 'I shall think it a dream to-morrow!' she cried. 'I shall not be able to believe that I have seen, and touched, and spoken to you once more. And yet, cruel Heathcliff! You don't deserve this welcome. To be absent and silent for three years, and never to think of me!'
>
> 'A little more than you have thought of me,' he murmured. 'I heard of your marriage, Cathy, not long since' (WH: 10, 92-93).

Nelly's summary, as usual, provides the lines along which the scene needs to be read:

> He had grown a tall, athletic, well-formed man; beside whom my master seemed quite slender and youth-like. His upright carriage suggested the idea of his having been in the army [probably in the American Revolution]. His countenance was much older in expression and decision of feature than Mr. Linton's; it looked intelligent, and retained no marks of former degradation." (WH: 10, 92)

The remark shows the landed gentry of England as being enfeebled, a standpoint that D.H. Lawrence would exploit in his novel *Lady Chatterley's Lover*.

The flower garden that Catherine the second and Hareton plan to plant at the Heights is a shorthand for miscegenation, cyphered in their transplantation of flowers from the Grange to the Heights, a move at first opposed by Heathcliff. He changes once he measures the fearlessness of Catherine the second in confronting him and standing her own ground about the garden and her and Hareton's right to the inheritance of the houses. It is this which makes Heathcliff desist in humiliating her, reminded as he is of the character of her mother. At this very moment Heathcliff, seemingly, gives up his revenge. This new Catherine also takes the education of Hareton in hand, in contrast to her mother, who had not believed in the possibility of Heathcliff's societal upgrade, which Catherine the second takes as her task to complete. Indeed, Hareton must learn the Ballad of Chevy Chase properly, the pathos-rich ballad relating the attack on the people of the North by the Earl of Northumberland for control of the Cheviot Hills chase, which Earl Douglas strongly defends. Brontë is probably underlining the fact that to defend oneself, one has to be educated enough to know one's rights and to take matters into one's own hands – a possibility that also Catherine the first does not pursue – given that there were no laws to legally rely on to defend her properties and rights in the first place. The ballad was republished around 1760 and it reappears in *The Minstrelsy of the Scottish Border* by Walter Scott (1802); previously, it had also been commented upon in Addison's *Spectator*, Nos. 70 and 74. It is the only piece of literature mentioned in the work and it urges to defend oneself vigorously if under attack. This is just what Hareton has to learn on top of acquiring an education; like Heathcliff, who always abides by the law, keeping strictly within its border in pursuing revenge through his atrocities but always "prevent[ing] the law by doing execution on myself" (WH: 10, 93), learning by heart what could harm him, interiorising the laws and abiding by them.

Notes

[1] Thomas Warton (1968 [1774, 1778, 1781]) *History of English Poetry*, 4 vols.; vol. 4 is included in vol. 3 (vol. 1 is dated 1774, vol. 2, 1778 and vol. 3, 1781, vol. 4 has only pp. 1-88) (New York and London: Johnson Reprints) (ed.) René Wellek, hereafter referred to with TW: vol. no., p. no. For this note, reference is TW: III, 390. It is of interest to note that R. Wellek, the undisputed authority on criticism up to the 1990s, edited in his series 'Classics in Art and Literary Criticism' only Warton's book and Lord Kames's *Elements in Criticism*, 3 vols.

[2] Thomas Warton, vol. 1, presents 'Of the Origin of Romantic Fiction in Europe. Dissertation I' that appears unnumbered in the text. After the Table of Contents ending on page IV, I have thus numbered the pages from 1 to 72, to facilitate the reader. Instead of appearing as (TW: I, s.p.) they will thus appear from here onwards with my pagination.

[3] Vijay Mishra (2007) *The Literature of the Indian Diaspora: Theorizing the Diasporic Imaginary* (London/New York: Routledge).

[4] Cf. C. Rinaker (1912) *Thomas Warton: A Biographical and Critical Study* (Urbana-Champaign: University of Illinois) and her article (1915) 'Thomas Warton and the Historical Method in Literary Criticism', *PMLA*, 30, 1, 79-109.

[5] Cf. S. Hall, (1990) 'Cultural Identity and Diaspora'. In J. Braziel, A. Mannur (eds) *Theorizing Diaspora* (Malden: Blackwell), pp. 233-47. See also (eds) S. Hall,

P. du Gay (1996) *Cultural Identity and Diaspora* (London: Sage).
[6] In the last remark he is referring, as explained in his note, to the Abbé Lebeuf, *Recherches, &c. Mem. de Litt.* tom. xvii. p. 718. edit. 4to.
[7] The work also appears with the title *Brut y Brenhined: The History of the Kings of Britain.*
[8] Warton's hypothesis that the *Brut y Brenhined* is the hypotext of the *Historia Regum Britanniae* by Geoffrey of Monmouth, rather than a hypertext is, controversially, confirmed by F.D. Reno (2000) *Historic Figures of the Arthurian Era: Authenticating the Enemies and Allies* (Jefferson: McFarland & Company), 'Prologue', pp. 1-40.
[9] E. Hobsbawm, T. Ranger (eds) (1983) *The Invention of Tradition* (Cambridge: Cambridge University Press), and his (1990) *Nations and Nationalism since 1780: Programme, Myth, Reality* (Cambridge: Cambridge University Press).
[10] V. Hart (1994) *Art and Magic in the Court of the Stuarts* (London: Routledge), p. 29. Hart states: "The renewal of the antique Golden Age by the British Court represented an essential counterpart to the scheme of church history which was formulated by Protestant theologians at the time of the Reformation, a scheme which cast the Pope as the Anti-Christ and the Protestant church as the prophetic restoration of a pure 'ancient theology' which Catholic tyranny had corrupted. (...) A necessary condition and setting for the return of Astraea and indeed Christ himself was the establishment, or rather re-establishment, by the Renaissance monarch of a Christian empire in succession to that governed by Rome. In line with this general northern imperial ambition — and most notably the claim made by Charles V to a renewal of the Holy Roman Empire — the British monarchy cultivated an imperial role" (p. 30). The fact was that the Stuart family derived their ancestry through the Tudor derivation, from Arthur, and their Stuart lineage through the British Prince Llewellin, in continuation with the Tudor tradition of using British material to strengthen and popularise their claim to the throne. On this, see the chapter on 'The Fairy Way of Writing'. Hart claims that: "Stuart expectations of a Golden Age and claims to Protestant imperial destiny were justified by Court apologists through reference to British legend, and to the tale of an Albion of magical virtue which would one day be restored. Indeed, through such legendary British magic, Renaissance Neoplatonism was itself seen as an aspect of this British antiquity restored. The principal legends of British national origins had been gathered together by the monk Geoffrey of Monmouth, and presented in the *Historia Regum Britanniae* of around 1130. In this the British were described as the heirs to a lost antiquity comprising the Trojan and later Arthurian land of Albion, for according to Geoffrey ancient British kings were descended from Brute, the grandson of Aeneas of Troy" (32). Protestants and Catholics united, for once, along the lines of religions for power reasons.
[11] Warton is here referring to the work of Evan Evans, a.k.a. Ieuan Prydydd Hir (1764) *Dissertatio De Bardis*: *Some Specimens of the Poetry of the Ancient Welsh Bards,* (London: Dodsley).

[12] See Murray G.H. Pittock (1997) *Inventing and Resisting Britain. Cultural Identities in Britain and Ireland, 1685-1789* (London: Macmillan) for the complex panorama of the various cultural and religious regional and marginal societies, in contrast to the Crown Culture (pp. 118-127), which Pittock contrasts to "selective adoption of the central English politico-cultural concerns of the past three hundred years (...) the teleological narrative of religious or economic integration through time" (p. 6). Pittock contests the "bloodlessness" of the 'Glorious Revolution' seeing it, via G.M. Trevelyan's ([1904] 1947) *England Under the Stuarts* (London: Penguin), pp. 402, 43, as evidence for the killings and the time being "an anachronistic drift back to 'the more barbarous methods of Elizabeth and the medieval kings'" (p. 3). This is, indeed, a good example of "history written by victors" as Walter Benjamin would call it, in his 'Theses on the Philosophy of History' where the Angelus Novus, by Klee, is always "turned towards the past" so to see it as "one single catastrophe" ready to be rewritten as "progress". Cf. W. Benjamin (1968 [1955]) (ed.) Hannah Arendt, *Illuminations. Essays and Reflections* (New York: Schocken), pp. 253-64: here 257-58.

[13] Thomas Percy, (1767) Antient Metr. Rom., (i.e. his *Reliques*) i., pp. 3-4.

[14] Warton quotes from Percy, Antient Metr. Rom., (i.e. his *Reliques*) i., pp. 3-4. edit. 1767.

[15] Warton quotes from Mallet, *Introduction a l'Histoire de Danemarc, & C*, tom. ii, p. 9 and tom. ii, ch. ix, p. 243.

[16] Warton is quoting from Hugh Blair, 'A Critical Dissertation on Ossian, the Son of Fingal'. In James Macpherson (1806) *The Poems of Ossian* (London: J.F. Dove), p. 77.

[17] The theory was recovered by T.S. Eliot, who links a "dissociation of sensibility" to the influence of Milton and Dryden. Cf. T.S. Eliot (1986 [1932]) 'The Metaphysical Poets', in *Selected Essays* (London: Faber and Faber), pp. 281-91.

[18] A. Fenner Jr. (1956) 'The Wartons 'Romanticise' their Verse', *Studies in Philology*, 53, 3, 501-08, 504.

[19] *ibid.*

[20] Cf. Kristine Louise Haugen (1998) 'Ossian and the Invention of Textual History', *Journal of the History of Ideas*, vol, 59, No. 2, pp. 309-27; Schmitt Cannon (1994) 'Techniques of Terror, Technologies of Nationality: Ann Radcliffe's "The Italian"', *ELH*, vol. 61, no. 4, pp. 853-76; David Durant (1982) 'Ann Radcliff and the Conservative Gothic', *Studies in English Literature*, 1500-1900, vol. 22, no. 3, pp. 519-30.

21 Patrick J. Geary (2003) *The Myth of Nations: The Medieval Origins of Europe* (Princeton: Princeton University Press), hereafter referred to in the text with GP: and p. no.

[22] Interesting, in this sense, is the Oriental hypothesis, besides the Southern and the Northern, posited by Howard D. Weinbrot, in his (1993) *Britannia's Issue. The Rise of British Literature from Dryden to Ossian* (Cambridge: Cambridge University Press), pp. 495-543, where he says that the first aborigines of the

English island were Jews, Phoenicians that settled in Cornwall, where they constructed Stonehenge, i.e. a Semitic population with a Hebrew language, that some early scholars see joining the Celts, and others refer to as being the aborigines of the island.

[23] See also J. Lucas (1971) *England and Englishness: Ideas of Nationhood in English Poetry: 1688-1900* (London: Methuen); J.M. Wright (2004) *Blake, Nationalism, and the Politics of Alienation* (Athens: Ohio University Press), K. Trumpener (1997) *Bardic Nationalism: The Romantic Novel and the British Empire*, Princeton: Princeton University Press), R. Samuel (1989) *Patriotism: The Making and Unmaking of British National Identity* (London: Routledge) 3 vols.

[24] Cf. on this literary period B. Willey (1980 [1940]) *The Eighteenth-Century Background: Studies on the Idea of Nature in the Thought of the Period* (London: Chatto & Windus); A.O. Lovejoy (1936, 1948) *Essays in the History of Ideas* (Baltimore: Johns Hopkins University Press); A.O. Lovejoy (1936) *The Great Chain of Being. A Study of the History of an Idea* (Harvard: Harvard University Press); R. Wellek (1941) *The Rise of English Literary History* (Chapel Hill: University of North Carolina Press); V. Papetti (1989) *Il Neoclassicismo* (Bologna: Mulino); F. Marenco (2000 [1996]) *Storia della civiltà letteraria inglese* (Torino: Utet), 4 vols.; M. McKeon (1987) *The Origins of the English Novel, 1600-1740* (Baltimore: John Hopkins University Press). For the major trends at work in the century, see James Sambrook (1993) *The Eighteenth Century: The Intellectual and Cultural Context of English Literature. 1700-1789* (London: Longman).

[25] W. Duff (1994 [1767]) *Essay on Original Genius* (London: Routledge/ Thoemmes), hereafter referred to in the text with WD and page no.

[26] For a further discussion of W. Duff's work, you can see my (2002) *Genio e immaginazione*, op. cit., pp. 44-50.

[27] Horace Walpole (1937 [1762-1771]) *Anecdotes of Painting in England with some Account on the Principal Artists and on Incidental Notes on other Arts*, F.W. Hilles, P.B. Daghlian (eds) (London: Oxford University Press) vol. 5 referred to in the text with HW5 and page no.

[28] Cf. T. Warton (1754) *Observations on the Faerie Queene* (London: Dodsley, Fletcher). Warton, however, repents of his Gothic past, but in the meantime twenty years have passed and the influence of the Neoclassicist Sir Joshua Reynolds has made itself felt. Cf. Walpole's work (1782) *Verses on Sir Joshua Reynolds' Painted Window at New College*, Oxford, especially the last verses, 105-106, where a fusion between the classical and the Gothic styles is wished for.

[29] Horace Walpole (1765) *Anecdotes of Painting in England with some Account on the Principal Artists and on Incidental Notes on other Arts*, G. Vertue, (Strawberry-Hill: Kirkgate) vol. 2, referred to in the text as HW2 and page no., here HW2: 1.

[30] Cf. K. Clark (1964 [1928]) *The Gothic Revival*, (Harmondsworth: Penguin), pp. 22-33, cf. also the chapter that Clark dedicates to Strawberry Hill, Horace Walpole's villa, the most blatant example of a Neo-Gothic that he also transposed

in literature in his (1996 [1764]) *The Castle of Otranto. A Gothic Story* (Oxford: Oxford University Press).
[31] Cf. also: Cannon Schmitt (1994) 'Technologies of Terror, Technologies of Nationality: Ann Radcliffe's "The Italian"', *ELH,* 61, 853-76.
[32] J. Bentham (1818) *Church of Englandism and its Catechism Examined* (London: Effingham Wilson).
[33]Richard Hurd (1762) *Letters of Chivalry and Romance* (London: Millar, Thurlbourne, Woodyer). Important letters for the recovery of the Celtic tradition of English literature are letters vi: 'Heroic and Gothic Manners', vii: 'Spenser and Milton', viii: 'The Faerie Queene'. These can be found also in the E.D. Jones (ed.) (1947 [1922]) *English Critical Essays: XVI-XVIII Centuries*, (Oxford and London: Oxford University Press,), pp. 312-26, edition, which I refer to as RH, letter no., and page (RH: viii, 320). On the chivalric imagination and its symbolic iconography, see Rodney Dennis (1975) *The Heraldic Imagination* (London: Barrie and Jenkins).
[34] Thomas Warton (1754) *Observations on the Faerie Queene* (London: J. Dodsley & J. Fletcher), hereafter referred to in the text as TWO and page no.
[35] Richard Hurd in his *Letters on Chivalry,* no. viii, connected the feast episode in *The Faerie Queene* with the real tournament that had been set up in Lisle in 1453, at the court of Philip the Good, Duke of Burgundy, to celebrate a victory over the Turks (RH: viii, 320).
[36] J. Addison, R. Steel (1891) *The Spectator. A New Edition Reproducing the Original Text both as First Issued and as Corrected by its Authors,* (ed.) Richard Morley, 3 vols. (London: Routledge).
[37] Thomas Warton (1754) *Observations on the Faerie Queene,* (London: J. Dodsley & J. Fletcher). The work is considered by critics to be "the first historical piece of criticism in the field of English criticism (…) and in the definitiveness of its revolt against the pseudo-classical criticism by rule marking the beginning of a new school", cf. Clarissa Rinaker 'Thomas Warton: A Biographical and Critical Study' *Illinois University Studies*, vol. 1, no. 2, 1912, and her 'Thomas Warton and the Historical Method in Literary Criticism', *PMLA*, vol. 30, no. 1 (1915), 79-109.
[38] C. Rinaker (1912) *Thomas Warton: A Biographical and Critical Study* (Urbana-Champaign: University of Illinois). p. 45, hereafter referred to in the text with RC and p. n.
[39] J.P. Ker (ed.) (1900) 'Discourse Concerning the Origin and Progress of Satire', *Essays of John Dryden* (Oxford: Clarendon Press), vol. 2, p. 28.
[40] Cf. Raymond D. Havens (1912) 'Romantic Aspects of the Age of Pope', *Modern Language Association of America, New Series,* vol. XX, 3, pp. 297-324, p. 319.
[41] Literary forgery is often linked to the rationale at the back of national state formations. In Scotland, for example, Macpherson's forgery of the *Ossian Poems*, and Thomas Chatterton's forgery of the poems of Rowley, well-studied by Anthony Grafton (1990) *Forgers and Critics: Creativity and Duplicity in Western Scholarship* (Princeton: Princeton University Press), and K.K. Ruthven (2001)

Faking Literature, (Cambridge: Cambridge University Press). Ruthven shows clearly that the aim behind the Ossian forgery was, first, to show that in the Gaelic tradition of Scotland, the Stuart Pretender, eventually defeated at Culloden (1745), had more right to the kingship of the nation than the Saxons, and second, to demonstrate that the real author of these poems was a Scot Bard called Ossian and not an Irish one called Oisean (cf. pp. 6-7), implicitly affirming that the "originating site of Gaelic culture in the third century AD was not Ireland but Scotland", p. 7. See also I. Haywood (1986) *The Making of History: A Study of the Literary Forgeries of James Macpherson and Thomas Chatterton in Relation to Eighteen-Century Ideas of History and Fiction* (London and Toronto: Associated University Presses).

[42] Thomas Percy (1926 [1765]) *Reliques of Ancient English Poetry* (London: Dent).

[43] P. Connell (2006) 'British Identities and the Politics of Ancient Poetry in Later Eighteenth-Century England', *The Historical Journal*, 49, 1, 161–92. Hereafter referred to in the text as PC and page number.

[44] T. Wein (2000) *British Identities, Heroic Nationalisms, and the Gothic Novel: 1764-1824* (Gordonsville VA: Palgrave), pp. 213-14, here p. 3. Cf. also: Murray G.H. Pittock (1997) *Inventing and Resisting Britain: Cultural Identities in Britain and Ireland: 1685–1789* (London: Macmillan); Katie Trumpener (1997), *Bardic Nationalism: The Romantic Novel and the British Empire* (Princeton: Princeton University Press), pp. 3–34.

[45] Typical examples of this are adventure novels, perceived as if they were children's literature whereas in reality they are being written for parents; the same happens with apparently unrealistic and neutral horror novels, such as *Dracula*, by Bram Stoker, which actually promote racist positions, or, again, in belletristic, entertaining novels that, like those of Chick-Lit, are read daily by thousands of readers and unobtrusively become the vehicles of values that 'high' literature tends to critique. That is why Cultural Studies advises us to study precisely this type of literature thoroughly, the best-sellers that are not easily comprised in university canons but that, seen "from afar off", as Franco Moretti (2005) has rightly pointed out in his *La letteratura vista da lontano* (Milano: Garzanti), in their wide dissemination often propagate values (money, success, beauty, often racism, etc.) that might become prevalent without this being noticed by intellectuals. See my reading of Bram Stoker's *Dracula* in Bezrucka: 2004: 137-46.

[46] Thomas Warton says "[T]he Saxon style [a development of "the old Gothic" p. 2], being the national architecture of our Saxon ancestors before the Conquest: the Normans only extended its proportion and enlarged its scale (...) The style which succeeded to this was not the absolute *Gothic*, or Gothic simply so called, but a sort of *Gothic* SAXON, in which the pure *Saxon* began to receive some tincture of the Saracen fashion", cf. T. Warton, J. Bentham, J. Milner (1800) *Essays on Gothic Architecture* (London: Architectural Library Holborn), p. 4. Francis Grose also classes three stages of the general appellation "Gothic": "Our modern antiquaries,

more accurately, divide (...) into Saxon, Norman, and Saracenic", in *ibid.*, p. 95.
[47] Cf. J.M. Wright (2004) *Blake, Nationalism, and the Politics of Alienation* (Athens: Ohio University Press).
[48] For the ancient vs. modern controversy in the British context, see J.M. Levine (1991) *The Battle of the Books: History and Literature in the Augustan Age* (Ithaca: Cornell University Press).
[49] See Roey Sweet (2004) *Antiquaries, The Discovery of the Past in Eighteenth-Century Britain* (Cambridge: Cambridge University Press), pp. 81-84, here 84, and the work of the antiquarian R. Gough (1780) *Anecdotes of British Topography: or, an Historical Account of what has been done for Illustrating the Topographical Antiquities of Great Britain and Ireland* (London: W. Richardson and S. Clark), which defines the English Gothic monuments and sets a possible Druidic origin of the Gothic: "One cannot enough regret the little regard hitherto paid to Gothic architecture, of which so many beautiful models are daily crumbling to pieces before our eyes. England can boast specimens of all its ages from the simplest to the most improved. We can go back even to the druids, who poised immense weights almost on nothing, yet wanted courage and contrivance to raise arches. At Stonehenge, they supplied their place with flat imposts of the same size with the uprights; all their other temples are but so many circles of pillars. It was reserved to the Norman architects to rear arches without centres and without those supports which a semicircle finds in itself, and which their bold magnificence betrays the want of, when, to furnish an equal pressure, their walls are obscured by massive buttresses" (p. XX).
[50] F. Grose (1773-1787) *The Antiquities of England and Wales* (London: Hooper & Wigstead).
[51] See Bezrucka: 2002:79-132, and Bezrucka: 2004: 61-103, where I examine his important 19th-century followers, amongst them Walter Pater and Oscar Wilde.
[52] J. Knowles, F.R.S. (1831), *The Life and Writing of Henry Fuseli*, Esq. M.A.R.A., 3 vols., (London: H. Colburn, R. Bentley), vol. III, p. 102.
[53] Anticipated in this affirmation by Oliver Goldsmith, in *Letters from a Citizen of the World to his Friends in the East*, where he *verbatim* says: "I now begin to fancy there is no universal-standard for beauty", Letter VIII, p. 38. Cf. Oliver Goldsmith (1820 [1762]) *Letters from a Citizen of the World to his Friends in the East* (London: J. Bungay and R. Childs), hereafter referred to in the text as CW and page no.
[54] This phase is the start of a very long process that climaxed in modernity with abstract or emphatic art, and was later superseded by the dictatorship of novelty as such. Nevertheless, postmodernist aesthetics can be considered the climax of aesthetic liberty, as I explain in Bezrucka: 1995b, 85-111.
[55] See Y. Bezrucka (ed.), *Regionalismo e antiregionalismo*, op. cit.
[56] Thomas Warton (1968 [1774, 1778, 1781]) *History of English Poetry*, 4 vols., (ed.) René Wellek (New York and London: Johnson Reprint Corporation), an anastatic copy of the London 3 editions, hereafter referred to as TW and vol. no.,

page no., here see TW: I, pp. I-VIII, VIII.
[57] Philological work on Warton's *History* has declined his "appropriation[s]". Cf. Richard Price's 'Introduction' to the 1824 edition of Warton's *History* (London: 1840 [1824], pp. 9-95, 42), who establishes his own tradition of romantic fiction by showing that its elements appear in all literatures of the four cardinal points.
[58] Cf. E.W. Soja (1989) *Postmodern Geographies. The Reassertion of Space in Critical Social Theory* (London: Verso), p. 122. See also Ann R. Markusen, who reads the characteristics of places as the result of "the dynamics of a process" rather than as the result of an essentialist logic in her article (1978) 'Regionalism and the Capitalist State: The Case of the United States', *Kapitalistate,* 7, 39-62, quoted in Soja, op. cit., p. 102.
[59] The evidence for Warton's hypothesis is to be found, as he says, in a mss. in the British Library, MSS. Harl. 978.107, and a set of old French tales of chivalry in verse, amongst which we find: *Tristram a Wales*, celebrated for his adventures in *Eliduc*, by the knight *Milun,* born in South Wales, and celebrated for his exploits in Ireland, Norway Gothland, Lotheringia, Albany, etc., and in Launval and in Guigemar. At the end of most of these tales, it is said that these lais were created by the poets of Bretaigne.
[60] Guy Alexis Lobineau (1707) *Histoire de Bretagne* (Paris: Muguet) 2 vols.
[61] The quote is referred in the notes as "MANSUS" but remains unspecified in the source of vol. 4. It refers to the Latin carme *Epitaphium Damonis*, p. 138, which John Milton dedicated to Giovanni Battista Manso, Marquis of Villa, who had had Milton as his guest and who is referred to in Milton's poem on page 139 in: Charles Symmons (1806) (ed.), *The Prose Works of John Milton with a Life of the Author*, 7 vols., vol. 7 (London: Bensley), p. 128, and final quote p. 130.
[62] Warton's note in TW: 1, 4 refers to Milton's *Paradise Lost*, I, 579.
[63] Charles Symmons (ed.) (1806), *The Prose Works of John Milton with a Life of the Author*, 7 vols., vol. 7 (London: Bensley), pp. 137-38, footnotes b and c.
[64] W.Y. Evans-Wentz (1911) *Fairy Faith in Celtic Countries* (London: Oxford U.P.). Hereafter referred to in the text as W and page no.
[65] On the role of Nature in the past, see my essay (2013) 'Nature as Oikos and Kepos: Ecocriticism as a Branch of Bioethics in Romantic Studies', *Nuovi Quaderni del CRIER*, X, (Verona: Fiorini), pp. 33-54.
[66] The suggestion that the folk-memory of the Druids and their magical practices is solely responsible for the Fairy-Faith can be found in James Currie (1803) *Scottish Scenery* (London: Cadell, Davies) and in Patrick Graham (1806) *Sketches Descriptive of Picturesque Scenery on the Southern Confines of Perthshire* (Edinburgh: P. Hill and W. Hunter).
[67] I have followed the issue of "critical regionalism" as an answer to the acritical, isolationist and excluding model in various works: Bezrucka: 2002 for aesthetic regionalism, and for cultural regionalism as both a negative strategy (essentialism) and a positive 'critical' one, motivated by an anti-colonial preservational response in Bezrucka: 2012, 2008, 2008 (a), 2006, 2005, 1995a and b, 1997, 1999a and b.

[68] Demons were used in the same way as saints were used by both the clergy and the kings to foster superstition in the people. St. Augustine (1871) speaks of Daemons in *The City of God* (Edinburgh: Clark), vol. 1, Bks. 8, 9, as aerial entities in which Plato, like Apuleius, believed "where interpreters and intercessors between the gods whom God made and men" (p. 346), cf. Bks. 13-22, from Bk. 23rd he speaks about the Egyptian Hermes Trimegistus who has different opinions from Apuleius, who believed that daemons were a superior order of intermediary beings, not as mighty as God and the Angels, but that were similar to human beings, although they were aerial creatures: "so humanity fashioned its own gods according to the liking of its own countenance (…) that are similar to "statues animated (…) prescient of future things, and foretelling them by lot, by prophet, by dreams, and many other things, who bring diseases on them and cure them again, giving them joy or sorrow according to their merits" (p. 340), but he also foresees the coming of Christianity which will overthrow all this "lying figments", concluding that "our forefathers have erred very much "they invented the art of making gods" (343).

[69] A good example of the kind of influence literary works have is provided by Bram Stoker's *Dracula*, a simple vampire book, as some people would describe it, that, nevertheless, rich in racist undertones, has done much to implement racist attitudes in the people who, unheedingly, absorb its message. Cf. my reading of the novel in (2005) *Oggetti e collezioni nella letteratura inglese dell'Ottocento* (Trento: Ares), pp. 137-146.

[70] See Patrick Brantlinger (1996) *Fictions of State. Culture and Credit in Britain, 1694-1994* (Ithaca: Cornell University Press), p. 4. Specifically, for the role of literature see Benedict Anderson (1983) *Imagined Communities. Reflections on the Spread of Nationalism* (London: Verso), pp. 25-36, and Patrick Brantlinger, *Rule of Darkness*, op. cit.; Homi Bhabha, 'Introduction: Narrating the Nation' in H. Bhabha (ed.) (1990) *Nation and Narration*, op. cit., p. 3. See also Simon During, 'Literature – Nationalism's other? The case for revision', in H. Bhabha (ed.) *Nation and Narration*, op. cit., pp. 142, et passim.

[71] Eric Hobsbawm, Terence Ranger (eds) (1992) *The Invention of Tradition* (Cambridge: Cambridge University Press), p. 8.

[72] Timothy Brennan (1990) 'The National Longing for Form'. In H. Bhabha (ed.) (1990) *Nation and Narration* (London: Routledge), p. 49.

[73] Morgan Prys, 'From a Death to a View: The Hunt for a Welsh Past in the Romantic Period'. In Hobsbawm, Eric, Ranger, Terence (eds) *The Invention of Tradition*, op. cit., p. 47.

[74] *ibid.*

[75] Hugh Trevor-Roper, 'The Invention of Tradition: The Highland Tradition of Scotland'. In Eric Hobsbawm, Terence Ranger (eds) *The Invention of Tradition*, op. cit., p. 44.

[76] *ibid.* p. 17.

[77] *ibid.* p. 18.

[78] M. Arnold (1891) *Celtic Literature* (London: Smith, Elder, & Co).
[79] W. Butler Yeats, in his work (1893, rev. 1902) *The Celtic Twilight* (London: Bullen) collected a series of stories about fairies and Celtic myths. This gave the name also to the late 19th- and 20th-century *Celtic Revival*, which centred around Lady Charlotte Guest's translation of the traditional Welsh materials collected in *The Mabinogion*. Yeats' great interest in the early Medieval Insular works is attested to in his essay 'The Celtic Element in Literature', in W. Butler Yeats (1985 [1961]), *Essays and Introductions* (London: Macmillan), pp. 173-88. Yeats tried to direct the attention of the people of Ireland to their early literature and their culture. He did the same by instituting, in collaboration with Lady Augusta Gregory, the Irish Theatre, and in pursuing an interest in the Theosophical Society where Kenneth Morris was active. Intellectuals that shared the interest in Celtic literature were: Ella Young, Æ (George WilliamRussell), Fiona Macleod (William Sharp), John Cowper Powys, Lord Dunsany, James Stephen, among others.
[80] Emily Brontë, (1949 [1847]) *Wuthering Heights* (Penguin, Harmondsworth), referred to as WH, chapter and relative page number.
[81] Emily Brontë's novel is a masterpiece in its vision of the consequences that ensue once aesthetic standards of taste are exported from the, only apparently, innocuous and safe realm of aesthetics, and are applied in the realm of peoples. Brontë clearly shows the discriminatory escalation which ensues once space-categories and imaginary borderlines are transformed into phenotypical, national, or racial typological standards. Brontë, that is, masterfully illustrates and foresees the havoc this wreaks.
[82] A later instance of this kind of escalation is Herbert Spencer's application of Charles Darwin's findings on the evolution of the species misusing it by applying it on the social level and distinguishing between more and less evoluted human beings and cultures, positing the white race at the top of the evolution chart, which is exactly what Brontë foresaw.
[83] J. Hillis Miller (1982) *Fiction and Repetition: Seven English Novels* (Cambridge MA: Cambridge University Press), pp. 42-72.
[84] Marc Augé (1995 [1992]) *Non-Places. Introduction to an Anthropology of Supermodernity* (orig. title *Non-Lieux*, tr. J. Howe (London: Verso).
[85] Michel Foucault (1984 [1967]) 'Des espaces autres'. In *Dits et écrits*, vol. 4, 752-62 (Paris: Gallimard), places where utopia is possible, a concept also developed in Hakim Beys' concept of the *TAF: Temporary Autonomous Zones* (1991), places where, for a given moment in time, control systems and episteme do not exist and where the imagination is totally free.
[86] I have named it thus in Bezrucka: 2002.
[87] See the contrasting points of view of William E. Buckler (1952) 'Chapter Seven of 'Wuthering Heights': A Key to Interpretation', *Nineteenth-Century Fiction*, 7, 52-55; see also John K. Mathison (1956) 'Nelly Dean and the Power of *Wuthering Heights*', *Nineteenth-Century Fiction*, 11, 106-29; Gideon Shunami (1973) 'The Unreliable Narrator in *Wuthering Heights*' *Nineteenth-Century Fiction*, 27, 106-

29, and in general on the role of the frames in the novel: Jeffrey Williams (1998) *Theory and the Novel. Reflexivity in the British Tradition* (Cambridge: Cambridge University Press), pp. 134-55, who sees this novel as an "inter-imbrication of narratorial relations" eschewing analogical framing structures (p. 145).

[88] Cf. Susan Meyer (1996) *Imperialism at Home: Race and Victorian Women's Fiction* (Ithaca and London: Cornell University Press), p. 98. In ch. 3 of this work, Meyer provides a very interesting reading of the implications of Heathcliff's origin for the development of the book.

[89] Terry Eagleton reads Heathcliff's aggressiveness as an emblem of capitalism intruding into rural values (1975) *Myths of Power: A Marxist Study of the Brontës* (London: Macmillan).

CONCLUSION

Our hypothesis of Northern aesthetics has examined the strong concentration of the geographical, cultural and climatic elements of the English environment and nature. We analysed a series of works that bear witness to the uneasiness English intellectuals feel when the Renaissance becomes a sort of Neoclassical cage used to measure whatever is produced in the arts in England in the 17th and 18th centuries.

Shakespeare was the first to rebel against Southern aesthetics and in his ingeniousness he was able to create an English counter-tradition and delineate and defend an aesthetics adherent to the prerogatives of his environment. He defends his liberty for doing so in at least two works: *A Midsummer Night's Dream* and *The Tempest*. In both, he explicitly points to the recovery of a tradition coming from popular culture and England's mythical past. This tradition he saw exemplified in the cultural heritage of the fairies. Fairies become, through his work, also a religious statement, being chthonic deities without proselytising aims, who were merely the protectors of nature and those positive humans who respect it. Their distinguishing characteristic is that they have a limited possibility to intervene in people's lives.

We then examined various works and established how the intelligentsia coalesced in a common effort to free themselves not only from the Ancients but also from the Southern aesthetics of beauty that they upheld. Beauty, as they came to realise, and some of them to defend, was an ideological vehicle for the monotheism they were questioning in the, only apparently peripheral, discussion of innatism, the concept that represented *in nuce* and in its essence, the core and stronghold of creationism.

Through Bacon, Locke, de Mandeville and Hume, the English empiricists challenged not only innatism but also other correlated concepts that endorsed the creationist hypothesis, upheld by the rationalists and the Neoplatonists. Empiricists attacked the idea of an inborn sense of morality and Grotius's belief in man's natural rights (de Mandeville), underlining the fact that there was no agreement between people from different cultures on what the word "natural" meant. They thus posited the theory of the mind as a blank slate, the *tabula rasa*, on which only the environment, experience, education and culture write.

Our analysis thus gives central importance to Addison's theory of the imagination (1712). Joseph Addison – the populariser of Locke's ideas – who ratified the intermediary role of the senses in our understanding of reality and posited the imagination as a faculty present in all people, there to be used and exercised, was, *de facto,* rejecting the deistic stronghold of the English Neoplatonists, who affirmed the inborn quality of God's gifts to artists and geniuses, the position that foremost endorsed creationism. Furthermore, Addison's request for a return to the autochthonous and unique tradition of England which he identified in the recovery of the fairy way of writing – the chthonic tradition of polytheism and magic which he saw as the origin and uniqueness of England – contributed to set, also in literary terms, the nationalistic, mythical, and now also magical, foundational past of the Celtic tradition of England, which folklore had never forgotten. At the same time, as I claim, with his work "The Pleasures of the Imaginations" (1712), he also established the all-in-one manifesto of Romanticism.

Reverend Gilpin focused on the elements he considered unique in his country, setting the picturesque as a proper style, a way of seeing and an epistemic filter for the detection of elements that the aesthetics of the South had thoroughly ousted: pleasing irregularity, intricacy, artificial naturality in contrast to artificial harmony. He thus adopted the geographical, or regionalist, change of perspective, which permitted people to look at England with different eyes and consequently to detect different qualities.

The specificities of reality were favoured also by Hogarth's *Analysis of Beauty* (1753), in which he posited the aesthetics of the shell as the passport for a no-choice acceptance of variety, which became embodied in Fielding's manifesto of the "comic-epic poem in prose" – the novel – as stated in *Joseph Andrews* (1742).

Edmund Burke's revision of the Greek stylistic theory of the sublime (1757) into an aesthetics of its own capitalised on Gilpin's picturesque. The sublime provided a further opportunity to see things differently. Authorising an upscaling of the morally contained pleasures of Addison, in focusing on the thoroughly personal perception that could comprise emotions and feelings like fear, ugliness and disquiet, Burke's work led to an entirely new literary panorama. Graveyard Poetry and the Gothic novel were the result of this new focus. Rewriting religious fears as mere superstitions, they provided a new perspective that dismantled the concept of *la belle nature* and the creationist idea that sustained it and with it, the idea of irrevocable perfection in aesthetics. Everybody was now free to perceive according to preference without borders or limits. The grand theory of beauty, which had posited a universal aesthetics by effacing the fact that it was itself regional – Western, Greek and Latin, space-time-specific – the cultural version of the beautiful was exposed, and the universality of beauty undermined and, eventually, dismantled by Francis Grose (1788).

Through Gilpin and Burke, English nature eventually had the chance to become attractive, even though the sun was scarce and the environment presented no symmetrical temples. The *Picturesque (Domestic) Anti-Grand-Tours* started to be preferred by the people who, through these men's work, had become educated to see their country through "the Eye of the Beholder" (JA: 412, 61). Irregular, intricate and picturesque natural sites became appreciated, and the further north one headed, the more picturesque nature became, climate notwithstanding.

Literature also came under fire: older autochthonous works were reclaimed as condensing a previously unseen Englishness in their non-compliance to the Southern aesthetics. Chaucer, Milton, Spenser and Shakespeare were reread and recast as authors whose works presented Gothic traits. Thomas Warton provided the passport for the new autochthonous tradition via the first *History of English Poetry* (1774-1781) and the canon that he established for the future. Gothic traits were now evident everywhere: in their stark, bulky, muscular qualities, in contrast with the harmonious but awkwardly gendered, feminine qualities of Palladian Neoclassicism, they represented the quintessence of this land.

Architecture became the new sister art of literature, a stronghold of the new aesthetics, despite the partly failed attempt made, later in time, to recover the Gothic for the Catholic High Church credo, by the architect Pugin, who transformed this into the hierarchical Gothic Perpendicular, emblematic of a top-down monotheistic religion. The Saxon-Gothic – the typically bulky architectural style before the Norman conquest, when Catholicism and the new, menacing vengeful God had not yet cancelled the magic lore of the past – became in the 18th century also a symbol of the Protestant and Northern reformed-religion and of the chthonic-religion of the Druids. This style reminded the people of England of Stonehenge and the primitive magical and polytheistic credo of its priests, of the laws of the Germans, of the equity tradition that Northern aesthetics emblematically cyphered. It also brought home to people the values of the chivalric tradition of King Arthur and his Round Table of equals: a miniature for the constitutional monarchy, echoed in the English garden blueprint.

The newly born Gothic genre was thus used in literature to debunk continental religious belief upheld by superstition, to undermine the undisputed authority that went with it. This it did by scoffing at those who could still believe in the ridiculous, extreme excesses of the genre – bleeding statues, falling arms, speaking mirrors, ghosts and so forth. This also explains why Walpole did not sign the first edition of his book – set in a canonical Catholic country, iLn Otranto, Apulia, Italy – because the critique was severe and he thought it would be immediately detected. Not only, however, did this not happen, the book even gave rise to a genre of its own, people being caught and interested in examining their fears, forgetting for a moment their beliefs. Once this book was successful, the second edition appeared under his name.

The Northern qualities of all these aesthetic choices have thus to be linked with the key importance that the English intelligentsia bestows on freedom: freedom from religious and political authority (via the fairies' tradition, King Arthur, the English garden, the Gothic novel), freedom to judge personally (empiricism), freedom to create new utopias for the future, the cult of the imagination and its outcome, Romanticism proper.

These positive outcomes unfortunately led to backyard consequences. Focusing mainly on difference, and setting a mythical moment in the past at its origin – the Celtic past and King Arthur as its representatives – it rooted the requests for freedom in the geographical and regional characteristics of the nation and its people, choosing to make it coincide with both the real and invented Celtic tradition of England, which erased the historical process of the peoples' identity issues, leading to this frozen and ahistorical, spatial outcome.

In the same way, the North/South opposition can easily be dismantled but this does not mean that in the 18th century it did not work. What I want to underline is that I am fully aware that the picturesque, grounded in nature, which intellectuals claimed as characteristic of England, provided one looked for it, was to be found everywhere, as were, also, the solar qualities of the South. Even the English garden was an invention of England but that did not mean that it was non-exportable. The same is true of the English defence of freedom from religious and political authoritarianism, which was also adopted by the French, and so on. In the same way, melancholy was also not an exclusive prerogative of the English but, as we have seen, they came to think of it like this, or, rather, decided to think so. Fostered by their different jurisprudence, the equity tradition and its pliability, in contrast to the continental written formulas based only on the letter of the law, English intellectuals perceived themselves as being more inclined to freedom and free-will, more enlightened than other peoples, who still languished in the dark of Continental superstition.

To conclude: this book tries to offer an original and fresh

understanding of 18th-century literature based on the well-backed-up hypothesis of the invention of a Northern aesthetics. It analyses the spatial regionalist politics used by the British intelligentsia to free themselves from the yoke of the Southern (Greek and Roman) tradition of beauty, which they felt to be non-adherent to their Northern environment and culture.

Scholars came to qualify the adjective "Northern" via a new art vocabulary directed at signalling the differences of the English nation from the nations of the Continent. Picturesque and sublime beauties were invented and new paradigms for variety created: aesthetic moves that were, nevertheless, soon transcodified into politics, i.e. into iconic and emblematic political symbols identified and demagogically deployed. English intellectuals, proud of having attained democracy (via the 'bloodless' Glorious Revolution), aptly decided to root their origins in a mythical past: that of King Arthur's chivalric shared model of government.

Northern aesthetics, which was initially linked to nature and taste issues, was upscaled and linked to the specific and, at this point, cultural differences that England contained: mainly its democratic tradition (*Magna Carta, Habeas Corpus*, Common Law jurisprudence), which scholars saw culminating in the constitutional monarchy, celebrating the predominance of the people over the king.

The other central element that the intelligentsia believed distinguished them from the continental nations was religion. Through their choice of adopting a scientific outlook, which came well before its time (The Royal Society, 1660) via detailed references to induction and the empiric philosophers (Bacon, Locke, de Mandeville, Hume), who had dismantled the innatist view of the mind and focused rather on the senses and their involuntary freedom, they came to favour, instead of ingeniousness, the faculty of the imagination, which was a talent common to all.

When, in 1774, Thomas Warton wrote the first *History of English Poetry*, he revised the *stemma codicum* of the chivalric romance, claiming for the Welsh bards of the court of King Arthur the authorship of the Arthurian works. The new Northern, in a general sense, and English canon (Chaucer, Spenser, Milton, Shakespeare), in a specific one, was thus created: literature proving to be a powerful ally of nationalism.

Alongside this literary autochthonous canon, the Puritan Reformation was deployed as the democratic religious model set against Catholicism and the gullibility of the continental nations – such as France and Italy – whose people could still believe in the blatant excesses of spirits and demonic forces of which, I claim, the mock-heroic Gothic novel makes fun.

These aesthetic and literary shifts were backed up with emblematic, cyphered nationalistic symbols: the English garden blueprint, King Arthur's Round Table, the reformed religion of England.

The focus on the country and its liberties made the English proud, so proud that they felt they should, as they later would, export their civilization, not realising that the various cultures of the world did not need their version of it. The Indian enterprise, which saw Queen Victoria proclaimed Empress of India, and the colonial agenda that went with it, are ideologically strong and rich in consequences, imperialistic translations of pride that find a good cypher in T.B. Macauley's *Minute on Indian Education* (1835).

This book downplays this nationalistic involution – masterfully depicted in *Wuthering Heights* – by following its 18th-century birth, offering a new outlook on the period and proposing to revise the definition of the 18th-century literary tradition, usually termed "The Long 18th Century" or "The Neoclassical Age", into "The Long Enlightened Romanticism". This move is fully justified by Addison's early essay on the topic (1712), which changed the literary tradition via the new English canon creation (Chaucer, Spenser, Milton, Shakespeare) that Thomas Warton (1774-1781) undertook and which culminates in English Romanticism.

To the studies of nationalism by Renan, Kohn, Ruthven, Anderson, Bhabha, During, Brennan and Brantlinger, to which I have referred, this work has added the fruitful cultural concept of regionalism to underline the presence of cultural varieties within each single nation, which should be considered to have greater relevance, before reducing cultural diversity into the homogenising concept of the "nation-as-one". The book, therefore, develops the point of a critical regionalism open to outside influences but also aware of the necessity of keeping the autochthonous cultural heritage alive, an autochthonous heritage that could prove to be a solid alternative to strong regionalism, i.e. populism and its legacies. This is also why we have chosen to follow the reading of history proposed by Patrick J. Geary, recasting the history of people as the ongoing history of their unfinished migration and diaspora. This we have named the ethnic cross-cultural engrafting of peoples on peoples producing new peoples.

BIBLIOGRAPHY

Abrams, M.H. (1971 [1953]) *The Mirror and the Lamp. Romantic Theory and the Critical Tradition* (Oxford: Oxford University Press).

—. (1973 [1971]) *Natural Supernaturalism. Tradition and Revolution in Romantic Literature* (New York: Norton).

Addison, J. (1907 [1711-1714]) 'The Pleasures of the Imagination'. In G. G. Smith (ed.) *The Spectator* (London: Dent), 54-96.

Aden, J.M. (1953) 'Dryden and Boileau: The Question of Critical Influence', *Studies in Philology*, 50, 3, 491-509.

Anderson, B. (1983) *Imagined Communities. Reflections on the Spread of Nationalism* (London: Verso).

Andrews, M. (1989) *The Search for the Picturesque: Landscape Aesthetics and Tourism in Britain, 1760-1800* (Stanford: Stanford University Press).

—. (1994) *The Picturesque. Literary Sources and Documents* (Mountfield: Helm).

Anglo, S. (1961) 'The British History in Early Tudor Propaganda', *Bulletin of the John Rylands Library,* 44, 1, 17-48.

Arac J., Ritv H. (eds) (1995) *Macropolitics of Nineteenth-Century Literature* (Durham and London: Duke University Press).

Aristotle (1961) *The Nicomachean Ethics* (tr. D. Ross) (Oxford: Oxford University Press).

Arnold D., Bending S. (eds) (2003) *Tracing Architecture* (Oxford: Blackwell).

Arnold, M. (1862) *On Translating Homer: Last Words* (London: Longman, Green, Roberts).

—. (1891) *The Study of Celtic Literature* (London: Smith, Elder, & Co).

Augé M. (1995 [1992]) *Non-Places. Introduction to an Anthropology of Supermodernity* (orig. title *Non-Lieux*, tr. J. Howe) (London: Verso).

Axelsson, K. (2007) *The Sublime: Precursors and British Eighteenth-Century Conceptions* (Bern: Peter Lang).

Bacon, F. (2000) *The New Organon* (ed.) L. Jardine (tr. M. Silverthorne) (Cambridge: Cambridge University Press).

Ball, M.J., Fife, J. (eds) (1993) *The Celtic Languages* (London and New York: Routledge).

Baridon, M. (1989) 'History, Myth, and the English Garden'. In G.

Jackson-Stops, et al. (eds), *The Fashioning and Functioning of the British Country House* (Washington: National Gallery of Art), pp. 373-91.

Barrell, J. (1983) *The Dark side of the Landscape* (Cambridge: Cambridge University Press).

Battisti, C. (ed.) (2010) *Parola e visione*, (Verona: Ombre Corte).

Baumgarten, A.G. (1961 [1750]) *Aesthetica* (Hildesheim: G. Olms).

Ben-Chaim, M. (2000) 'Locke's Ideology of Common Sense', *Studies in History and Philosophy of Science*, Part A 31, 3, 473-501.

Bending S. (2003) 'Every Man is Naturally an Antiquarian: Francis Grose and Polite Antiquities'. In Arnold D., S. Bending (eds) (2003) *Tracing Architecture* (Oxford: Blackwell), pp. 100-110.

—. (2013) *Green Retreats: Women, Gardens and Eighteenth-Century Culture* (Cambridge: Cambridge University Press).

Benjamin, W. (1968 [1955] (ed. Hannah Arendt) *Illuminations. Essays and Reflections* (New York: Schoken).

Bentham, J. (1789 [1780]) *An Introduction to the Principles of Morals and Legislation* (Oxford: Clarendon Press).

—. (1800) Bentham, J., Milner J., Warton T., (eds) *Essays on Gothic Architecture* (London: Architectural Library Holborn).

—. (1818) *Church of Englandism and its Catechism Examined* (London: Effingham Wilson).

Berger, M. (ed.) (1964) *Madame de Staël. On Politics Literature and National Character* (New York: Doubleday).

Beys, H. (1991) *TAF: Temporary Autonomous Zones* (New York: Autonomedia New Autonomy Series).

Bezrucka, Y. (1993) *Virginia Woolf's Artists: The Influence on Her Work of the Aesthetics of Roger Fry and Clive Bell*, PhD, Royal Holloway Bedford New College, University of London.

—. (1994) 'Assenza, violenza, proliferazione dei sensi in 'Between the Acts' di Virginia Woolf', *Quaderni del Dipartimento di Letterature Straniere Moderne dell'Università di Verona*, 19, 1994, 97-107.

Bezrucka, Y. (ed.) (1995a) *Tra passato e futuro. Assaggi di teoria dell'architettura* (Trento: Autem).

Bezrucka, Y. (ed.) (1995b) 'Il postmodernismo: l'accettazione ironica del doppio senso'. In Y. Bezrucka (ed.) *Tra passato e futuro. Assaggi di teoria dell'architettura*, (Trento: Autem), pp. 85-111.

Bezrucka, Y. (ed.) (1997) *Le identità regionali e l'Europa* (Trento: Luoghi/Edizioni).

Bezrucka, Y. (ed.) (1999a) *Regionalismo e antiregionalismo* (Trento: Luoghi/Edizioni).

Bezrucka, Y. (ed.) (1999b) *Forme e caratteri del regionalismo. Mitteleuropa ed oltre* (Trento: Luoghi/Edizioni).
Bezrucka, Y. (2002) *Genio ed immaginazione nel Settecento inglese* (Università degli Studi di Verona: Valdonega).
—. (2004) *Oggetti e collezioni nella letteratura inglese dell'Ottocento* (Trento: Ares).
—. (2006) 'Albert Wendt's 'Flying-Fox in a Freedom Tree': Contagious Infection and 'Regional' Dissenting Bodies'. In Righetti, A. (2006) (ed.) *Theory and Practice of the Short Story: Australia, New Zealand, The South Pacific* (Valdonega: Università di Verona), pp. 245-63.
—. (2007) 'Law *vs.* Equity: Jarndyce *vs.* Jarndyce in Charles Dickens's "Bleak House"'. In D. Carpi (ed.) (2007) *The Concept of Equity. An Interdisciplinary Assessment* (Heidelberg: Winter), pp. 269-78.
—. (2008a) '"The Well-Beloved": Thomas Hardy's Manifesto of "Regional Aesthetics"', *Victorian Literature and Culture*, 36.1, (Cambridge: Cambridge University Press), 227-45.
—. (2008b) 'Representation and Truth: Law and Equity in Robert Browning's "The Ring and the Book"', *Pólemos*, 21-34.
—. (2008c) 'Otello e la retorica visuale del Moro di Venezia', *Studi Culturali* (Bologna: Mulino), 3/2008, 375-406.
—. (2008d) 'Virginia Woolf: Life Living and Life Writing – Collage, "Planes, Parallels, Montage and Design"'. In Righetti A. (2008) (ed.) *The Protean Forms of Life Writing. Auto/Biography in English: 1680-2000* (Napoli: Liguori), pp. 213-28.
—. (2010) 'Regimi scopici e tassonomie visuali: da Virginia Woolf a Italo Calvino'. In C. Battisti (ed.) *Parola e visione* (Verona: Ombre Corte) 2010, pp. 92-104.
—. (2011) 'Bio-Ethics Avant la Lettre: Nineteenth-Century Instances in Post-Darwinian Literature'. In D. Carpi (ed.) *Bioethics and Biolaw through Literature* (Berlin: De Gruyter) pp. 188-202.
—. (2013) 'Nature as *Oikos* and *Kepos*: Ecocriticism as a Branch of Bioethics in Romantic Studies', *Nuovi Quaderni del CRIER*, X, (Verona: Fiorini), 33-54.
—. (2016) 'Beehive-Images and Politics in Bernard de Mandeville's 'The Fable of the Bees': Empiricism *vs.* Innatism', *The Cardozo Electronic Law Bulletin*, Research Paper Series, 1-26.
Bhabha, H. (ed.) (1990) *Nation and Narration* (London: Routledge).
Bindella, M.T. (1979) *Scena e figura nella poesia di Thomas Hardy* (Pisa: Pacini).
Bicknell, P. (1981) *Beauty, Horror and Immensity: Picturesque Landscape in Britain, 1750-1850* (Cambridge: Cambridge University

Press).
Blair, H. (1806) 'A Critical Dissertation on Ossian, the Son of Fingal'. In James Macpherson, *The Poems of Ossian* (London: J.F. Dove), pp. 74-160.
Blake, W. (1998 [1804]) *Jerusalem. The Emanation of the Giant Albion* (ed.) M. D. Paley (Princeton: Princeton University Press).
Bloom, H. (2002) *Genius: A Mosaic of One Hundred Exemplary Creative Minds* (New York: Warner).
Boswell, J. (1785) *The Journal of a Tour to the Hebrides with Samuel Johnson* (London: Henry Baldwin).
Boileau-Despréaux, N. (1972 [1694, 1713]) *Preface to His Translation of Longinus and Critical Reflections on Longinus* (tr. John Ozell) (Sheffield: University of Sheffield).
Brantlinger, P. (1988) *Rule of Darkness: British Literature and Imperialism 1830-1914* (Ithaca: Cornell University Press).
—. (1996) *Fictions of State. Culture and Credit in Britain. 1694-1994* (Ithaca: Cornell University Press).
Braziel, J., Mannur A. (2003) (eds) *Theorizing Diaspora* (Malden: Blackwell).
Brennan, T. (1990) 'The National Longing for Form'. In H. Bhabha (ed.) *Nation and Narration* (London: Routledge) pp. 44-70.
Brewer, J. (1997) *The Pleasure of the Imagination. English Culture in the Eighteenth Century* (Bath: Harper Collins).
Brilli, A. (1995) *Quando viaggiare era un'arte. Il romanzo del Grand Tour* (Bologna: il Mulino).
Brinkley, R.F. (2015 [1932]) *Arthurian Legend in the Seventeenth Century* (London: Routledge).
Brome, J. (1707 [1700]) *Travels over England and Wales* (London: Goslin).
Brontë, E. (1949 [1847]) *Wuthering Heights* (Harmondsworth: Penguin).
Buelow, G.J. (1990) 'Originality, Genius, Plagiarism in English Criticism of the Eighteenth Century', *International Review of the Aesthetics and Sociology of Music*, 2, 2, 117-28.
Buckler, William E. (1952) 'Chapter Seven of *Wuthering Heights*: A Key to Interpretation', *Nineteenth-Century Fiction*, 7, 52-55.
Burke, E. (1827 [1757]) *A Philosophical Enquiry into the Origin of our Ideas of the Sublime and the Beautiful* (London: Dove).
Burlingame, A.E. (1969 [1920]) *The Battle of the Books in its Historical Setting* (New York: Bilo and Tannen).
Burnet, T. (1684 [1681]) *The Sacred Theory of the Earth* (London: R. Norton).

Burton, R. (1883 [1617]) *Anatomie of Melancholy* (Philadelphia: Claxton).
Bussles, S., Delbeke, M. Pieters J., Van Eck, C.A. (eds) (2012) *The Early Modern Reception and Dissemination of Longinus' 'Perì Hupsous'* (Leiden: Brill).
Camaiora, Conti, L. (1993) *The Letters and Poems of John Keats's Northern Tour* (Europrint: Milano).
Carpi, D. (ed.) (2007) *The Concept of Equity. An Interdisciplinary Assessment* (Heidelberg: Winter).
Carpi, D., Leiboff, M., (eds) (2016) *Fables of the Law* (Berlin: De Gruyter).
Carpi, D. (ed.) (2011) *Bioethics and Biolaw through Literature* (Berlin: De Gruyter).
Carpi, D., Franci, G., Silvani G. (eds) (1993) *Raccontare i giardini* (Milano: Guerini)
Carpi, D., Fiorato S. (2011) (eds) *Iconologia del potere. Rappresentazione della sovranità nel Rinascimento* (Verona: Ombre Corte).
Carpi, D., (1993) 'Il giardino come metafora e metamorfosi in 'The Virgin in the Garden' di A.S. Byatt.' In Carpi D., Franci, G., Silvani G. (eds) (1993) *Raccontare i giardini* (Milano: Guerini), pp. 117-30.
Carpi, D., Gaakeer, J. (eds) (2013) *Liminal Discourses. Subliminal Tensions in Law and Literature* (Berlin, Boston: De Gruyter).
Carpi, D., 'The Sublime of Law'. In Carpi, D. (ed.) *Liminal Discourses. Subliminal Tensions in Law and Literature* (Berlin, Boston: De Gruyter), pp. 1-14.
Carruthers, G., Rawes A. (eds) (2003) *English Romanticism and the Celtic World* (Cambridge: Cambridge University Press).
Cassirer, E. (1953) *The Platonic Renaissance in England* (Austin: University of Texas Press).
Chadwick, N. (1964) 'The Celtic Background of Early Anglo-Saxon England'. In K. Jackson, P. Hunter Blair, B. Colgrave, B. Dickins, J. Taylor, H. Taylor, C. Brooke, N.K. Chadwick (eds) *Celt and Saxon. Studies in the Early British Border* (Cambridge: Cambridge University Press), pp. 323-52.
—. (1976) *The British Heroic Age: The Welsh and the Men of the North* (Cardiff: Wales University Press).
Chambers, E.K. (1958) *Shakespeare: A Survey* (New York: Hill and Wang).
Cheyne, G. (1733) *The English Malady or, a Treatise of Nervous Diseases of all Kinds; as Spleen, Vapours, Lowness of Spirits, Hypochondriacal, and Hysterical Distempers, Etc*. (London: G. Strahan).
Clark, K. (1964 [1928]) *The Gothic Revival* (Harmondsworth: Penguin).

Clifford, J.L. (ed.) (1955) *Eighteenth-Century English Literature. Modern Essays in Criticism* (Oxford: Oxford University Press).

Coleridge, S. T. (1956 [1817]) *Biographia Literaria* (London: Dent).

Collin de Plancy, J.-A.-S. (1863) *Dictionnaire Infernal* (Paris: Furne Jouvet).

Collins P.A.W. (1984 [1982]) 'Shakespeare Criticism'. In B. Ford (ed.) *From Dryden to Johnson* (Harmondsworth: Penguin), pp. 378-80.

Connell, P., Leask N. (eds) (2009) *Romanticism and Popular Culture in Britain and Ireland* (United Kingdom: Cambridge University Press).

Cooper, A.A., 3rd Earl of Shaftesbury (1709) *Sensus Communis. An Essay on the Freedom of Wit and Humour* (London: Sanger).

—. (1976) 'The Moralist, A Philosophical Rhapsody, a Recital of Certain Conversations on Natural and Moral Subjects'. In A. Hofstadter and R. Kuhns (eds), *Philosophies of Art and Beauty: Selected Readings in Aesthetics from Plato to Heidegger* (Chicago: Chicago University Press).

—. (1981) *Sämtliche Werke*, (eds) G. Hemmerich, W. Benda (Stuttgart: Frommann- Holzboog).

—. (2001 [1732]) *Characteristicks of Men, Manners, Opinions and Time* (ed.) Douglas Den Uyl (Indianapolis: Liberty Fund).

Copley S., Garside P. (eds) (1994*) The Politics of the Picturesque* (Cambridge: University Press).

Crimmins, J.E. (2015) 'Jeremy Bentham'. In E.N. Zalta (ed.) *The Stanford Encyclopedia of Philosophy* (cf. https://plato.stanford.edu/archives/spr2015/entries/bentham/).

Currie, J., Byrne, W. and Walker, G. (1803) *Scottish Scenery* (London: T. Cadell, W. Davies).

Crystal, D. (2010) *The Cambridge Encyclopaedia of Language* (Cambridge: Cambridge University Press).

Cunliffe, B.W. (2003) *The Celts. A Very Short Introduction* (Oxford: Oxford University Press).

D'Agnone, L. (2017) *A Triple-Faced Janus: Tom Jones as Bastard, Pretender, and Cowan*, Phd Thesis (University of Verona).

Dainotto, R.M. (2000) *Place in Literature. Regions, Cultures, Communities* (Ithaca, London: Cornell University Press.

Danius, S., Jonsson, S. (1993) 'An Interview with Gayatri Chakravorty Spivak', *Boundary 2*, 20, 2, 24-50.

Davenport Adams, W.H. (1889) *Witch, Warlock, and Magician* (London: Chatto & Windus).

Davies, H. (ed.) (1983 [1966]) *Pope. Poetical Works* (Oxford: Oxford University Press).

De Certeau, M. (1986) *Heterologies: Discourse on the Other* (Manchester: Manchester University Press).
De Givry, E.G. (1931) *Witchcraft Magic and Alchemy* (tr. J. Courtenay Locke) (London: Harrap).
Delbeke, M., Pieters, J., Van Eck, C.A., Bussles, S. (eds) (2012) *The Early Modern Reception and Dissemination of Longinus' 'Perì Hupsous'* (Leiden: Brill).
De Mandeville, B. (1924) *The Fable of the Bees, or Private Virtues, Publick Benefits* (ed.) F. B. Kaye (Oxford: Clarendon Press).
De Montfaucon, N.P.H, Abbé de Villars (1670) *Le Comte de Gabalis, ou Entretiens sur les sciences secrètes* (Paris: Claude Barbin).
Delattre, F. (1912) *English Fairy Poetry: From the Origins to the Seventeenth Century* (London: Henry Frowde).
Descartes, R. (1986) *Meditations on First Philosophy with Selections from the Objections and Replies*, (tr. J. Cottingham) (Cambridge: Cambridge University Press).
Dewitt, T.C. (1935) 'Addison's Theory of the Imagination as "Perceptive Response"', *Papers of the Michigan Academy of Science, Arts and Letters*, 21, 509-530.
D'Israeli, I. (1796) *Miscellanies; or, Literary Recreations* (London: Cadell and W. Davies).
Drake, N. (1838) *Shakespeare and His Times* (Paris: Baudry).
Draper, J.W. (1931) *Eighteenth-Century English Aesthetics: A Bibliography* (Heidelberg: Winter).
Dryden, J. (1674) *The State of Innocence and the Fall of Man* (London: Henry Hills).
—. (1679) 'Preface', *Troilus and Cressida, or Truth Found too Late, a Tragedy* (London: J. Tonson, A. Swall).
—. (1982[1668]) *An Essay on Dramatic Poesy* (New York: Irvington).
Duff, D. (2013) *Romanticism and the Uses of Genre* (Oxford: Oxford University Press).
Duff, D., Jones C. (2007) *Scotland, Ireland, and the Romantic Aesthetic* (Lewisburg: Bucknell University Press.
Duff, W. (1994 [1767]) *Essay on Original Genius* (London: Routledge/Thoemmes).
Du Gay P., Hall, S. (eds) (1996) *Questions of Cultural Identity* (London: Sage).
Dunbar, J. (1780) *Essays on the History of Mankind* (London: Strahan, Cadell, Carfour).
Duncan I., Leith, D., Sorensen J. (eds) (2006 [2004]) *Scotland and the Borders of Romanticism* (United States of America: Cambridge

University Press).
During, S. (1990) 'Literature – Nationalism's other? The Case for Revision'. In H. Bhabha (ed.) *Nation and Narration* (London: Routledge), pp. 138-53.
Eagleton T. (1975) *Myths of Power: A Marxist Study of the Brontës* (London: Macmillan).
Evans, E., a.k.a. Ieuan Prydydd Hir (1764) *Dissertatio De Bardis*: *Some Specimens of the Poetry of the Ancient Welsh Bards* (London: Dodsley).
Evans-Wentz, W.Y. (1911) *Fairy Faith in Celtic Countries* (London: Henry Frowde, Oxford University Press).
Fenner, A., Jr. (1956) 'The Wartons 'Romanticise' their Verse', *Studies in Philology*, 53, 3, 501-08.
Ferris, I. (2002) *The Romantic National Tale and the Question of Ireland* (Cambridge: Cambridge University Press).
Fielding, H. (1983 [1742] *Joseph Andrews and Shamela* (London: Dent).
Fiorato S., Carpi D. (2011) (eds) *Iconologia del potere. Rappresentazione della sovranità nel Rinascimento*, (Verona: Ombre Corte).
Fjagesund, P. (2014) *The Dream of the North: A Cultural History to 1920* (New York: Rodopi).
Foucault, M. (1984 [1967]) 'Des espaces autres'. In *Dits et écrits*, vol. 4, 752-762 (Paris: Gallimard).
Fletcher, F.T.H. (1934) 'Climate and Law. Influence of Montesquieu on British Writers', *Geography*, 19, 1, 29-36.
Frye, N. (1956) 'Towards Defining an Age of Sensibility', *English Literary History*, 23, 2, 144-52.
—. (1971) *Anatomy of Criticism* (Princeton: Princeton University Press).
Furst, L.R. (2005) 'Lighting Up Night'. In M. Ferber (ed.) *A Companion to European Romanticism* (Oxford: Blackwell), pp. 505-21.
Garside P., Copley S. (eds) (1994) *The Politics of the Picturesque* (Cambridge: University Press).
Gaskill, H. (1986) 'Ossian's Macpherson: Towards a Rehabilitation', *Comparative Criticism*, 8, 113-46.
Geary, P.J. (2003) *The Myth of Nations: The Medieval Origins of Europe* (Princeton: Princeton University Press).
Gifford, G. (1931 [1603]) (ed.) B. White, *A Dialogue Concerning Witches and Witchcrafts* (London: Oxford University Press).
Gill, S. (1984) *William Wordsworth* (New York: Oxford University Press).
Gilpin W. (1768) *Essay Upon Prints: Containing Remarks upon the Principles of Picturesque Beauty; the Different Kinds of Prints; and the Characters of the Most Noted Masters: Illustrated by Criticisms*

upon Particular Pieces: to which are added, some Cautions that may be Useful in Collecting Prints (London: G. Scott).
—. (1792) *Three Essays: on Picturesque Beauty, on Picturesque Travel, and on Sketching Landscape, to which is added a Poem on Landscape Painting* (London: R. Blamire).
—. (1748) *A Dialogue upon the Gardens of the Right Honourable the Lord Viscount Cobham at Stowe in Buckinghamshire* (Buckingham: B. Seeley).
Gilroy, A. (ed.) (2000) *Romantic Geographies: Discourses of Travel, 1775-1844* (Manchester: Manchester University Press).
Gilroy A. (ed.) (2004) *Green and Pleasant Land: English Culture and the Romantic Countryside* (Leuven: Peeters).
Glendening J. (1997) *The High Road: Romantic Tourism 1720-1820* (New York: St. Martin's Press).
Goethe, J.W. (1772) *Von deutscher Baukunst* (Frankfurt am Main: Deinet).
Goldsmith, O. (1759) *An Enquiry into the State of Polite Learning in Europe* (London: Dodsley).
—. (1820 [1762]) *Letters from a Citizen of the World to his Friends in the East* (London: J. Bungay and R. Childs).
Gough, R. (1780) *Anecdotes of British Topography: or, an Historical Account of what has been done for Illustrating the Topographical Antiquities of Great Britain and Ireland* (London: T. Payne and J. Nichols).
Grafton, A. (1990) *Forgers and Critics: Creativity and Duplicity in Western Scholarship* (Princeton: Princeton University Press).
Graham, P. (1806) *Sketches Descriptive of Picturesque Scenery on the Southern Confines of Perthshire* (Edinburgh: P. Hill and W. Hunter).
Grady, H. (2008) '*A Midsummer Night's Dream* – Eros and the Aesthetic', *Shakespeare Quarterly*, 59, 3, 274-302.
Greenlaw, E. (1918) 'Spenser's Fairy Mythology', *Studies in Philology*, 15, 2, 105-22.
Grose, F. (1787) *A Provincial Glossary, with a Collection of Local Proverbs and Popular Superstitions* (London: S. Hooper).
—. (1773-1787) *The Antiquities of England and Wales* (London: Hooper & Wigstead).
—. (1791 [1753]) 'Rules for Drawing Caricaturas: with an Essay on Comic Painting'. In W. Hogarth, *The Analysis of Beauty* (London: S. Bagster), pp. 1-24.

Hagstrum, J.H. (1974 [1958]) *The Sister Arts: The Tradition of Literary Pictorialism and English Poetry from Dryden to Gray* (Chicago: Chicago University Press).

Hall, R., Woolhouse, R. (1983) *Eighty Years of Locke Scholarship: A Bibliographical Guide* (Edinburgh: Edinburgh University Press).

Hall, S. (2003) 'Cultural Identity and Diaspora'. In *Theorizing Diaspora*, 2003, pp. 233-47.

Hall, S., Du Gay P. (eds) (1996) *Questions of Cultural Identity* (London: Sage).

Halliwell-Philipps, J.O. (1879) *Memoranda on the Midsummer Night's Dream* (Brighton: Fleet and Bishop).

Hamilton, A.C. (ed.) (1990) *The Spenser Encyclopaedia* (Toronto: Toronto University Press).

Hardy, F.E. (1928) *The Early Life of Thomas Hardy: 1840-1891* (London: Macmillan).

Hart, V. (1994) *Art and Magic in the Court of the Stuarts* (London: Routledge).

Hartley, D. (1749) *Observations in Man, his Frame, his Duty and his Expectations* (London: S. Richardson).

Havens, R.D. (1912) 'Romantic Aspects of the Age of Pope', *Modern Language Association of America*, 27, 3, 297-324.

Haywood, I. (1986) *The Making of History: A Study of the Literary Forgeries of James Macpherson and Thomas Chatterton in Relation to Eighteen-Century Ideas of History and Fiction* (London and Toronto: Associated University Presses).

Hazlitt, W. (2004) *Selected Essays of William Hazlitt: 1778 to 1830* (ed.) G. Keynes (Whitefish: Kessinger Publishing).

Herder, J.G., (1784) *Ideen zur Philosophie der Geschichte der Menschheit* (Riga, Leipzig: Kartknoch).

Herman, P.C. (2014) 'Equity and the Problem of Theseus in *A Midsummer Night's Dream*: Or, the Ancient Constitution in Ancient Athens', *Journal for Early Modern Cultural Studies*, 14, 1, 2014, 4-31.

Hewitt, A. (1934) 'The Fairy Lore of the Elizabethans', *The Elementary English Review*, 11, 1, 1-4.

Hipple, W.J., Jr. (1957) *The Beautiful, The Sublime, and The Picturesque in Eighteenth-Century British Aesthetic Theory* (Carbondale: Southern Illinois University Press).

Hobbes, T. ([1642]) 1651) *De Cive* (London: R. Royston).

—. (1651) *Leviathan, or the Matter, Forme, & Power of a Common-Wealth Ecclesiasticall and Civill* (London: Andrew Crooke).

Hobsbawm, E., Ranger, T. (eds) (1983) *The Invention of Tradition*

(Cambridge: Cambridge University Press).
Hobsbawm E. (1990) *Nations and Nationalism since 1780: Programme, Myth, Reality* (Cambridge: Cambridge University Press).
Hoeveler, D.L. (2014) *The Gothic Ideology: Religious Hysteria and Anti-Catholicism in British Popular Fiction, 1780-1880* (Cardiff: University of Wales Press).
Hogarth, W. (1791 [1753]) *The Analysis of Beauty* (London: S. Bagster).
Hope, Nicholson, M. (1997 [1959]) *Mountain Gloom and Mountain Glory: The Development of the Aesthetics of the Infinite* (Washington: Washington University Press).
Howard, H., Earl of Northampton (1583) *Defensative against the Poyson of Supposed Prophecies* (London: I. Charlewood).
Hudson, N. (1996) 'From 'Nation' to 'Race': The Origin of Racial Classification in Eighteenth-Century Thought', *Eighteenth-Century Studies*, 29, 3, 247-264.
Hulme, P., Youngs, T. (eds) (2013 ([2002]) *The Cambridge Companion to Travel Writing* (Cambridge: Cambridge Press University).
Hume, D. (1819) *The History of England from the Invasion of Julius Caesar, to the Revolution of 1688* (London: Millar).
—. (1965 [1739]) *A Treatise of Human Nature: Being an Attempt to Introduce the Experimental Method of Reasoning into Moral Subjects* (ed.) L.A. Selby-Bigge (Oxford: Clarendon).
—. (2009 [1779]) *Dialogues Concerning Natural Religion*, Gutenberg, June 20, 2009 [EBook #4583].
—. (1818 [1748 Bodl. Ed. D]) 'Of National Characters' *Essays Moral, Political and Literary* (eds) T.H. Greene, T.H. Grose (London: *sine ed.*).
Hunt, D.J. (ed.) (1995 [1780]) *The History of the Modern Taste in Gardening* (New York: Ursus).
Hunter, J.P. (1990) *Before Novels. The Cultural Contexts of the Eighteenth-Century English Fiction* (London: Norton).
Hurd, R. (1971 [1765]) *Letters on Chivalry and Romance* (New York: Garland).
Hussey, C. (1967) *The Picturesque. Studies in a Point of View* (London: Frank Cass & Co).
Hutcheson, F. (1990 [1725]) *An Inquiry into the Originals of our Ideas of Beauty and Virtue; in Two Treatises. In which the Principles of the late Earl of Shaftesbury are Explain'd and Defended, Against the Author of the 'Fable of the Bees': and the Ideas of Moral Good and Evil are Establish'd, According to the Sentiments of the Ancient Moralists. With an Attempt to Introduce a Mathematical Calculation in Subjects of*

Morality (Zürich, New York: Georg Olms).

Iser, W. (1978 [1976]) *The Act of Reading: A Theory of Aesthetic Response* (Baltimore: Johns Hopkins University Press).

Jackson, K. *et al.* (1963) 'Angles and Britons in Northumbria and Cumbria'. *In Angles and Britons: O'Dunnell Lectures* (Cardiff: University of Wales Press), pp. 60-84.

James I (King) (1603) *Demonology* (London: Arnold Hatfield).

Johnson, S. (1755) *A Dictionary of the English Language* (London: W. Strahan).

Johnson, S., Todd, H. J., Chalmers, A. and Walker, J. (1835) *Johnson's English Dictionary as improved by Todd and abridged by Chalmers with Walker's Pronouncing Dictionary* (Boston: Nathan Hale).

Jones C., Duff, D. (eds) (2007) *Scotland, Ireland, and the Romantic Aesthetic* (Lewisburg: Bucknell University Press).

Jones, E.D. (1934 [1922]) *English Critical Essays, XVI-XVIII Centuries* (London: Oxford University Press).

Jones, W. (1990) 'Stories of Desire in the Monk', *ELH*, 57, 1, 129-50.

Kames, H.H., Lord, (1762) *Elements of Criticism* (London, Edinburgh: A. Miller, A. Kincaid & J. Bell).

Kant, I. (1911 [1790]) *Kant's Critique of Aesthetic Judgement,* (ed.) Henry Frowde (*Kritik der Urteilskraft*, tr. J.C. Meredith) (Oxford: Clarendon Press).

Kant, I. (1991 [1790]) *Kritik der Urteilskraft* (ed.) Gerhard Lehmann (Stuttgart: Reclam).

Kant, I. (1991 [1764]) 'Of National Characteristics, so far as they Depend upon the Distinct Feeling of the Beautiful and Sublime'. In *Observations on the Feeling of the Beautiful and Sublime* (tr. ed.) John T. Goldthwait (Berkeley: California University Press), pp. 97-116.

Kantorowicz, E.H. (1958) *The King's Two Bodies: A Study in Mediaeval Political Theology* (Princeton: Princeton University Press).

Kedourie, E. (1960) *Nationalism* (Essex: Anchor Press).

Kehler D. (1998) (ed.) *A Midsummer Night's Dream. Critical Essays* (New York: Garland).

Ker, J.P. (ed.) (1900) *Essays of John Dryden* (Oxford: Clarendon Press).

Kilburn, F.W. (1910) *Alterations and Adaptations from Shakespeare* (Boston: Gerham).

King, J.N. (1990) 'Queen Elizabeth I: Representations of the Virgin Queen', *Renaissance Quarterly,* 43, 30-74.

Kipling, R. (1899) 'The White Man's Burden: The United States and the Philippine Islands', *McClure's Magazine*, 12, 4, 290-91.

Kipperman, M. (1995) 'Macropolitcs of Utopia: Shelley's Hellas in

Context'. In J. Arac, H. Ritvo (eds) (1995) *Macropolitics of Nineteenth-Century Literature* (Durham and London: Duke University Press), pp. 86-101.

Kirk, R. (2008 [1893]) *The Secret Commonwealth of Elves, Fauns, and Fairies* (London: Dover).

Knight R.P. (1972 [1795]) *The Landscape. A Didactic Poem in Three Books addressed to Uvedale Price* (Farnborough: Gregg).

—. (1972 [1805]) *An Analytical Enquiry into the Principles of Taste* (Farnborough: Gregg).

Knoepflmacher, U.C., Tennyson G.B. (eds) *Nature and the Victorian Imagination* (Berkeley, Los Angeles: California University Press).

Knowles, J.F.R.S. (1831) *The Life and Writing of Henry Fuseli, Esq. M.A.R.A.* (London: H. Colburn, R. Bentley).

Koch, J.T. (2006) *Celtic Culture: A Historical Encyclopedia* (Oxford: ABC-CLIO).

Kott, J. (1998) 'Titania and the Ass's Head'. In Kehler D. (ed.) *A Midsummer Night's Dream. Critical Essays* (New York: Garland), pp. 107-26.

Kuhn, T. (1962) *The Structure of Scientific Revolutions* (Chicago: Chicago University Press).

Langley, B. (1972 [1728]) *New Principles of Gardening* (New York: Garland).

Lassels, R. (1670) *An Italian Voyage, or a Compleat Journey through Italy* (Paris: Du Moutier).

Latham, M.W. (1930) *The Elizabethan Fairies: The Fairies of Folklore and the Fairies of Shakespeare* (New York: Colombia University Press).

Law, W. (1732) *Origin of Honour*, commented by F.B. Kaye (1924). In de Mandeville's *Fable of the Bees*, Bk. II (Oxford: Oxford University Press).

Lawrence, K.R. (1994) *Penelope Voyages: Women and Travel in the British Literary Tradition*, (Ithaca, NY: Cornell University Press).

Leibniz, G.W. (1710) *Essais de Théodicée sur la bonté de Dieu, la liberté de l'homme et l'origine du mal* (Amsterdam: Isaac Troyel).

—. (1988) *Discourse on Metaphysics and Related Writings* (tr. eds) R. N. D. Martin, S. Brown (Manchester: Manchester University Press).

—. (1996 [1764]) *New Essays on Human Understanding* (tr., eds) P. Remnant and J. Bennett (New York: Cambridge University Press).

Leiboff, M., Carpi, D. (eds) (2016) *Fables of the Law* (Berlin: De Gruyter).

Leith, D., Duncan I., J. Sorensen (eds) (2006 [2004]) *Scotland and the*

Borders of Romanticism (Cambridge: Cambridge University Press).
Lennard, J.D. (1983) *Factual Fictions. The Origins of the English Novel* (New York: Columbia University Press).
Levack, B.P. (1995 [1987]) *The Witch-Hunt in Early Modern Europe* (London: Longman).
Levine, J.M. (1991) *The Battle of the Books: History and Literature in the Augustan Age* (Ithaca: Cornell University Press).
Lewis, M.G. (1796) *The Monk* (Waterford: J. Saunders).
Lill, V.J. (1954) *Dryden's Adaptations from Milton, Shakespeare, and Chaucer* (Urbana: University of Minnesota Press).
Lobineau, G.A. (1707) *Histoire de Bretagne* (Paris: Muguet).
Locke, J. (1689a) *A Letter Concerning Toleration* (London: A. Churchill).
—. (1689b) *Two Treatises of Government: In the Former, The False Principles, and Foundation of Sir Robert Filmer, and His Followers, Are Detected and Overthrown. The Latter Is an Essay Concerning the True Original, Extent, and End of Civil Government* (London: A. Churchill).
—. (1997 [1690]) *An Essay Concerning Human Understanding* (London: Penguin).
—. (1999) *The Reasonableness of Christianity and Paraphrases of St. Paul's Epistles* (ed.) J. Higgins-Biggle (Oxford: Clarendon).
Longinus (1652 [ca. I c. B.C.E.]) *Peri hypsous, or Dionysius Longinus of the Height of Eloquence Rendred out of the Originall. By J. H. Esq,* (London: Roger Daniel for Francis Eaglesfield).
Longinus Dionysius (1735) *On the Sublime* (tr. ed.) William Smith (London: J. Watts).
Loomis, C. 'The Arctic Sublime.' In Knoepflmacher, U.C., Tennyson G.B. (eds) *Nature and the Victorian Imagination* (Berkeley, Los Angeles, California University Press), pp. 95-112.
Lovejoy, A.O. (1936, 1948) *Essays in the History of Ideas* (Baltimore: Johns Hopkins University Press).
—. (1936) *The Great Chain of Being. A Study of the History of an Idea* (Harvard: Harvard University Press).
Lowe, J.E. (1995) *Locke* (London: Routledge).
Loewenstein, D., M. Witmore (2015) (eds) *Shakespeare and Early Modern Religion* (Cambridge: Cambridge University Press).
Lucas, J. (1971) *England and Englishness: Ideals of Nationhood in English Poetry, 1688-1900* (London: Methuen).
Luckombe, P. (1769) *The Beauties of England* (London: Davis and C. Reymers).
MacAulay, D. (1992) 'The Celtic languages: An Overview'. In D.

MacAulay (ed.) *The Celtic Languages* (Cambridge: Cambridge University Press), pp. 1-8.
—. (1992) (ed.) *The Celtic Languages* (Cambridge: Cambridge University Press).
MacLean, K. (1962) *John Locke and English Literature of the Eighteenth Century* (New York: Russell & Russell).
Macpherson, J. (1760) *Fragments of Ancient Poetry Collected in the Highlands of Scotland, and Translated from the Galic or Erse Language* (Edinburgh: Hamilton, Balfour).
—. (1818 [1763]) *Temora: An Epic Poem by Ossian* (Perth: Morison).
—. (1806) *The Poems of Ossian* (London: J.F. Dove).
—. (1762 [1761]) *Fingal, An Ancient Epic Poem, In Six Books: Together with Several Other Poems, Composed by Ossian the Son of Fingal* (London: T. Becket, P. A. De Hondt).
MacRitchie, D. (1890) *The Testimony of Tradition* (London: Kegan Paul, Trench, Trübner).
Malinowsky, B. (2013 [1935]) *Coral Gardens and Their Magic: A Study of the Method of Tilling the Soil* (Hamburg: Severus Verlag).
Malone, E. (1800) (ed.) *The Critical and Miscellaneous Works of John Dryden* (London: Baldwin and Son).
Mannur A., Braziel, J. (2003) (eds) *Theorizing Diaspora* (Malden: Blackwell).
Marenco, F. (2000 [1996]) (ed.) *Storia della civiltà letteraria inglese* (Torino: Utet) 4 vols.
Markusen, A.R. (1978) 'Regionalism and the Capitalist State: The Case of the United States', *Kapitalistate,* 7, 39-62.
Mason, J. (1612) *Anatomie of Sorcerie* (London: I. Legatte).
Mathison, J.K. (1956) 'Nelly Dean and the Power of *Wuthering Heights*', *Nineteenth-Century Fiction*, 11, 106-29.
McIlwain, C.H. (ed.) (1887 [1616]) *The Political Works of James I* (Cambridge MA: Harvard University Press).
McKeon, M. (1987) *The Origins of the English Novel, 1600-1740* (Baltimore: John Hopkins University Press).
McMahon, D. (2013) *Divine Fury: A History of Genius* (Philadelphia: Basic Books).
Meyer, S. (1996) *Imperialism at Home: Race and Victorian Women's Fiction* (Ithaca and London: Cornell University Press).
Miller J.H. (1982) *Fiction and Repetition: Seven English Novels* (Cambridge MA: Cambridge University Press).
Millican, C.B. (2014 [1932]) *Spenser and the Table Round. A Study in the Contemporaneous Background for Spenser's Use of the Arthurian*

Legend (Harvard: Harvard University Press).
Millner, J. (1800) Bentham, J., Warton T., (eds) *Essays on Gothic Architecture* (London: Architectural Library Holborn).
Mishra V. (2007) *The Literature of the Indian Diaspora: Theorizing the Diasporic Imaginary* (London, New York: Routledge).
Monk, S.H. (1935) *The Sublime: A Study of Critical Theories in XVIII-Century England* (New York: Modern Language Association of America).
Montagu Wortley, M. (2004 [1716-1718] *Turkish Embassy Letters* (London: Virago).
Montesquieu, Charles-Louis de Secondat, Baron de La Brède et de Montesquieu (1748) *De l'Esprit des Lois* (Geneva: Barrillot).
Montrose, L. (2006) *The Subject of Elizabeth. Authority, Gender, and Representation* (Chicago: University of Chicago Press).
—. (1998), 'A Kingdom of Shadows'. In Kehler D. (1998) (ed.) *A Midsummer Night's Dream. Critical Essays* (New York: Garland), pp. 217-40.
Morden, R. (1701) *New Description and State of England* (London: R. Morden, T. Cockerill & R. Smith).
Moretti, F. (2005) *La letteratura vista da lontano* (Milano: Garzanti).
Murray, P. (ed.) (1989) *Genius. The History of an Idea* (Oxford: Blackwell).
Murray, S. (1799) *A Companion and Useful Guide to the Beauties of Scotland* (London: George Nicol).
Newman, G. (1997 [1987]) *The Rise of English Nationalism: A Cultural History, 1740-1830* (London: Macmillan).
Newton, I. (1704) *Opticks, or a Treatise of the Reflexions, Refractions, Inflexions and Colours of Light: also Two Treatises of the Species and Magnitude of Curvilinear Figures* (London: Smith and Walford).
Nuttall, A.D. (2000) '*A Midsummer Night's Dream*: Comedy as Apotrope of Myth', *Shakespeare Survey 53,* 49–59.
Ost, F. (2005) *Sade et la loi* (Paris: Odile Jacob).
Ousby, I. (1990) *The Englishman's England. Taste, Travel and the Rise of Tourism* (Cambridge: Cambridge University Press).
Papetti, V. (1989) *Il Neoclassicismo* (Bologna: Mulino).
Parrinder, P. (2006) *Nation & Novel. The English Novel from its Origin to the Present Day* (Oxford: Oxford University Press).
Pask, K. (2013) *The Fairy Way of Writing. Shakespeare to Tolkien*, (Baltimore: Johns Hopkins University Press).
Pater, W. (1986 [1873]) *The Renaissance* (Oxford: Oxford University Press).

Paton, L.A. (1960) *Studies in the Fairy Mythology of Arthurian Romance* (New York: Burt Franklin).

Patrides, C.A. (ed.) (1980) *The Cambridge Platonists* (Cambridge: Cambridge University Press).

Paulson, R. (1991) *Hogarth: 'The Modern Moral Subject' 1697-1732* vol. 1 (New Brunswick and London: Rutgers University Press).

—. (1992) *Hogarth: High Art and Low 1732-1750,* vol. 2 (New Brunswick: Rutgers University Press).

—. (1993) *Hogarth: Art and Politics 1750-1764*, vol. 3 (Cambridge: Lutterworth).

Percy, T. (1926 [1765]) *Reliques of Ancient English Poetry* (London: Dent).

Perrault, C. (1692) *Parallèle des anciens et des modernes en ce qui regarde les arts et les sciences, avec le Poème du siècle de Louis le Grand et une Epitre en vers sur le génie* (Paris: Coignard).

Perry, R. (2004) *Novel Relations: The Transformation of Kingship in English Literature and Culture, 1748-1818* (Cambridge: Cambridge University Press).

Petit, A. (1997) 'Ralph Cudworth, un Platonisme Paradoxal: La Nature dans la "Digression Concerning the Plastick Life of Nature"'. In G. A. J. Rogers, J. M. Vienne and J. C. Zarka (eds) *The Cambridge Platonists in Philosophical Context. Politics, Metaphysics and Religion*, (Dordrecht: Kluwer), pp. 101-10.

Pieters, J., Delbeke, M., Van Eck, C.A., Bussles, S. (eds) (2012) *The Early Modern Reception and Dissemination of Longinus' 'Perì Hupsous'* (Leiden: Brill).

Pittock, M.G.H. (2008) *Scottish and Irish Romanticism* (Oxford: Oxford University Press).

—. (1997) *Inventing and Resisting Britain: Cultural Identities in Britain and Ireland: 1685–1789* (London: Macmillan).

Plato (1950 [c. 360 BCE]) *Republic* (Harmondsworth: Penguin).

Pope, A. (1714 [1712]) *The Rape of the Lock* (London: Bernard Lintott).

—. (1978 [1966]) 'An Essay on Man'. In A. Pope, *Complete Poetical Works*, (ed.) H. Davies (Oxford: Oxford University Press).

—. (1978 [1966]) *Complete Poetical Works*, (ed.) H. Davies (Oxford: Oxford University Press).

Porter, J.I. (2016) *The Sublime in Antiquity* (Cambridge: Cambridge University Press).

Primer, I. (ed.) (1975) *Mandeville Studies: New Explorations in the Art and Thought of Dr. Bernard de Mandeville* (The Hague: Martinus Nijhoff).

Prys, M. (1983) 'From a Death to a View: The Hunt for a Welsh Past in the Romantic Period'. In Hobsbawm, E., Ranger, T. (eds) *The Invention of Tradition* (Cambridge: Cambridge University Press), pp. 43-100.

Pseudo-Longinus (1992) *Il Sublime* (Palermo: Aesthetica).

Punter, D. (2001) *A Companion to the Gothic* (Hoboken: Wiley-Blackwell).

Ralph, J. (1728) *Night: A Poem* (London: C. Ackers).

Reese, W. (1963) 'Survival of Ancient Celtic Customs in Medieval England'. In Jackson, K., *et al.* (1963) (ed.) *Angles and Britons* (Cardiff: Wales University Press), pp. 148-68.

Reid, T. (1764) *Inquiry into the Human Mind, on the Principles of Common Sense* (London: Millas).

Renan, Ernest (1882) 'What is a Nation?' In Bhabha, H. (ed.) (1990) *Nation and Narration* (London: Routledge), pp. 8-22.

Reno, F.D. (2000) *Historic Figures of the Arthurian Era: Authenticating the Enemies and Allies of Britain's Post-Roman King* (Jefferson: McFarland & Company).

Reynolds, H. (1972 [1632]) *Mythomystes, wherein a Short Survey is Taken of the Nature and Value of True Poesie, and Depth of the Ancients above our Moderne Poets* (Menston: Scholar Press).

Reynolds, J. (1992 [1797]) *Discourses* (Harmondsworth: Penguin).

Richetti, J.J. (1969) *Popular Fiction Before Richardson, Narrative Patterns 1700-1739* (Oxford: Clarendon).

Righetti, A. (ed.) *Theory and Practice of the Short Story: Australia, New Zealand, The South Pacific* (Università di Verona: Valdonega).

—. (2008) (ed.) *The Protean Forms of Life Writing. Auto/Biography in English: 1680-2000* (Napoli: Liguori).

Rinaker, C. (1912) *Thomas Warton: A Biographical and Critical Study* (Urbana-Champaign: University of Illinois).

—. (1915) 'Thomas Warton and the Historical Method in Literary Criticism', *PMLA*, 30, 1, 79-109.

Ritson, J. (1875 [1831]) *Fairy Tales, Now First Collected: to which are prefixed Two Dissertations: I. On Pygmies. 2. On Fairies* (London: F. & W. Kerslake).

Ritv H., Arac J. (eds) (1995) *Macropolitics of Nineteenth-Century Literature* (Durham and London: Duke University Press).

Roberts, A. (2015) *The Celts* (London: Heron Books).

Robertson, J.M. (1900 [1711]) *Characteristics of Men, Manners, Opinions and Times.* 2 vols. (London: Grant Richards).

Rodney, D. (1975) *The Heraldic Imagination* (London: Barrie and

Jenkins).

Rogers, G.A.J. (1979) 'Locke, Newton, and the Cambridge Platonists on Innate Ideas', *Journal of the History of Ideas*, 40, 191-215.

Rogers P. (1993) 'Faery Lore and *The Rape of the Lock*'. In Rogers P. *Essays on Pope* (Cambridge: Cambridge University Press), pp. 70–84.

Rosenkrantz, K. (1990 [1853]) *Ästhetik des Hässlichen* (Leipzig: Reclam).

Rousseau, J.J. (1782-1789) *Les Confessions de Jean-Jacques Rousseau* (Genève).

Ruskin, John (1903-1912) *The Works of John Ruskin*, (ed.) E.T. Cook and A. Wedderburn, 39 vols. (London: Allen).

—. (1960 [1853]) *The Stones of Venice* (ed.) J.G. Links (London: Penguin).

Ruthven, K.K. (2001) *Faking Literature* (Cambridge: Cambridge University Press).

Rymer, T. (1693) *A Short View of Tragedy; It's Original Excellency and Corruption with Some Views on Shakespear and Other Practitioners for the Stage* (London: Baldwin).

Sabor, P., Yachnin, P.E. (eds) (2008) *Shakespeare and the Eighteenth Century* (Aldershot: Ashgate).

Samuel, R. (1989) *Patriotism: The Making and Unmaking of British National Identity* (London: Routledge).

Sambrook, J. (1993) *The Eighteenth Century: The Intellectual and Cultural Context of English literature. 1700-1789* (London: Longman).

Schmitt C. (1994) 'Technologies of Terror, Technologies of Nationality: Ann Radcliffe's 'The Italian', *ELH,* 61, 853-76.

Scot, R. (1584) *The Discovery of Witchcraft* (London: William Brome).

Scott, W. (1807 [1802]) *Minstrelsy of the Scottish Border, Consisting of Historical and Romantic Ballads, collected in the Southern Counties of Scotland; With a Few of Modern Date, founded upon Local Tradition,* vol. 2 (Edinburgh: Black).

—. (1813) *Minstrelsy of the Scottish Border, Consisting of Historical and Romantic Ballads, collected in the Southern Counties of Scotland; With a Few of Modern Date, founded upon Local Tradition*, vol. 1. (Philadelphia: M. Carey).

—. (1995 [1871]) *Rob Roy* (London: Penguin).

Scott, W. (ed.) (1821) *The Works of John Dryden*. 4 vols. (Edinburgh: Constable).

Seeber, E.D. (1944) 'Sylphs and Other Elemental Beings in French Literature since Le Comte de Gabalis (1670)', *PMLA*, 59, 1, 71-83.

Seligmann, K. (1948) *The Mirror of Magic* (New York: Pantheon).

Shakespeare, W. (1993 [or. text 1595 ca. pub. 1600]) *A Midsummer Night's Dream* (ed.) H. F. Brooks (London: Arden, Routledge).
Shell, A. (2015) 'Delusion in *A Midsummer Night's Dream*'. In D. Loewenstein and M. Witmore (eds) *Shakespeare and Early Modern Religion* (Cambridge: Cambridge University Press), pp. 81-95.
Sharpe, W. (1755) *A Dissertation upon Genius: or, an Attempt to shew that several Instances of Distinction, and Degrees of Superiority in the human Genius are, not fundamentally, the Result of Nature, but the Effect of Acquisition* (London: C. Bathurst).
Shesgreen, S. (1973) *Engravings by Hogarth* (New York: Dover).
Shunami G. (1973) 'The Unreliable Narrator in *Wuthering Heights*' *Nineteenth-Century Fiction*, 27, 106-29.
Smith, A. (1759) *Theory of Moral Sentiment* (London: A. Millar).
Smollett, T.G. (1771 [1967]) *The Expedition of Humphry Clinker* (London: Penguin).
Soja, E.W. (1989) *Postmodern Geographies. The Reassertion of Space in Critical Social Theory* (London: Verso).
Sontag, S. (1967) 'The Pornographic Imagination', *The Partisan Review*, 181-212.
Sorensen J., Duncan I., Leith, D. (eds) (2006 [2004]) *Scotland and the Borders of Romanticism* (Cambridge: Cambridge University Press).
Spenser, E. (1596) *A View of the Present State of Ireland* (electr. text: Oregon University).
—. (1596) *The Faerie Queene*, 12 Bks (London: Ponsobie).
Spivak, G.C. (1988) 'Can the Subaltern Speak?'. In L. Grossberg and C. Nelson (eds) *Marxism and the Interpretation of Culture*, (Basingstoke: Macmillan), pp. 271-313.
Standish, H. (1969) 'The Fairies of *A Midsummer Night's Dream*', *Shakespeare Quarterly*, Vol. 20, No. 4, 484-85.
Stoddart, A.M. (1915) *The Life of Paracelsus* (London: Rider).
Stoker, B. (1996) *Dracula* (Oxford: Oxford University Press).
Sullivan III, C. W. (1989) *Welsh Celtic Myth in Modern Fantasy* (Westport: Greenwood Press).
Swales, K. (2016) *Understanding the Leave Vote*, NatCen Social Research that works for Society (London: NatCen).
Sweet, R. (2004) *Antiquaries: The Discovery of the Past in Eighteenth-Century Britain* (Cambridge: Cambridge University Press).
Swift, J. (1898) *The Prose Works of Jonathan Swift* (ed.) S. Temple (London: Bell and Sons).
—. (1901 [1696]) *The Battle of the Books* (Dublin: E. Ponsonby).
Switzer, S. (1982 [1718]) *Iconographia Rustica or the Nobleman,*

Gentleman and Gardener's Recreation (New York: Garland).
Symmons, C. (ed.) (1806) *The Prose Works of John Milton with a Life of the Author* (London: Bensley).
Tacitus, Cornelius (1894) *Tacitus The Agricola and Germania* (ed.) Townshend, R.B. (London: Methuen)
Tatarkiewicz, W., (1974 [1962-67]) (ed.) Petsch, D., *History of Aesthetics* (Berlin: de Gruyter).
Temple, W. (1709 [1690]) 'An Essay upon Ancient and Modern Learning'. In *Miscellanea,* part II (London: Tonson), pp.129-30.
—. (1720) 'Upon the Gardens of Epicurus: Or, of Gardening in the Year 1685'. In J. Swift (ed.) *The Works of Sir William Temple, Bart.: In Two Volumes* (London: A. Churchill), pp. 170-90.
—. (1909 [1690]) *On Ancient and Modern Learning and On Poetry* (ed.) J.E. Spingarn (Oxford: Clarendon).
Tennyson, G.B., Knoepflmacher, U.C., (eds) *Nature and the Victorian Imagination* (Berkeley, Los Angeles, California University Press).
Thomas, K. (1983) *Man and the Natural World. Changing Attitudes in England 1500-1800* (London: Penguin).
Thompson, C. (2011) *Travel Writing* (Abingdon: Routledge).
Thomson, J. (1735) *The Four Seasons and Other Poems* (London: Millan).
Tillyard, E.M.W. (1981 [1943] *The Elizabethan World Picture* (Harmondsworth: Penguin).
Toland, J. (1696) *Christianity not Mysterious* (London: Buckley).
Toscano, A. (1991) 'Charles Batteux: Les Quatre Poëtiques', *Rivista di Estetica*, 39, 67-78.
Tregear, S.G. (29.8.1837) *The Queen Bee in her Hive*, in Y. Bezrucka (2016) 'Beehive-Images and Politics in Bernard de Mandeville's 'The Fable of the Bees': Empiricism vs. Innatism', *The Cardozo Electronic Law Bulletin*, Research Paper Series, 1-26.
Trevor-Roper, Hugh, 'The Invention of Tradition: The Highland Tradition of Scotland'. In Eric Hobsbawm, Terence Ranger (eds) *The Invention of Tradition*, pp. 15-41.
Trumpener, K. (1997) *Bardic Nationalism: The Romantic Novel and the British Empire* (Princeton: Princeton University Press).
Tulloch, J. (1872) *Rational Theology and Christian Philosophy in the Seventeenth Century* (Edinburgh and London: W. Blackwood).
Turner, S. (1820 [1799-1805]) *Anglo-Saxons: Comprising the History of England, from the Earliest Period to the Norman Conquest* (London: Longman).
Tuveson, E. (1960) *The Imagination as a Means of Grace: Locke and the Aesthetics of Romanticism* (Berkeley: University of California Press).

Van Eck, C.A., Pieters, J., Delbeke, M., Bussles, S. (eds) (2012) *The Early Modern Reception and Dissemination of Longinus' 'Perì Hupsous'* (Leiden: Brill).

Vernon, J. (2017) *Modern Britain: 1750 to the Present* (Cambridge: Cambridge University Press).

Von Hohemheim, Theophrastus, (1616) a.k.a Paracelsus, *Book of Nymphs, Sylphs, Pygmies, and Salamanders, and Kindred Beings* (Strassburg s.e.) tr. of ([1566]) 1608) '*Liber de Nymphis, sylphis, pygmaeis et salamandris et de caeteris spiritibus', Opera*, vol. 2, 388-98, Genève.

Von Ofterdingen, H., a.k.a. Novalis ([1800] 1951*) Hymnen an die Nacht. Die Christenheit oder Europa* (Wiesbaden: Insel).

Walker, D. P. (1972) *The Ancient Theology* (London: Duckworth).

Wallis, J. (1769) *The Natural History and Antiquities of Northumberland* (London: W. and W. Strahand).

Walpole, Horace (1937 [1762-1771]) *Anecdotes of Painting in England with some Account on the Principal Artists and on Incidental Notes on other Arts*, F.W. Hilles, P.B. Daghlian (eds) (London: Oxford University Press), vol. V.

Walpole, H. (1765) *Anecdotes of Painting in England with some Account on the Principal Artists and on Incidental Notes on other Arts,* (ed.) G. Vertue (Strawberry Hill: Kirkgate), vol. II.

—. (1888 [1780]) 'On Modern Gardening'. In *Anecdotes of Painting in England with some Account on the Principal Artists and on Incidental Notes on other Arts* (London: Hazell, Watson & Viney), pp. 63-92.

—. (1798 [1762-65]) *Anecdotes of Painting in England* (London: Robinson), vol. III.

—. (1996 [1764]) *The Castle of Otranto. A Gothic Story* (Oxford: Oxford University Press).

Warton, J. (1756) *Essay on the Genius and Writings of Pope* (London: M. Cooper).

Warton, T. (1777) 'Ode X: The Grave of King Arthur'. In T. Warton, *Poems: A New Edition, with Additions* (London: T. Becket).

—. (1782) *Verses on Sir Joshua Reynolds' Painted Window at New College* (Oxford: J. Dodsley).

—. (1968 [1774-1778- 1781]) *History of English Poetry* (ed.) R. Wellek, 4 vols. (I, II, III-IV) (New York and London: Johnson Reprint Corporation).

—. (1840 [1824]) (ed.) *History of English Poetry* (ed.) Price, R. (London: Tegg), 4 vols.

—. (1754) *Observations on the Faerie Queene* (London: Dodsley, Fletcher).

—. (1800) Bentham, J., Milner J. (eds) *Essays on Gothic Architecture* (London: Architectural Library Holborn).

Wein, T. (2002) *British Identities, Heroic Nationalisms, and the Gothic Novel, 1764-1824* (Gordonsville: Palgrave Macmillan).

Weinbrot, H.D. (1993) *Britannia's Issue: The Rise of British Literature from Dryden to Ossian* (Cambridge: Cambridge University Press).

Wendorf, R. (ed.) (1983) *Articulate Images. The Sister Arts from Hogarth to Tennyson* (Minneapolis: University of Minnesota Press).

West, Thomas (2008 [1779]) *A Guide to the Lakes of Cumberland, Westmorland and Lancashire* (Cumbria: Unipress).

Willey, B. (1967) *Seventeenth Century Background; Studies in the Thought of the Age in Relation to Poetry and Religion* (New York: Columbia University Press).

—. (1980 [1940]) *The Eighteenth-Century Background: Studies on the Idea of Nature in the Thought of the Period* (London: Chatto & Windus).

Williams, J. (1998) *Theory and the Novel. Reflexivity in the British Tradition* (Cambridge: Cambridge University Press).

Williams, R. (1973) *The Country and the City* (London: Chatto and Windus).

—. (1983 [1976]) *Keywords: A Vocabulary of Culture and Society* (Oxford: Oxford University Press).

Witmore M., Loewenstein, D. (2015) (eds) *Shakespeare and Early Modern Religion* (Cambridge: Cambridge University Press).

Wollstonecraft, M. (1970 [1796]) *Letters Written During a Short Residence in Sweden, Norway and Denmark* (Fontwell: Centaur).

Wordsworth, W. and Coleridge, S. T. (1798) *Lyrical Ballads* (London: Arch).

Wright, J.M. (2004) *Blake, Nationalism, and the Politics of Alienation* (Athens: Ohio University Press).

Yachnin, P.E., Sabor, P. (eds) (2008) *Shakespeare and the Eighteenth Century* (Aldershot: Ashgate).

Yeats, W.B. (1902 [1893]) *The Celtic Twilight* (London: Bullen).

—. (1985 [1961]) 'The Celtic Element in Literature'. In *Essays and Introductions* (London: Macmillan), pp. 173-88.

Yolton, J. W. (1956) *John Locke and the Way of Ideas* (Oxford: Oxford University Press).

—. (2004) *The Two Intellectual Worlds of John Locke: Man, Person, and Spirits in the Essay* (Cornell: Cornell University Press).

Young, A. (1770) *A Six Months Tour Through the North of England* (London: W. Strahan and W. Nicholl).

Young, E. (1759) 'Conjectures on Original Composition in a Letter to the Author of Sir Charles Grandison'. In E. D. Jones (ed.), *English Critical Essays, XVI-XVIII Centuries* (London: Oxford University Press).

Youngs, T., Hulme, P. (eds) (2013 ([2002]) *The Cambridge Companion to Travel Writing* (Cambridge: Cambridge Press University).

Youngs, T. (2013) *Cambridge Introduction to Travel Writing* (Cambridge, New York: Cambridge University Press).

Zipes, J. (2000) *The Oxford Companion to Fairy Tales* (Oxford: Oxford University Press).